COMMUNICATION FOR THE
CLASSROOM TEACHER

SEVENTH EDITION

COMMUNICATION FOR THE CLASSROOM TEACHER

PAMELA J. COOPER
Northwestern University

CHERI J. SIMONDS
Illinois State University

Boston   New York   San Francisco
Mexico City   Montreal   Toronto   London   Madrid   Munich   Paris
Hong Kong   Singapore   Tokyo   Cape Town   Sydney

Executive Editor: *Karon Bowers*
Editorial Assistant: *Jennifer Trebby*
Marketing Manager: *Mandee Eckersley*
Editorial-Production Service: *Omegatype Typography, Inc.*
Composition and Prepress Buyer: *Linda Cox*
Manufacturing Buyer: *JoAnne Sweeney*
Cover Administrator: *Linda Knowles*
Electronic Composition: *Omegatype Typography, Inc.*

For related titles and support material, visit our online catalog at www.ablongman.com.

Library of Congress Cataloging-in-Publication Data

Cooper, Pamela J.
    Communication for the classroom teacher / Pamela J. Cooper, Cheri J. Simonds. — 7th ed.
      p. cm.
    Includes bibliographical references (p.) and index.
    ISBN 0-205-35955-8 (alk. paper)
     1. Teacher–student relationships.   2. Interaction analysis in education.   3. Oral communication.   4. Communication in education.   I. Simonds, Cheri.   II. Title.

    LB1033 .C64   2003
    371.10'23—dc21

                                              2002020213

Printed in the United States of America

10 9 8 7 6 5 4 3 2   07 06 05 04 03 02

Credits start on page 333, which constitutes a continuation of the copyright page.

To my parents—who will always be my favorite teachers

—P.C.

To the memory of my father,
Floyd Wayne Morris—who taught me always to be grateful

—C.S.

CONTENTS

CHAPTER THREE
Listening   64

CHAPTER SEVEN
Small Group Communication   180

CHAPTER TEN

Communication Concerns   246

PREFACE

> I have decided that real learning involves a change of attitude and behavior no less than does real teaching. I have come to believe that teaching is more of a calling forth of wholeness to be a better person than just a jamming in of information, that it must deal with the entire person, not just the mind. Teaching should make students and teachers aware of their sacredness, give them high expectations of themselves, and change their lives.
>
> —Schmier, 1995, p. 21

Teachers and students become aware of the sacredness of which Louis Schmier writes through communication with one another. This text is about communication—the very essence of teaching and learning. It provides prospective and in-service teachers the means to analyze, develop, and facilitate their own and their students' communication behaviors. It is designed to be both theoretical and pragmatic, providing teachers the rationale for using certain communication strategies and the practical means to employ those strategies in the classroom. The text's discussions are supported by numerous and varied activities.

There are numerous changes to this seventh edition of *Communication for the Classroom Teacher*. First, although we have updated material that was key to current classroom practices, we made a conscious decision to maintain information from renowned educators, to maintain the historical value of the textbook. In doing so, we added information on culture, students with special needs, technology, and ethics, as well as sexism and racism in the classroom. We also reorganized materials on communication apprehension and students with special needs to create more conceptual cohesiveness and to balance chapter lengths. Finally, we attempted to make the seventh edition more student friendly. Based on student reviews of the previous edition, we relocated (to boxes) some of the more lengthy lists, which can now be used as guides for future reference.

As you read this text, please be aware of the following styles and treatments. First, we have chosen to avoid the somewhat awkward "he/she" construction. Instead, we have used "he" and "she" alternately throughout the text. Second, even though this is a coauthored text, in some instances, we have chosen to write the text in the first person singular when personal stories and examples are used. Finally, this text, like teaching, is highly personal. Much of what we have written comes from our own experiences in the classroom, both as students and as teachers. What you will read are guidelines, ideas we have found to work.

Many people have contributed to this seventh edition of *Communication for the Classroom Teacher*. Our students continue to influence our ideas about teaching and learning, and hence the text itself. They have challenged, criticized, and sometimes praised us. We are grateful for their insights and their enthusiasm for the teaching–learning process.

Our colleagues Kathleen Galvin, Gus Friedrich, and Steve Hunt have influenced our ideas about classroom communication. They have stimulated our thinking, challenged our conclusions, and helped us to find our own sacredness.

The staff at Gorsuch Scarisbrick Publishers was invaluable in assisting and encouraging us with five previous editions. We are truly grateful to them. We are also grateful to the staff at Allyn & Bacon, and in particular to our editor, Karon Bowers, and Editor-in-Chief, Karen Hanson. They "took us on" and supported our endeavors. In addition, we would like to thank our graduate student assistants John Hooker and Allison Rattenborg who helped in the task of preparing these revisions. Your assistance and support have not gone unnoticed.

We would also like to thank the reviewers of this edition: Melanie Bloom, California State University–Fresno; Virginia Chapman, Anderson University; and Judith Olson-Fallon, Case Western Reserve University.

Finally, our families deserve a very special thanks—our husbands, Rick and Brent, for teaching us that love gives strength, beauty, and meaning to life; our children, Jenifer, Bryan, Jamie, Dylan, and Addison, for teaching us a whole new meaning of the word "teacher;" and our grandchildren, Emma and Jack, who remind us that teaching is indeed sacred and gives us another chance.

COMMUNICATION FOR THE CLASSROOM TEACHER

UNIT **I**

COMMUNICATION COMPETENCE

You communicate with your students, and you also communicate with parents, administrators, and fellow teachers. Sometimes your interactions with these various groups will be under less than ideal circumstances. For example, a parent may need to be consulted concerning a student's behavior or academic difficulty. An administrator may discuss a student's dissatisfaction with your class. A fellow teacher may complain to you about the lack of fairness of the educational system, about a student he dislikes, or his work load. On other occasions your interactions will be very enjoyable.

Regardless of the circumstances surrounding your interactions, the more competent a communicator you are, the more effective you can be.

What is communication competence? Competent communicators are concerned with

> (1) enlarging their repertoire of communication acts; (2) selecting criteria for making choices from the repertoire; (3) implementing the communication acts chosen; and (4) evaluating the effectiveness of communication employed. (Wood, 1977, p. 2)

To be effective communicators, we must be flexible and possess a repertoire of communication acts. Different communication behaviors may be required depending on the situation, the people involved, the topic being discussed, and the task at hand. The competent communicator can perform five different types of communication acts.

1. *Controlling*—We are often in a situation in which we need to persuade others. Similarly, others try to persuade us. You might need to persuade parents that their child needs counseling; convince the principal that your band members, not the football team, should get new uniforms this year; or your team teacher may try to persuade you to present a lecture you think should be omitted from the unit of study.

2. *Feeling*—Often we need to express our feelings and attitudes or respond to those of others. You might, for example, praise another teacher, express your

1

attitude concerning new discipline procedures in the school, or indicate to a parent your approval or disapproval of her child's classroom work.

3. *Informing*—These are communication acts in which you seek or give information. You may need to ask a counselor for a student's score on an aptitude test or explain your grading procedures to a parent.

4. *Ritualizing*—These communication acts serve to maintain social relationships and to facilitate social interaction. Included here are the actions of greeting, leave-taking, taking turns in conversations, and demonstrating culturally appropriate amenities. To understand the importance of these communication acts, think how frustrating it is to communicate with someone who never lets you have a chance to talk or who continually moves toward the door, but never actually leaves!

5. *Imagining*—These are communicative acts in which you cast yourself and the other participants into imaginary situations. It might be helpful to speculate or theorize with parents concerning why their son or daughter misbehaves. You might then use the imagining act to speculate on what behaviors you and the parents could employ to help the student, and what the student's reactions to those behaviors might be.

In terms of classroom communication, the National Communication Association has outlined the communication competencies teachers need in order to be effective (Cooper, 1988). These are listed in Table 1. In addition, we know that effective teachers:

1. Make clear their instructional goals.
2. Know their content and the strategies for teaching it.
3. Communicate to their students what is expected of them and why.
4. Use existing instructional material expertly to devote more time to practices that enrich and clarify content.
5. Know their students, adapt instruction to students' needs, and anticipate misconceptions in students' existing knowledge.
6. Teach students metacognitive strategies and give them opportunities to master them.
7. Address higher-level as well as lower-level cognitive objectives.
8. Monitor students' understanding by offering regular, appropriate feedback.
9. Integrate their instruction with that in other subject areas.
10. Accept responsibility for student outcomes.
11. Reflect on their practice.

Much of the research reviewed in this text suggests that teaching effectiveness is intrinsically related to the way one communicates. The basis of communication effectiveness is the appropriateness of the communication act. The competent communicator carefully examines the components of the communication situation—the participants, the setting, the topic, and the task. Based on an analysis of these components, the competent communicator chooses the appropriate communication act.

TABLE 1   Communication Competencies for Teachers

I. **Informative Messages.** Teachers should demonstrate competence in sending and receiving messages that *give or obtain information.*
   A. To *send* these messages effectively:
      1. Structure information by using devices such as preview questions and comments, transitions, internal summaries, and concluding summaries.
      2. Amplify information graphically through the use of verbal and audiovisual supporting materials. *clearcuts suggesting keen alertness*
      3. Ask incisive questions to assess how well students understand the information given in lectures.
      4. Present information in an animated and interesting way.
   B. To *receive* these messages effectively:
      1. Identify the main point of students' informative messages.
      2. Discern structural patterns and problems in the information they present.
      3. Evaluate the adequacy of one's verbal and audiovisual supporting material in terms of the students' responses.
      4. Formulate questions that probe for the informative content.
      5. Differentiate between informative messages that students deliver in an interesting manner and those that are dull—but still say something.

II. **Affective Messages.** Teachers should demonstrate competence in sending and receiving messages that *express or respond to feelings.*
   A. To *send* these messages effectively:
      1. Reveal positive and negative feelings about self to students.
      2. Express positive and negative feelings about students to students.
      3. Offer opinions about classroom content, events, and real-world occurrences.
      4. Demonstrate openness, warmth, and positive regard for students.
   B. To *receive* these messages effectively:
      1. Recognize verbal and nonverbal cues that reveal students' feelings.
      2. Invite students to express their feelings.
      3. Be nonjudgmental in responding to their feelings.
      4. Ask open-ended questions in response to their expressions of feelings.
      5. If necessary, offer advice tactfully.

III. **Imaginative Messages.** Teachers should demonstrate competence in sending and receiving messages that *speculate, theorize, or fantasize.*
   A. To *send* these messages effectively:
      1. Use vivid descriptive language.
      2. Use expressive vocal and physical behavior when creating or recreating examples, stories, or narratives.
   B. To *receive* these messages effectively:
      1. Respond to students' use of imagination with appreciation.
      2. Be nondirective when encouraging their creativity.

IV. **Ritualistic Messages.** Teachers should demonstrate competence in sending and receiving messages that *maintain social relationships and facilitate interaction.*
   A. To *send* these messages effectively:
      1. Demonstrate appropriate behavior in performing everyday speech acts such as greeting, taking turns in conversation, and leave-taking.
      2. Model appropriate social amenities in ordinary classroom interaction.
      3. Demonstrate speaking and listening competence when participating in or role-playing interviews, conversations, problem-solving and legislative groups, and public ceremonies.

(continued)

TABLE 1   Continued

    B. To *receive* these messages effectively:

      1. Comment favorably when students perform everyday speech acts appropriately.

      2. Acknowledge appropriate performance of social amenities; diplomatically correct inappropriate behavior.

      3. Recognize competence and incompetence when students participate in interviews, conversations, problem-solving and legislative groups, and public ceremonies.

V. Persuasive Messages. Teachers should demonstrate competence in sending and receiving messages that *seek to convince.*

    A. To *send* these messages effectively:

      1. Differentiate between fact and opinion.

      2. Be aware of audience factors that may encourage or constrain acceptance of ideas, such as peer pressure, fatigue, bias, and so on.

      3. Offer sound reasons and evidence in support of ideas.

      4. Recognize underlying assumptions in one's own arguments.

    B. To *receive* these messages effectively:

      1. Admit one's own bias in responding to ideas.

      2. Question the adequacy of reason and evidence given.

      3. Evaluate audience evidence and reasons presented.

      4. Recognize underlying assumptions in the arguments of others.

From *Communication Competencies for Teachers,* by Pamela Cooper, 1988. Used by permission of the National Communication Association.

Imagine for a moment that you and another teacher, Ms. Smith, are alone in the faculty lounge after school. Ms. Smith is complaining loudly to you about a student who is disruptive in class—refuses to work, arrives late to class every day, whispers constantly to other students, and "talks back" when Ms. Smith tells him to "behave." You have the student in a class and have had no difficulties with him. You know that Ms. Smith has the reputation among students of being "incompetent" and is perceived by the faculty as unable to "keep order" in her classroom. Ms. Smith, after complaining at length, turns to you and asks, "What shall I do?" Several communication choices are open to you. Some of them include persuading Ms. Smith to quit teaching, informing her of how students and faculty perceive her, accepting her feelings of anger and telling her you understand, and theorizing with her about what she might do to solve the problem. Based on your analysis of the communication situation, you choose one of the possible choices—the one you think most appropriate.

After choosing from the repertoire of possible communicative acts, you'll implement the one you've chosen. Finally, you'll evaluate the effectiveness of the choice you implemented. Was it appropriate to the communication situation? Was it satisfactory to you? To the other person? The judgments you make concerning the effectiveness of your communication choice will depend on feedback from others as well as information from your personal experiences.

Poor parent–teacher, administrator–teacher, and teacher–teacher communications can seriously interfere with your relationship with your students. Remember the systems perspective. If you respond inappropriately to a parent, for example, you may foster defensiveness or hostility that the parent, intentionally or not, may communicate to the student. This, in turn, affects how the student behaves in your classroom. Thus, possessing a large repertoire of communicative acts—controlling, feeling, informing, ritualizing, and imagining—and using them appropriately will enhance your interaction with others in the educational environment.

In the next unit, several communication variables are discussed. Paying particular attention to these variables can enhance your communication competence in the educational environment.

■ ■ ■ ■ ■

CHAPTER ONE

FOUNDATIONS OF CLASSROOM COMMUNICATION

Objectives

After reading this chapter, you should be able to:

- Define communication.
- Describe the components of communication.
- Describe the nature of communication.
- Discuss the socialization model.
- Differentiate between a supportive and defensive classroom climate.
- Describe the values of a supportive classroom climate.
- Describe ways to create a supportive classroom climate.
- Discuss the importance of understanding cultural diversity in the classroom.
- Discuss the importance of understanding students with special needs.

Although many variables affect classroom learning, one variable most educators agree is paramount is communication. The essence of the teaching–learning process is effective communication. Without communication, teaching and learning would be impossible.

COMMUNICATION: DEFINITION AND COMPONENTS

Communication scholars have long pondered the question: What is communication? The term *communication* is abstract, and like all words, has several meanings. For purposes of our discussion, classroom communication consists of the verbal and non-verbal transactions between teachers and students and between or among students.

In order for us to communicate, several components are necessary. We know from the previous definition of communication that we need *interactants* and a *message*. We also need *channels* (hearing, sight, and the other senses) through which the message can be sent and received. In addition, because the interactants in communication affect one another, feedback is also a necessary component. *Feedback* is the message sent in response to other messages. This feedback can be either verbal or nonverbal.

Another important component of the communication process is noise. *Noise* is any signal that disrupts the accuracy of messages being sent. Noise may be physical (someone tapping a pencil on a desk, chalk scraping on a blackboard) or psychological (daydreaming, personal problems, attitudes). These are all distractions that can cause inaccuracy in communication—preventing the message sent from being the message received. In the English classroom, for example, a student's dislike for the subject could function as noise by prohibiting the student from accurately receiving messages concerning, say, Shakespeare. Regardless of what messages the teacher sends about Shakespeare and his relevance today, the student will find it difficult to receive any messages that would enhance his liking for Shakespeare.

Finally, the environment in which the communication takes place is important. In the educational context, this environment is termed *classroom climate*. The climate is the atmosphere of the classroom. It is contingent on both verbal and nonverbal communication.

Much of what is discussed in this text concerns how to build a supportive classroom climate through communication. A supportive classroom climate is important because it promotes fuller development of a student's positive self-image and enhances self-concept.

We discuss ways to build a supportive classroom climate in more depth later in this chapter as well as throughout the text. For now, keep in mind that a supportive classroom climate is one characterized by

- openness rather than defensiveness
- confidence rather than fear
- acceptance rather than rejection
- trust rather than suspicion
- belonging rather than alienation
- order rather than chaos
- control rather than frustration
- high expectations rather than low expectations

THE NATURE OF COMMUNICATION

Based on our definition of communication, several axioms or truths concerning communication are apparent: Communication is a transactional process that is complex, symbolic, and has both a content and a relational component. The next section discusses each of these in depth.

Communication Is a Transactional Process

The transactional process of communication is depicted in Figure 1.1 (Wenburg & Wilmot, 1973, p. 5). This perspective stresses that communication takes place between persons, not roles. In other words, if our communication is to be truly effective, I must think of you as a person, not simply as another student. Similarly, you

FIGURE 1.1   A Transactional Model of Communication.

From *The Personal Communication Process*, John Wenburg and William Wilmot, Copyright © 1973 by John Wiley & Sons, Inc. Reprinted by permission of John Wiley & Sons, Inc.

must think of me as a person, not simply another teacher. This requires that we be person oriented rather than role oriented. The transactional view suggests that to be an effective communicator, I must not only concentrate on my performance as a teacher and be aware of you as a student but I must also be aware of you as a person—treat you as an individual and not an object.

Each of the elements in your classroom—the students, the teacher, the environment, the teaching strategies—interact and mutually affect one another. Thus, a change in one of these will produce changes in the others. For example, suppose you decide to give your students a "pop quiz"—all other elements of the classroom are affected by your decision. Or, if one student engages in disruptive behavior, the entire classroom is disrupted. Thus, all members of a classroom are affected by the actions of each of the other members.

Communication Is Complex

It's been said that when two people interact, there are really six: my me, my you, my impression of the way you see me, your you, your me, and your impression of how I see you. Suppose two people are communicating—we'll call them Alex and Jackson. The "people" in their communication transaction are diagrammed in Figure 1.2. When we multiply this by thirty students and a teacher, we soon realize how complex classroom communication can be. All these "people" enter into the messages sent and received. No wonder communication problems arise! Remember also that in addition to these six "people" (and their attitudes, beliefs, moods) there are also factors such as time, place, and other circumstances that affect communication and make it even more complex.

Communication Is Symbolic

Communication is the symbolic means through which we relate our experiences and perceptions to others. The symbols we use are words (verbal messages) and behaviors (nonverbal messages). In order to relate our experiences and perceptions, we must share common meanings. The problem is that meanings are not transferable; only messages are. Stated in other terms, meanings are in people, not

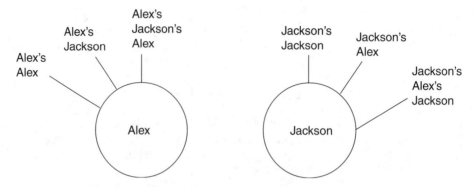

FIGURE 1.2   The Six "People" Involved in a Communication Transaction.

Adapted from *Dimensions in Communication: Readings,* edited by James Campbell and Hal Hepler. Belmont, CA: Wadsworth, 1970.

in words. For example, when a teacher says to a student, "See me after class," the student provides the meaning. Thoughts such as "What did I do wrong?" or "Oh, no, she found out!" may go through the student's mind. The student doesn't know if the teacher means "You've done something wrong" or "I think you did a great job and I want to compliment you." As Combs (1965) indicates, "The discovery of meaning...can only take place in people.... This is the human side of learning" (p. 165). Just as words don't have a single meaning, neither do nonverbal aspects of communication. The clothes you wear, the expressions on your face, the gestures you use may communicate different meanings than you intend.

Communication Has Both a Content and a Relational Component

Whenever we communicate, we do so on two levels—the content level and the relationship level. To understand these two levels, consider the following example. You are a teacher and a student enters your office to discuss a problem he's having with an assignment. He knocks on your slightly opened door and asks, "Do you have a few minutes?" As you continue with your work, not even looking up at him, you answer, "Yes. Come on in." Your content message indicates a specific behavior the student should perform—he should walk in. However, your relationship message states quite clearly that you don't wish to be disturbed. The relationship message can indicate how you view the other person, how you view yourself, and how you view the relationship between you and the other person.

The importance of the relationship message for teachers is evident. The relationships we create with our students affect us, our students, and the educational outcomes of our instruction. When a teacher's communication response to students is one of "I accept you," the relationship is positive and learning is enhanced (Trymier & Houser, 2000).

THE SOCIALIZATION MODEL

Consistent with the transactional perspective of communication is the notion of teacher and student socialization. Socialization is a process where people "selectively acquire the values and attitudes, the interests, skills and knowledge—in short, the culture-current in groups to which they are, or seek to become a member" (Merton, Reader, & Kendall, 1957, p. 287). The classroom can be viewed as a secondary socialization process where already socialized individuals are placed into new social situations. Thus, each time teachers and students change classes, they undergo secondary socialization involving learning knowledge relevant to a particular role (Berger & Luckman, 1966) and a particular situation (i.e., the classroom). Both teachers and students must learn about their role in the classroom and the culture of their school. Thus, teachers and students find themselves in a transactional relationship where they help to socialize each other. In this sense, "socialization is a process of mutual influence in which the teacher impacts students, students influence the teacher, and students affect one another" (Staton, 1990, p. 15). However, the socialization experience is somewhat different for teachers and students.

Teacher Socialization

First, teachers must undergo occupational or role socialization. That is, they must acquire the skills and knowledge necessary to teach and to become a part of the culture of teachers (Staton & Darling, 1986). They must not only learn the content they want to teach but also the skills of being a teacher. Because teachers must communicate their content in a way that students understand, communication becomes an integral part of becoming an effective teacher. Hurt, Scott, and McCroskey (1978) aptly state that the difference between knowing and teaching is communication. This book addresses the communication skills that all teachers need to effectively socialize into their roles as teachers.

Second, teachers must learn the culture of the school system in which they plan to teach. According to Zeichner (1980), cultural socialization involves a constant interplay between individuals and the institution into which they are socialized. Teachers must not only be concerned with teaching their own classes, but with "fitting" in with colleagues, supervisors, support staff, students, and so on. Teachers are often unprepared to deal with the complexities they encounter with their roles as teachers, their place in school, and especially their relationship with students.

Staton and Hunt (1992) found that communication is the key to effective socialization. They developed a model of teacher socialization that includes biography, agents, changes, and context. For example, prospective teachers come into training with their own ideas and attitudes about what it means to be a teacher (biography). Through communication with colleagues, supervisors, students, and others (agents) and dilemmas (changes) that create uncertainty, they work their way through a program (context). Students are the primary agents of socialization in the classroom.

Student Socialization

When students and teachers come together for the first time, the teacher is the only one who knows, in advance, what the expectations of that particular classroom are; thus, "classrooms are communicative environments with teachers as the only native" (Friedrich, 1982, p. 5). The students must learn to make sense of teacher expectations. Because students have a vested interest in the outcome of the class, they attempt to share ownership of the culture and become active agents in establishing, maintaining, and changing the conventions of the classroom culture (Littlejohn, 1989). The role of the student is developed through interactions with the teacher and other students (Staton, 1990). The resulting relationships between students and teachers help define the culture of the classroom.

CLASSROOM COMMUNICATION CLIMATE

As we suggested earlier in this chapter, a supportive classroom climate fosters fuller development of a student's positive self-image and enhances self-concept. In addition, when students are free of disruptive anxiety, fear, anger, or depression, they are more likely to make desirable cognitive and affective gains. More than any other person, the teacher sets the classroom climate. Productive pupil behavior is related to the following teacher characteristics: understanding/friendly teacher behavior, stimulating/imaginative teacher behavior, student-centered educational philosophy, favorable attitudes toward students, and democratic classroom procedures (Cooper & Galvin, 1983).

In his book *The Geranium on the Window Sill Just Died but Teacher You Went Right On*, Cullum (1971) writes of what students experience in a nonsupportive classroom climate:

It's September again
—the time of jumping when you call,
doing cartwheels for you,
nodding yes.
It's September again
—standing on my head for you,
leaping high
hoping to please.
It's September again
—taking your tests,
finding my lost pencil,
losing ground.
It's September again
—hiding behind my reading book,
breathing quietly,
afraid!

So what specifically and behaviorally can you do as a teacher to create a supportive classroom climate and, therefore, positive attitudes in your students? You want to focus on the positive, not the negative. Mayer (1968, p. 47) defines these concepts for us; an aversive or negative consequence is "any event that causes physical or mental discomfort. It is an event that causes a person to think less highly of himself, that leads to a loss of self-respect or dignity, or that results in a strong anticipation of any of these. In general, any condition or consequence may be considered aversive if it causes a person to feel smaller or makes his world dimmer."

Pain, anxiety, fear, frustration, embarrassment, boredom, and physical discomfort are all aversive stimuli and encourage a defensive classroom climate. Box 1.1 provides examples of aversive stimuli.

A positive consequence or condition is "any pleasant event that exists during the time the student is in the presence of the subject matter, or that follows his approach to the subject matter. In the way that an aversive condition or consequence causes the student's world to become dimmer or causes him to think less highly of himself, a positive condition or consequence causes the student to think a little more highly of himself, causes his world to become a little brighter" (Mayer, 1968, p. 58). Box 1.2 provides examples of positive stimuli.

Personal feedback, the use of praise, and the lack of blame increase student participation and performance. These practices communicate respect for students, or indicate to students that they are valued. It's important to remember that simply providing feedback or praise is not sufficient in itself. The feedback must be

■ ■ ■ ■ ■

BOX 1.1
AVERSIVE STIMULI

1. Loss of self-esteem, as in failing to understand an idea or solve a problem correctly.
2. Physical discomfort, such as sitting too long, trying to hear in a room with poor acoustics, or having to see a blackboard or a screen that is too far away for the size of what is being shown.
3. Frustration from not being able to obtain feedback.
4. Being told that one is unlikely to understand something.
5. Having to stop work in the middle of an interesting activity.
6. Trying to learn material that is too difficult for one's present level of ability or understanding.
7. Having one's request for help go unmet by the teacher.
8. Having to go too fast to keep up with students better than oneself at what is being learned.
9. Being graded on a curve.
10. Having to sit through a dull teacher presentation, one that is repetitive, boring, insufficiently challenging, banal, platitudinous, or too easy.

▪ ▪ ▪ ▪ ▪ ▬

BOX 1.2

POSITIVE STIMULI

1. Acknowledging students' responses, whether correct or incorrect, as attempts to learn, and following them with accepting rather than rejecting comments ("No, you'll have to try again," rather than "How could you make such an error").
2. Providing instruction in increments that will allow success most of the time.
3. Providing enough signposts so that the student always knows where he or she is and where he or she is expected to go.
4. Providing the student statements of your instructional objectives that he can understand when he first sees them.
5. Detecting what the student already knows and dropping that from her curriculum, thereby not boring her with redundancy.
6. Providing feedback that is immediate and specific to the student's response.
7. Giving the student some choice in selecting and sequencing subject matter.
8. Relating new information to old, within the experience of the student.
9. Treating the student as a person rather than as a number in a faceless mass.
10. Making use of those variables known to be successful in attracting and holding human attention, such as motion, color, contrast, variety, and personal reference.
11. Expressing genuine delight at seeing the student succeed.

effective. Suggestions for effective feedback are presented in Box 1.3 (Curwin & Mendler, 1988, p. 70).

Classroom climate has two dimensions: supportiveness and defensiveness (Gibb, 1961). A supportive climate has few distortions, effective listening behaviors (a topic we turn to in detail in Chapter 3), and clear message transmission (Darling & Civikly, 1987). A supportive climate reduces defensiveness and allows students to focus on the content and structure of the message (Gibb, 1961). In contrast, a defensive climate interferes with the communication process and creates an atmosphere in which the sharing of ideas is stifled (Gibb, 1961, pp. 142–148). Table 1.1 lists Gibb's definitions of each of the components of both climates.

Most students feel defensive. Our educational environments have fostered this defensiveness through the different status and roles in classrooms and the use of grades. Students often feel controlled by the teacher, who is in a superior, "always right" position. They also feel strategies are used to manipulate them and that teachers often behave neutrally toward their problems. Rosenfeld (1983) examined coping mechanisms used by students when they felt defensive. He summarizes his findings:

> In disliked classes, characteristic coping mechanisms are "daydreaming" and "resisting the teacher's influence." In general, the coping mechanisms used by students in disliked classes fall into two categories: active and passive. "Resisting the teacher's influence," "retaliating against the teacher," and "forming alliances against the

BOX 1.3
EFFECTIVE FEEDBACK

1. *Make your messages clearly your "own" by using the first person singular pronouns I and my.* Personal ownership includes clearly taking responsibility for the ideas and feelings that are expressed. People disown their messages when they use terms such as "most people," "some of our friends," and "our group."
2. *Make your messages complete and specific.* Include clear statements of all necessary information the student needs in order to comprehend the message. Being complete and specific seems so obvious, but often people do not communicate the frame of references they are using, the assumptions they are making, the intentions they have in communicating, or the leaps in thinking they are making.
3. *Make your verbal and nonverbal messages congruent.* Every face-to-face communication involves both verbal and nonverbal messages. Usually these messages are congruent, so if a person is saying that he has appreciated your help, he is smiling and expressing warmth nonverbally. Communication problems arise when a person's verbal and nonverbal messages are contradictory.
4. *Be redundant.* Repeating your messages more than once and using more than one channel of communication (such as pictures and written messages as well as verbal and nonverbal cues) will help the student understand your messages.
5. *Ask for feedback concerning the way your messages are being received.* In order to communicate effectively you must be aware of how the student interprets and processes your messages. The only way to be sure is to continually seek feedback as to what meaning the receiver attaches to your messages.
6. *Make sure your feedback is helpful and nonthreatening:*
   a. *Focus your feedback on the person's behavior, not on her personality.* Refer to what the person does, not to what you imagine his traits to be. Thus you might say, "you talked too much in class" rather than saying "you are a loudmouth." The former is a statement of what you see and hear, and the latter is an inference about, or interpretation of, the person's character.
   b. *Focus your feedback on descriptions rather than on judgments.* Refer to what occurred, not to your judgments of right or wrong, good or bad, or nice or naughty. You might say, "you speak too softly to be heard," rather than "you are a poor public speaker." Judgments arise out of a frame of reference or value system and should be avoided, whereas description represents, as much as possible, neutral reporting.
   c. *Focus your feedback on a specific situation rather than on abstract behavior.* What a person does is always related to a specific time and place. Feedback that ties behavior to a specific situation and is given immediately after the behavior has occurred increases self-awareness. Instead of saying, "Sometimes you have very interesting ideas," say "When you have done your homework and thought about the assignment, you have very interesting ideas."
   d. *Focus your feedback on the "here and now" not on the "there and then."* The more immediate the feedback, the more helpful it is. Instead of saying, "Three weeks ago you didn't hand in your homework," say "You didn't hand in your homework today. Is something wrong?"

(continued)

BOX 1.3   CONTINUED

e. *Focus your feedback on sharing your perceptions and feelings rather than on giving advice.* By sharing perceptions and feelings you leave other people free to decide for themselves—in the light of their own goals in a particular situation at a particular time—how to use the perceptions, reactions, and feelings. When you give advice, you tell other people what to do with the information and thereby take away their freedom to determine for themselves what is for them the most appropriate course of action. Let other people decide for themselves what behavior they want to change. You can give feedback such as, "You don't do well in this class when you don't do your homework," without giving advice such as "You are failing. Do your homework."

f. *Do not force feedback on people.* Feedback is given to help people become more self-aware and to improve their effectiveness in relating to other people. If other people do not want to hear your feedback, do not force it on them. Even if you are upset and want more than anything else to give a student some feedback, do not give it if the student is too defensive or uninterested to understand it.

g. *Do not give people more feedback than they can understand at the time.* If you overload people with feedback, it reduces the chances that they will use it.

7. *Make the message appropriate to the receiver's frame of reference.* The same information will be explained differently to an expert in the field than to a novice, to a child than to an adult, or to a boss than to a co-worker.

8. *Describe your feelings by name, action, or figure of speech.* When communicating your feelings, it is especially important to be descriptive. You may describe your feelings by name ("I feel sad"), by actions ("I feel like crying"), or by figures of speech ("I feel down in the dumps"). The description will help communicate your feelings clearly and unambiguously.

9. *Describe other people's behavior without evaluating or interpreting.* When reacting to the behavior of other people, be sure to describe their behavior ("You keep interrupting me") rather than evaluating it ("You're self-centered and won't listen to anyone else's ideas").

---

teacher," are active strategies for coping with a hostile environment, whereas "not doing what the teacher asks," "hiding feelings," and "daydreaming," are passive strategies for accomplishing the same end. (p. 173)

Civikly (1982) lists six factors necessary for a supportive communication climate. You might analyze the communication climate in your classroom by answering the questions posed in Table 1.2.

CULTURAL DIVERSITY

There is a wide diversity of cultural backgrounds in today's classrooms and every indication is that this diversity will continue to increase. Yet, the classroom culture is, to a great extent, an extension of mainstream American culture (Condon, 1986;

TABLE 1.1 Defensive versus Supportive Communication Climates

Defensive Climates	Supportive Climates
1. *Evaluation.* To pass judgment on another; to blame or praise; to make moral assessments of another; to question another's standards, values, and motives and the affect loadings of the person's communication.	1. *Description.* Nonjudgmental; to ask questions that are perceived as genuine requests for information; to present "feelings, events, perceptions, or processes that do not ask or imply that the receiver change behavior or attitude." If we use "you" language—"You are not doing your best"—we are evaluating. If we use "I" language—"When you don't do as well as I think you can, I get frustrated"—we are describing.
2. *Control.* To try to do something to another; to attempt to change an attitude or the behavior of another; to try to restrict another's field of activity; "implicit in all attempts to alter another person is the assumption of the change agent that the person to be altered is inadequate."	2. *Problem Orientation.* The antithesis of persuasion; to communicate "a desire to collaborate in defining a mutual problem and in seeking its solution" (thus, tending to create the same problem orientation in the other); to imply that he has no preconceived solution, attitude, or method to impose on the other; to allow "the receiver to set his own goals, make his own decisions, and evaluate his own progress—or to share with the sender in doing so." Control is an "I know what's best for you" attitude. Problem orientation is "We have a problem. What can we do to solve it?" attitude.
3. *Strategy.* To manipulate others; to use tricks to "involve" another, to make her think she was making her own decisions, and to make her feel that the speaker had genuine interest in her; to engage in a stratagem involving ambiguous and multiple motivation.	3. *Spontaneity.* To express guilelessness; natural simplicity; freedom from deception; having a "clear id"; having unhidden uncomplicated motives; straightforwardness and honesty. Whenever we try to trick or manipulate another person into doing what we want, we are using a strategy. Spontaneity is expressing ourselves honestly. How many of us wish for a simple, honest "I just didn't get the paper done" instead of the "My dog ate the paper" excuse!
4. *Neutrality.* To express lack of concern for the welfare of another; "the clinical, detached, person-is-an-object-of-study attitude."	4. *Empathy.* To express respect for the worth of the listener; to identify with his problems, share his feelings, and accept his emotional values. Students feel defensive when they perceive our neutrality—"She doesn't really care about me. I'm just another student to her." Being empathic—putting ourselves in another's shoes—can communicate to students that we care about them personally. Remember, being empathetic doesn't mean we agree with the student's feelings—only that we respect those feelings.
5. *Superiority.* To communicate the attitude that one is "superior in position, power, wealth, intellectual ability, physical characteristics, other ways" to another; to tend to arouse feelings of inadequacy in the other; to impress the other that the speaker "is not willing to enter a shared problem-solving relationship, that he probably does not desire feedback, that he does not require help, and that he will be likely to try to reduce the power, the status, or the worth of the receiver."	5. *Equality.* To be willing to enter into participative planning with mutual trust and respect; to attach little importance to differences in talent, ability, worth, appearance, status, and power. We have all had teachers who constantly remind us that they are the teacher—the superior intellectual being in the classroom. Remember how thrilled you were when the teacher made a mistake? A teacher who believes in equality communicates that everyone has value—regardless of their intellectual capabilities. In addition, such a teacher communicates that everyone makes mistakes and that everyone—teacher and students—can learn from one another.

(handwritten annotations in margin: "should go first!!!", "contrast of ideas by parallel arrangement Ex: They promised freedom and provided slavery.")

(continued)

TABLE 1.1 Continued

Defensive Climates	Supportive Climates
6. *Certainty.* To appear dogmatic; "to seem to know the answers, to require no additional data"; and to regard self as teacher rather than as co-worker; to manifest inferiority feelings by needing to be right, wanting to win an argument rather than solve a problem, seeing one's ideas as truths to be defended.	6. *Provisionalism.* To be willing to experiment with one's own behavior, attitudes, and ideas; to investigate issues rather than taking sides on them, to problem solve rather than debate, to communicate that the other person may have some control over the shared quest or the investigation of ideas. "If a person is genuinely searching for information and data, he does not resent help or company along the way." We have all known people who are always right—who believe they have a corner on ultimate truth. Generally, we expend a great deal of energy trying to prove these people wrong. In provisionalism, although the person may have a strong opinion, she is willing to acknowledge another's viewpoint.

Adapted from J. Gibb, "Defensive Communication," *Journal of Communication 11* (1961), pp. 142–148. Copyright © 1961 by Oxford University Press. Used by permission.

Samovar & Porter, 2001). For example, the values of the classroom are those of mainstream America—independence, competition, individualism, and concern for relevance and application. As a result, students whose backgrounds are different from this dominant culture often have a difficult time adjusting to the classroom culture. For example, many Hispanics and Asian cultures expect students to learn by listening, observing, and imitating. Compare this to the U.S. educational system where critical thinking, active discussion, and question asking are expected. In the United States students are taught to answer questions quickly. In contrast Asian and Native American students are taught to consider all sides of an issue before answering a question. And, to compound the problem such differences make in classroom learning, teachers often aren't trained in how to teach to a multicultural student body (Cole, 1995).

Culture influences both behavior and psychological processes. It affects the way we perceive the world and the way we communicate. Culture "forms a prism through which members of a group see the world and create 'shared meanings'" (Bowman, 1989, p. 118). Yet, teaching in a multicultural classroom is also challenging and rewarding. One way to improve the possibility that communication will be effective is to be sensitive to the "stumbling blocks" to intercultural communication. These stumbling blocks have been defined as the following (Barna, 1988):

1. *Assuming similarity instead of difference.* There seem to be no universals of "human nature" that can be used as a basis for automatic understanding. Each of us is so unconsciously influenced by our own culture that we assume the basic needs, desires, and beliefs of others are the same as our own.

2. *Language.* Even words as simple as "yes" and "no" can cause trouble. When a Japanese person hears, "Won't you have some tea?" she tends to listen to the literal

TABLE 1.2   Analyzing Classroom Climate

Classroom Factor	Summary	Questions to Pose to Self
Challenge	"A good way to create challenge is to wait until the chances of success are good, and then say, 'This is hard work, but I think that you can do it.'"	Do I provide challenging problems to the students and encourage their efforts at solving the problem? Do I encourage creative alternative solutions to problems and questions?
Freedom	"What freedom means to the teacher is that students will learn, provided the material appears to be relevant to their lives and provided they have the freedom to explore and to discover its meaning for themselves."	Do I encourage students to try something new and to join in new activities? Do I allow students to have a voice in planning and do I permit them to help make the rules they follow?
Respect	"The rule seems to be that whenever we treat a student with respect, we add to his self-respect, and whenever we embarrass or humiliate him, we are likely to build disrespect in him both for himself and for others."	Do I have genuine respect for the students and for each student's contribution to the class? Do I communicate this respect to the students, and demonstrate this respect in classroom discussions and one-to-one interactions with each student?
Warmth	"A warm and supportive educational atmosphere is one in which each student is made to feel that he belongs in school and that teachers care about what happens to him. It is one in which praise is used in preference to punishment, courtesy in preference to sarcasm, and consultation in preference to dictation."	Do I spread my attention around and include each student, keeping special watch for the student who may need extra attention? Do I notice and comment favorably on the things that are important to students? Do I practice courtesy with my students?
Control	"Classroom control does not require ridicule and embarrassment. The secret seems to be in the leadership qualities of the teacher. When he (she) is prepared for class, keeps on top of the work and avoids the appearance of confusion, explains why some things must be done, and strives for consistency, politeness and firmness, then classroom control is likely to be maintained."	Do I remember to see small disciplinary problems as understandable, and not as personal insults? Do I have, and do my students have, a clear idea of what is not acceptable in my class?
Success	"Perhaps the single most important step that teachers can take in the classroom is to provide an educational atmosphere of success rather than failure."	Do I permit my students some opportunities to make mistakes without penalty? Do I set tasks that are, and that appear to the student to be, within his or her abilities? Do I provide honest experiences of success for my students?

From J. Civikly (1982), "Self-Concept, Significant Others, and Classroom Communication," in L. Barker (Ed.), *Communication in the Classroom.* Copyright © 1982 by Allyn and Bacon. Reprinted by permission.

meaning of the sentence and answers "no," meaning she wants some. Also, in some cultures it is polite to refuse the first or second offer of refreshment. Many foreign guests have gone hungry because their U.S. host or hostess never presented the third offer—another case of "no" meaning "yes" (Barna, 1988, p. 326).

3. *Nonverbal misinterpretations.* When we enter into another culture, we need to be able to hear its "special hum and buzz of implication" (Frankel, 1965, p. 103). When we misinterpret or do not comprehend the nonverbal cues, communication will be ineffective.

4. *Preconceptions and stereotypes.* These reduce the chance for effective communication because they interfere with our ability to objectively view the situation.

5. *Tendency to evaluate.* When we approve or disapprove the actions or statements of another, rather than try to comprehend, effective communication is difficult. We need to remain open-minded. Otherwise, communication may be "cut-off" before we really understand the other person. Because we are all ethnocentric to some degree, that is, we think our cultural ways are "right" or "best," we evaluate other cultures as "not as good" or "wrong."

6. *High anxiety.* Going into new, unfamiliar, or uncertain situations is difficult for many of us. We become anxious, and as a result, may become defensive. Jack Gibb (1961) tells us that defensiveness prevents us from concentrating on the message. In addition

> Not only do defensive communicators send off multiple value, motive, and affect cues, but also defensive recipients distort what they receive. As a person becomes more and more defensive, he becomes less and less able to perceive accurately the motives, the values, and the emotions of the sender. (Gibb, 1961, p. 142)

It is impossible to outline the cultural characteristics of every ethnic group here. Teachers must identify the groups present in their classrooms and learn about the characteristics of each. In terms of our focus, the communication variables that "are identifiable as culturally determined, as constituting ethnic communication styles, and as being influenced in shaping interactions among members of different ethnic groups" (Gay, 1978, p. 52) are

attitudes
social organization (status of people within the structure)
patterns of thought
role prescription (how people are supposed to behave)
language
use and organization of space
vocabulary
time conceptualizations
nonverbal expressions

Thus, the preceding list constitutes the categories of knowledge you will need about a particular ethnic group in order to communicate effectively with that group.

Anderson and Powell (1988), in their article on cultural influences on education processes, review research that highlights intercultural differences. For example, there is virtually no classroom interaction in Vietnamese, Mexican, or Chinese classrooms. In contrast, in an Israeli kibbutz students talk among themselves, address teachers by their first names, and criticize when they feel teachers are wrong.

In Italian classrooms, children greet their teacher with a kiss on both cheeks, and students and teachers touch one another frequently. African American children may use back channeling—a vocal response that is meant to encourage or reinforce the speaker ("yeah," "go on," "right on," etc.). Often European American teachers view this interaction as an interruption rather than a reinforcer. Looking at the teacher is a sign of disrespect in Jamaican and some African cultures, but a sign of respect in the United States.

Whereas European American culture values punctuality and a monochronic view of time, other cultures may not. This can cause problems in the educational process. For example, Latino students are not conditioned to use every moment in a productive, task-oriented way. Native Americans have a polychronic view of time—things are done when the time is right, not by a time on a clock or a date on a calendar.

The cultural differences among students are important to understand for two major reasons: (1) cultural differences may result in differences in learning style and (2) understanding cultural differences can help us communicate more effectively with students.

Gay (1978) indicates that two cognitive patterns are evident from research on ethnic learning styles. The *analytic style* is detail specific, impersonal, requires sustained attention, and uses an elaborate syntactic code. This style seems to be characteristic of European and Jewish Americans. The *relational style* employs self-centered orientations, determines word meanings by situational contexts, focuses on global characteristics of stimuli, uses a descriptive mode of abstracting information from stimuli, and uses a restricted syntactic code. This style seems to be characteristic of Mexican Americans, Asian Americans, African Americans, and some Native Americans.

In the past decade, considerable research has focused on students' learning styles. Students appear to have preferences for the ways in which they process information (for example, concretely or abstractly) as well as the ways in which they receive information (for example, listening or seeing).

Bond (1991) in his text, *Beyond the Chinese Face*, provides an excellent example of the Chinese learning style. Matched samples of Taiwanese and American children were tested on their approaches to grouping objects. The children were presented with arrays of three familiar objects taken from a variety of categories, such as people, food, tools, and so forth. Each child was asked to select two of the three objects that were alike or went together and to state the reason for their grouping. Chinese children more often grouped objects on the basis of an assumed relationship or interdependence between the two items, for example, "because the man is married to the woman" or "because the mother takes care of the baby." The Chinese were also slightly more likely to pair objects on the basis of similarities in the total appearance of the objects, such as "because both people are fat." The American children, by contrast, preferred the analytic style of grouping. That is, they identified some attribute, be it descriptive, such as "because both animals have fur" or inferential, such as "because both animals are mammals." In short, the Chinese tend to perceive on the basis of the overall pattern uniting the objects; Americans on the basis of a characteristic shared by the objects. American children join the objects after decomposing them into parts; Chinese children join the objects after considering them as wholes.

In general, the research supports the conclusion that Latino, Native American, African American, and female students respond better to teaching methods that emphasize holistic thinking, cooperative learning, a valuing of personal knowledge, a concrete orientation, the oral tradition, and a reliance on imagery and expressiveness. This learning style is quite different from that of most college instructors, Asian Americans, and the majority of students, whose learning style is characterized by an abstract, independent, written, technical orientation (see, for example, Anderson, 1988; Banks, 1988; Calloway-Thomas, Cooper, & Blake, 1999; Hilliard, 1989; Pemberton, 1988; Samovar & Porter, 2001).

Remember that although general statements such as these can be made as a result of existing research, careful attention must be given to individual differences to avoid stereotyping. That is why it is imperative for teachers to understand the cultural differences of their students in order to communicate effectively with them.

In order to understand our communication in the culturally diverse classroom, we need to consider the following (adapted from Condon, 1986):

1. *Our expectations for appropriate student behavior.* We may, for example, expect students to use standard English in both speaking and writing.
2. *The student's actual behavior.* The student may or may not use standard English.
3. *Our feeling about the student's behavior as well as the basis for this feeling.* "I'm angry because the student refuses to learn standard English."
4. *Our explanations for the behavior.* We must remember that these explanations reflect our cultural values ("The student isn't motivated to learn").
5. *Our response to the student's behavior.* We may reprimand the student—either publicly or privately. Again, our response reflects our cultural values and norms.

When we are aware of the cultural differences in our classrooms, understand our attitudes concerning them, and understand the five steps previously outlined, we can begin to structure our classroom so that we communicate effectively with multicultural students. We can, for example, respect the ethnic background of our students. We can read stories with varied ethnic and racial content in literature class. We might have students study world events from different cultural perspectives in social studies class. However, multicultural education is not content alone. Your attitude toward culturally diverse students and how you communicate that attitude is extremely important.

When one of the authors of this text was teaching Chinese students at the Chinese University of Hong Kong, she learned that our American teaching strategies can be problematic for the Chinese. For example, never ask Chinese students, "Are there any questions?" To ask a question would show one's ignorance, and a loss of face would result. However, if a teacher asks, "Have I explained this clearly?" students are free to ask questions because it is the teacher's "fault" that they don't understand. If she explained clearly, there would be no need for questions.

In addition, because of the high status of teachers, Chinese students are very uncomfortable with the informality, common in college-level American classrooms, of referring to a teacher by first name. Interestingly, one of the Chinese words for disobedience consists of two characters, which roughly translated mean "mouth back." As one might expect, students show their respect by keeping quiet in class. Thus, Asian students may be uncomfortable with a teaching strategy such as discussion or small groups.

African American students, whose culture emphasizes verbal skills and expressiveness, show greater emotion and theatrical behavior; demonstrate faster responses, higher energy, and more animation; and are persuasive and more active in the communication process. European American teachers often view these behaviors as confrontational because they are more passive in their communication style (Shade & New, 1993).

From a transactional perspective, problems arise because the African American student perceives the communication of the European American teacher as dissuasive and distancing, whereas the teacher sees the African American student's communication as disruptive or confrontational (Shade & New, 1993).

These examples tell us that teaching in a culturally diverse classroom is not an easy task. Teachers need special training. In preparing to teach a diverse group, Chism and her associates (1989) suggest the following:

1. Understand nontraditional learning styles.
2. Learn about the history and culture of nontraditional groups.
3. Research the contributions of women and ethnic minorities.
4. Uncover your own biases.
5. Learn about bias in instructional materials.
6. Learn about your school's resources for nontraditional students.

Finally, use a variety of teaching methods. Provide opportunities for students to work cooperatively as well as individually. Supplement lectures with audiovisual materials; use discussion, simulation, role playing, and active, hands-on experiences. Give students choices in how to complete an assignment—a paper, an art project, an oral report. (For additional ideas, see Cano, Jones, & Chism, 1991; Kepler, Royse, & Kepler, 1996).

STUDENTS WITH SPECIAL NEEDS

In addition to students from varying cultural backgrounds, you will also have students with special needs. Space does not allow an in-depth discussion here of students with special needs; however, books have been written on these students, referenced throughout this chapter. Following is a brief discussion of several types of students with special needs and some suggestions for teaching these students.

Students with Learning Disabilities

Students with learning disabilities often have poor self-concepts and are less accepted and more overtly rejected than their peers without learning disabilities; they frequently have problems interacting with teachers and parents and exhibit problem behaviors in general. Many youth with learning disabilities exhibit negative verbal interactions and misinterpret nonverbal communications.

Students with learning disabilities usually exhibit discrepancies between their actual level of performance and their intellectual potential. These students have difficulty processing auditory and visual stimuli, the result of which is a faulty interpretive response. Learning disabilities can occur in the following areas:

Memory—inability to remember newly presented information

Visual–auditory discrimination—inability to see or hear likenesses and differences

Visual–auditory association—inability to associate visual and auditory stimuli

Perceptual–motor skills—inability of visual, auditory, tactile, and kinesthetic channels to interact appropriately with motor activity

Spatial orientation—inability to master temporal, spatial, and orientation factors

Verbal expression—inability to express ideas, communicate, or request information

Closure–generalization—inability to extrapolate beyond an established set of data or information

Attending—inability to attend selectively or focus on tasks

Generally, students who are learning disabled need a structured classroom environment, which encourages cooperative efforts among students and teachers (Carnahan, 1994; Rothman & Casden, 1995). When working with learning disabled students, teachers should

- Increase attention span by removing distractions, including any materials other than those necessary for the assigned task.
- Teach the student how to organize desk belongings and materials.
- Try to improve one behavior at a time, rewarding appropriate behavior, and involving the student in recording behavioral progress. Discuss appropriate ways to expend extra energy.
- Carefully structure the learning environment and tasks with specific standards, limits, and rules.
- Make consistency an important ingredient—in rules, directions, and the like. Make consequences for rule infractions clear.
- Assign one task at a time, at first using a step-by-step procedure. This means short, sequential assignments, with breaks between tasks.

- Use a variety of media to present content (films, tapes, printed material, etc.).
- Use active methods (simulation games, experiments, role playing, etc.) in the instructional strategies.
- Employ materials for differing learning patterns (pictures, tapes, concrete objects).

Students Who Are Intellectually Gifted

Intellectually gifted students often progress academically one and a fourth or more years within one calendar year. Usually gifted students possess some of the following characteristics:

- an interest in books and reading
- large vocabularies and an ability to express themselves verbally in a mature style
- a wide range of interests
- a high level of abstract thinking
- a curiosity to learn

Instructional materials and programs for the gifted are numerous. In general, the following instructional procedures should prove helpful:

- Make use of trade (library) books in the program.
- Develop units of work that provide opportunity for in-depth and long-term activities, as well as library research.
- Use special tables and bulletin boards for interesting and challenging problems, puzzles, worksheets, and so on.
- Use special enrichment materials appropriate to the content areas.
- Encourage oral and written reports on topics under discussion and related topics.
- Challenge creative thinking by using games and simulation.
- Provide opportunities for participation in special clubs or groups designed to challenge gifted students. (Roe, Ross, & Bums, 1984, p. 183)

In terms of teaching gifted students, several traits of effective teachers of the gifted have been identified (Martin–White & Staton–Spicer, 1987). These include building and maintaining interpersonal relationships with students, skill in problem-solving strategies, skill in conducting group discussions, using debate and controversy to involve students in discussion, communicating with children at their level of understanding, and asking questions to elicit higher-level cognitive responses.

The voluminous research on gifted and talented youth demonstrates that gifted students need accelerated, challenging instruction in core subject areas that parallel their special aptitudes, opportunities to work with other gifted students, and highly competent teachers (Feldhusen, 1989).

Students Who Are Mainstreamed

Mainstreaming is the practice of integrating students into the regular classroom who had previously been enrolled in special education classes. Prior to these students entering your classroom, an Individualized Educational Program (IEP) must be devised for each pupil who is disabled.

According to law, each IEP should be made up by a team of specialized personnel, parents, and classroom teachers yearly. It should contain (1) a statement of the pupil's present educational levels; (2) the educational goals for the year; (3) specifications for the services to be provided and to what extent the pupil should be expected to take part in the regular program; and (4) the type, direction, and evaluative criteria for the services to be provided. You should have an active role in the preparation of these specifications for the students who are disabled assigned to your classes. You will have the major responsibility for carrying out the specifications.

Regardless of the nature of the disability, the following guidelines should prove helpful in dealing with the mainstreamed student (Roe, Ross, & Bums, 1984, pp. 197–198):

1. *Build rapport with the student who has a disability.* Let the student know you are genuinely interested in seeing that he overcomes his difficulties. A comfortable, relaxed atmosphere also enhances rapport (see, for example, Hart & Williams, 1995).
2. *Formulate a plan for alleviating the difficulty as much as possible.* Instruction must be tailored to meet the needs of the individual student. Skills to be taught must relate to the student's learning characteristics and potential. Different approaches will succeed with different students, so you must be flexible in your approaches and familiar with many different approaches.
3. *Adjust the length of the instructional session to fit the student's attention span and needs.* In fairly long sessions you will need frequent changes of activities or rest periods.
4. *When necessary, identify the basic life skills and relate them to subject content.* For example, in mathematics, note skills related to such everyday areas of usage as these: newspaper advertisements, price tags, money values, the calendar, road signs, road maps, recipes, timetables, measurement units, thermometers, clocks, sales slips, making change, budgeting money, planning meals, and balancing a checkbook.
5. *The mainstreamed student's interests need to be utilized.* A student interested in a particular topic (hobby, game, sport, or the like) will tend to put forth a great deal of effort to master a concept or skill that relates to that interest.

Physical Disabilities

The National Organization on Disabilities reports that more than 49 million Americans have a disability (Cohen, 1998). These may range from a "hidden" disability, such as a learning disability, to a visible physical disability, such as a person in a wheelchair. In terms of the classroom, students with disabilities, particularly those with visible physical disabilities, report negative attitudes of faculty as a primary reason they fail at the postsecondary level (see research reviewed in Bilke and Ya-sel, 1999). Indeed, the classroom climate does not seem to be a supportive one for students with physical disabilities. Beilke and Yasel (1999) report that these students often find faculty willing to make instructional accommodations but encounter less than a supportive classroom climate.

When able-bodied persons encounter a person with a physical disability, the able-bodied person often feels uncomfortable. They are not sure what to say or do (Braithwaite, 1990, 1991, 1996; Higgins, 1992). In addition, able-bodied people hold many stereotypes about people with disabilities:

> For example, they often perceive them as dependent, socially introverted, emotionally unstable, depressed, hypersensitive, and easily offended, especially with regard to their disability. In addition, disabled people are often presumed to differ from able-bodied people in moral character, social skills, and political orientation. (Coleman & DePaulo, 1991, p. 69)

Braithwaite and Braithwaite (2000, p. 144) provide guidelines for communicating with persons with disabilities. These are presented in Box 1.4.

Students at Risk

In a very real sense, all of the groups discussed previously are at risk. However, for our purposes, the at-risk student is defined as "one who is in danger of failing to complete his or her education with an adequate level of skills" (Slavin & Madden, 1989, p. 4). Risk factors include low achievement, behavior problems, low self-esteem, lack of social skills, poor attendance, retention in grade, low socioeconomic status, and attendance at schools with large numbers of poor students (Richman & Bowman, 1997). According to Slavin and Madden (1989, p. 4)

> Each of these factors is closely associated with the dropout rate; and by the time students are in 3rd grade, we can use these factors to predict with remarkable accuracy which students will drop out of school and which will stay to complete their education.

In their book on at-risk learners, Lehr and Harris (1988, p. 11) identify the necessary skills and competencies to teach students at-risk. These are summarized in Box 1.5.

In addition, cooperative learning has been found to improve academic and social skills of at-risk students. Slavin (1986, p. 126) summarizes the effectiveness of cooperative learning:

> The research on cooperative learning methods supports the usefulness of these strategies for improving such diverse outcomes as student achievement at a

---

BOX 1.4

COMMUNICATING WITH PERSONS WITH DISABILITIES

DO NOT
- Assume persons with disabilities cannot speak for themselves or cannot do things for themselves.
- Force your help on persons with disabilities.
- Avoid communication with persons who have disabilities simply because you are uncomfortable or unsure.
- Use expressions such as *handicapped, physically challenged, crippled, victim,* and so on unless requested to do so by persons with disabilities.
- Assume that a disability defines a person.

DO
- Assume persons with disabilities can do something unless they communicate otherwise
- Let persons with disabilities tell you if they want something, what they want, and when they want it. If a person with a disability refuses your help, don't go ahead and help anyway. The goal is to give the person with the disability control in the situation.
- Remember that persons with disabilities have experienced others' discomfort before and understand how you might feel.
- Use expressions such as *people with disabilities* rather than *disabled people*. The goal is to stress the person first before introducing the disability.
- Treat persons with disabilities as *persons first,* recognizing that you are not dealing with a disabled person but with a *person* who *has* a disability. This means actively seeking the humanity of the person you are speaking with, and focusing on the person's characteristics instead of the superficial physical attribute. Without diminishing the significance of a physical disability, you can selectively attend to many other aspects of a person during communication.

---

variety of grade levels and in many subjects, inter-group relations, relations between mainstreamed and normal-progress students, and student self-esteem. Their widespread and growing use demonstrates that in addition to their effectiveness, cooperative learning methods are practical and attractive to teachers. The history of the development, evaluation, and dissemination of cooperative learning is an outstanding example of educational research resulting in directly useful programs that have improved the education experience of thousands of students and will continue to affect thousands more.

Research suggests the importance of supportive communication for at-risk students (Richman, Rosenfeld, & Bowen, 1998; Rosenfeld & Richmond, 1999; Rosenfeld, Richmond, & Bowen, 1998). In general this research examines supportive communication and school outcomes. Supportive communication can take eight forms as described in Table 1.3 (Rosenfeld, Richman, & Bowen, 1998, p. 311).

BOX 1.5

NECESSARY SKILLS AND COMPETENCIES TO TEACH AT-RISK STUDENTS

PERSONAL SKILLS AND COMPETENCIES

Teachers need to be

- accepting
- caring, concerned, empathetic, loving, respecting, humanistic
- enthusiastic and energetic
- humorous
- patient
- effective communicators with students and parents
- creative
- flexible

PROFESSIONAL SKILLS AND COMPETENCIES

Teachers need to

- be professional (reliable, punctual, dedicated)
- use resources from other teachers and the community

MATERIALS

Teachers need to

- adapt materials to appropriate levels
- develop and use manipulatives
- use a wide range and variety of materials

METHODS

Teachers need to

- set realistic goals and objectives for students (high expectations)
- diagnose, prescribe for, and evaluate students (formally and informally)
- make learning relevant
- individualize instruction
- utilize small group instruction
- utilize a variety of techniques and methods
- reteach and give students time to practice the skill or concept—meaningful repetition is essential
- have a thorough knowledge of all content areas
- have training in special education

LEARNING ENVIRONMENT

Teachers need to

- be "cheerleaders"
  - be positive
  - use motivational strategies
  - enhance self-concepts
  - ensure successful experiences
- create a warm, inviting learning environment
- be firm, consistent, and fair in classroom management
- consider the total student (mental, physical, and emotional)

TABLE 1.3   **Types of Support**

Type of Support	Description Perception that the other is
Listening	Listening without giving advice or being judgmental
Emotional	Providing comfort and caring
Emotional challenge	Challenging the support recipient in order to encourage her/him to evaluate her/his attitudes, values, feelings
Reality confirmation	Helping to confirm the support recipient's perspective of the world
Task appreciation	Acknowledging the support recipient's efforts and expressing appreciation for the work she/he is doing
Task challenge	Challenging the support recipient's way of thinking about a task or activity in order to motivate the support recipient to greater creativity, involvement, or excitement
Tangible assistance	Providing the support recipient with either financial assistance, products, or gifts
Personal assistance	Providing services or help, such as running an errand

In terms of at-risk students, Rosenfeld, Richman, and Bowen (1998) found that for middle school students, various types of support were related to school outcomes. Technical appreciation and reality confirmation were related to the student avoiding school problems (e.g., being "kicked out" of class, fighting). Emotional support and emotional challenge support were related to higher school engagement (e.g., finding school fun, looking forward to learning new things). Technical challenge was related to higher school satisfaction (e.g., liking classes, enjoying coming to school). High school students who received emotional support, emotional challenge support, and personal assistance support reported studying more hours than students who did not receive these types of support. In addition, higher school engagement was related to task assistance support, whereas task challenge support and emotional challenge support were related to higher attendance (Rosenfeld & Richman, 1999). Thus, it appears that teachers should strive to be as supportive as possible in their communication with at-risk students.

Finally, teachers need to consider how to motivate at-risk students. Brophy outlines principles for motivating students (Table 1.4). These are particularly important in teaching at-risk students.

IN SUM

This chapter has provided a basic introduction to classroom communication. The nature of communication as a transactional, complex, symbolic process involving both content and relational components was also discussed. Several important topics that provide the foundations for our study of classroom communication were presented: socialization, classroom climate, cultural diversity, and students with special needs. These ideas are important. Yet, we would caution that teachers

TABLE 1.4   Highlights of Research on Strategies for Motivating Students to Learn

Research on student motivation to learn indicates promising principles suitable for application in classrooms, summarized here for quick reference.

Essential Preconditions

 1. Supportive environment
 2. Appropriate level of challenge/difficulty
 3. Meaningful learning objectives
 4. Moderation/optimal use

Motivating by Maintaining Success Expectations

 5. Develop program for success
 6. Teach goal setting, performance appraisal, and self-reinforcement
 7. Help students recognize linkages between effort and outcome
 8. Provide remedial socialization

Motivating by Supplying Extrinsic Incentives

 9. Offer rewards for good (or improved) performance
10. Structure appropriate competition
11. Call attention to the instrumental value of academic activities

Motivating by Capitalizing on Students' Intrinsic Motivation

12. Adapt tasks to students' interests
13. Include novelty/variety elements
14. Allow opportunities to make choices or autonomous decisions
15. Provide opportunities for students to respond actively
16. Provide immediate feedback to student responses
17. Allow students to create finished products
18. Include fantasy or simulation elements
19. Incorporate gamelike features
20. Include higher-level objectives and divergent questions
21. Provide opportunities to interact with peers

Stimulating Student Motivation to Learn

22. Model interest in learning and motivation to learn
23. Communicate desirable expectations and attributions about students' motivation to learn
24. Minimize students' performance anxiety during learning activities
25. Project intensity
26. Project enthusiasm
27. Induce task interest or appreciation
28. Induce curiosity or suspense
29. Induce dissonance or cognitive conflict
30. Make abstract content more personal, concrete, or familiar
31. Induce students to generate their own motivation to learn
32. State learning objectives and provide advance organizers
33. Model task-related thinking and problem solving

must consider all these ideas in relationship to their students. As Hugh Prather (1970, p. 20) reminds us:

> Ideas are clean. They soar in the serene
> supernal. I can take them out and look
> at them, they fit in books, they lead
> me down that narrow way. And in the
> morning they are there. Ideas are straight—
> But the world is round, and a
> messy mortal is my friend.
> Come walk with me in the mud…

ACTIVITIES

1.1   Term Project: Your Communication Journal. Keep a journal in which you enter notes from your readings, as well as observations, articles, poems, short stories, cartoons, and other materials on communication. The purpose of this journal is to help you analyze your own communication behavior and that of others. It should include anything that will help you meet this objective.
     In your journal write on one of the following:

1. Choose one of the following and write a brief opinion paper (one page).

   - The most critical issue in education is…
   - The most exciting challenge for teachers is…
   - Every teacher is a teacher of communication because…
   - Answer the question, "Why teach?"

2. Much has been written of late concerning metaphors about teaching. Complete the sentence, "Teaching is…"
     Ask several of your classmates to complete the sentence as well. What do such metaphors tell us about the teaching–learning process?

3. Read any of the following books about teachers' lives and write a one-page reaction. What did you learn about the role of communication in the classroom?

   Freedman, S. G. (1990). *Small victories: The real world of a teacher, her students and her high school.* New York: Harper and Row.

   Kidder, T. (1989). *Among school children.* Boston: Houghton Mifflin.

   McLaren, P. (1989). *Life in schools.* New York: Longman.

   Palmer, P. (1993). *To know as we are known: Education as a spiritual journey.* San Francisco: Harper and Row.

   Rose, M. (1989). *Lives on the boundary: The struggles and achievements of America's underprepared.* New York: The Free Press.

Sacher, E. (1991). *Shut up and let the lady teach: A teacher's year in a public school.* New York: Poseidon Press.

4. What are some behaviors you engage in when you enjoy a class: arriving on time? asking questions? What are some behaviors you engage in when you don't enjoy a class: arriving late? hesitating to participate?

5. As a teacher concerned with a supportive communication climate, what general changes would you make in course curricula (e.g., learning vehicles, group activities, and class asignments) to help accommodate students with physical disabilities? With learning abilities? With special needs?

6. Think of the types of support discussed by Rosenfeld and his colleagues (1998, 1999). How might you demonstrate each of those in the classroom?

7. Choose a folktale or proverb from another culture. What does it tell you about the values of that culture? How do these values compare with the values of your own culture? What problems might result from differences in values? How could communication help solve them?

FURTHER READING

Arnett, R. C. (1992). *Dialogic education: Conversation about ideas and between persons.* Carbondale, IL: Southern Illinois University Press.

Although a somewhat difficult read, a worthwhile one—a conversation about ideas between caring persons as they nourish relationships and then create nondefensive climates in the classroom.

Bertrand, Y. (1995). *Contemporary theories and practice in education.* Madison, WI: Magna.

This text provides an introduction to the principal contemporary theories of education. Each theory is accompanied by reflections about the goals of education, the roles of the instructor, the place of the student, the scope of course content, and the sociocultural relevance of education.

Bertrand, J., & Stice, C. (Eds.). (1995). *Empowering children at risk of school failure: A better way.* Norwood, MA: Christopher Gordon.

This resource uses detailed classroom profiles to show how a student failing in school can flourish in a holistic classroom.

Borman, K., Swami, P., & Wagstaff, L. (Eds.). (1991). *Contemporary issues in U.S. education.* Norwood, NJ: Ablex.

This text focuses on understanding social and policy issues and initiating political action to confront and solve them.

Braithwaite, D. O., & Thompson, T. L. (Eds.). (1999). *Handbook of communication and people with disabilities: Research and application.* Mahwah, NJ: Erlbaum.

This book is an excellent resource for understanding communication with people with disabilities.

Calloway-Thomas, C., Cooper, P., & Blake, C. (1999). *Intercultural communication: Roots to routes.* Boston: Allyn & Bacon.

Chapter 11 discusses intercultural communication in the educational context.

Daly, J., Friedrich, G., & Vangelisti, A. (Eds.). (1999). *Teaching communication: Theory, research and methods* (2nd ed.). Hillsdale, NJ: Erlbaum.

Written by some of the most outstanding communication scholars, this is the first text in the field of communication to integrate the conceptual and practical issues related to communication instruction.

Houston, R. (Ed.). (1990). *Handbook of research on teacher education.* New York: Macmillan.

The purpose of this 925-page book is to explore and delineate the accumulated research and scholarship pertinent to teaching.

Landis, D., & Bhagat, R. (Eds.). (1996). *Handbook of intercultural training* (2nd ed.). Beverly Hills, CA: Sage.

This is a "one of a kind" in terms of its comprehensiveness and coverage of a variety of issues and contexts.

Nyquist, J., & Wulff, D. (Eds.). (1992). *Preparing teaching assistants for instructional roles: Supervising TAs in communication.* Annandale, VA: Speech Communication Association.

This text provides various viewpoints on teaching assistantship supervision, competencies, and programs. Case studies of successful training programs are included.

O'Neill, K. L., & Todd–Mancillas, W. R. (1992). "An investigation into the types of turning point events affecting relational change in student–faculty interactions." *Innovative Higher Education 16,* 227–290.

This article describes research that suggests students need and want faculty who communicate well.

Rose, M. (1995). *Possible lives.* Boston: Houghton Mifflin.

A refreshing book that focuses on what is right about education.

Schmier, L. (1995). *Random thoughts: The humanity of teaching.* Madison, WI: Magna.

A compilation of the author's thoughts about teaching—from cheating to class size.

Siccone F. (1995). *Celebrating diversity: Building self-esteem in today's multicultural classrooms.* Boston: Allyn & Bacon.

This text helps teachers build self-esteem in students and encourages students to appreciate cultural diversity through 75 carefully chosen activities.

Sleeter, C., (Ed.). (1991). *Empowerment through multicultural education.* Albany, NY: University of New York Press.

Chapters 1–4 illustrate how schools disable many children, 5–12 describe strategies for empowering students, and 13–14 address issues in teacher education for multicultural classrooms.

Studer, S. C. (1999). *The teacher's book of days.* Rocklin, CA: Prima Publishing.

This book includes a short "inspirational" reading for each day of the year. Contains interesting and creative ideas for use in the classroom.

Tiedt, P., & Tiedt, I. (1990). *Multicultural teaching: A handbook of activities, information and resources* (3rd ed.). Boston: Allyn & Bacon.

This text is full of helpful ideas on how to prepare to understand and teach effectively within a multicultural environment.

CHAPTER TWO

INTERPERSONAL COMMUNICATION

Objectives

After reading this chapter you should be able to:

- Define interpersonal communication.
- Explain the importance of good interpersonal relationships in the classroom.
- Define self-concept.
- Define self-esteem.
- Outline the process by which we develop our self-concept.
- Explain how a teacher's self-concept can affect a student's self-concept and vice versa.
- Define self-disclosure.
- Discuss the concept of immediacy in intercultural classrooms.
- Define communication style.
- Discuss the two dimensions of teacher credibility.
- Describe the process of teacher expectancy.
- Outline how teacher expectancies can be communicated.
- Describe necessary teacher expectancies.
- Define student expectancies.
- Discuss seven guidelines for parent–teacher conferences.
- Discuss the advantages and uses of communicating electronically.

Carl Rogers (1962) suggests that in our work with students it's the quality of our relationship with them, not the content we teach, that is the most significant element determining our effectiveness. When asked to rate behavior they consider important to effective teaching, teachers often cite interpersonal communication and relationship skills. For example, Swinton and Bassett (1981) note that personality characteristics such as warmth, supportiveness, and openness, along with interpersonal and relationship skills, are rated highest among secondary school teachers.

How do we build relationships in the classroom? We build these relationships through communication with our students—through interpersonal communication.

From a transactional perspective, this means that interpersonal communication is concerned with the relational as well as the content message of our communication. It is through communication that we develop, maintain, and terminate relationships. A teacher must possess a well-developed repertoire of interpersonal communication skills in order to establish, maintain, and promote effective interpersonal relationships in the classroom.

RELATIONSHIP DEVELOPMENT

Several writers have analyzed the stages in developing and terminating relationships. Although the number of stages and the terminology used to describe them vary from writer to writer, the basic stages of relationship development are initiating, experimenting, and intensifying. The termination stages are deterioration and dissolution. It is important to note that communication changes as people progress through the stages.

According to Knapp and Vangelisti (1996) our communication becomes more broad, unique, efficient, flexible, smooth, personal, spontaneous, and overt as we progress through the stages of relationship development. Knapp and Vangelisti also speculate that as relationships deteriorate, communication becomes more narrow, stylized, difficult, rigid, awkward, public, and hesitant, and overt judgments are suspended.

Relationship Stages

Initiating.   This first stage is one of first encounters. On the first day of class we begin initiating our relationships with students. Much goes into this first stage. Our prior knowledge of the students and theirs of us, our mutual expectations, and our initial impressions all affect the initiation stage.

Much has been written in teacher education concerning the importance of the first day of class. First impressions have a great impact on how the student–teacher relationship progresses. First impressions are difficult to change. The first impression I have of a class or a student determines my expectations of how effective or pleasant future interactions will be.

Getting off on the wrong foot—either as a teacher or a student—can have very detrimental effects (Friedrich & Cooper, 1990; Goza, 1993).

Experimenting.   In this stage, students and teachers test one another and try to discover the unknown. Students experiment with behaviors—"How much can I get away with?" and "How can I please this teacher?" Teachers seek to identify the teaching methods and classroom management techniques that work best. Each person is trying to answer questions such as "Who are you?" "What do we have in common?" and "What do you expect from me?"

Much of the communication in this stage is stereotypical. Teachers aren't perceived by students as unique individuals, but only in their role as teachers. In like fashion, students are viewed in their role and not as individuals with unique ways of behaving or learning.

Intensifying.   In the intensifying stage, teachers and students communicate on a more interpersonal level. That is, communication is not role-to-role but person-to-person. A larger variety of topics may be discussed in greater depth than in the experimenting stage. Behavior is more easily predictable and explainable because teachers know students better and vice versa. For example, at this stage of the student–teacher relationship, a teacher will be able to predict how a particular student will react to humor or criticism and to adapt communication accordingly.

Deterioration and Dissolution.   We often consider termination of relationships as negative. However, in the student–teacher relationship, the termination stages of deterioration and dissolution are a natural phenomenon. Classes end and students leave. Patrick Walsh (1986), in his book *Tales Out of School*, describes the feelings many teachers experience as the school year ends:

> Nowadays I make my June farewells to students by writing them notes on the blackboard. A couple of years ago I was checking the roll for the last time when I suddenly got choked up. I made a quick exit, returned, but had to leave again. The next year, confident I'd be able to control my emotions, I started to tell a fourth-period how much I'd enjoyed teaching them. I got about five words out and had to stop.
> Another time I was collecting the last set of tests when it hit me that this would be the last time these kids would come together as "my" students. I could feel the tears starting, so I turned and pretended to look for papers on my desk. Finally, I grabbed some chalk and scribbled a note on the blackboard: "You've been one of the most talented, wild, fun classes I've ever taught. Thanks for a great year." As I finished writing, I thought of a line from T. S. Eliot: "It is impossible to say just what I mean." (p. 211)

COMMUNICATION VARIABLES IN INTERPERSONAL RELATIONSHIPS

Several communication variables contribute to building a positive relationship between student and teacher. The following variables are discussed in this chapter—self-concept, self-disclosure, immediacy, communication style, credibility, and teacher expectancy.

Listening is discussed in Chapter 3, and perception, language, general semantics, and nonverbal communication in Chapter 4.

Self-Concept

Basic to all interpersonal communication is the question, "Who am I?" Finding the answer to this question is prerequisite to being able to communicate effectively with others. Only when we know who we are can we proceed to communicate effectively with others.

Definition.   Your self-concept is your total image of yourself. It is made up of four parts:

1. How you perceive yourself intellectually, socially, and physically.
2. How you would like to be.
3. How you believe others perceive you.
4. How others actually perceive you.

Although we'll use the term *self-concept* throughout this chapter, it's important to remember that this term is somewhat misleading. Many self-concepts make up our general self-concept. For example, a student may have a concept of self as an athlete and a concept of self as a math student. For each of these concepts, the student has ideas about the four parts previously listed. You not only describe yourself, but also appraise or evaluate yourself. This appraisal reflects your self-esteem. In other words, I have a concept of myself as a teacher: I am dedicated and hard working. If I value those qualities, I will have high self-esteem. If I do not value my concept as a teacher, I will have low self-esteem. When people have high self-esteem, they feel likable, productive, and capable.

Communication and Self-Concept.   A reciprocal relationship exists between communication and self-concept: communication affects our self-concept, and our self-concept affects how and what we communicate. A model by Kinch (1963, p. 482) demonstrates this reciprocal relationship (Figure 2.1).

We can begin looking at this model at any of the four circles. Beginning with (P), our perceptions of how others see us influence our self-concept (S). Our self-concept influences our behavior (B). Our behavior (B) in turn influences the actions of others toward us (A). These actions influence our perceptions of how others see us, and we are back to the starting point again. As a teacher you can affect the self-concepts of students by the nature of the communication you direct toward them. Several researchers have found support for this idea. For example, Cooper, Stewart, and Gudykunst (1982) conducted studies that demonstrate that students with high and low self-concepts as public speakers perceive messages differently and that these perceptions are related to changes in their self-concept, their motivation to achieve, and their rating of both the instructor and their relationship with the instructor. Thus, how we perceive the communication we receive from others influences our self-concept and our subsequent communication.

One of the major ways self-concept affects communication in the classroom is through the self-fulfilling prophecy. Self-concept influences behavior. In other words, we behave in accordance with our self-concept. Consider the student who believes he is "dumb" in math. His attitude might be, "I don't do well, so why try?" As a result, he doesn't do math homework, doesn't study for exams, and doesn't pay attention in class. Because of these behaviors, he subsequently fails math. He has fulfilled his own prophecy, "I don't do well in math."

In summary, self-concept affects communication because we communicate and behave in accordance with our self-concept. Our self-concept is formed, to a large extent, by the communication we receive from others.

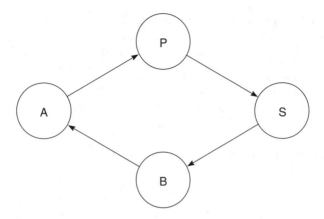

P = Perception of others' responses
S = Self-concept
B = Behavior
A = Actual responses of others

FIGURE 2.1   Kinch's Model of the Relationship between Self-Concept and Communication.

From "A Formalized Theory of Self-Concept," by J. W. Kinch, *American Journal of Sociology 68* (January 1963), pp. 481–486. Copyright © 1963 by The University of Chicago Press. Used by permission.

The power to produce an effect

Self-Concept and Academic Performance.   A logical question at this point is, "What effect does self-concept have on academic performance?" Bassett and Smythe (1979) outlined the characteristics of a student who demonstrates high academic achievement and the characteristics of a student who demonstrates low academic achievement. (See Table 2.1.) These authors indicated that many of the variables affecting academic achievement are related to student self-concept. If this is the case, it becomes crucial to consider the impact that teachers can have on student self-concepts.

   In general, teachers who appear to enjoy teaching and facilitate good student–student interaction, shared decision making, and positive student–teacher interactions foster more positive self-concepts in students. For example, your concept of self can greatly affect your teaching effectiveness. One way that this can happen is through a concept known as *teacher efficacy* which is a teacher's belief that he/she can influence how well students learn (Guskey & Passaro, 1994, p. 4). Researchers have found that teachers who have a high sense of efficacy were more satisfied with teaching, experienced less stress (Burley, Hall, Villeme, & Brockmeier, 1991), and exhibited greater enthusiasm for teaching and levels of planning and organization (Allinder, 1994). High teacher efficacy has also been shown to be related to student achievement and motivation (Midgley, Feldlaufer, & Eccles, 1989), increased self-esteem (Borton, 1991), improved self-direction (Rose & Medway, 1981), and more positive attitudes toward school (Miskel, McDonald, &

TABLE 2.1 Characteristics of Students Demonstrating High and Low Academic Achievement

Students Demonstrating High Academic Achievement	Students Demonstrating Low Academic Achievement
1. Have high regard for themselves	1. Have unfavorable attitudes toward school and teachers
2. Are optimistic about their potential for success in the future	2. Do not assume responsibility for learning
3. Possess confidence in their competence as persons and students	3. Have low motivation
4. Believe they are hard workers	4. Have low morale and are dissatisfied with their school experience
5. Believe other students like them	5. Participate in class infrequently
	6. Act in ways that create discipline problems
	7. Have high dropout rates
	8. Have difficulty adjusting personally and socially

Bloom, 1983). According to Czubaj (1996), when teachers tend to operate at the "higher," self, their students' self-esteem and motivation improved. More important, when students operated at the "higher" self, there was a reduction in failure, teenage pregnancies, and discipline referrals. It appears that teacher efficacy is somewhat contagious and cyclical. It works like this: a teacher who has confidence in his ability will have more positive interactions with students, who will, in turn, do better in school. It should be noted that the reverse is also true. A low sense of efficacy can create a self-defeating and demoralizing cycle of failure (Bandura, 1997). In this way, a teacher's concept of self has a great impact on student success.

Teachers with positive self-concepts have a flexibility that allows them to foster pupil autonomy and accept pupil ideas. Without this freedom from self, teachers cannot perceive or address the needs and concerns of their students. Research by Klein (1971) suggests that student reactions indeed influence teachers' self-concepts. She found that positive behavior (agreement, attentiveness, cooperation) on the part of students elicited positive behavior from teachers. Based on what we know about the relationship between self-concept and behavior, it's probable that teachers engaged in the positive behavior because they felt positive about themselves.

Not only does positive student behavior affect our self-concepts as teachers but negative student behavior can also influence the way we feel about ourselves as teachers. One of your authors, Dr. Cooper, shares the following:

> Recently I began teaching a class in communication and socialization. I had never taught the class before and was somewhat nervous. One student began to argue with me about the requirements for the course and became quite hostile. Perhaps because she was not completely confident about this new course, she left class

questioning my ability to teach this course effectively. As teachers we all have days when we don't get positive reactions from students. Often when we receive negative reactions, we feel inadequate. At this point, it is necessary to honestly reevaluate our teaching techniques and skills. However, it's just as important to keep things in perspective and not overreact to unpleasant situations. As I reflected on the student's hostile behavior and reevaluated what I wanted to accomplish in the course on communication and socialization, I decided I had been correct in my choice of requirements for the course. One student's negative behavior had thrown me temporarily, but a reevaluation of myself and the situation convinced me I was still adequate as a teacher.

Self-Disclosure

Self-disclosure—voluntarily giving others information about ourselves that they are unlikely to know or discover from other sources—is important in the development of relationships. If we're going to communicate effectively with our students, we need to know how they view themselves (their self-concepts). The only way to really know how students view themselves is through their self-disclosures. Likewise, if our students are going to communicate effectively with us, they need to know how we view ourselves. The underlying assumption of interpersonal communication is that the more we know about another, the more effective our communication will be with that person.

Although the focus in this chapter is on verbal self-disclosure, you should remember that we disclose information about ourselves nonverbally as well as verbally. The clothes you wear, the way you walk, and your smile all communicate things about you—your likes and dislikes, your emotional states, and so forth. We discuss nonverbal communication in Chapter 4.

The more information you have about how students view themselves, the better able you'll be to see the world through their eyes and thus better understand their responses to you, to other students, and to the instructional process.

Effective Self-Disclosure.   A major characteristic of effective self-disclosure is appropriateness. To be effective communicators we consider the timing of our disclosure, the other person's capacity to respond, the short-term effects, the motives for disclosure, how much detail is called for, whether the disclosure is relevant to the current situation, and the feelings of the other person as well as our own.

Another characteristic of self-disclosure is that it occurs incrementally. It's unlikely a student will come into your office following the first day of class and tell you anything very personal. In order to self-disclose, we have to trust the other person, and it takes time to build trust in a relationship. We must believe that the other person will not reject us, but will accept us for who we are. In addition, we must trust that they will respect the confidentiality of the information. As soon as someone violates our trust, self-disclosure stops or decreases significantly.

Self-disclosure is reciprocal. We disclose to the people who disclose themselves to us. It's primarily up to the teacher to begin this reciprocal process. If we are willing to share ourselves with our students, they'll be more willing to share themselves with us. The effect of this reciprocity is that a more positive classroom atmosphere can be developed and effective communication will be enhanced.

Factors Influencing Self-Disclosure.   Numerous factors influence self-disclosure. Self-disclosure occurs more readily under some circumstances than others. For example, *audience size* affects self-disclosure. The smaller the number of people, then the more likely it is that self-disclosure will occur.

Pair

Usually people are more comfortable disclosing information about themselves in a dyadic relationship than in a more public setting, such as a small group. Powell (1990), in the book *Why Am I Afraid to Tell You Who I Am?*, indicates the reason self-disclosure is scary: "If I tell you who I am, you may not like who I am, and it is all that I have" (p. 20).

Remember our discussion of communication complexity—complexity increases with each additional person. The more people present, the harder it is to monitor people's reactions to our disclosures. What happens if some people in a small group are accepting of us and others aren't? Do we continue to disclose or do we stop? The decision is difficult. Thus, students are more likely to disclose to us on a one-to-one basis. To request disclosures in any other context may be unwise.

Children disclose more than adolescents or *adults*. Elementary school teachers receive some rather interesting (and unsolicited) information concerning a student's home life, likes and dislikes, fears, and so on. However, children learn to temper their disclosures so that by the time students reach adolescence, they are fairly secretive.

Females disclose more than *males*. Men have traditionally been seen as the stronger of the sexes physically as well as emotionally. Many men don't cry or reveal their feelings, because this would seem to show weakness. As traditional sex roles are reevaluated, this tendency may well begin to disappear.

Finally, *race, culture,* and *nationality* affect self-disclosure. European American students have been found to disclose more information than African American students. U.S. students disclose more than similar students in Puerto Rico, Great Britain, West Germany, or the Far East.

What does all this information on self-disclosure have to do with classroom communication? We know that academic as well as social experiences during school have direct effects on self-concept development. Nussbaum and Scott's (1979, 1980) research suggests that students perceive teachers as intentionally and unintentionally revealing information about themselves in the classroom. These self-disclosures are linked to affective learning and teacher effectiveness. Holladay (1984) asked students to recall self-disclosures by teachers. These self-disclosures were most often about the teachers' education, experience as teachers, family, friends, beliefs and opinions, leisure activities, and personal problems. Downs, Javidi, and Nussbaum (1988) investigated the extent to which teacher self-disclosures are a part of their regular classroom behavior. Teachers' classes were audiotaped, and the researchers categorized the self-disclosing statements by general topic (teacher education, teacher experience, family, friends and colleagues, beliefs and opinions, leisure activities, personal problems, and others) and purpose (not relevant to course contents, clarifying course content, and promoting discussion). Seventy percent of teacher self-disclosing messages were used to clarify course content, and the general topic of the disclosures was most often related to teacher beliefs and opinions. The researchers also report data that suggests that moderate amounts of self-disclosing statements are most effective.

Javidi and Long (1989) found that experienced teachers used self-disclosing statements more often than inexperienced teachers. The researchers suggest this is true because more experience (which may be related to increased familiarity with course content, refinement of syllabi, and decreased tension due to increased classroom teaching time) may positively affect the use of self-disclosure.

Sorensen (1989a) was interested in the relationship between a teacher's self-disclosing statements and students' perceptions of the instructor's competence. She gave students 150 statements and asked them to evaluate each for the likelihood that a good (or poor) teacher would make the statement in the classroom. Disclosing statements that (1) were positively worded and (2) expressed sentiments that referred to caring were perceived by students to be used by good teachers. (For example, "I care about my students" versus "I do not like people who smile all the time.") If teachers use these types of disclosing statements, it can be expected that they will increase students' affective learning.

Finally, we know that in general, award-winning teachers self-disclose more than nonaward-winning teachers. Most of the self-disclosures of award-winning teachers are concerned with teaching experiences and are related to course content (Javidi, Downs, & Nussbaum, 1988).

Research has clearly demonstrated that the attitudes teachers have toward students affect the quality and quantity of communication teachers have with students. In addition, students' behavior toward you can affect how you feel about yourself as a teacher. This feeling can, in turn, influence your teaching, which can influence student learning. Remember the transactional perspective—each individual in the system affects every other individual. Two poems, one from the student's perspective (Cullum, 1971, p. 52) and one from the teacher's perspective (Cullum, 1978, p. 52) reflect the role of self-concept in the classroom:

> Teacher, give me back my "I" ——
> You promised, teacher,
> You promised if I was good you'd give it back.
> You have so many "I's" in the top drawer of your desk,
> You wouldn't miss mine.
>
> Do you love your teacher, children?
> Do you think I'm important?
> Do you think I'm best?
> Tell me boys and girls, tell me:
> Am I the fairest one of all?...

Immediacy

Immediacy behaviors (positive affect) are "nonlinguistic actions which send four simultaneous and complementary messages" (Andersen & Andersen, 1982).

Immediacy behaviors include the following: (1) approach behaviors, (2) signals of availability for communication, (3) typically multichanneled, and (4) communications of interpersonal closeness and warmth.

Immediacy can be communicated in a variety of ways both verbally and nonverbally. Varying voice pitch, loudness, and tempo; smiling; leaning toward a person; face-to-face body position; decreasing physical distance between teacher and student; arriving on time to class; removing physical barriers (such as standing or sitting behind a desk); gesturing; using overall body movements; and being relaxed and spending time with someone can all communicate immediacy.

Teachers who lecture from the same notes year after year; leave school immediately at the end of the day; rarely appear at school functions such as athletic, musical, or theatrical events; and rarely interact with students outside the classroom may communicate not only a dislike of students but also a dislike of the educational environment generally.

Immediate teachers are viewed as approachable, friendly, open, and responsive to student needs (see, for example, Andersen, 1979; McCroskey, Richmond, Plax, & Kearney, 1985; and Richmond et al., 1986). In addition, immediate teachers are perceived as warm and relaxed. Nonimmediate teachers are perceived as cold, distant, and unfriendly (see, for example, Kearney, Plax, Smith, & Sorensen, 1988). Nonverbal immediacy has been found to be perceived positively by students. Perceptions of teacher credibility and teachers' use of affinity-seeking strategies were found to be positively related to students' motivation to study. The affinity-seeking strategies that were positively related were listening, dynamism, inquiring about students' interests and opinions, creating a classroom environment in which learning is enjoyable, optimism, communicating empathy, being polite, displaying confidence in self and others, nonverbal immediacy (frequent eye contact, forward leans, smiling), telling students about self and accomplishments, and trustworthiness (Frymier & Thompson, 1992). In addition to nonverbal immediacy, researchers have examined verbal immediacy. For example, Gorham (1988) found that students' perceptions of teacher immediacy are influenced by verbal behaviors, and these behaviors contribute positively to learning:

> The teacher's use of humor in class appears to be of particular importance, as are his/her praise of students' work, actions, or comments and frequency of initiating and/or willingness to become engaged in conversations with students before, after, or outside of class. In addition, a teacher's self-disclosure ("uses personal examples or talks about experiences she/he has had outside of class"); asking questions or opinions; following up on student-initiated topics ("gets into discussion based on something a student brings up even when this doesn't seem to be a part of his/her lecture plan"); reference to class as "our" class and what "we" are doing; provision of feedback on students' work; asking how students feel about assignments, due dates, or discussion topics; and invitations for students to telephone or meet with him/her outside of class if they have questions or want to discuss something all contribute meaningfully to student-reported cognitive and affective learning. (p. 47)

A great deal of research has investigated the immediacy variable. In general, findings indicate that teacher immediacy (vocal expressiveness, smiling, gestures, eye contact, movement around the classroom, and a relaxed body position) is associated with cognitive learning (Gorham, 1988; Richmond, McCroskey, & Payne, 1987), affective learning (Andersen, 1979; Gorham, 1988; Kearney, Plax, Richmond, & McCroskey, 1985), recall of information (Kelley & Gorham, 1988), classroom management (Kearney, Plax, Richmond, & McCroskey, 1984; Kearney et al., 1988; Richmond, 1990), humor (Gorham & Christophel, 1990), motivation (Christophel, 1990; Christophel & Gorham, 1995; Frymier, 1994a; Gorham & Christophel, 1992; Richmond, 1990), and positive evaluation of the teacher by students (Thweatt & McCroskey, 1996).

Why does teacher immediacy have such a positive impact? As Frymier and Shulman (1995) suggest:

> Initially, an immediate teacher gains students' attention. Immediate teachers move about the classroom, make eye contact, use vocal variety, and address students by name, all of which are attention getting. Use of immediacy behaviors may also help to build confidence in students. An immediate teacher seems to produce liking and positive feelings among students, which creates an environment where success may seem more likely. Students with such a teacher are also likely to be more satisfied with the learning experience than are students with a low immediacy teacher (Frymier, 1994b).... Immediacy behaviors are likely to increase motivation because of their positive impact on (a) attention, (b) confidence, and (c) satisfaction. (p. 41)

Interestingly, from the transactional perspective, students are more likely to respond reciprocally to immediate teachers (Plax, Kearney, McCroskey, & Richmond, 1986). In other words, students affirm teachers who affirm them.

In sum, the use of immediacy in the classroom creates positive outcomes for students in terms of enhanced learning and motivation. Teachers who are immediate are evaluated more positively than those who are not.

One word of caution is necessary. Several researchers suggest that immediacy is influenced by culture. For example, Fayer, Gorham, and McCroskey (1993) examined teacher immediacy in the United States and in Puerto Rico. They found immediacy to be positively related to affective and cognitive learning in both cultures, but more so for U.S. students than for Puerto Rican students.

Collier and Powell (1990) found significant differences in the ways European Americans, Hispanic Americans, African Americans, and Asian Americans evaluated teacher immediacy. Although all four groups perceived a positive relationship between immediacy and teacher effectiveness, immediacy cues functioned differently across groups. For European Americans, the degree to which the teachers oriented their body positions toward the students contributed significantly to teacher effectiveness. For Hispanic Americans, smiling, vocal expressiveness, and body position were most important. Teacher relaxedness and smiling were perceived by African Americans to be important contributors to teacher effectiveness. Finally, for Asian Americans, vocal expressiveness, smiling, and teacher relaxedness contributed significantly to their perception of teacher effectiveness.

For all ethnic groups, seven immediacy behaviors were positively associated with cognitive learning: encouraging students to talk, using humor, having discussions with students outside of class, soliciting alternative viewpoints, praising students' work, not using a dull voice, and smiling at students. Some of these cues

Animated
dramatic
friendly
open
attentive

were particularly strong predictors for only certain groups. For example, although encouraging students to talk and using humor were significant predictors for all ethnic groups, they were particularly important to African American students, whereas willingness to have discussions outside of class was particularly salient to Asian American students.

Six immediacy behaviors were significant predictors of affective learning for all ethnic groups: using humor, asking students about assignments, soliciting viewpoints from students, praising student work, maintaining eye contact, and smiling at students. Again, differences in terms of significance were found between ethnic groups. For example, maintaining eye contact was very important to Hispanic American students and less so to African American students, whereas the reverse was true for asking about assignments.

Only two immediacy cues were significant predictors of behavioral learning across cultural groups: asking student names and maintaining eye contact.

Based on data drawn from the cultures of Australia, Finland, Puerto Rico, and the United States, McCroskey, Richmond, Sulliven, Fayer, and Barraclough (1995) found that nonverbal teacher immediacy behaviors related to positive teacher evaluation and willingness to take another course with the teacher in all four cultures. Immediacy behaviors that contributed to higher teacher evaluations were vocal variety, relaxed body position, eye contact with students, and smiling at students. Moving around and gesturing were also viewed positively by students (less so by Australian students) but were less important in students' evaluations of teachers. McCroskey, Fayer, Richmond, Sulliven, and Barraclough (1996) found that increased teacher immediacy was associated with increased affective learning across the cultures of the United States, Puerto Rico, Australia, and Finland.

These studies suggest that teachers need to be concerned with being both verbally and nonverbally immediate to their students. Perhaps what these multicultural studies suggest is that a large repertoire of immediacy behaviors are necessary for a teacher in order to be perceived as immediate by all students.

Communication Style

Communication style can affect interpersonal communication in the classroom. It is "the way an individual verbally and paraverbally interacts to signal how literal meaning should be taken, interpreted, filtered, or understood" (Norton, 1978). Communication style can be classified in terms of eleven independent variables: whether the speaker is precise, contentious, relaxed, dominant, dramatic, open, attentive, animated, and friendly, and the voice and impression she leaves. Communication style also consists of one dependent variable—communicator image. In his research, Norton (1977) found strong evidence that students' perceptions of effective teaching are related to a teacher's communication style. The effective teacher was rated as attentive, relaxed, not dominant, friendly, and precise; further, this study found that effective teachers created positive, lasting impressions on their students.

tendency to quarrels and disputes

Potter and Emanuel (1990), in their research with students in grades 8 through 12, found that adolescents identify the instructor communication styles of friendly, attentive, and relaxed as the most desirable and the styles of dominant and contentious as the least desirable. Potter and Emanuel refer to these three styles as Human, Actor, and Authority. The Human teacher is one who carefully listens to student needs, talks to them on a friendly and informal basis, and is open to changing the course to meet student needs. The Actor teacher is a good storyteller who moves around a lot with gestures and facial expressions. The Authority is well organized, has a command of all details, and puts students on the spot with probing questions and difficult arguments.

To give you a better understanding of each communication style, the items related to each variable are presented in Table 2.2. Norton (1983) examined the question of which of these variables strongly profile the ineffective teacher. He found that the ineffective teacher is not very animated or lively, does not show enough attentiveness or friendliness, does not have a very precise style, is not very relaxed, and does not use a dramatic style.

In addition, Norton examined the dramatic style more closely and found that the teacher with a highly dramatic style always scored high on three variables: (1) uses energy; (2) catches attention; and (3) manipulates moods. Norton makes the following recommendations to help ineffective teachers do a better job of teaching:

- *Use more energy when teaching.* The primary problem at this point is defining what constitutes energy. It probably entails being more dynamic, active, open, mentally alert, enthusiastic, and forceful. The dynamic speaker employs vocal variety (emphasis, intonation, rate) and nonverbal variety (gestures) to increase expressiveness.
- *Anticipate how to catch attention.* The classes of communicative behaviors to do this include use of humor, curiosity, suspense, emotion, analogy, metaphors, surprise, and narratives.
- *Learn how to make a class laugh.* This is not to say that the teacher needs to become a clown. The more important dynamic entails audience analysis. Learning how to make someone laugh requires understanding shared premises. Even if laughter is never evoked, thinking about the problem is useful. A teacher might use humor to reduce tension, facilitate self-disclosure, relieve embarrassment, disarm others, save face, entertain, alleviate boredom, or communicate goodwill. The assumption is that humor enhances student–teacher relationships and thus enhances learning.

Gorham (1988) found that the amount of humor teachers are perceived to use is positively related to the students' perceptions of how much they learn and how positive they feel about the course content, instructor, and the behaviors recommended in the course. Examining students' perceptions of teachers' humor, Gorham and Christophel (1990) found that male and female students perceive humor differently, and the effect of humor on learning differs by student gender. Females seem to prefer the use of stories or anecdotes, particularly personal stories related to the topic. Male students seem to prefer tendentious comments, reporting

biased, in tendency in favor of a particular point of view

TABLE 2.2   **Communicator Style Variables**

Communicator Style Variable	Questionnaire Item
Attentive	This person can always repeat back to someone else exactly what was said.
	This person deliberately reacts in such a way that people know that he or she is listening to them.
	This person really likes to listen very carefully to people.
	This person is an extremely attentive communicator.
Impression making	What this person says usually leaves an impression on people.
	This person leaves people with an impression that they definitely tend to remember.
	The way this person says something usually leaves an impression on people.
	This person leaves a definite impression on people.
Relaxed	This person has no nervous mannerisms in his speech.
	This person is a very relaxed communicator.
	The rhythm or flow of this person's speech is not affected by nervousness.
	Under pressure this person comes across as a relaxed speaker.
Not dominant	In most social situations this person (does not) generally speak very frequently.
	This person is (not) dominant in social situations.
	This person (does not) try to take charge of things when she is with other people.
	In most social situations this person (does not) tend to come on strong.
Friendly	This person readily expresses admiration for others.
	To be friendly, this person habitually acknowledges others' contributions verbally.
	This person is always an extremely friendly communicator.
	Whenever this person communicates, he tends to be very encouraging to people.
Precise	This person is a very precise communicator.
	In an argument this person insists on very precise definitions.
	This person likes to be strictly accurate when he or she communicates.
	Very often this person insists that other people document or present some kind of proof for what they are arguing.

Adapted from R. W. Norton, *Communicator Style: Theory, Applications, and Measures.* Copyright © 1983 by Sage Publications, Inc. Reprinted by permission of Sage Publications, Inc.

these as things their teachers did to "show he/she had a sense of humor." Darling and Civikly (1987) and Stuart and Rosenfeld (1994) found that humor was positively related to classroom climate.

Observational and experimental research indicates humor is capable of improving student perception of teachers, facilitating student–teacher rapport, reduc-

transmission

ing negative affective states, and enhancing perceptions of competence, appeal, delivery, perceived intelligence, character, and friendliness. High school teachers use humor less frequently than college teachers. High school teachers use humor as a way of putting students at ease, as an attention getter, as a way of showing they are human, and to make learning fun. In other words, humor is used as a way to make the classroom environment more conducive to learning (Neuliep, 1991).

One note of caution is necessary. Downs, Javidi, and Nussbaum (1988) found that award-winning college teachers used less humor than did a comparison group of nonaward-winning teachers. The researchers suggest that "too much humor or self-disclosure is inappropriate and moderate amounts are usually preferred" (p. 139). It should also be noted that the majority of communication style research has been conducted in the United States. Thus, little is known about teacher communication style from an intercultural perspective. For example, strategies usually proposed in the United States to enhance teacher effectiveness may be anxiety provoking and misunderstood by Asian American students. In addition, Eastern Europeans experience difficulties in classrooms when teachers are perceived as being too informal and friendly (Borisoff, 1990).

Credibility

A teacher's credibility has two dimensions: competence and character. Competence is perceived knowledge and expertise in an area; character refers to perceived trustworthiness, goodness as a person, ability to be sympathetic, and willingness to act in the best interest of others.

Research evidence suggests that increasing a teacher's credibility has a positive impact on learning outcomes for students (Beatty & Zahn, 1990; Teven & McCroskey, 1996; Wheeless, 1974, 1975). You can get a sense of your credibility by having students complete the credibility scale in Figure 2.2.

What affects the perception of credibility? Research indicates that the communication variables previously discussed—namely communicator style and immediacy—can affect student's perceptions of teacher credibility. For example, Rubin and Feezel (1986) found that teacher credibility and teacher effectiveness were best predicted by the communication style variables of making an impression and being relaxed. Beatty and Behnke (1980) found that a teacher's consistent verbal and nonverbal messages lead to perceptions of greater character, whereas positive vocal cues predict perceptions of competence.

More recently, Thweatt and McCroskey (1998) found that students perceive instructors with high immediacy to have more credibility. They also note that students perceive nonimmediacy as a form of teacher misbehavior and suggest that teachers engage in immediate behaviors to protect their credibility.

What else can teachers do to enhance their credibility? One thing appears to be the use of affinity-seeking behaviors. Affinity is "a positive attitude toward another person" (McCroskey & Wheeless, 1976, p. 231), including perceptions of credibility, attraction, and similarity. In their study of twenty-five affinity-seeking strategies, Frymier and Thompson (1992) found twelve that were positively correlated with both dimensions of credibility. These twelve strategies were: *listening*—paying close

FIGURE 2.2   **Measure of Source Credibility.**

DIRECTIONS: On the following scales, please indicate your feelings about your teacher. Circle the number between the adjectives that best represents your feelings. Numbers "1" and "7" indicate a very strong feeling. Numbers "2" and "6" indicate a strong feeling. Numbers "3" and "5" indicate a fairly weak feeling. Number "4" indicates you are undecided or do not understand the adjectives themselves. There are no right or wrong answers.*

COMPETENCE	Reliable	7 6 5 4 3 2 1	Unreliable
	Uninformed	1 2 3 4 5 6 7	Informed
	Unqualified	1 2 3 4 5 6 7	Qualified
	Intelligent	7 6 5 4 3 2 1	Unintelligent
	Valuable	7 6 5 4 3 2 1	Worthless
	Inexpert	1 2 3 4 5 6 7	Expert
CHARACTER	Virtuous	7 6 5 4 3 2 1	Sinful
	Honest	7 6 5 4 3 2 1	Dishonest
	Unfriendly	1 2 3 4 5 6 7	Friendly
	Pleasant	7 6 5 4 3 2 1	Unpleasant
	Selfish	1 2 3 4 5 6 7	Unselfish
	Awful	1 2 3 4 5 6 7	Nice

* To compute your scores for competence and character, simply add up the numbers you circled for each measure separately.

Competence Total ___5 1___   Character Total _____

Adapted from "Ethos: A Confounding Element in Communication Research," by James C. McCroskey and Robert E. Dunham, *Speech Monographs 33* (1966), pp. 456–463. Used by permission of the National Communication Association.

attention to what the student says and querying to ascertain if the student's intended meaning is the interpreted meaning; *facilitate enjoyment*—developing a classroom environment that is enjoyable, an environment in which learning is both interesting and entertaining; *dynamism*—physically indicating to the students that one is dynamic, active, and enthusiastic via physical and vocal animation; *elicit other's disclosure*—inquiring about the student's interests and opinions and providing positive reinforcement for responses; *optimism*—presenting a positive outlook of one's self as someone who is pleasant to be around, someone who will not be self-critical or critical of others; *sensitivity*—communicating empathy, sympathy, and an "I care about you as a person and what you think about" attitude; *conversational rule-keeping*—following the cultural norms for socializing, being polite, and demonstrating interest in what the student says; *comfortable self*—displaying confidence in the setting, oneself, the students, and presenting oneself as a relaxed, contented individual; *nonverbal immediacy*—smiling, making frequent eye contact with students, exhibiting forward leans and other nonverbal cues indicating interest; *altruism*—attempting to be of assistance to the student by doing things for her or him or giving advice; *present interesting self*—highlighting of past accomplishments, sharing positive qualities, and demonstrating one's knowledge; and *trustworthiness*—letting the student know that as a teacher he or she is responsible, reliable, fair, honest, sincere, consistent in beliefs and behaviors, and will fulfill promises. This cluster of affinity-seeking strategies indicates that teachers who demonstrate that they care about students and have a sincere interest in and respect for them may be more likely to have motivated students in their classrooms. This, in turn, should lead to more opportunities for learning to occur (pp. 397–398).

Affinity-seeking not only appears to be positively related to perceived teacher credibility but also to motivation (Frymier & Thompson, 1992), a supportive classroom climate (Meyers, 1995), perceived cognitive learning (Beebe & Butland, 1993; Frymier, 1994b; Frymier & Thompson, 1992; Richmond, 1990; Thomas, 1994), liking for the instructor (Dolin, 1995; Frymierb, 1994), affect toward the subject matter (Gorham, Kelley, & McCroskey, 1989; Richmond, 1990), affect toward the instructor (Richmond, 1990), and students' motivation to study (Beebe & Butland, 1993; Frymier, 1994b; Richmond, 1990). Finally, teacher affinity seeking has been positively related to student willingness to accommodate their instructors' requests (Dolin, 1995).

Expectancy

Teacher Expectancies.   With the publication of Rosenthal and Jacobson's *Pygmalion in the Classroom* in 1968, a controversy began about the effect of teachers' expectations on students. Basically, the expectancy process works as follows:

1. Teachers expect certain behaviors from certain students.
2. These expectations influence the teacher's behavior toward these students.
3. The teacher's behavior indicates to the students what the teacher expects of them. These expectations affect the students' self-concept, motivation to achieve, and achievement.
4. If the teacher's behavior is consistent over time and the students do not resist it, high-expectation students will achieve well and low-expectation students will not.

Although much disagreement has been generated about the teacher expectancy issue, the evidence does suggest that teacher expectations can be self-fulfilling.

One of the clearest models of teacher expectancy is proposed by Braun (1976). The model suggests that, based on the teacher's perceptions of student ability and background (input), expectations are formed (see Figure 2.3). These expectations are then communicated to students in various ways (output). Students read and internalize the teacher's output and form a self-expectation. The student's output, based on the self-expectation, produces new input (represented by the dotted line in the model), and the cycle continues.

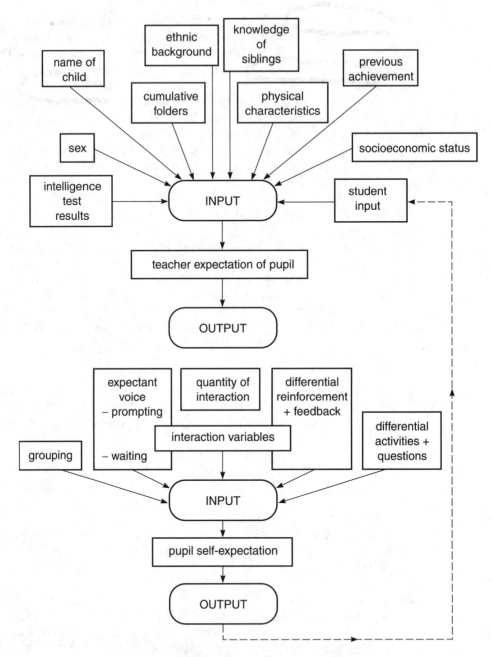

FIGURE 2.3   A Model of the Expectation Process.

From "Teacher Expectation: Sociopsychological Dynamics," by C. Braun, in *Review of Educational Research 46* (1976), p. 206. Copyright © 1976 by the American Educational Research Association. Reprinted by permission of the publisher.

Good and Brophy (1987) suggest several specific methods by which expectations can be communicated in Box 2.1. Teachers may inadvertently communicate high or low expectations in students simply by the way they respond to them. The methods outlined in Box 2.1 will be useful to you as you begin to interact with students in your own classroom. For example, if a student appears to be a low achiever, you can reflect on this list to determine if you might be discouraging high achievement based on your expectations of that student.

Should the teacher strive to have only positive expectations? The preceding section may seem to suggest this. However, appropriate expectations, not necessarily high expectations, are what you as a teacher should strive for, according to Good and Brophy (1987):

> Expectations should be appropriate rather than necessarily high, and they must be followed up with appropriate behavior. This means planned learning experiences that take students at the level they are now and move them along at a pace they can handle. The pace that will allow continued success and improvement is the correct pace and will vary with different students. Teachers should not feel guilty or feel that they are stigmatizing slower learners by moving them along at a slower pace. As long as students are working up to their potential and progressing at a steady rate, the teacher has reason to be satisfied. There will be cause for criticism only if the slower children are moved along at a slower pace than they can handle because the teacher's expectations for them are too low, are never tested out or re-evaluated, and consequently, are unalterable. (p. 42)

Certain teacher expectations are recommended for an effective learning experience. Without them, teachers would not be very effective. Box 2.2 provides a useful list of things that you as a teacher should expect of yourself and your students. As you reflect on this list (both now and when you begin teaching), consider how these expectations will influence the way you approach teaching and your students. Consider how your approach will affect your continued desire to teach and your student's motivation to learn.

Student Expectancies.   Remember that expectancies exist on the part of students as well as teachers. Lim (1996) asked fifty of his students their expectations for an outstanding professor. Their expectations are provided in Box 2.3.

The profiles in Box 2.3 provide a set of guidelines that can prompt careful self-evaluation and motivate instructors toward "A" professor behaviors (pp. 3–4).

Students avoid some teachers and flock to others based on their expectations of what a particular teacher's class will be like. The expectancies a student has for a teacher will affect communication in the classroom. Students will communicate more with teachers they expect to be positive in responding. Student expectancies can affect student perceptions of a teacher's messages. If students expect to receive negative feedback, chances are they'll perceive messages from the teacher as negative. If they expect to receive positive messages, they'll perceive the teacher's communication as positive. For example, if a student raises her hand and is not called on, she may perceive the message negatively—"Ms. Miller never calls on

---

BOX 2.1

COMMUNICATING EXPECTATIONS TO STUDENTS

1. *Waiting less time for lows to answer.* Teachers have been observed to provide more time for high-achieving students to respond than for low-achieving students. The determinants of this behavior might include excessive sympathy for the student, teacher anxiety, or lack of probing skills, among others. As with the other variables discussed later, the determinants of such behavior are largely unknown.

2. *Staying with the lows in failure situations.* In addition to waiting less time for lows to begin their response, teachers in replicated studies have been found to respond to lows' (more so than highs') incorrect answers by giving them the answer or calling on another student to answer the question. High-achieving students in failure situations are much more likely to have the teacher repeat the question, provide a clue, or ask them a new question. Thus, teachers have been found to accept mediocre performance from lows but to work with and demand better performance from highs.

3. *Rewarding inappropriate behavior of lows.* In some studies, teachers have been found to praise marginal or inaccurate student responses. Praising inappropriate substantive responses (as opposed to perseverance, and so on) when the student's peers know the answer may only dramatize the academic weakness of such students.

4. *Criticizing lows more frequently than highs.* Somewhat at odds with the previously noted findings is that in some studies teachers have been found to criticize lows proportionately more frequently than highs when they provide wrong answers. This is indeed a strong finding, for it suggests that lows' expression of risk-taking behavior and general initiative is being discouraged. One would expect that lows might receive more negative feedback (but not necessarily criticism) simply because they emit more wrong answers. But the analyses alluded to here were controlled for the frequency of wrong answers and found that on a percentage basis, lows were more likely to be criticized than highs. It is possible that the quality of lows' responses may have been lower, but criticism for a serious attempt to respond is an inappropriate strategy in any case. The seeming discrepancy between items 3 and 4 may reside in differing teachers' personalities. Teachers who praise inappropriate answers from lows may be mired in sympathy for these students, whereas hypercritical teachers may be irritated at them for delaying the class or providing evidence that the teaching has not been completely successful.

5. *Praising lows less frequently than highs.* Also in contrast to item 3, some research has shown that when lows provide correct answers, they are less likely to be praised than highs even though they provide fewer correct responses. The situation is clear for lows in certain classes. If they respond, they are more likely to be criticized and less likely to be praised; thus, the safest strategy is to remain silent, because here the teacher is likely to call on someone else.

6. *Not giving feedback to public responses of lows.* Teachers in some studies have been found to respond to lows' answers (especially correct answers) by calling on another student to respond. Failing to confirm their answers seems undesirable in that these students in particular may be unsure about the adequacy of their response.

7. *Paying less attention to lows.* Studies have shown that teachers attend more closely to highs (and, as we noted previously, provide more feedback). Some data exists to suggest that teachers smile more often and maintain greater eye contact with highs than lows. Studies also show that teachers miss many opportunities to reinforce lows simply because they do not attend to their behavior. Such studies provide support for part of Rosenthal and Jacobson's (1968) original explanation of the Pygmalion results: positive expectations increase a student's salience and his or her opportunity for appropriate reinforcement.

8. *Calling on lows less often.* Relatedly, teachers have been found to call on high-achieving students more frequently than low-achieving students. Although much of the difference can be explained by student differences, the data show that few teachers compensate for these student differences. The difference in public participation becomes more sharply differentiated with increases in grade level.

9. *Differing interaction patterns of highs and lows.* Interestingly, contact patterns between teachers and lows are different in elementary and secondary classrooms. In elementary classrooms highs dominate public response opportunities, but highs and lows receive roughly the same number of private teacher contacts. In secondary classrooms highs become even more dominant in public settings, but lows begin to receive more private contacts with the teacher. Perhaps at this level private conferences with teachers are a sign of inadequacy, especially if the teacher does not initiate many private contacts with highs.

10. *Seating lows farther from the teacher.* Studies have suggested that when students are grouped randomly within classrooms, undesirable discrepancies in teacher behavior between high and low achievers are less likely. Perhaps this is because lows are sitting next to highly salient or "liked" students so that teachers are more likely to notice them and to maximize treatment of them as individual learners. Seating pattern studies have sometimes found that lows tend to be placed away from the teacher (creating a physical barrier). Random placement seems to reduce the physical isolation of lows and the development of sharp status differences among peers.

11. *Demanding less from lows.* Several studies have suggested that this is a relevant variable. It can be seen as an extension of the more focused "giving up" variable discussed previously. This is a broader concept suggesting such activities as giving these students easier tests (and letting the students know it) or simply not asking the student to do academic work. Also, sometimes if a low-achieving student masters the elementary aspects of a unit, he or she may be neglected until the elementary aspects of the next unit are dealt with. Teachers set different mastery levels for students. At times, however, being less demanding may be appropriate if initial low demands are coupled with systematic efforts to improve performance.

me"—if she expects a negative message. If a positive expectation is present, the student could interpret the message, "Ms. Miller wanted to give someone else a chance to talk."

Finally, student expectations can affect learning. Consider how learning might be affected by such expectations as, "You never have to do anything. Just go to class and you'll get an A," or "Mr. Brommel really knows his stuff. You'll learn a lot."

■ ■ ■ ■ ■ ■

BOX 2.2

TEACHER EXPECTATIONS

1. *The teacher should enjoy teaching.* Teaching brings many rewards and satisfactions, but it is a demanding, exhausting, and sometimes frustrating job. It is hard to do well unless you enjoy doing it. If you enjoy teaching, you'll show this in your classroom behavior.

2. *Teachers should understand that their main responsibility is to teach.* Your job involves many roles besides that of instructing students. Many of these have been discussed in previous chapters. Although these other roles are necessary aspects of your job, they are subordinate to and in support of the major role of teaching—instruction.

3. *Teachers should understand that the crucial aspects of teaching are task presentation, diagnosis, remediation, and enrichment.* Failure to be clear about crucial aspects of teaching characterizes teachers who favor high achievers over low achievers or who pay more attention to answers than to the thinking processes a student goes through in reaching an answer. Such teachers sometimes act as if the students are expected to learn on their own with no help from them. If a student does not catch on immediately after one demonstration or does not do his work correctly after hearing the instructions one time, they react with impatience and frustration.

   reading problems

4. *Teachers need to assess student understanding regularly.* There may be disparity between what teachers think they have communicated and what students actually heard. Teachers should monitor the work of their students regularly and talk to them about their understanding of classroom instruction. Unfortunately, many teachers become relatively passive during seatwork and deny themselves the opportunity to discover gaps or confusion in student understanding. It is important for teachers to assess the effects of instruction immediately (rather than waiting for an exam) to prevent students from practicing errors and developing misunderstandings.

   disparity
   difference

5. *Teachers should expect all students to meet at least the minimum specified objectives.* Although all students cannot be reasonably expected to do equally well, reasonable minimal objectives can be established for each of your classes. Naturally, most students will be capable of going considerably beyond minimal objectives, and you should try to stimulate this development as far as their interests and abilities allow. However, remember that remedial work with students who have not yet met minimal objectives should not be delayed in favor of enrichment activities with those who have.

6. *Teachers should expect students to enjoy learning.* Teachers can and should expect students to enjoy learning activities and communicate this expectation to students. This is one of the most common areas where teacher expectations become self-fulfilling. When you do have the appropriate attitude toward your subject, you present it in ways that make your students see it as enjoyable.

7. *The teacher should expect to deal with individuals, not groups or stereotypes.* As a rule, you should think, talk, and act in terms of individual students. You may practice grouping or use terms such as "slow learner." These practices and labels should be used only as a means to meet the needs of individual students or to think about ways to teach individuals better. In the final analysis, you are teaching Johnny and Susie, not Group A or "slow learners." The way you talk about your students is an indication of how you think about them and how you'll relate to them.

8. *The teacher should assume good intentions and a positive self-concept.* Teachers must communicate to their students the expectation that the students want to be—and are trying to be—fair, cooperative, reasonable, and responsible. This includes even those who consistently present the same behavior problems. Your basic faith in the student's ability to change is a necessary (but often not sufficient) condition for such change. If students see that you do not have this faith in them, they will probably lose whatever motivation they have to keep trying.

9. *The teacher should expect to be obeyed.* Obedience is usually obtained rather easily if you establish fair and appropriate rules, are consistent in what you say, say only what you really mean, and follow up with appropriate action whenever this is necessary. This produces credibility and respect; the students are clear about what you expect of them and know that they are accountable for meeting those expectations.

PARENT–TEACHER CONFERENCES

Interaction between the school and the home seems to be increasing, so that the home environment affects the classroom. For this reason, and because parent–teacher conferences are one of the most important interpersonal communication events, we discuss these briefly. Because parents and teachers each hold the other primarily responsible for school-related problems, parent–teacher conferences deserve special attention. Your goal during a parent–teacher conference is to discuss a student's progress. In order to meet that goal, you and the parents must communicate effectively. Several guidelines should prove helpful:

1. *Know the child's home background.* Does she live in a single-parent home or with a parent or stepparent? Such information will often influence how you structure the conference.

2. *Create a positive atmosphere.* Make sure your meeting room is clean and attractive. Choose furniture that is all the same height. If you sit in a higher chair and remain seated behind your desk, parents may feel intimidated.

3. *Make the right comments.* Don't outline all of a student's shortcomings. Choose those essential to the student's improvement. State your "problem" in positive terms: "Jane did not finish her assignment because she was reading the school newspaper" rather than "Jane is lazy."

4. *Offer practical, realistic suggestions.* Ask parents for their suggestions and solutions for solving a problem. Your attitude ought to be: "How can we best work together to help Jane?"

5. *Listen to parents.* Don't get defensive. If a conflict arises, remember the behaviors discussed earlier about managing conflict and apply them to this situation.

6. *Conclude the conference by asking parents questions that will tell you whether or not your message was clearly understood.* Make sure you understood them correctly also.

STUDENT EXPECTATIONS

THE "A" PROFESSOR—AN OUTSTANDING PROFESSOR

Preparation: "A" professors are able to prepare very well-organized syllabi and follow them. They always bring a complete set of notes to class and are prepared to lecture the materials thoroughly and efficiently.

Enthusiasm: "A" professors are enthusiastic about teaching. They make students feel welcome when seeking help, be it personal or academic. They have a genuine desire and interest in the subject they are teaching.

Clarity: "A" professors answer their students' questions clearly, accurately, and specifically. They make homework assignments clear and to the point.

Research: "A" professors are always up-to-date with new information. They are able to introduce the latest research into classrooms and always keep an eye on the latest technology and prepare their students for the future.

Assignments: "A" professors give out assignments regularly to reinforce class materials. Their assignments are challenging and pertain to class discussions. They always make sure that the students have the tools and knowledge to finish the assignments on time. They grade the assignments promptly and make adequate comments on homework and tests.

Humor: "A" professors have a sense of humor that makes the class more fun to attend. They bring to the class a level of dynamics that helps to maintain the interest of students when the materials become dry.

Fairness: "A" professors are fair in treating students. They grade students according to the students' performance and efforts. They are not biased, but assign grades impartially.

THE "C" PROFESSOR—AN AVERAGE OR TYPICAL PROFESSOR

Preparation: "C" professors do not prepare their lectures well. They do not have syllabi that students can follow. They often misplace their notes or forget to bring them to class. They frequently find themselves trying to figure out where they were previously. They do not have a clear plan about what to cover.

Enthusiasm: "C" professors usually do not show a strong commitment toward the class. They will be half-hearted when it comes to teaching, and they usually are not focused on the task at hand.

Clarity: "C" professors present their lectures in such a way that the students feel lost. They are vague about the requirements for assignments.

Research: "C" professors are not up-to-date in their field of study. They do not have full command of the subject and often try to conceal it.

Assignments: "C" professors give minimal assignments, and they do not grade the assignments for weeks after. They pile up assignments and assign all of them at once without proper warning. They give assignments that are unreasonable, expecting students to know more than they do. They also give poor guidance on assignments.

Humor: "C" professors present the materials in a monotone voice and manner that could make an interesting subject boring. They appear aloof and intimidating.

Fairness: "C" professors are not necessarily fair in treating students. They favor students that they know prior to class and give some sense of inequality in the classroom.

7. *Don't leave a parent "hanging."* Request a follow-up conference if necessary or report back to parents on their child's progress.

Parent–teacher conferences can be very enjoyable and helpful. Much of what occurs during the conference will be your responsibility. By following these guidelines, most of your conferences should prove to be very productive.

Box 2.4 provides a letter from a parent to a teacher discussing how she views the parent–teacher conference. In this letter, a concerned parent provides useful suggestions about how to communicate during the "dreaded" parent–teacher conference. Notice how many of these suggestions support the guidelines previously suggested. Also keep in mind that many parents will feel just as anxious as you will about this encounter (as the letter in Box 2.4 intimates). In the future, you may want to refer to this letter just prior to your first parent–teacher conference.

COMMUNICATING ELECTRONICALLY

Earlier in this chapter, we discussed the relationship between immediacy and learning as well as student perceptions of teacher credibility. Recall that immediacy includes verbal and nonverbal behaviors that signal approachability, availability, and warmth. Recently, researchers have begun to investigate the relationship between immediacy and student willingness to communicate with instructors outside of the classroom setting (Fusani, 1994; Jaasma & Koper, 1999). With the prevalence of personal home computers and increasing student computer literacy, one form of extraclass communication can take place via e-mail. Waldeck, Kearney, and Plax (2001) found that when teachers are immediate, students are more willing to communicate on-line. When doing so, students interacted with their teachers (1) to clarify course material and procedures, (2) for personal/social reasons, and (3) because it was convenient. There are many advantages to communicating with administrators, colleagues, students, and parents using e-mail (Dorman, 1998). First, e-mail is convenient and efficient because you can send and receive messages on your own time and to many people at once. Second, e-mail provides opportunities for increased contact between students and parents when school is not in session. Third, e-mail can provide a central source of information where you can announce assignments or special events, respond to frequently asked questions, and provide feedback to individuals or groups. Fourth, e-mail can facilitate communication with parents and is a cost-effective way to ensure parents obtain information that may get lost between school, a student's backpack, and home.

When using e-mail, however, there are several issues to consider. If requiring the use of e-mail as an opportunity for extended learning, you will need to be sure that all students have both access and the skills necessary to use this medium. Keep in mind that e-mail leaves a permanent record of your interactions and that information that should be confidential should be protected. In addition, e-mail does not contain a nonverbal component and some messages could be misinterpreted.

BOX 2.4

LETTER FROM A CONCERNED PARENT

Dear Mrs. McCrea,

About that conference next week.... It's a week until our conference about David, and I already have a knot in my stomach. Even having sat behind the desk as a teacher doesn't make it any easier when it's my child. I still have a knot.

I guess I'm like most people in that I don't deal very well with the unknown. I start weaving dreadful fantasies, anticipating the worst. Oh, I know David is a terrific kid. The question is, do you? I also know I shouldn't get anxious; when I'm anxious, I don't listen very well, and that's not a great way to go into a conference that's supposed to be for my benefit, is it? So I've been trying to think of ways to make our getting together a little easier for me, and maybe for you, too. Here are a few suggestions:

Information in advance about what we'll be talking about would definitely help loosen that knot in my stomach. You might send a general note to all the parents outlining the topics you usually cover—and maybe even ask us what we'd like to hear about on a tear-off at the bottom (that way you won't have to wait and wonder what I'm going to spring on you!). If you have a sense of what's on the agenda, I can pull my thoughts together and formulate reasonable-sounding questions (my words just get jumbled up if I don't have a chance to plan a bit). I could also talk with David's father about his ideas, and bring them along, since he can't always get away for daytime meetings.

It would help if you went over, at the outset of the meeting, what you plan to cover during the meeting—as well as what you don't plan to discuss. That way I'll know what to expect and can dispel those dreadful fantasies right from the start. At the same time, it would be useful if you told me how you want to structure the meeting. Should I interrupt with questions or wait until you ask for them? Will there be things for me to look at or read? How much time will we have? Much as I hate to admit it, we parents are a bit like students when it comes to parent–teacher conferences. The more that's laid out for us at the beginning of the lesson, the more we're apt to learn.

What I really want to know about David is how he's doing—both in relation to his own ability (and certainly I want to know if he's slacking off), and in comparison with other children. I know comparisons aren't supposed to be important, but I do wonder where he stands. Eventually he'll be getting some kind of comparative grades; I don't want to be taken by surprise. Hearing for years that "he's working up to his ability" in spelling won't prepare me for his official low grade in the subject. I want to know as much as you can tell me about my child's schoolwork.

If you do have bad news for me, tell me at the start, so I don't have to spend my time waiting for the other shoe to drop. Let me know exactly what you see to be the problem. Show me the papers, tell me the episodes, put everything out for me to look at, I'll probably be upset, but I'll react more calmly if I get clear, specific information. I'd like to know how serious you think the problem is, too. Is it a big issue that you think will have long-term effects, or do you see it as a minor annoyance that will go away by itself? Is it a part of a larger concern, or is it an isolated event? Help me to keep my perspective by telling me just how worried I should be.

Please tell me, too, what you plan to do about any problem David is having—and how I can help. The worst feeling for me is helplessness. If you can give me some guidance about what David needs (a special tutor, less help with homework, whatever), I'll have something to do besides worry.

Which brings me to another point. Even though I think I know what "fine motor skills" and "set theory" mean, some real-world examples will help me to be sure we agree on their meaning and purpose. I like seeing David's work. I'm also interested in what you see in his writing and art. Don't worry about boring me with lots of examples; where my child's progress is concerned, I'd rather see his work than listen to lots of fancy talk about it.

Finally, please plan to reserve some time to listen to me. I want to be able to tell you how I think David's doing, to ask you some questions, to respond to what you've told me. I know that I do go on at times, so I won't mind if you remind me that we have only a few minutes left and ask if I have any last things to say. If I feel there's a lot more to talk about, I hope we can schedule another conference.

If all this makes you think I'm an overly concerned parent, well, maybe I am. I admit I'm something of a zealot where David's skills, competence, and progress are concerned. I want what's best for him, of course. I've put him under your care and tutelage for six hours a day. Now I expect to know what's been going on during that time, how he's doing, and what I can do to help. I think we can be a terrific team—if I can just untie that knot in my stomach. (Gerritz, 1983, p. 46)

Finally, e-mail has a unique set of rules or norms (DeFleur, Kearney, & Plax, 1998) commonly referred to as "netiquette." These rules recommend that e-mail users keep messages brief, avoid using all upper case letters, use correct spelling and grammar, use "emoticons" to convey emotion (e.g., "LOL for "I'm laughing out loud" and ":-)" for "I'm smiling"), and avoid hostility or "flaming."

IN SUM

Teaching is not simply talking, just as learning is not simply listening. Rather, teaching and learning involve a communication relationship. Research suggests that good teachers differ from poor teachers in that good teachers

1. Have generally more positive views of others—students, colleagues, and administrators.
2. Are less prone to view others critically or to attack people as having ulterior motives; rather, they see them as potentially friendly and worthy in their own right.
3. Have a more favorable view of democratic classroom procedures.
4. Have the ability and capacity to see things from the other's point of view.
5. Don't see students as persons "you do things to" but rather as individuals capable of doing for themselves once they feel trusted, respected, and valued.

Good teachers are able to communicate what they know in a way that makes sense to their students. They are good also because they view teaching as primarily a human process involving interpersonal communication in human relationships.

ACTIVITIES

2.1   Mark on the scales below your perceptions of yourself as a teacher.

Expert	:_____:_____:_____:_____:_____:_____:_____:	Inexpert
Unintelligent	:_____:_____:_____:_____:_____:_____:_____:	Intelligent
Qualified	:_____:_____:_____:_____:_____:_____:_____:	Unqualified
Boring	:_____:_____:_____:_____:_____:_____:_____:	Interesting
Nervous	:_____:_____:_____:_____:_____:_____:_____:	Poised
Calm	:_____:_____:_____:_____:_____:_____:_____:	Anxious
Honest	:_____:_____:_____:_____:_____:_____:_____:	Dishonest
Bad	:_____:_____:_____:_____:_____:_____:_____:	Good
Kind	:_____:_____:_____:_____:_____:_____:_____:	Cruel
Undependable	:_____:_____:_____:_____:_____:_____:_____:	Dependable
Powerful	:_____:_____:_____:_____:_____:_____:_____:	Powerless
Bold	:_____:_____:_____:_____:_____:_____:_____:	Timid
Silent	:_____:_____:_____:_____:_____:_____:_____:	Talkative
Aggressive	:_____:_____:_____:_____:_____:_____:_____:	Meek
Organized	:_____:_____:_____:_____:_____:_____:_____:	Disorganized
Awful	:_____:_____:_____:_____:_____:_____:_____:	Nice
Unpleasant	:_____:_____:_____:_____:_____:_____:_____:	Pleasant
Irritable	:_____:_____:_____:_____:_____:_____:_____:	Good-natured
Cheerful	:_____:_____:_____:_____:_____:_____:_____:	Gloomy

From "An Instrument for Measuring Source Credibility of Basic Speech Communication Instructors," by J. C. McCroskey, W. Holdridge, and J. K. Toomb, *Speech Teacher 23* (1974), p. 30. Used by permission of the National Communication Association.

2.2   To what degree have the teachers of your classes revealed themselves to you so that you may communicate effectively with them? To what degree have you revealed yourself to your teachers so they may communicate effectively with you?

2.3   Consider the teacher who has influenced you the most. What sort of person was this teacher? Why was this teacher's influence so great?

2.4   Think about the classrooms in which you've been a student. Consider the most negative experience you've had in the classroom. Why was it so negative? What could the teacher have done to make it less negative? Consider the most positive experience you've ever had as a student. Why was it so positive? What role did the teacher play in making it so positive?

2.5   What expectations did you have for this class? From where did these expectations come?

Do you think you communicated these expectations to your teacher? How? What effect did these expectations have on

1. Your perceptions?
2. Your learning?

3. Your communication?
4. Other variables, such as your motivation, satisfaction with the class, where you sat in the class, how much out-of-classroom contact you had with the teacher, and so on?

2.6   Microteach a five-minute lesson. Choose any teaching method you desire. Try to communicate positive expectations previously outlined in this chapter. When you're finished microteaching, consider the following:

1. How did you communicate your expectations?
2. Did you feel comfortable communicating these expectations? Why or why not?

2.7   Formulate a description for each of two students. One should describe a student as physically attractive, highly verbal in class, well dressed, and from a high socioeconomic status. The other should describe a student who is just the opposite. Show both descriptions to ten teachers. Ask the question, "Which of the following would you expect to do well academically and why?" What do the results of this mini-experiment tell you about teacher expectancy?

FURTHER READING

Booth-Butterfield, M. (1992). *Interpersonal communication in instructional settings.* Edina, MN: Burgess.

The emphasis of this text is on the ways in which interpersonal communication and relationships influence classroom communication. The chapter on the structure of relationships and the chapter on attribution are particularly interesting.

Canfield, J., & Siccone, F. (1993). *101 ways to develop student self-esteem and responsibility.* Boston: Allyn & Bacon.

This volume provides activities that prepare teachers to coach students to accept themselves and responsibility for their lives.

Canfield, J., & Wells, H. (1994). *100 ways to enhance self-concept in the classroom* (2nd ed.). Boston: Allyn & Bacon.

This text offers teachers many activities, cartoons, and quotations that can be used to help students enhance their self-concepts

Perinbanayagam, R. S. (1991). *Discursive acts.* New York: Aldine De Gruyter.

This text examines, in a highly readable style, the relationships among social interaction, language use, and self-concept.

Richmond, V., & Gorham, J. (1992). *Communication, learning and affect in instruction.* Edina, MN: Burgess.

Chapter 8 concerns student self-concept, and Chapter 12 discusses teacher self-concept. Strategies for enhancing self-concept are included.

Saunders, W., Goldenberg, C., & Hamann, J. (1992). "Instructional conversations beget instructional conversations." *Teaching and Teacher Education, 8,* 199–218.

This article describes a mode of instruction designed to emphasize active student involvement in goal- and meaning-oriented discussions.

CHAPTER THREE

LISTENING

Objectives

After reading this chapter, you should be able to:

- Define listening.
- Designate reasons that good listening is important.
- List, define, and provide examples of three types of listening.
- Describe the steps to empathy.
- Discuss the barriers to effective listening.
- Discuss active listening.
- Improve your own listening skills.

> After too many days of
> "learning"
>   I stopped long enough
>   to simply LISTEN,
>   It was then that I found that
>   LEARNING is
>   that soft
>   quiet thump
>   beneath the
>   fall
>   of
>   the
>   leaf
> (Welch, 1991, p. 7)

Listening is a key component of the teaching–learning process. Most of us need to improve our listening skills. In this chapter we discuss not only methods of improving our listening but also the importance of listening, types of listening, and barriers to effective listening. Most people have some misconceptions about listening. These misconceptions can greatly reduce our effectiveness as listeners and, therefore, should be eliminated.

WHAT IS LISTENING?

If communication is the difference between knowing and teaching (Hurt et al., 1978), then listening is the difference between hearing and learning. The following scenario exemplifies this notion:

Student: What do you mean the unit test is today? I thought you said it was Friday! We always have unit tests on Fridays!

Teacher: As we discussed last week, the test is today because we have an assembly scheduled during this period on Friday. I know you heard me explain that!

The teacher involved in this conversation is operating under the misconception that hearing and listening are the same activity. However, listening is much more than simply hearing. Hearing is only the first step in the listening process—the physical step of sound waves hitting your eardrums. After hearing sounds, three more steps must be completed before the listening process is complete: the interpretation of the sound waves (leading to understanding or misunderstanding), the evaluation of what was heard (when you decide how you'll use the information), and, finally, the response step (reacting to what you heard).

Listening, then, is a four-step process. If any of the four steps is not completed, effective listening has not occurred. There are no shortcuts to effective listening. It is an active, difficult, time-consuming activity. Thus, although a teacher must learn to communicate effectively in order to teach, students must learn to listen effectively in order to learn. How else can educators be held responsible for the learning outcomes of instruction if students do not take the responsibility to fulfill the teaching–learning cycle? Conversely, teachers must listen to their students to determine the pace and complexity of instruction that is consistent with the transactional perspective of the communication process and this text.

THE IMPORTANCE OF LISTENING

Why is effective listening important? First of all, we spend a great deal of time listening. Research demonstrates that 70 percent of our waking time is spent participating in some form of communication. Of that time, 9 percent is spent writing, 16 percent reading, 30 percent talking, and 42 to 57 percent listening.

Interestingly, although listening is the type of communication we engage in the most and learn first, it requires a skill we are taught the least. The following chart shows the order in which we learn the four types of communication, the degree to which we use them, and the extent to which we are taught how to perform them (Steil, 1980):

	Listening	Speaking	Reading	Writing
Learned	1st	2nd	3rd	4th
Used	45%	30%	16%	9%
Taught	Least	Next least	Next most	Most

In the classroom, listening is the main channel of instruction. Estimates of the amount of time students are expected to listen range from 53 to 90 percent of their communication time (Galvin, 1985). When such a large portion of time is spent listening, ineffective listening can be quite costly to students. Most of us are inefficient listeners, retaining only about 20 percent of what we hear.

Finally, listening is important because it is a survival skill. For example, in the business community, listening is cited as one of the top skills necessary for effective performance (Wolvin & Coakley, 1991). We acquire knowledge, develop language, increase our communication ability (the good listener is also a good communicator), and increase our understanding of ourselves and others through listening. Listening, then, is an important skill to develop and improve because we cannot be effective in our relationships or our professions without it.

Listening is also a very important way to communicate respect. One of your authors, Dr. Simonds, shares the following:

> In the first year of my teaching career, I had a parent visit me after class who was apparently quite upset. She stormed into my classroom in a very heated manner, and with a raised voice, to discuss her daughter's sudden sense of apathy toward the drama program I was directing and school in general. My first thought was to defend myself immediately, but I held back that instinct when I remembered my own rules of listening: look people directly in the eye when they are talking, smile and nod, and avoid interrupting. In other words, I demonstrated active listening skills to allow the parent to express her concern. I noticed that as I engaged in these behaviors, the parent softened in her approach and by the time she was done communicating with me, she thanked me for listening and admitted that her daughter's apathy probably had little or nothing to do with my teaching.

TYPES OF LISTENING

There are basically three types of listening: appreciative, informative, and therapeutic. However, these categories are not mutually exclusive. We may engage in all three in any given communicative situation.

We engage in *appreciative* listening when we listen for enjoyment. We may simply want to gain a sensory impression of the tone, mood, or style of another person. For example, we've all heard teachers or speakers we like to listen to because their voices are pleasant or because they are stylistically unique. Much of the listening we do is *informative*. Whenever we listen to gain and comprehend information, discriminate between fact and opinion, or evaluate whether to accept or reject ideas, we are engaging in informative listening. Obviously, this type of listening is particularly important in the classroom. Errors in informative listening can be extremely detrimental to classroom learning.

The final type of listening is *therapeutic*. In this type, we are listening for the feelings of another person. Often we are simply sounding boards; people say, "Thank you for listening. I guess I just needed someone to talk to." Thus, in therapeutic listening we may not be asked to provide any service other than simply listening. This should indicate how important listening is. And when we need someone to listen to us, we are grateful when that person gives us the full attention we seek.

As we become more familiar with students we will find ourselves increasingly engaging in therapeutic listening. A student came to one of the authors for some personal advice on a problem she was having at home. She talked and talked. Suddenly, she jumped up and said, "Thanks for all your help. I know now what I need to do!" She had thought through her problem and had come to a solution with no input except a willingness to let her verbalize her thoughts and feelings.

EMPATHY

Empathy, a concept closely linked to therapeutic listening, is not an easy concept to define (Weaver & Kintley, 1995). For our purposes, empathy is the capacity of a person to put himself into the shoes of another, to see things from another's viewpoint. The empathic listener strives to thoroughly and accurately understand the person communicating. This doesn't direct the conversation but encourages the other person to share her ideas and feelings. The empathic listener doesn't impose her own opinions and values. When you listen empathically, you don't evaluate. Instead you promote honest, engaged communication through total other-centered involvement in the encounter (Brownell, 1996). From a transactional perspective, empathy involves two steps:

1. Predicting accurately the motives and attitudes of others.
2. Communicating in ways that are rewarding to the other person who is the object of prediction.

Let's examine each of these.

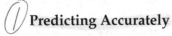 Predicting Accurately

The first step—predicting accurately—involves an awareness of what the other person is like and what can realistically be expected from him. However, just because we accept another person for "who they are" doesn't mean we agree with what they say or do. For example, you can accept students' feelings, ideas, and behavior as legitimate and still not agree with them. However, students appreciate empathic understanding—the realization that they are understood, not evaluated or judged, but understood from their own point of view rather than the teacher's.

② Communicating Empathy

In terms of the second component of empathy—communicating empathy to students—several guidelines should be followed:

1. *Be willing to become involved with the student.* When students who are graduating from high school or college are asked to identify the best teachers they had,

they often identify teachers who were available or accessible to them. The willingness to become involved with another person can be more important at times than the quality of the interaction itself. Knowing that someone who is important to you cares enough about you to devote time to the relationship and to focus on matters of mutual interest can make quite a difference.

2. *Communicate positive regard for the student.* Positive regard for another person is expressed not so much by the specific content of our remarks when we interact as it is by the general way we treat that person. If we are manipulative, if we attempt to control or to coerce the other person, or if we prevent the other person from saying or doing things that displease us, then we are not displaying positive regard. Positive regard for another person can be said to exist when we treat that person with a basic respect as a person of integrity, regardless of the specific things that person says or does.

3. *Communicate a supportive climate.* A supportive climate is one in which the emphasis is on understanding rather than on judging the behavior of others.

4. *Listen to the person's nonverbal as well as verbal communication.* Effective listening requires that we respond to the content of the message and the metacommunication, or the information about the message, as well.

5. *Accurately reflect and clarify feelings.* There is a tendency to respond more to the content of what others say—the ideas, thoughts, opinions, and attitudes conveyed—than to the feelings that others are expressing. Feelings are harder to respond to because in our culture most of us get less experience responding to feelings than to ideas.

6. *Be genuine and congruent.* We are not as likely to develop a good relationship with others if we communicate in a false and misleading way. Facades are difficult to maintain and ultimately not very attractive. A constructive relationship is one in which the participants respond to each other in an honest and genuine manner. Our communication is congruent when the things that we do and say accurately reflect our real thoughts and feelings.

BARRIERS TO EFFECTIVE LISTENING

It's no wonder most of us are poor listeners. The factors that keep us from listening as effectively and efficiently as we could are numerous. These factors fall within four major categories: factual distractions, semantic distractions, mental distractions, and physical distractions.

Factual Distractions

Factual distractions occur because we listen for facts rather than for the main ideas and feelings behind the message. As a result, we fail to integrate what we hear into a whole, or we lose sight of "the big picture." Students sometimes have a problem pulling together facts into a coherent whole, particularly in essay exams, because they listen for facts but fail to analyze the ways in which the facts fit together. The same problem often occurs when students take notes. Thus, repeating only the main points of our lectures can help students integrate facts into a complete framework.

Semantic Distractions

Semantic distractions occur when the other person uses unfamiliar terminology or when we react emotionally to words or phrases. Both of these semantic distractions result from the fact that meanings are in people, not words.

The following exchange illustrates the confusion that can result if someone is using a term in a manner unfamiliar to you:

What Did You Knott Say?

Hello, who's speaking?
This is Watt.
I'm sorry. What's your name?
Yes, Watt's my name.
Is this a joke? What is your name?
John Watt.
John what?
Yes. Look, who's this? Are you Jones?
No, I'm Knott.
Will you tell me who you are?
Will Knott.
Why not?
My name is Knott.
Not what?
(Littell & Littell, 1972, p. 19)

When we hear words that carry emotional overtones for us, our anger, frustration, or resentment can impair our ability to listen. For some students, the word *math* has a negative connotation. If students have not done well in math, they may continue to fail because they believe failure is inevitable and, therefore, they do not listen in class.

Mental Distractions

Mental distractions are caused by intrapersonal factors. One form of mental distraction occurs when we focus on ourselves. We may be formulating what we will say when it's our turn to speak; we may be engrossed in our own problems or needs; we may be concentrating on our own goals and plans; we may be simply daydreaming.

Mental distractions can also occur when we focus on the other person, allowing our preconceived attitudes about the other to prematurely determine the value of what the person is saying. For example, we often listen more closely and with more interest to those we perceive as attractive. If the person belongs to a group we value, we may listen more closely and more positively. Other nonverbal factors, such as vocal cues, can also affect our listening.

Most of us stereotype others at some time or another. Often we aren't as tolerant of those who fit a stereotype we don't value. For example, if I stereotype a student as a *low-level* student and don't find any value to students with low academic ability, I will be reluctant to listen to the student's ideas. To be effective listeners, we have to consciously "unteach" ourselves prejudices and stereotypes—or at least understand that they may be affecting the extent to which we are willing to listen to others.

Finally, focusing on the status of the other person can cause a mental distraction that keeps us from listening. Sometimes we fail to listen critically to those we view as of a higher status. The ideas of teachers may be accepted simply because they are "experts." Similarly, we rarely listen to those we perceive as having lower status: "Jane's really artistic, but she's so quiet and boring. Let's ask Maria, the head cheerleader, to help with decorations instead."

Physical Distractions

The final barrier to listening, physical distractions, can take many forms. The color of the room, the time of day, uncomfortable clothing, and noises can all be physical distractions that interfere with one's ability to listen.

IMPROVING LISTENING SKILLS

Several behaviors can help you improve your listening skills. Some are fairly easy to master. Others will take a great deal of effort on your part.

1. *Remove, if possible, the physical barriers to listening.* You might simply move to another room, or move the furniture in the room, turn the thermostat up or down, or close the door to your classroom. Manipulate your environment to fit your needs.

2. *Focus on the speaker's main idea.* You can always request specific facts and figures later. Your initial purpose as a listener should be to answer this question: "What is this person's main idea?"

3. *Listen for the intent, as well as the content, of the message.* Ask yourself, "Why is this person saying this?"

4. *Give the other person a full hearing.* Don't begin your evaluation until you've listened to the entire message. When a student tells you that his homework is not finished, allow the student to complete his explanation before you respond. Too often as listeners we spend our listening time creating our messages rather than concentrating on the content and intent of the other's message.

5. *Remember the adage that meanings are in people, not in words.* Ask for clarification when necessary. Try to overcome your emotional reactions to words. Focus on what you can agree with in the other's message, and use this as common ground as you move into more controversial issues.

6. *Concentrate on the other person as a communicator and as a human being.* All of us have our own ideas, and we have deep feelings about those ideas. Listen with all your senses, not only with your ears. The well-known admonition to "stop, look, and listen" is an excellent one to follow when listening. Focus on questions such as, "What does she mean verbally?", "Nonverbally?", "What's the feeling behind the message?", and "Is this message consistent with those she has expressed in previous conversations?"

ACTIVE LISTENING

The process of listening isn't completed until you have made some active response—verbal or nonverbal—to the other person. Your response can have an important impact on the communication climate.

The concept of active listening has been around for a number of years. The main idea of active listening is that the listener must get involved in the communication transaction. In other words, listening is not passive; rather, it is as active and behavioral as speaking. And, of course, the primary indicator of active listening is active responding. Several methods of active response are important.

Paraphrasing

Paraphrasing is a restatement of both the content and the feelings of another person's message. It is not, however, simply parroting another's words. Often, understanding a speaker's feelings is even more important to understanding his or her message than simply comprehending the actual words spoken. Thus, paraphrasing restates both the content and the feelings components of the message.

Suppose a student says to you, "I don't see how I can possibly finish this report by tomorrow. I have two major tests tomorrow. Boy, I've really gotten myself into a bind." Your paraphrase might be something such as, "It sounds like things are really hectic for you, and you feel frustrated."

If paraphrasing sounds trite, uncomfortable, or clumsy to you, keep in mind two important ideas. (1) Anytime you learn a new skill, it initially feels funny. Remember how clumsy you felt when you were first learning to ride a bike? Remember also, that with practice, riding a bike became easier and very natural. The same is true of paraphrasing. The more you practice and use the skill, the easier it will become. (2) Paraphrasing is not always appropriate or necessary. If someone says to you, "Wow, what fantastic weather!" there's no need for paraphrasing. Paraphrasing should be used to help you avoid confusion and misunderstanding. Overuse of the paraphrasing technique is just as detrimental to effective communication as its underuse.

Perception Checking

A second technique of active responding is perception checking. Perception checking is similar to paraphrasing—both seek to clarify the speaker's meaning. But a perception check, unlike paraphrasing, is not limited to the last utterance of the speaker. Perception checking refers to behavior over an extended period of time.

A perception check consists of stating three ideas: (1) sensory data that describes what you have heard and seen to lead to your conclusion; (2) the conclusion you've drawn; and (3) a question that asks the other person whether your conclusion is accurate.

Suppose you are a science teacher and one of your students has, for the past week, been late for class every day, been extremely disruptive, and failed to hand in homework. You have decided to call the student into your office to talk. How might you use perception checking?

You might say, "Martin, I am aware that you've been late every day this week, you have ridiculed other students when they answer questions, and your work has not been up to par. I suspect all this might mean you are having a problem—either with this class or at home. Is there any truth to that?"

The basic purpose of perception checking is to clarify our perceptions of another's thoughts, feelings, or intentions. Because it's impossible to communicate with others without making some inferences, it's important that we check on those inferences in order to make our communication as effective as possible.

Ask Questions

One of the communication strategies we all use less than we should is asking questions. Whenever we are not sure we have understood another person's content or relationship messages, we need to ask questions. A word of caution here: avoid questions that pry into irrelevant areas or issue a challenge to the other person in any way.

Say More

Closely related to asking questions is a technique discussed by Stewart and Thomas (1990) called "Say more," encouraging your conversation partner to keep talking. When ideas seem unclear or you're not sure you really understand what your partner means, ask that person to "Say more" or "Keep talking."

Beware of Cultural Differences

Remember that cultural background can affect listening behavior. Nishida (1985) suggests that the most effective intercultural listeners have a high tolerance for ambiguity. In other words, they can see many points of view and they remain open-minded when confronted with information that contradicts their previously held beliefs.

In addition, the competent intercultural listener recognizes differences in nonverbal systems and does not make assumptions about what various nonverbal behaviors mean. For example, in the United States, we often signal that we are listening to someone when we maintain eye contact, smile and nod, and physically lean toward the person who is speaking. The competent intercultural communicator understands that not all cultures interpret attentiveness in the same way. In some Asian, Latin American, and African cultures, for instance, direct eye contact is considered rude, threatening, and disrespectful, especially when communicating with a person of higher status, such as a teacher (Samovar & Porter, 2001). As teachers of the dominant Western culture, we appreciate when students look at us during the communication process so that we can gauge their level of understanding and comprehension through feedback. In fact, we might even become suspicious that students are not listening when we cannot see this behavior. But we should not assume that a student is not listening simply because she is not looking at us. Rather, the student may be showing a sign of respect and fully comprehending our message.

IN SUM

Listening is an active process. It requires practice and concentration. Because it is a process in which you spend a great deal of time, it's important to do it well. As one author suggests, "A failure to listen probably creates more interpersonal problems than any other aspect of human behavior" (Barker, 1971). As a teacher, try to adhere to the following "Code for Listening" in order to avoid interpersonal problems and foster a supportive communication climate in your classroom.

Code for Listening

As a teacher I shall

1. Be a good listener myself.
2. Use a classroom voice that is relaxed, unhurried, and nonthreatening.
3. Use sincere, varied, expressive facial expressions that promote accurate listening.
4. Get everyone's attention before speaking.
5. Teach students that directions and instructions will be given only once.
6. Not repeat a student's contributions, answers, or remarks but encourage students to listen to each other.
7. Ask questions that require more than "yes," "no," or other short answers.
8. Take time to listen to my pupils before and after school as well as in school.
9. Create an emotional and physical atmosphere conducive to good listening.
10. Establish with my students the purpose for which they should listen to each activity.
11. Be well prepared for the material to be taught or the activity to be directed.

12. Vary my classroom program to include a variety of listening experiences, such as sound films, discussions, individual and group reports, dramatic activities, and demonstrations.
13. Teach my students the value and importance of good listening.
14. Build a program in which listening skills are consistently taught and practiced: for example, interpreting unknown words through context, noting details, finding main and subordinate ideas, evaluating expressed points of view in relation to facts or propaganda, and making valid inferences.
15. Teach my students to form desirable listening habits: for example, disregarding distractions and mannerisms of speakers, exercising mental curiosity about what is heard, and being courteous to speakers by looking for something interesting about speaker and subject.

ACTIVITIES

3.1 Maintain a communication log for one day. Construct a time chart divided into 15-minute intervals. Code your communication as speaking (S), writing (W), reading (R), and listening (L). If you engage in more than one type of communication during a 15-minute interval, code that interval according to the type of communication you engaged in the majority of the time. At the end of the day, tabulate the percentage of time you spent in each type of communication. What do your results tell you about the importance of listening?

	Percentage
Reading	_____
Writing	_____
Speaking	_____
Listening	_____

3.2 Read the following case study. Analyze the barriers to listening—factual, semantic, mental, and physical—that Ms. Sawyer and Rosa encountered.

Ms. Sawyer is lecturing to her students about the fall of the Roman Empire. The students know this is an important lecture. The information is not available in the text, and Ms. Sawyer has indicated the information will be included in the unit exam.

One of Ms. Sawyer's students, Rosa, has had a difficult week. She has problems at home, and she just found out she did not make the list of finalists for a scholarship. Rosa is certain she has an *A* in Ms. Sawyer's class and that she doesn't need to worry about the upcoming exam. In addition, the room is hot and stuffy.

Rosa tries to concentrate on Ms. Sawyer's lecture. However, as the lecture continues, Rosa begins to daydream, mentally planning what she needs to get done this weekend.

Suddenly, Rosa is jolted back to the present when Ms. Sawyer asks her to summarize the major points of the lecture.

3.3   Consider a recent classroom transaction in which you engaged in poor listening. Briefly describe the communication transaction, the listening skills you used, and what you could have done to eliminate your poor listening behavior:

Description of communication transaction:

People involved:

Topic:

Environment in which transaction took place:

The listening skills you used:

Ways to have improved your listening in this transaction:

3.4   Think of someone who is a good listener. What characteristics does that person display?

Characteristics of a Good Listener
1.
2.
3.
4.
5.

3.5   To help you become more comfortable with paraphrasing, write paraphrased responses for the following situations.

"I really feel uncomfortable talking to large groups of people. I wonder if I could get Mr. Amtson to let me present my speech for him alone rather than for the entire class."

"I really hate this school. Everyone here tells me what to do. I don't have any freedom."

3.6   Read the following article. Discuss with your classmates whether or not Bozik's (1989, p. 7) suggestions would be helpful.

When working to develop student listening skills, one area worthy of special attention is teaching students to listen to teachers talk. Lessons are more meaningful if they relate to real-life situations in students' lives. Preparing students to be successful in-class listeners provides clear motivation for student learning and an opportunity for immediate and relevant application.

Effective comprehensive listening requires that listeners ask themselves questions. By learning to ask the right questions, students can be taught to anticipate the type of evaluation the teacher may use and thus make a more accurate assessment of what materials need to be remembered and studied. Any questions that cannot be easily answered should prompt the student to ask the teacher a question.

Encourage students to ask themselves the following questions when listening to a lecture or other teacher presentation. Use your own lectures to demonstrate the technique, stopping to discuss how the questions relate to what you are saying. For example, stop occasionally to ask the class, "What idea am I talking about now?"

Discuss how students can phrase and ask appropriate questions if the answer to any of the questions is, "I don't know." Teach students that teachers are usually pleased to be asked questions and view them as a sign of student interest and desire to learn (p. 72).

Questions and Comments

1. What is the teacher talking about? Keep reminding yourself what the topic is. If you can't easily answer the question, raise your hand and ask, "Can you remind me what topic this relates to?"

2. What is the main idea? The teacher has something to say about the topic; keep focusing on the message. If in doubt, ask, "What is the main thing we should remember about this?"

3. What ideas or details has the teacher said two or more times? Repetition is one technique teachers use to emphasize important concepts and to be sure students understand important ideas and information. These are items that are most likely to be on tests.

4. When does the teacher stop to ask if there are any questions? Asking for questions usually indicates the teacher is particularly concerned you understand the material just presented. This material is likely to appear on a test.

5. What is an example of the idea about which the teacher is talking? Teachers often give examples; write these in your notes. If you cannot think of an example, ask the teacher for one. Asking for examples is a common test item.

6. How does what the teacher is talking about relate to yesterday's topic? You should see a connection between the two topics; there may be none, but that would be rare. If you cannot state to yourself how the two ideas are related, ask the teacher, "How does this relate to what we talked about yesterday?"

7. How does this topic relate to the course subject? Remind yourself of the connection between the small idea of today's class and the big idea of the course. For example, "What do 'Causes of the Civil War' have to do with American history?"

8. What did I learn today? Review in your mind what was new to you. Things you already know, you will remember. New material will require study.

9. If I were the teacher, what would I ask on a test? You might write a few test questions at the end of your notes. For example, "Name four causes of the Civil War." Put a star next to likely test material in your notes. Do the same for material on handouts.

3.7   By learning to listen carefully and think about the relationship between the lecture and the evaluation, students can begin to study immediately and prepare themselves for successful performance on a test or other evaluation tool.

Bohlken (1991, p. 7) created the following inventory to help make students more aware of the importance of listening skills in lectures. The inventory also provides teachers with information on what they can do to improve student listening.

Note: there are no right or wrong answers to the inventory questions. Instead, the questions provide insight and stimulate discussion.

Classroom Listening Inventory

_____   1. What classroom characteristic interferes most   *Comments*
with your listening to a classroom lecture?
   a. temperature
   b. chalkboard and wall colors
   c. outside noise
   d. noise created by other students in class
   e. other

_____   2. What characteristics of mine interfere most
with your listening to my classroom lectures?
   a. voice, speech rate, and/or accent
   b. thought organization
   c. appearance
   d. movement and behavior
   e. vocabulary

_____   3. In the classroom where you listen best, where
do you usually sit?
   a. front left
   b. front center
   c. front right
   d. middle
   e. back

_____   4. In the classroom where you listen best, how
often does the instructor look at you?
   a. very often
   b. often
   c. sometimes
   d. seldom
   e. very seldom

_____   5. How often do I look at you while I am lecturing?
   a. very often
   b. often
   c. sometimes
   d. seldom
   e. very seldom

_____   6. What personal characteristic interferes most
with your listening to my class lectures?
   a. tired
   b. hungry
   c. daydreaming
   d. preoccupied
   e. not interested in subject
   f. other

_____   **7.** In the classroom where you listen best, how do you respond to the course?
- **a.** eye contact with teacher
- **b.** nod and acknowledge the teacher's comments with facial expressions
- **c.** take notes
- **d.** ask questions
- **e.** anticipate what will be said
- **f.** other

_____   **8.** How do you respond to me while I am lecturing?
- **a.** make eye contact
- **b.** nod and acknowledge my comments with facial expressions
- **c.** take notes
- **d.** ask questions
- **e.** anticipate what I will say next
- **f.** other

_____   **9.** At what time of the day do you listen best to classroom lectures?
- **a.** early morning
- **b.** midmorning
- **c.** around noon
- **d.** midafternoon
- **e.** evening

_____   **10.** Why did you choose this time for this course?
- **a.** only one available
- **b.** fit my schedule
- **c.** considered my best time to listen
- **d.** instructor
- **e.** other

_____   **11.** What is the nature of the lecture content to which you listen best?
- **a.** personally relevant
- **b.** dynamic
- **c.** familiar vocabulary and organization
- **d.** visually aided
- **e.** well supported with examples and comparisons

_____   **12.** For what purpose do you listen in the class in which you listen best?
- **a.** to pass a test
- **b.** to relate to the instructor
- **c.** to satisfy an interest in the subject
- **d.** to learn new knowledge
- **e.** to apply information to self-improvement

_____   **13.** For what purpose do you listen in this
                classroom?
                a. to pass a test
                b. to relate to instructor
                c. to satisfy an interest in subject
                d. to learn new knowledge
                e. to apply information to self-improvement

_____   **14.** When you take notes in this class, do you
                a. write down terms?
                b. use a sentence outline?
                c. paraphrase?
                d. use topic outline?
                e. other?

_____   **15.** What single factor influences your listening
                behavior most in this lecture?
                a. the room
                b. the instructor
                c. your purpose/attitude
                d. your physical and mental states
                e. other students

FURTHER READING

Hunsaker, D. (1997). *Listening.* Annandale, VA: SCA.

> This text presents a brief discussion of listening theory and research. The second half of the text presents activities for teaching listening.

Hynds, S., & Rubin, D. (1990). *Perspectives on talk and learning.* Urbana, IL: National Council of Teachers of English.

> The underlying premise of this text is that oral communication—both speaking and listening—plays a central role in the learning process. Topics such as questioning, group work, collaborative learning, student performances, and language diversity are discussed.

Phelan, P. (1989). *Talking to learn.* Urbana, IL: National Council of Teachers of English.

> This text describes successful classroom practices that use oral communication to develop student confidence in a variety of speaking and listening suggestions.

CHAPTER FOUR

VERBAL AND NONVERBAL COMMUNICATION

Objectives

After reading this chapter, you should be able to:

- Explain the process of perception.
- Describe the characteristics of language.
- Explain the statement, "Meanings are in people."
- Describe techniques used by general semanticists.
- Explain the importance of nonverbal communication in the classroom.
- Explain the functions of nonverbal communication in the classroom.
- Define the categories of nonverbal communication.
- Provide examples of how each category affects classroom communication.
- Discuss the impact of physical attractiveness on classroom communication.
- Define kinesics.
- Explain the significance of kinesic behavior in the classroom.
- Define paralanguage.
- Explain the significance of paralanguage in the classroom.
- Discuss the relationship of teacher nonverbal behavior to teacher effectiveness.

In the first chapter we defined classroom communication as the verbal and nonverbal transaction between teachers and students and between or among students. In this chapter we examine more specifically the verbal component and the nonverbal component. However, we first discuss the perception process—the basis of our verbal and nonverbal communication.

PERCEPTION

Why is it that in a classroom consisting of twenty students and a teacher there can be twenty-one different perceptions or descriptions of the class? The answer is that we select, organize, and interpret the stimuli we receive through our senses into a meaningful picture of the world around us. This process is called perception and is the basis of communication. In addition, our perceptions of others affect how we relate to them. W. V. Haney (1967) suggests, "We never really come into contact with reality. Everything we experience is a manufacture of our nervous system" (p. 52). In other words, what we perceive may not be reality. Through symbolic interactions, each of us constructs his or her reality such that our reality is not necessarily the same as yours. However, we communicate from our reality and you communicate from yours. An experiment will make this idea clear.

Examine Figure 4.1. How old do you think the person is? Some people see a woman of about twenty years; some see a woman around eighty years old. Although this stimulus is the same for everyone, not everyone perceives the picture similarly. Each person constructs his or her own reality.

Differences in Perception

What causes these differences in perception? John Steinbeck suggests one reason in the following passage from *Travels with Charley* (1962):

> I've always admired those key reporters who can descend on an area, talk to key people, ask key questions, take samplings of opinions, and then set down an orderly report very much like a road map. I envy this technique and at the same time do not trust it as a mirror of reality. I feel that there are too many realities. What I set down here is true until someone else passes that way and rearranges the world in his own style. In literary criticism, the critic has no choice but to make over the victim of his attention into something the size and shape of himself.... So much there is to see, but our morning eyes describe a different world than do our afternoon eyes, and surely our wearied evening eyes can only report a wary evening world. (pp. 69–70)

**FIGURE 4.1   Testing Perception:
A Young Woman or An Old Woman?**

Perception begins with our senses. Some people see better than others, hear better than others, smell better than others, and so forth. Our senses can make our perceptions different from other people's.

Steinbeck also suggests another limiting factor to our perceptions—differing internal states. How we feel, our past experience, our opinions, values, and beliefs can all affect our perceptions.

Finally, differing environments can affect our perceptions. A good example of this problem is the generation gap. Other examples include communication between the sexes and interracial and cross-cultural communication. Because of differing environments, people may perceive people and/or events differently. In terms of teacher–student communication, the classroom is perceived differently by each person in it. Student teachers often comment, "Boy, it really gives you a different perspective when you're the teacher! I always thought teachers had it easy and only students worked!"

If communication is to be effective, we must be aware that our perceptions are not reality, but our view of reality. Haney (1967) suggests that perception can be equated with a window. This window is the only means by which we can see the world. Inherent in this analogy is the realization that the window has limitations (our senses, internal states, past experiences, environment, etc.) and that what we can see from our window is not exactly the same as what someone else can see from their window. The outside world may not be different, but our perceptions (our view through our window) may be different from other people's.

The Process of Perception

How does this process of perception work? There are basically five steps in the process:

1. We observe the available data in our environment.
2. We choose what data we see/hear/feel/smell/taste and process it (selective perception).
3. We define the person or event and build expectations of future behavior.
4. Our expectations help determine our behavior toward the person.
5. Our behavior affects the other person's perceptions.

Obviously, the data we select from all the available data is affected by our personal experiences, our psychological states, our values, our culture, and many other factors. Selective perception in the classroom affects both teachers and students. We make judgments concerning students based on those perceptions and communicate accordingly. Students do the same. If either students or teachers misperceive, or interpret reality differently, communication problems may result.

Perceptions consist of three components: the attributive, the expectative, and the affective. The attributive component consists of those characteristics we attribute to the person or object or event. These characteristics may or may not be present. However, based on our experiences, we perceive them as being there. We may view students as hard working, eager, and intelligent. Or, we may view them as lazy, unmotivated, and unintelligent.

The expectative component consists of the expectations we have of the things we perceive. We expect college professors to read different kinds of books than construction workers. We also expect them to dress differently. Based on the characteristics you attribute to students, you'll expect certain behaviors. For example, if you view students as hard working, eager, and intelligent, you'll expect them to complete assignments on time, get *A*s, and contribute to class discussions.

Finally, we have feelings about the objects and people we perceive—the affective component of perception. The feelings are derived from our experiences with whatever we're perceiving, the characteristics we attribute to whatever we're perceiving, and our expectations concerning whatever we're perceiving. If you have the first view of students previously presented, you'll probably feel positively toward students. If you have the second view, you'll no doubt dislike students.

Perceptions and Classroom Communication

Kelley (1950) conducted an experiment that demonstrates the ways our perceptions can affect our classroom communication. Students were given a brief biographical note concerning a lecturer they were about to hear. Unknown to the students, half of them received this biographical note, "People who know him consider him to be a rather warm person, industrious, critical, practical, and determined." The other half of the class received this brief note, "People who know him consider him to be a rather cold person, industrious, critical, practical, and determined." When the lecturer left the room after speaking, students were asked to evaluate him. Students who received the "warm" description perceived the lecturer as social, popular, and informal; those who received the "cold" description perceived the lecturer as formal and self-centered. Among those students receiving the "warm" description, 56 percent participated in classroom discussion. Only 32 percent of those students receiving the "cold" description participated. Thus, our perceptions of others can determine the kind of communication that takes place as well as how much communication takes place.

Improving Perception Skills

The effective teacher knows that students are individuals bringing with them into the classroom a multitude of perspectives. This leads to unpredictability in the classroom. As Shulman (1987) reminds us, "The uncertainties inherent in any simple act of tutoring are multiplied enormously as one attempts to teach a room full of thirty mindful bodies" (p. 382). All students bring their own perceptions, and because the classroom is a system, the myriad of perceptions are interdependent.

As a teacher, it's imperative that you begin to improve your perception skills. The more accurate your perceptions, the more effective your communication. Perhaps the best way to improve your perception skills is to "look before you leap." Draw your conclusions based on the best evidence available. Remember that our perceptions should be conditional. We should be open to changing them as new evidence becomes available.

Make a commitment to accurate perception. Unless you really want to increase your perception skills, you never will. Making a commitment to perception that is as accurate as possible involves making a conscious effort to seek out all possible information. It means being open—allowing others to disclose themselves to you and being willing to disclose yourself to them, realizing that this disclosure adds information needed in order for you to perceive accurately. Making a commitment to accurate perception involves a willingness to expend the time such a commitment necessitates. It's much easier to make snap judgments than it is to hold off judgments until more information is gathered. The danger in snap judgments is illustrated in the following excerpt from Sunny Decker's *An Empty Spoon* (1969).

> One day when I was feeling ugly, I asked him a question about the book we were reading. He didn't say a word. I thought of all the things I should have done, but no—I had to get belligerent. I asked the question again. Then I waited for an interminable length of time. Nothing.
>
> "If you can't answer when you're spoken to, you can leave."
>
> I hated the way I sounded. But I was too wrapped up in my own frustration to cope with anything Arthur might feel. He left. And I had to find out from a far more patient teacher than I that there wasn't anything personal in the kid's apathy. He couldn't read. His mother was insane, and there was no place to send her. The two babies at home hadn't eaten in a couple of days. I was just a very small ugliness in Arthur Wesson's ugly world. At least he'd found someone in school he could cry to. Except for selfishness, it might have been me. Every time I saw him, I hated myself all over again. I was too ashamed to look him in the eye.
>
> It's not all that hard to do the right thing. But it takes so much effort to think of the kid first, especially when you really need to explode. Arthur Wesson sat in my class for a month and never opened his mouth. (pp. 79–80)

SHARED LANGUAGE AND MEANING

> Each man lives within his own Tower of Babel. Forming the highest reaches is the myth through which he looks out on life. To evolve into something near his potential he must interlace this myth with the feelings which are his foundations—to let things reveal themselves to him, to "talk of their nature, and be able to respond to them, to answer." Yet he cannot do this alone. To know what he means he must talk and listen to others whose revelations are different. (Brown & Keller, 1979, pp. 133–134)

Characteristics of Language

This quotation suggests that we need language in order to communicate, but language can also be a barrier to communication. This paradox exists because language is symbolic. Words *stand for* or symbolize things; they are not the actual things. Words, therefore, can have several meanings. Consider the word *frog*, for example. What comes to your mind? A tailless amphibian? A hoarseness in your throat? A small holder placed in a vase to hold flower stems in position? An ornamental fastening for the front of a coat? A mass of elastic, horny substance in the middle of the sole of a horse's foot? It should be obvious that what you think of when you hear the word *frog* may not be the same as what another person might think of.

Not only are words symbolic, but they are also arbitrary. Words have no meaning in and of themselves. They derive their meaning from the people who use them. There is nothing inherent in a chair that necessitates us calling it by that name. We could call it anything we desire. Figure 4.2 illustrates the symbolic, arbitrary nature of words (Ogden & Richards, 1927, p. 11).

A *symbol* (lower left-hand corner) is a word. The apex of the triangle is the *thought*—the concept you have of an object or event. The *referent* (lower right-hand corner) is the actual object. For example, you see a chair and say "chair." The word you speak is the symbol, the thought is your image of the chair, and the referent is the actual chair. Notice that the line connecting the symbol and the referent is broken. This indicates that the symbol and the referent have no connection except that which you make in your mind—in your thoughts.

Meanings and Perception

The symbolic and arbitrary nature of words suggests that words don't impart meaning, people do. In other words, meanings are in people, not in words. Notice the confusion that can result because of this axiom of communication:

> Here the Red Queen began again. "Can you answer useful questions?" she said. "How is bread made?"
>
> "I know that!" Alice cried eagerly. "You take some flour—."
>
> "Where do you pick the flower?" the White Queen asked. "In a garden or in the hedges?"
>
> "Well, it isn't picked at all," Alice explained, "it's ground—."
>
> "How many acres of ground?" said the White Queen. "You mustn't leave out so many things."

We may tie this "meanings are in people" concept to our earlier discussion of the three components of perception. Our perceptions of things are influenced by

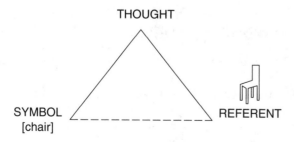

FIGURE 4.2   **The Triangle of Meaning.**

the words we use to label them. If you are labeled a *teacher*, certain characteristics are attributed to you, certain behaviors are expected from you, and certain feelings are generated toward you. If you are labeled *good*, these characteristics, expectancies, and feelings will be different than if you are labeled *bad*. Remember, however, that your meaning for *good* and another's may not be the same, and our attributions, expectancies, and feelings about good teachers may differ because meanings differ. Thus, perception, language, and meaning are interdependent.

For example, many gender or racial/ethnic stereotypes shape our perceptions. When you think of a teacher, what race or gender is that person? When you think of a doctor, what race or gender is that person? When you think of a civil rights leader, what race or gender is that person? The words we use to describe certain people are somewhat based on our stereotypes of what that role should be. In other words, language serves to create the social reality in which we live. For instance, years ago firefighters were referred to as "firemen." As such, very few women, if any, ever thought it possible to become one. And, if a women were to have such aspirations, she most likely had to work very hard to prove herself capable of the job. Because it has become more commonplace to refer to this role as a "firefighter," more women have entered into this particular workforce.

Language used in the classroom context can affect learning. In general, positive language is more effective in terms of learning and creating a supportive classroom climate than is negative language. Good and Brophy (1991, pp. 234–235) provide excellent examples of the use of positive versus negative language (Table 4.1).

Research on teacher effectiveness (both from the student's and the teacher's perspectives) seems to suggest that communication variables such as humor, warmth, openness, enthusiasm, and attentiveness are extremely important in classroom interaction and in building a supportive classroom climate.

GENERAL SEMANTICS

When we discussed perception, we noted that it is impossible to focus on all the stimuli that bombard us; we have to zero in on certain stimuli if we are to make sense of our environment. Similarly, we must organize and order our world by using language to classify things into general categories, thus helping make our world predictable. This is called the process of abstraction. For example, we classify some people into the category of student. We abstract from each of these people the characteristics they have in common. This abstraction notes the similarities and overlooks the differences among students. Based on this abstraction of student, we make predictions about what students might do to get an *A*, how they'll behave during exams, and whether they are trustworthy.

However, abstraction can cause problems in interpersonal communication. We often overlook the differences in people and things simply because they fall into the same category. If we respond to the stereotype or the abstraction rather than to the person with whom we are trying to communicate, we can become very ineffective communicators.

TABLE 4.1   Positive Versus Negative Language

Positive Language	Negative Language
Close the door quietly.	Don't slam the door.
Try to work these out on your own without help.	Don't cheat by copying your neighbor.
Quiet down—you're getting too loud.	Don't make so much noise.
Sharpen your pencil like this (demonstrate).	That's not how you use a pencil sharpener.
Carry your chair like this (demonstrate).	Don't make so much noise with your chair.
Sit up straight.	Don't slouch in your chair.
Raise your hand if you think you know the answer.	Don't yell out the answer.
When you finish, put the scissors in the box and bits of paper in the wastebasket.	Don't leave a mess.
These crayons are for you to share—use one color at a time, then put it back so others can use it too.	Stop fighting over those crayons.
Use your own ideas. When you do borrow ideas from another author, be sure to acknowledge them. Even here, try to put them in your own words.	Don't plagiarize.
Speak naturally, as you would when talking to a friend.	Don't just read your report to us.
Note the caution statements in the instructions. Be sure you check the things mentioned there before proceeding to the next step.	Take time when doing this experiment, or you'll mess it up.
Be ready to explain your answer—why you think it is correct.	Don't just guess.

From *Looking in Classrooms*, 5th ed., by Thomas L. Good and Jere E. Brophy. Copyright © 1991 by HarperCollins Publishers, Inc. Reprinted by permission of Addison Wesley Educational Publishers Inc.

General semanticists (people interested in how humans use their language and how language relates to behavior) present us with some devices to aid in avoiding the dangers inherent in abstraction. The first device is called *dating*. People, objects, events—everything is constantly changing. Thus, the *you* in 1998 is not the same as the *you* of 1970 or 2003. *Cheri* 1991 is not *Cheri* 2002. Even *Pam* 10:00 is not *Pam* 11:00. If you mentally attach a date to such statements as "Pam is grouchy" (by saying "Pam is grouchy now"), you'll keep from assuming that Pam is always grouchy. You'll refrain from communicating as if people and events are static. Remember that one thing can be different at two different times.

Indexing is closely related to dating. Indexing helps us account for individual differences. People, as well as objects and events, differ from one another. Thus, *Student 1* is not *Student 2*. If we index, we keep from making such generalizations as, "All students are lazy." If you've seen one, you haven't seen them all!

Both indexing and dating point to the fact that the verb *is* should be used with care. When we say *is*, we imply a static, unchanging phenomenon. This negates the concept that communication is a dynamic, continuous, and ever-changing process. There's a difference between saying, "That student is cheating," and "That student appears to be cheating." When we say that the student "is" cheating, we leave ourselves open for misevaluation.

Finally, the use of mental quotation marks reminds us that meanings are in people, not in words. When you say, "We're going to have a quiz on Tuesday," you may mean an evaluation instrument of fifty questions. Your students may think of a quiz as fifteen items. That difference in meaning could cause problems! If you use mental quotation marks—"quiz"—you'll be reminded that your students may need that term clarified.

NONVERBAL COMMUNICATION

Some researchers indicate that 65 percent of the meaning we get from a given message is communicated nonverbally (Birdwhistell, 1970). Others suggest that the percentage is not nearly so high (Lapakko, 1997). However, researchers do agree that the role of nonverbal cues in the communication process is extremely important. Nonverbal communication includes such areas as proxemics (the use of space), environmental factors, chronemics (the use of time), physical characteristics, artifacts, kinesics (body movement), touch, and paralanguage.

Nonverbal communication is important to the classroom teacher. A teacher's nonverbal behavior is an important factor in students' attitude formation toward school. When teachers are trained in using nonverbal communication in the classroom effectively, student–teacher relationships improve. In addition, student cognitive learning and affective learning improve.

An important axiom of communication is that one cannot *not* communicate.[1] When we are perceived by another person, we communicate. Remember also that every communicative message has both a content and a relationship component. As we will see, nonverbal gestures, facial expressions, touch, and so on can affect the content message. In addition, the relationship aspect of a message is communicated primarily through nonverbal means. Thus, students will discern how you view your relationship with them by analyzing your nonverbal communication.

Perhaps the most famous study in nonverbal communication in the classroom is reported in Rosenthal and Jacobson's *Pygmalion in the Classroom* (1968). These researchers randomly labeled some elementary school children as high achievers and others as low achievers. This information was given to teachers. Students who were labeled as high achievers had raised their IQ scores signifi-

---

[1]A series of interesting articles argues for a reexamination of this axiom: M. Motley, "On Whether One Can(not) Not Communicate: An Examination via Traditional Communication Postulates," *Western Journal of Speech Communication* 54 (1990): 1–20; "Forum: Can One Not Communicate?" *Western Journal of Speech Communication* 54 (1990): 593–624; P. Andersen, "When One Cannot Not Communicate: A Challenge to Motley's Traditional Communication Postulates," *Communication Studies* 42 (1991): 309–325; M. Motley, "How One May Not Communicate: A Reply to Andersen," *Communication Studies* 42 (1991): 325–339; T. Clevenger, "Can One Not Communicate? A Conflict of Models," *Communication Studies* 42 (1991): 340–353; J. Stewart, "A Postmodern Look at Traditional Communication Postulates," *Western Journal of Speech Communication* 55 (1991): 354–379.

cantly from the beginning of the school year to the end. Rosenthal and Jacobson (1968) suggest the role nonverbal communication may have played:

> We may say that by what she [the teacher] said, by how and when she said it, her facial expressions, postures, and perhaps her touch, the teacher may have communicated to the children of the experimental group that she expected improved intellectual performance. Such communication...may have helped the child learn. (p. 181)

This finding is substantiated in research study after research study (Cooper & Tom, 1984). Similarly, much research suggests that teachers need to learn to use nonverbal behaviors in order to improve the quality of classroom communication (see, for example, Brophy, 1983; Cooper & Good, 1983; Woolfolk & Brooks, 1983). For example, recent research suggests that some students who have behavior problems may be suffering primarily from difficulties in interpreting nonverbal cues. Emory University psychologist Stephen Norwick found that students with behavioral problems could often process verbal information with little difficulty, but often misinterpreted nonverbal cues. For example, these students mistook a friendly gesture for a hostile one and then acted in ways that set off a series of negative events (Arnold, 1983).

NONVERBAL COMMUNICATION AND CULTURE

As we examine nonverbal communication in the classroom, it is important to remember that few nonverbal norms are universal. According to Samovar and Porter (2001), "many of your nonverbal actions are touched and altered by culture" (p. 164). These authors also point out three parallels between culture and nonverbal communication: both are invisible, omnipresent, and learned. First, most people are not consciously aware of their nonverbal behavior much like their culture. In addition, culture is all-pervasive (it is everywhere and in everything) as is nonverbal communication. Finally, both culture and nonverbal behavior need to be learned. That is, you are not born knowing the specific signals that constitute nonverbal communication, and you are not born knowing the norms or values associated with your culture. For example, Samovar and Porter (2001) clearly demonstrate how nonverbal communication and culture are inextricably linked in the following passage:

> In the United States people greet by shaking hands. Arab men often greet by kissing on both cheeks. In Japan, men greet by bowing, and in Mexico they often embrace. Touching one's ear is protection against the evil eye in Turkey. In southern Italy, it denotes jeering at effeminacy, and in India, it is a sign of repentance or sincerity. In most Middle and Far Eastern countries, pointing with the index finger is considered impolite. In Thailand, to signal another person to come near, one moves the fingers back and forth with the palm down. In the United States, you beckon someone to come by holding the palm up and moving the fingers toward your body. In Vietnam that same motion is reserved for someone attempting to summon their dog. The Tongans sit down in the presence of superiors; in the West, you

stand up. Crossing one's legs in the United States is often a sign of being relaxed; in Korea, it is a social taboo. In Japan, gifts are usually exchanged with both hands. Muslims consider the left hand unclean and do not eat or pass objects with it. Buddha maintained that great insights arrived during moments of silence. In the United States, people talk to arrive at the truth. (p. 4)

FUNCTIONS OF NONVERBAL COMMUNICATION IN THE CLASSROOM

Nonverbal communication serves many functions in the classroom. As in any context, a nonverbal message can repeat, substitute for, complement, contradict, or regulate the verbal message. However, in the classroom context, nonverbal communication also plays a significant role in several areas. These include self-presentation, identification of rules and expectations, feedback and reinforcement, liking and attitude, regulation of conversational flow, and classroom control. Let's briefly examine each of these.

Self-Presentation

If you were asked to describe teaching, you would have little difficulty describing what a teacher does and how a teacher acts. How we define the job of teaching influences how we present ourselves. For example, if you view teachers as authoritative information givers, your nonverbal cues will present this image. You will stand erect, speak in a commanding voice, and lecture from the front of the room. Students, too, present a particular image. They may nod their heads, take notes, and look very attentive. Your image of yourself, both as a teacher and a student, will affect your nonverbal behaviors in the classroom.

Identification of Rules and Expectations

Although most teachers will verbally state classroom rules to their students ("No late papers will be accepted. Class participation is expected. Misbehavior will not be tolerated."), most rules are communicated nonverbally. A gaze that connotes disapproval or the wagging finger tells you that your behavior is inappropriate, even though the teacher may never have verbally said so.

Similarly, expectations are communicated, in large part nonverbally. Rarely does a teacher say to you, "I expect you to do very well in this class." However, as we discussed in Chapter 2, teachers' expectations for student achievement are most often communicated by such nonverbal cues as eye contact, seating arrangement, body orientation, and facial expressions.

Feedback and Reinforcement

Even when a teacher fails to tell us, "Good job," we know how we are doing by the teacher's facial expressions, gestures, and body movements. A smile, an affirmative head nod, or a pat on the shoulder can all communicate approval. Similarly, a frown, quizzical look, or shake of the head can tell us we are not "on the right track."

Reinforcement has a powerful effect on a student's perception of self, school, and instructor. Smiles, frowns, eye contact, touch—all give students a message about how worthwhile they are. This is an example of how nonverbal messages tell us the most about the relationship level of a message. Most of us can remember teachers we didn't like or teachers we felt didn't like us. Obviously the teacher did not say, "I don't like you," but nonverbally we got the message.

Liking and Affect

As we discussed in Chapter 2, nonverbal immediacy is perceived positively by students and is related to numerous student outcomes. You might want to review that information again.

Regulation of Conversational Flow

Because of their power position in the classroom, teachers determine who talks, how often, how long, and when. As Andersen (1986, p. 46) suggests:

> Nonverbally, instructors signal that it is a student's turn to talk by dropping their pitch, dropping gestures, relaxing and leaning back slightly, and ending a vocal phrase by looking directly at the student expected to respond. An instructor can shorten student responses and acquire the speaking floor more quickly by nodding his or her head rapidly, opening his or her mouth as if to talk, inhaling, gesturing, leaning forward, and verbalizing during the first pause that is accompanied by eye contact.

Teachers can also use nonverbal cues to signal that it is not time to talk. Sometimes a particular student will want to answer every question. Instead of ignoring the student, the teacher might make eye contact while in the middle of an utterance. Eye contact timed in this way recognizes the student, but does not invite her to participate verbally. After the teacher finishes talking he can avoid eye contact with the overly verbal student and focus eye contact directly on another student.

Classroom Control

Nonverbal communication can be used both to encourage desirable student behavior and control undesirable student behavior. Often nonverbal behavior is more effective than verbal behavior in controlling the classroom. None of us likes to be verbally reprimanded. Nonverbal behaviors create less of the "me against you" attitude that often occurs with verbal reprimands. Suppose three or four students are talking together while you are lecturing. Increasing your eye contact with these students or moving in their direction may be enough to stop their talking. Such nonverbal movements are far less likely to disrupt other students who have been listening than, "Juan, Mary, Kim, please be quiet."

A major research focus in the communication literature is the power variable. Because this is discussed at length in Chapter 9, we only briefly discuss it here. This research constitutes an effort to determine those strategies teachers employ to gain student on-task compliance. Because the single best predictor of learning is simply academic engagement time, a greater amount of active time spent on specific academic tasks consistently results in higher achievement gains. The teacher uses power to keep students working on their tasks. Power can be prosocial (based on reward, expert, and referent power) or it can be antisocial (based on coercive and legitimate power). The use of prosocial as opposed to antisocial messages to alter student behavior has been shown to increase perceptions of teacher immediacy, which lead to greater affective (Plax, Kearney, McCroskey, & Richmond, 1986) and cognitive (Richmond, McCroskey, Kearney, & Plax, 1987) learning. In addition, teachers' nonverbal behavior may play a major role in establishing and maintaining student cooperation in the classroom. Head nodding, smiling, and touching appear to operate as reinforcers of on-task behavior. These teacher immediacy cues signal to students that on-task compliance is expected and valued.

Researchers have developed a typology of power strategies based on five bases of teacher power: reward, coercive, legitimate, referent, and expert power (French & Raven, 1960; Kearney, Plax, Richmond, & McCroskey, 1985; McCroskey, Richmond, Plax, & Kearney, 1985).

1. *Reward* power, based on the target's perception that the agent has the ability to mediate rewards for her or him.
2. *Coercive* power, based on the target's perception that the agent has the ability to mediate punishments for her or him.
3. *Legitimate* power, based on the target's perception that the agent has a legitimate right to prescribe or proscribe behavior for her or him.
4. *Referent* power, based on the target's identification with the agent.
5. *Expert* power, based on the target's perception that the agent has some special knowledge or expertness.

In terms of classroom control, research indicates that college students' perceptions of the behavior alteration techniques used by their teachers is affected by their teachers' nonverbal immediacy orientation. Students perceive that their more immediate teachers use primarily prosocial behavior alteration techniques and their nonimmediate teachers rely on antisocial behavior alteration techniques. Students resist immediate teachers less. In other words, students are more willing to comply with teachers they like than those they dislike. Immediate teachers who employed prosocial behavior alteration techniques were resisted less than immediate teachers who employed antisocial techniques. However, a nonimmediate teacher who employed prosocial techniques was resisted more than a nonimmediate teacher who used antisocial strategies. Researchers interpret this finding:

> Students may perceive their more nonimmediate teachers' prosocial attempts to gain compliance as insincere. Claiming that "you'll find it a rewarding and mean-

ingful experience," or that "it will help you later on in life," nonimmediate teachers may be perceived as communicating sarcasm or ridicule. Moreover, students may not assign reward-based power to the nonimmediate teacher. Given the negative affect associated with nonimmediacy, students may not believe that such teachers can deliver on promises of rewarding consequences. (Kearney, Plax, Smith, & Sorensen, 1988, p. 64)

Burroughs, Kearney, and Plax (1989) examined the messages students communicate in order to resist teacher influence. The researchers found that students constructed significantly more resistance messages when the teacher was nonimmediate as opposed to when the teacher was immediate. Thus, immediacy seems to be related both to the messages teachers use to gain compliance and the amount of resistance they receive.

Often teachers want to increase student participation in their classrooms. Teachers need to do more than say, "I'd like us all to participate in this discussion." Their nonverbal behaviors such as eye contact, facial expressions, and gestures need to encourage participation. For example, smiling, gesturing, being vocally expressive, pausing to wait for student comments, and reducing spatial barriers can do much to encourage participation. One teacher I observed increased participation by doing three simple things: she had her students sit in a semicircle, she moved from behind her desk to sit in the semicircle with them, and she paused several seconds after asking a question so students could respond and participate.

CATEGORIES OF NONVERBAL COMMUNICATION

Nonverbal communication can be categorized in several ways. In the next section, we examine the following categories of nonverbal communication: proxemics, spatial arrangements, environmental factors, chronemics, physical attractiveness, artifacts, kinesics, touch, and paralanguage.

Proxemics

Proxemics is the study of how people use space. It includes territoriality and personal space. Territoriality is fixed space. You usually sit in the same place in the classroom, even if the seats aren't assigned. I have noticed this phenomenon in mass lectures of 300 students as well as in classrooms of twenty-five or thirty students. Personal space has been compared to a bubble surrounding us that we carry with us wherever we go and that expands or contracts depending on the situation.

If our personal space is invaded we usually become very uncomfortable unless, of course, we know the person well and he or she is special to us. For most encounters in the classroom, more distance is needed for students and teachers to be comfortable. Consider how you feel when a teacher stands over you while you're working at your desk. As teachers, we need to be careful of invading the personal space of our students.

Spatial Arrangements

Think about the various classroom environments you have experienced and the effect these spatial arrangements had on the communication that occurred. Spatial arrangements (a form of territoriality) affect such communication factors as who talks to whom, when, where, for how long, and about what.

You may choose any of several different spatial arrangements for your classroom. The most common is the traditional row arrangement. The effect this arrangement has on communication is pictured in Figure 4.3. Notice that the percentage of participation is greater for students in the front and center rows. In a straight row arrangement, students most willing to communicate will tend to sit front and center. Those less willing to communicate will tend to sit further from the teacher and on the sides.

Two other common classroom arrangements are the horseshoe and the modular. Probable participation level according to seat location in each of these arrangements is designated in Figures 4.4 and 4.5 (McCroskey & McVetta, 1978).

Sommer (1969), interested in comparing student participation in the row arrangement with other types of arrangements, studied four varieties of seating arrangements for one semester. The rooms selected were

- two seminar rooms with horseshoe or open-square arrangements
- two laboratories with straight rows
- one windowless room with rows
- one room with rows, full of windows

Sommer (1969) concluded that

> although a higher proportion of people participated in the laboratory, there was a trend for greater absolute participation in the seminar rooms in terms of the larger

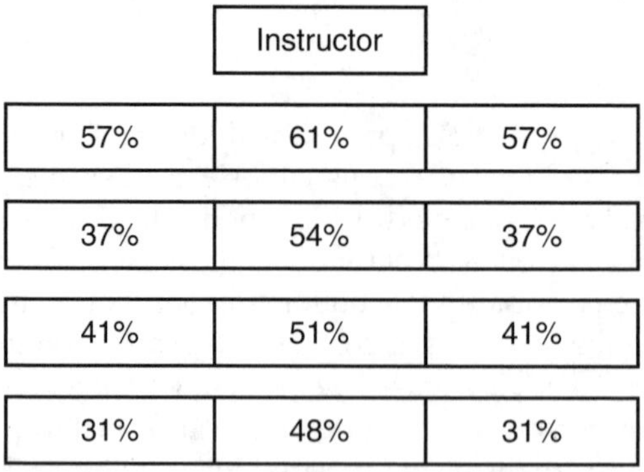

	Instructor	
57%	61%	57%
37%	54%	37%
41%	51%	41%
31%	48%	31%

FIGURE 4.3   The Traditional Classroom
Spatial Arrangement: Rows. Percentages
Indicate Degree of Participation in Classroom.

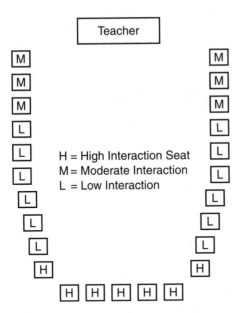

FIGURE 4.4   **The Horseshoe Arrangement.**

total number of statements per class period. The implication is that a few people say more in a seminar arrangement, whereas participation is more widespread with the straight row arrangement. There were no differences in participation between the open and windowless rooms. (p. 114)

Consider Figure 4.6. Psychologist Feitler (1971) and two fellow researchers showed this figure to 276 graduate and undergraduate students at Syracuse University's School of Education and asked them the following questions:

1. Which of the following classroom seating arrangements would you find the most and least comfortable if you were a student?
2. Which would you find the most and least comfortable if you were the teacher?

Responses to the questions indicated that, whether the students thought of themselves as students or teachers, setting four was most comfortable. Settings three and seven were also chosen as comfortable. Least comfortable for both teacher and student were settings one and six. The researchers interpreted these results as indicating the need for teacher control. Perhaps, however, the results can be explained by remembering that students and teachers have little experience with seating arrangements other than those in which the teacher has control.

McCroskey and McVetta (1978) conducted research to answer the question, "Does the type of course being taught affect student preferences for classroom

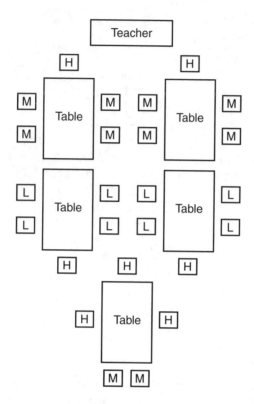

H = High Interaction Seat, M = Moderate Interaction, L = Low Interaction

FIGURE 4.5   The Modular Arrangement.

Figures 4.3–4.5 from "Classroom Seating Arrangements: Instructional Communication Theory versus Student Preferences," by J. C. McCroskey and R. W. McVetta, *Communication Education* 27 (March 1978), pp. 101–102. Used by permission of the National Communication Association.

arrangements?" By using the traditional row, horseshoe, and modular arrangements, they found that students preferred the traditional arrangement over the horseshoe and modular arrangements for required courses and preferred horseshoe and modular arrangements over the traditional arrangement for elective courses.

As a teacher, you need to be aware of how each of the three arrangements affects communication in the classroom. Your own experience as a student should tell you that the traditional row arrangement promotes teacher–student interaction. Very little communication occurs among students because the teacher dominates the classroom in this type of arrangement. The horseshoe arrangement increases student–student interaction. The modular arrangement promotes the most student–student interaction. The arrangement you desire depends on many factors—the content you are teaching, the teaching style you use, the amount you want your students to communicate, and so forth.

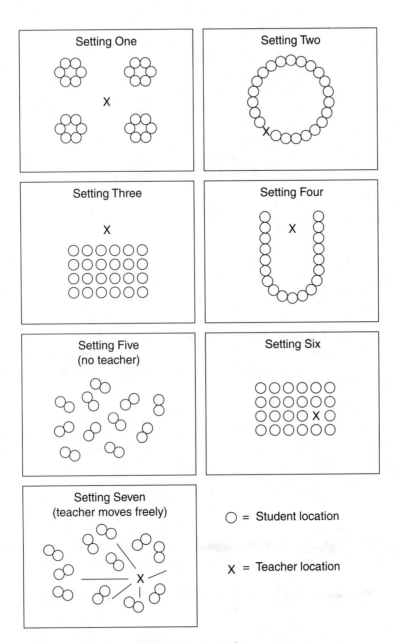

FIGURE 4.6   Figure for Feitler's Spatial Arrangement Questionnaire.

From "Tie Line," by Kenneth Goodall, *Psychology Today 5* (September 1971), p. 12. Reprinted with permission from *Psychology Today Magazine*. Copyright © 1971 (Sussex Publishers, Inc.).

Research suggests that a student's preference for a particular seat is determined by personality characteristics. Studies indicated that students who sat in seats of high participation (in the traditional arrangement) scored higher on measures of imagination than students who chose nonparticipation seats (Totusek, 1978; Totusek & Staton-Spicer, 1982). Students who are apprehensive about communicating will choose seats of low participation. Koneya (1976), interested in whether certain types of students prefer certain areas of the classroom, found that low verbalizers avoid seats that promote communication more often than high verbalizers.

Interestingly, occupancy of seats in high-participation areas affects, in a positive manner, not only how students view themselves but also how they are perceived by their teacher and peers. However, some sex and age differences are apparent: teachers regard males sitting in the rear and females sitting forward more positively in the early grades and less positively in the later grades.

Environmental Factors

Maslow and Mintz (1956) conducted a now-classic study in which they compared the interaction of people in an ugly versus a beautiful room. They found that

> the ugly room was variously described as producing monotony, fatigue, headaches, discomfort, sleep, irritability and hostility. The beautiful room, however, produced feelings of pleasure, comfort, enjoyment, importance, energy, and desire to continue in the activity. (p. 256)

Several studies have confirmed this finding in the classroom. Sommer and Olsen (1980) remodeled a traditional classroom to create a "soft" classroom, one with cushioned benches, carpeting, and various decorative items. The percentage of students voluntarily participating was greater in the soft classroom (79 percent) than in the traditional classroom (51 percent). In addition, the mean number of comments per student doubled (2.5 per student in the traditional classroom compared to 5 per student in the soft classroom).

In a recent study, Teven and Comadena (1996) examined the effects of the aesthetic quality of faculty offices on students' perceptions of teacher credibility and communication style. Their research indicates that interactions outside of the classroom, especially those conducted in an instructor's office, may mediate students' perceptions of teacher credibility and communication style. Participants who visited an aesthetically pleasing office of an instructor prior to evaluating a videotape of that instructor's classroom behavior, compared to those who visited an office of low aesthetic quality or who had no office exposure at all, reported the instructor to be more friendly, more animated, more relaxed, more open, and more able to leave an impression on others. In addition, the aesthetically pleasing office produced higher ratings of trustworthiness and authoritativeness than the office of low aesthetic quality or the no office control condition (p. 105).

Todd-Mancillas (1982) reviewed research demonstrating that color, lighting, and temperature all affect the classroom climate. For example, warmer colors (yellows and pinks) are best for classrooms of younger children; cool colors (blues and blue–greens) are best for classrooms of older students. Summarizing previous color research, Malandro and Barker (1983) emphasized the effect of color:

> One school was left unpainted, a second school was finished in the usual institutional color scheme of light buff walls and white ceilings, and the third was painted in accordance with the principles of color dynamics. In the third school the corridors were painted a cheerful yellow with gray doors; classrooms facing north were done in a pale rose; classrooms facing south depicted cooler shades of blue and green; front walls were darker than side walls; the art room was a neutral gray so as to avoid interfering with the colorful work that it contained; and green chalkboards were used to reduce glare. Over a two-year period, behavior in each school was observed. The results were clear; students in the third school showed greatest improvement on several variables measured—social habits, health, safety habits, and scholastic aptitude in language, arts, arithmetic, social studies, science, and music. Those in the unpainted school showed the least improvement in these areas and those in the traditional school fell somewhere in between. (pp. 189–190)

Lighting can affect student–teacher communication. Poor lighting can lead to eye strain and fatigue, resulting in frustration and even hostility. Thompson (1973) suggests three guidelines for classroom lighting:

> Maintain high levels of illumination. When students must expend energy just to see, they will have little left to understand what is being said. All areas of the room should be balanced in brightness. Factory and assembly-line workers have their work well illuminated. Industry has known for a long time that eye fatigue plays havoc with production schedules. To avoid sharp contrast, the visual field around the task should be only one-third as bright as the work area. No part of the visual field should be brighter than the immediate vicinity of the task. Avoid glare either from direct light sources or from reflecting surfaces. (p. 81)

Another environmental factor affecting classroom communication is temperature. If the classroom is too hot, learning may be affected because students become irritable and anxious to leave. If the room is too cold, it's difficult to concentrate on learning. The classroom temperature for optimal student performance appears to be 66° to 72° Fahrenheit.

The implications for teachers are obvious. If you value some of the behaviors and attitudes that environmental factors have been found to influence, then you should consider your classroom environment. Changes in classroom environment may lead to changes in classroom climate. Eventually, these changes may lead to changes in achievement (Fouts & Myers, 1992). At any rate, it's important for students to feel comfortable in the learning environment, and you can have a significant impact on how the environment is arranged. Keep in mind that any educational environment should

1. Ensure a variety of stimuli.
2. Present a feeling of comfort and security.
3. Be adapted to the activity.
4. Allow for some privacy and individuality.

Chronemics

Chronemics is the study of people's use of time. Schools are organized temporally as well as spatially. Students often are admonished not to waste time, and classes are scheduled to meet at certain times and for specific lengths of time. The teacher's use of time in the classroom can greatly affect the communication that occurs. For example, the amount of time a teacher waits for a student to answer a question can affect interaction between teacher and student. Too often teachers fail to wait long enough for students to respond to questions—in fact, they seldom wait longer than five seconds. Silence certainly is not viewed as being golden in the classroom! Teachers seem to be afraid of silence and therefore answer their own questions or move rapidly from one student to another. This has a great impact on the communication interaction in the classroom. Few students will be willing to interact in such an environment—only those who are highly verbal will respond. In addition, when students know the teacher will answer his own questions if they simply wait long enough, the teacher will find himself doing just that!

Another area of chronemics involves the time spent on different subjects. The amount of time you spend on a given topic area communicates to students the importance of that area. How many times have you heard someone say, "I don't need to study that for the exam. The teacher spent hardly any time on it in class."

Time spent with individual students communicates our attitudes toward them. Teacher expectancy research indicates that high-expectancy students receive more teacher communication time than low-expectancy students. For example, teachers talk more to (praise more and have more academic interactions) and are more nonverbally active (head nods, smiles, supportive gestures) with high-expectation students.

Time can affect students in a number of other ways as well. College professors often comment that students achieve better and participate more in their 10:00 A.M. classes or 2:00 P.M. classes than in their 8:00 A.M. or 4:00 P.M. classes. In addition, students may be either monochronic or polychronic; that is, they may work best when one activity, assignment, or project is scheduled at a time, or they may be able to engage in several activities at once. Students' *biological clocks* also affect their classroom performance. Morning-active students generally have higher academic achievement than those students who are most alert later in the day. Your awareness of the ways in which students are affected by time can enable you to meet their individual needs more effectively.

Finally, students use time to communicate. Putting away pencils and packing up books signals the instructor that the class period is nearly over. As we often tell our teachers in training: you don't need a clock in your classroom. Students will let you know what time it is!

Physical Characteristics

Physical characteristics and artifacts (objects in contact with the interacting persons—perfume, jewelry, clothes, and so on) can also affect classroom communication and learning.

Physical Attractiveness.   As an eighth grader, I had an English teacher whose appearance completely prohibited learning:

> She was very attractive and quite well-endowed physically. She also wore very tight skirts and sweaters. From the very beginning of the year we learned little because we could not get beyond her appearance. Chaos reigned in that classroom all year! We were a very rowdy, uncooperative, defiant group of students. She had simply lost control of the classroom. As I look back, although I'm sure she was quite knowledgeable in her subject area, I'm not sure what exactly we thought of her. I do remember, however, that because of her manner, her dress, and her general appearance, she communicated something to us that made us sure we could get away with murder, and we did!

Teachers who are rated more attractive are also rated more competent and are more likely to motivate students than are teachers who are rated unattractive. A recent study explored the impact of teachers' physical appearances and teaching philosophies on other people's perceptions of their competence. The attractive female authoritarian teacher was rated less negatively than other types of teachers (Buck & Tiene, 1989).

Research has examined attractiveness and its relationship to achievement (see, for example, Gibson, 1982; Richmond & McCroskey, 1984; Schlossen & Algozzine, 1980). A positive relationship has been found between attractiveness in first-year college female students and high grades received from their male professors. Several researchers have found that teachers react more favorably to students they perceive as attractive than to those they perceive as unattractive. Teachers also interact less with students perceived to be unattractive.

Recent studies have examined the relationship between depression and adolescents' perceptions of their bodies' attractiveness (Rierdan, Koff, & Stubbs, 1988, 1989). Depressed adolescents had poorer body images than their nondepressed peers. They viewed their bodies' as less attractive and less competent. Gender differences in body image appeared among nondepressed adolescents, with boys more satisfied with their bodies than girls. A negative body image also appeared to be a good predictor of the persistence of adolescent girls' depression.

In addition, body image has been found to affect academic competence and self-concept in early adolescence (see, for example, Lerner, Delaney, Hess, Javonovic, & Von Eye, 1990; Lerner, Lerner, Hess, Schwab, Javonovic, Talwan, & Kucher, 1991; Page, 1992). Body type is another aspect of physical attractiveness that can affect classroom communication. There are three general body types: (1) the ectomorph—tall and thin; (2) mesomorph—bony and muscular; and (3) endomorph—soft and round. Much evidence suggests that your body type influences how others perceive you and communicate with you. Ectomorphs are perceived to be anxious, tense, self-conscious, and reticent. Mesomorphs are perceived to be energetic, talkative, and dominant. Endomorphs are perceived to be jolly, warm, and complacent. What does all this have to do with you, the teacher? Physical attractiveness is important in the classroom. The standard for attractiveness seems to be the mesomorph, and students may interact with you on the basis of this image. Richmond, McCroskey, and Payne (1987) summarize the effect of body type in the classroom:

> Body type will determine how a person is perceived by others. The ectomorphic student will be perceived by the teacher as being high-strung, anxious, nervous, but probably competent. They might be perceived by their peers as being "nerdy." The endomorphic student might be perceived by the teacher as being slow, lazy, not too bright, but nice and funny. The mesomorphic student will be perceived as dependable, intelligent, competent, dominant, and appealing by the teacher. They are also often perceived as the ones who will do the best in athletics.
>
> Teachers who are ectomorphic will be perceived by students as being anxious, not composed, but perhaps intelligent. The endomorphic teacher will be perceived by students as being slow, lazy, underprepared, and not dynamic in the classroom. Lastly, the mesomorphic teacher will be perceived as credible, dependable, likeable, and competent, but possibly tough and dominant. (p. 244)

Artifacts.   One of the authors, Dr. Cooper, writes the following:

> I was recently reminded of the impact of artifacts in the classroom. I always wear an ankle chain. I entered a classroom on the first day of class wearing a business suit. One girl later told me she was "put off" by my clothing. It communicated a stiff, unyielding personality. But, she said, "I knew you would be human when I saw your ankle chain!"

An interesting study suggests the effects clothes can have in the classroom. High school boys who had much better achievement scores than some of their peers but wore "unacceptable" clothing (as deemed by their peers) had lower grade point averages than those boys who wore clothing deemed "acceptable" by their peers (Knapp & Hall, 1996). Anecdotal evidence suggests that students are ostracized if their clothing is tattered or out of fashion (Parsons, 1997).

In the classroom, researchers have examined student perceptions of "informally/casually dressed" and "formally dressed" teachers. "Formally dressed" teachers are perceived as more organized, more knowledgeable, and better prepared. Informally dressed teachers are perceived as more friendly, more sympathetic, fair, enthusiastic, and flexible (Richmond, McCroskey, & Payne, 1987).

Morris, Gorham, Cohen, and Huffman (1996) had four graduate teaching assistants (two males and two females) present a guest lecture in a section of the basic psychology course. The students were dressed one of three ways when they presented the lecture: formal professional (business dress), casual professional (for men, no jacket or tie; for women, a sweater and skirt instead of a suit), or casual (jeans, a tee shirt, and a plaid flannel shirt worn open). Following the presentation, the students rated the lecturer on scales measuring teacher competence, character, sociability, composure, and extroversion, as well as perceptions of how informed and how interesting the presentation was. Instructors who were dressed casually were rated as being less competent than those who dressed formally or in a casual but professional manner. But neither composure nor knowledge ratings showed any difference because of dress. Results indicated that casual dress resulted in higher ratings of sociability, extroversion, and making an interesting presentation; there were no differences on rating of character, however.

Students tended to favor presentations by the male instructors who wore the casual professional, or typical teaching assistant dress, over similarly dressed female instructors. Female students tended to rate male instructors more favorably if they dressed casually, but they rated female instructors more favorably if they dressed formally.

Children's names have been shown to be a boost or a barrier to their school success. Developmental psychology professor S. Gray Garwood (1983) of Tulane University asked teachers to list desirable and undesirable names. Garwood found sixth graders with those names and examined their achievement and self-concept scores. Students with desirable names had higher self-concept scores and, according to Garwood, had a better chance for higher achievement.

In a similar study psychologists Herbert Harari and John McDavid (1983) gave a set of essays to eighty San Diego elementary school teachers. The teachers gave a higher grade to an essay written by David or Michael than to the same essay with the name Elmer or Herbert on it.

Kinesics

Kinesics is the study of body movement, gestures, facial expressions, eye contact, and so on. Ekman and Friesen (1969) classified kinesic behavior according to the following categories:

1. *Emblems* are nonverbal behaviors that have direct verbal translations. For example, "I don't know," may be communicated emblematically by a shrug of the shoulders and raised eyebrows.
2. *Illustrators* are nonverbal behaviors that are tied directly to speech. During a geography lesson a teacher might illustrate where a city is located by pointing to that city on a map.
3. *Affect displays* are facial expressions that communicate emotional states. Your frown may communicate displeasure with a student's answer. A confused expression or bored expression may communicate a certain emotional state in one of your students.
4. *Regulators* are nonverbal behaviors used to control and maintain verbal interactions. Rapid head nods may communicate, "Yes, I understand. Go ahead with the next portion of the lesson."
5. *Adapters* are nonverbal behaviors developed in childhood as adaptive behaviors to satisfy emotional or physical needs. Students, when they feel anxious or bored, may chew their pencils, bite their nails, click their pens, or tap their pencils on the desks. All of these are ways to adapt to their boredom or anxiety.

When we compare the nonverbal behaviors of effective and average teachers, we find that effective teachers use more motions than average teachers to facilitate student-to-instructor interaction, to focus student attention on key points, and to demonstrate and illustrate concepts to students. In addition, nonverbally active teachers elicit more positive perceptions from students than do inactive teachers.

The teacher's kinesic behavior also influences student achievement. A teacher's use of kinesic behavior is positively related to student achievement. In other words, the more movement and gestures the teacher uses, the higher the achievement. Wycoff (1973) found that, for secondary students, teacher movement resulted in better test scores on the material presented. However, elementary students exposed to more vigorous teacher movement scored lower on a comprehension test than did students learning from a less active instructor. Wycoff suggests that increased stimulus variation is attention catching for older students, but distracting for younger children.

Your kinesic behavior can communicate that you like or dislike your students. Liking, compared to disliking, is characterized by more forward leaning, more pleasant facial expressions, and more openness of arms and body. Teachers who are perceived as "warm" smile, use direct eye contact, and tend to lean toward the other person. Warmth cues, along with verbal reinforcers ("mm-hmm"), increase verbal output from the other person.

In addition to liking and disliking, kinesic behavior can communicate how much you trust your students. For example, when monitoring a test, do you walk around the room, watching what the students are doing, or do you sit at a desk and work, occasionally glancing up?

Eye Contact.   One important area of kinesic behavior is eye contact. Eye contact signals that communication lines are open—that you're willing to communicate with another. Think about what you do when a teacher asks a question and you don't know the answer. You look down at your book, doodle, rearrange materials on your desk—anything to avoid looking at the teacher and thereby risking being called on!

In addition to this signaling function, eye contact may also be used to seek feedback or to convey information about relationships—for example, dominance and submission or liking and disliking. Students indicate they are more comfortable with a person who, when speaking, listening, or sharing mutual silence, looks at them 50 percent of the time than one who looks at them 100 percent of the time. Thus, teachers who stare at students lengthily may create anxiety or even hostility.

Teachers who use moderate eye contact monitor and regulate their classrooms more easily. Have you ever received the "evil eye" from a teacher when you were being disruptive? Generally, when students feel teachers looking at them, they will stop their disruptive behavior.

Although constant eye contact is discomforting, eye contact has been found to enhance comprehension. In addition, direct eye contact usually communicates interest and attention, whereas lack of direct eye contact communicates disinterest and inattention. Studies reviewed by Beebe (1980) suggest that eye contact has a significant effect on student retention of information, attitudes toward the teacher, attention, and classroom participation.

Facial Expression.   A teacher can use facial expressions to manage interactions in the classroom (a "dirty look" may be enough to stop a student from whispering, for example), regulate communication, signal approval or disapproval, and reinforce or not reinforce. As teachers we need to consider what messages we are sending with our faces. Are we sometimes communicating messages we would rather not send? Learning to control our facial expressions may be a requirement of our profession. Sometimes we do not want to communicate what we're thinking. Increased sensitivity to and control over our display of emotions can improve the communication between teacher and students.

The teacher's facial expressions communicate much in the classroom. The teacher who smiles and has positive facial affect will be perceived as approachable and immediate. A teacher's dull facial expression may be perceived by students as indicating disinterest in them or the subject matter.

In theory, a teacher should be able to use student facial expressions and gestures to determine their understanding of material being discussed. However, neither novice nor experienced teachers are able to judge student understanding based on facial expressions and gestures alone. Sometimes we can read nonverbal kinesic cues wrong. Students are very adept at looking interested and awake when their minds are a million miles away!

Touch

Touch is a "touchy" subject in our society. Touch can communicate many things— emotional support, tenderness, encouragement—and is an important aspect in most human relationships. Montagu (1971) in his book *Touching: The Human Significance of the Skin* indicates the importance of touch in the development of healthy, happy individuals:

> When affection and involvement are conveyed through touch, it is those meanings, as well as the security-giving satisfactions, with which touch will become associated. Inadequate tactile experience will result in a lack of such associations and a consequent inability to relate to others in many fundamental human ways. (p. 292)

The amount of touching between student and teacher declines steadily from kindergarten through sixth grade, but is still greater than most adults engage in. Junior high students engage in about half as much touching as do students in the elementary grades. Most touching occurs between same-sex pairs.

As teachers we should be aware that touch in the elementary grades can be used as an effective means of communicating caring and understanding. Research indicates that children who are touched often have higher IQs than those who don't receive a lot of touch. However, we must be aware that as students grow older, they equate touch with intimacy. Thus, although a teacher's touch is usually inappropriate with older students and will probably create a barrier to effective communication, remember that a pat on the shoulder or back may be appropriate at times and may be very much appreciated by a student.

Paralanguage

The final nonverbal aspect we'll discuss is paralanguage. Paralanguage includes

Vocal qualifiers—intensity (loud, soft), pitch height (high, low), and extent (drawl, clipping)

Vocal qualities—pitch, range, rhythm, articulation, resonance, tempo

Vocal characterizers—laughing, sobbing, whispering

Vocal segregates—"shh," "uh," "um," "uh-huh"

The combined effects of these four major components are the unique sound that is your vocal signature.

Consider how important paralinguistic cues are to the overall image of the communicator. Have you ever talked to a blind date over the telephone and created an image of what the person looked like? When you met the person, how accurate had your fantasy been? Our voice helps shape the image others have of us.

Your paralinguistic cues can communicate your attitude. For example, if you say "Great job!" in an upbeat, somewhat loud, somewhat high pitch, you communicate your approval. If you say the same phrase in a lower, softer, sarcastic tone, you communicate your disapproval.

Your voice also communicates your feelings toward yourself or others. Generally, the more positive your feelings, the faster the rate, louder the volume, and more varied the pitch will be.

Vocal cues can create the mood of a classroom. Obviously, other nonverbal cues also contribute to the classroom's mood, but because teachers talk so often, paralinguistic cues no doubt carry quite a bit of weight! A harsh, threatening voice is much less conducive to learning than a pleasant, warm voice.

The effect of paralinguistic cues on comprehension is somewhat unclear. Some studies indicate that comprehension seems to be affected by vocal inflection combined with variation of voice quality, rate, and volume. Perhaps variations in these qualities help maintain audience interest and this, in turn, increases comprehension. However, other researchers have found that vocal pitch variations do not improve comprehension. Generally, research in paralanguage suggests that listeners judge the credibility of a speaker in accordance with the speaker's vocal behavior. Vocal inflection, for example, has been found to relate to a speaker's perceived effectiveness.

It appears, then, that both the teacher's and students' paralanguage can affect perceptions of their personalities. These perceptions can, in turn, influence classroom communication patterns (Gill, 1994).

For example, students rated a monotone voice as the most objectional behavior of teachers. Students perceived the monotone voice as communicating boredom, noncaring, and nonimmediacy. As a result, students were less interested in the class, liked the class less, and learned less (Richmond, Gorham, & McCroskey, 1986).

IMPROVING NONVERBAL COMMUNICATION

As stated in the introduction to this chapter, the impact of nonverbal cues on learning is not completely clear. Therefore, we cannot tell you the right nonverbal moves to make in the classroom. However, the following is an instrument used to record nonverbal behavior. The instrument was developed by two researchers, Love and Roderick, after considerable observation of elementary and secondary teachers. Thus, these behaviors seem to represent some of the important nonverbal teaching practices. Studies using this instrument reveal two fairly consistent findings: (1) teachers who are nonverbally active are more effective (perceived as more interesting and informative) and (2) teachers can be trained to improve their nonverbal behavior.

Love–Roderick Nonverbal Categories and Sample Teacher Behaviors

1. *Accepts student behavior.* Smiles, affirmatively shakes head, pats on the back, winks, places hand on shoulder or head.
2. *Praises student behavior.* Places index finger and thumb together, claps, raises eyebrows and smiles, nods head affirmatively and smiles.
3. *Displays student ideas.* Writes comments on board, puts students' work on bulletin board, holds up papers, provides for nonverbal student demonstration.
4. *Shows interest in student behavior.* Establishes and maintains eye contact.
5. *Moves to facilitate student–student interaction.* Physically moves into the position of group member, physically moves away from the group.
6. *Gives directions to students.* Points with the hand, looks at specified area, employs predetermined signal (such as raising hands for students to stand up), reinforces numerical aspects by showing that number of fingers, extends arms forward and beckons with the hands, points to student for answers.
7. *Shows authority toward students.* Frowns, stares, raises eyebrows, taps foot, rolls book on desk, negatively shakes head, walks or looks away from the deviant, snaps fingers.
8. *Focuses students' attention on important points.* Uses pointer, walks toward the person or object, taps on something, thrusts head forward, thrusts arm forward, employs a nonverbal movement with a verbal statement to give it emphasis.
9. *Demonstrates or illustrates.* Performs a physical skill, manipulates materials and media, illustrates a verbal statement with a nonverbal action.
10. *Ignores student behavior.* Lacks nonverbal response when one is ordinarily expected. (This is sometimes appropriate, particularly in classroom management.)

IN SUM

The areas of verbal and nonverbal communication are important ones for teachers. Our verbal and nonverbal communication affect students' perceptions of the classroom that, in turn, affect how students view the educational environment, the people in it, and how much they desire to communicate.

A final comment about nonverbal communication. Although we have isolated it from the verbal component of communication, such an isolation distorts the process of communication. Nonverbal communication can be used to reinforce, contradict, substitute for, accent, complement, or regulate the flow of verbal communication. Remember that the two systems—verbal and nonverbal—work together in the classroom.

ACTIVITIES

4.1   Consider the words *student* and *teacher*. List as many meanings of these two words as you can. Compare your list of meanings with other students' lists in class.

4.2   Think about a communication problem or misunderstanding you've had with a teacher or student lately. Briefly describe the problem. How might your awareness and use of the techniques discussed here—dating, indexing, mental quotation marks, and using the word *is* sparingly—have helped in resolving the problem or avoiding it altogether?

4.3   Now that you have considered different classroom arrangements, it's time to experiment with them. Try each arrangement as both teacher (with your class on varying days) and student (possibly through the use of role playing). Were your perceptions and conclusions about each arrangement accurate? You can get additional feedback from your students by copying Figure 4.6 and asking them to state which are most and least comfortable for them. Compare their answers with yours. In your journal keep a record of each arrangement that you use in your teaching (or those you observe) and note how the arrangement may have affected the success of the lesson.

4.4   Draw the seating arrangement in this class. How does this arrangement affect the communication taking place? Where do you sit? What does this tell you about your own communication?

4.5   What is your body type? How do you think your body type affects your classroom communication?

4.6   The way teachers move about the classroom has a profound effect on the messages they convey to students, on the ways in which they relate to students, and ultimately on the learning that occurs. Their movements demonstrate how teachers feel about students; at the same time, movements have a determining effect on their relationships with students. For example, teachers who always sit or stand behind a desk put a physical barrier between themselves and their students. If they remain behind the desk because they feel uncomfortable relating closely to students, students will probably perceive them as being emotionally as well as physically distant. Students are not likely to attempt to relate more closely with such teachers, so the emotional distance is thereby increased. Thus, the very action of remaining behind a desk (which may not have been a conscious action on the part of a teacher) reinforces the original feeling that motivated the action. Even if teachers are aware of the emotional distance between themselves and their students, they are unlikely to bridge that distance until they realize how their physical deportment is contributing to it.

Let's look at another example: if a generally active teacher moves throughout the classroom but consistently avoids one corner, it may be because a student in that corner makes the teacher uncomfortable. By avoiding that corner the teacher conveniently avoids the student, while at the same time creating even greater distance from that student. Unless the teacher becomes aware of this pattern of movement, confronting and changing the feelings of discomfort are impossible.

Objectives

1. To help you monitor your movement in a classroom.
2. To help you identify the possible effects of your classroom movement on students.
3. To assist you in making your physical movement contribute to your goals.

Directions

For a specified period of time (perhaps one period or one hour), ask a colleague observer to map on paper your movement about the classroom, using the following technique:

1. Draw a map of the classroom, including the furniture arrangement (see, for example, Figure 4.7).
2. Chart with a pencil the teacher's location at the beginning of class, and follow the teacher's movement throughout the agreed on time period.
3. Consecutively number places at which the teacher stops.
4. Draw concentric circles around places at which the teacher remains for significant time periods: one circle for every three minutes.

For example, a map of a traditionally arranged classroom with a teacher who spends most of the time in front of the class might look something like the one shown in Figure 4.5.

Questions

1. In which areas of your classroom did you spend most of your time?
2. Did you neglect any area(s)?
3. Did the students' activities determine your movements in any way?
4. What effect did the seating arrangement have on your movements?
5. What effect might your movement have had on students?
6. Do you want to make any changes in your movement pattern based on the information you now have? Why or why not?

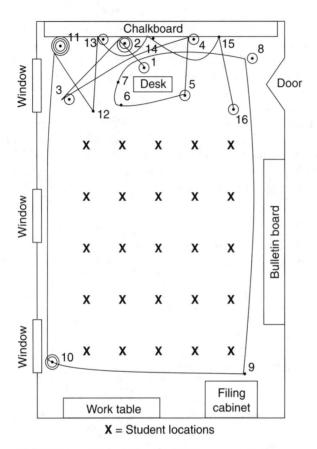

X = Student locations

FIGURE 4.7   **Map of Teacher's Movement during Class Period. Stops Are Numbered Consecutively; Each Circle Next to a Number Indicates a Stop of Three Minutes.**

Follow-Up

A teacher's movement in the classroom can have a significant effect on the learning that occurs. It follows, then, that becoming aware of your movement, analyzing its possible effects, and selecting movements that facilitate your goals should become part of your planning process. Your lessons may determine some or all of your movements in the classroom. For example, if you consistently include references to a pull-down or posted map in your lesson plans, or if you consistently use the chalkboard, your movements will be somewhat limited. You can spend less time at the map or at the board by providing dittoed maps or other materials to students, thus freeing yourself to move in different ways. The lessons you plan should allow you as many options for movement as possible and should free, rather than restrict, your movement in the classroom.

Use the information gained from having your movement monitored and mapped to devise a plan of movement for a lesson you will use in the next few days. Be as specific in your plan as appropriate for the lesson. Use the following questions to assist your planning:

1. Does the lesson itself dictate your movement in any way? For example, do you have to remain in one place in order to use audiovisual aids? Specify those elements of your lesson that require you to move in specific ways.
2. What effect might the movements you cited previously have on the learning that occurs?
3. How else can you plan the lesson to give yourself greater choice of movement in the classroom?

Following the lesson for which you planned your movement, evaluate for yourself how your movements might have affected the learning that occurred.

FURTHER READING

Knapp, M., & Hall, J. (1996). *Nonverbal communication in human interaction* (4th ed.). New York: Holt, Rinehart & Winston.

This text provides an excellent review of the theory and research of nonverbal communication.

Richmond, V. (1992). *Nonverbal communication in the classroom.* Edina, MN: Burgess.

This text presents an overview of nonverbal communication and its effect on classroom learning.

INSTRUCTIONAL STRATEGIES

A variety of teaching strategies exist from which teachers can choose—lecture, discussion, independent study, programmed learning, computer-assisted instruction, small group instruction, peer instruction, and so forth. During any one day, a teacher may use several of these strategies. None of these strategies has been found to be consistently superior to any other. How, then, can teachers choose the "best" strategy for their students?

CHOOSING A TEACHING STRATEGY

The choice of a teaching strategy is not an easy task. However, there are certain guidelines a teacher should follow. Four are discussed here. Keep in mind that no teaching method is inherently good or bad. However, given the guidelines presented here, you should be able to choose the appropriate strategy for your particular needs.

The Teacher

The first consideration in determining which teaching strategy to use is the personality and expertise of you—the teacher. Anyone who has taught knows that he has more adaptability and skill in some approaches than in others. Some teachers feel most comfortable when lecturing, others feel quite capable of stimulating a class discussion. A teacher's ability to tolerate high levels of ambiguity, willingness to relinquish some of the control over the classroom, and ability to tolerate low levels of organization and structure will influence that teacher's liking of the discussion method.

To a certain extent, you should use the approach with which you feel most comfortable. However, we would encourage you to experiment with a variety of teaching strategies. You might find you enjoy and do well with several approaches.

Objective of the Lesson

A second important factor to consider is the objective of the lesson. If the objective is information acquisition, the lecture method would be one appropriate method. If the objective is to have students develop their critical thinking abilities, a discussion method would be more appropriate. It's imperative that you formulate objectives for each lesson and then use the teaching strategy that will best enable your students to meet those objectives.

The Students

Students—their age, intelligence, motivational level, and previous learning of the subject matter—are an important consideration in choosing a particular teaching strategy. For example, the attention span of elementary school children is limited. Thus, the lecture method will not be as appropriate as some other teaching methods. Most researchers recommend only ten to twenty minutes of lecturing for any age group. In addition, students who are below average in intelligence or educational experience may have difficulty learning via the lecture method. In contrast, students who are not highly motivated may benefit from the lecture method, because it affords them the structure they need in order to learn.

The Environment

Finally, the environment in which learning is to take place must be considered. The environment includes such variables as time, class size, and furniture arrangements. How much time will you have for the lesson itself? To adequately evaluate and respond to students' needs takes more instructional time with some teaching methods than with others. Class size is a factor to consider. For example, the larger the class, the more difficult it will be to use the discussion method. Some classrooms do not lend themselves to using small instructional groups. If chairs in a straight row arrangement are bolted to the floor (as was the case in a classroom in which one of the authors taught), it's impossible to rearrange furniture spatially in a manner conducive to small group communication. Remember that the classroom is a system. All these factors—teacher, objectives, student, environment—interact to affect your decision on which teaching strategy is best for a particular lesson.

Keeping these general guidelines in mind, the next few chapters examine specific teaching methods—the lecture, discussion, use of small groups, storytelling, and communicative reading. It's important to remember that these methods are examined from a communication perspective. In other words, we'll be concerned with the communication interaction that occurs when each of these methods is used, as well as communication skills necessary in order to teach via each of these methods.

ADVANTAGES AND DISADVANTAGES OF THE LECTURE METHOD

Following is a list of the advantages and disadvantages of the lecture method. Notice that the major advantage of lecturing is that vast amounts of information can be presented in a relatively expedient manner. The major idea permeating the disadvantages is that the communicative interaction among students and between students and teacher is limited.

Although teachers of elementary schoolchildren will not use this method to the extent that teachers of older students will, the principles discussed can be used for any information sharing function in the classroom—giving direction, providing explanations, and conducting reviews.

Lecturing is advantageous because

1. It presents a human model.
2. It is inexpensive because the student–teacher ratio is quite large.
3. It is flexible in that it can be adapted easily to a particular group of students, subject matter, and so on.
4. It can cover vast amounts of information
5. It provides for reinforcement.

   a. Teachers are rewarded by the attention they receive. As one instructor indicates

   I enjoy the lecture method. It is the most dramatic way of presenting to the largest number of students a critical distillation of ideas and information on a subject in the shortest possible time. The bigger the class the better I perform intellectually. How else in teaching can you share with so many a lifetime of looking at and loving art? You stand on a stage in front of a screen on which the whole history of art is projected. You can be an explorer of African art, an interpreter of Greek sculptures, a spokesman for cathedral builders, an advocate of Leonardo, a political theorist for palace architects, an analyst of Picasso and philosopher of Sung painting. No other subject is as visually exciting in the classroom, and this is what keeps me turned on lecture after lecture, year after year. With that supporting cast and if he knew his lines, who wouldn't want to perform in front of a large audience? (Elsen, 1969, p. 21)

   b. The humor, warmth, and enthusiasm bestowed on students by the effective lecturer can serve as reinforcement to them.

Lecturing is disadvantageous because

1. Lectures are usually used when class size is fairly large, thus prohibiting student–teacher interaction as well as student–student interaction. Students often feel they are "just a number." This depersonalization may impair learning.
2. Students can become easily confused because of a large amount of information being covered. If, as a lecturer, you don't pay close attention to nonverbal feedback from students, you won't know which material needs to be clarified.
3. It is a difficult method by which to probe deeply into material that is abstract or theoretical in nature.
4. It is difficult for students to maintain attention in such an inactive role for more than fifteen to twenty minute intervals.
5. Lecture audiences are heterogeneous; therefore, it is difficult to gear material to all audience members.

When to Lecture

These advantages and disadvantages of the lecture method suggest there are times when lecturing is appropriate and times when other methods are perhaps more advantageous. The following list presents conditions under which the lecture is appropriate and inappropriate.

Lecturing is appropriate when

1. The basic instructional purpose is to disseminate information.
2. The information is not available elsewhere.
3. The information must be organized and presented in a particular way.
4. It is necessary to arouse learner interest in a subject.
5. It is necessary to introduce an area of content or provide directions for learning tasks that will be developed via some other teaching method.

Lecturing is inappropriate when

1. The basic instructional purpose involves forms of learning other than the acquisition of information.
2. The instructional objective involves higher cognitive levels, such as analysis, synthesis, and evaluation.
3. The learning task involves initiating or changing attitudes, values, beliefs, and behavior.
4. The information acquired must be remembered for a long period of time.
5. The information is already available, abstract, or detailed.
6. Learner participation is essential to the achievement of the instructional objective.

ADVANTAGES AND DISADVANTAGES OF THE DISCUSSION METHOD

As is the case with any teaching method, there are times when the discussion method will be appropriate and other times when it will not be. Some of the first considerations in determining the discussion method's appropriateness are those parts of the classroom discussed earlier—you, the teacher; your students; and the educational environment. In addition to these considerations, the discussion method is appropriate when the teacher is striving to do the following:

1. Use the resources of members of the group.
2. Give students opportunities to work out ways to apply the principles being discussed.
3. Get prompt feedback on how well the teaching objectives are being reached.
4. Help students learn to think in terms of the subject matter by giving them practice in thinking.
5. Help students learn to evaluate the logic of, and evidence for, their own and others' positions.

6. Increase students' awareness of class readings and lectures, and help them formulate questions that require them to seek information from the readings and lectures.
7. Gain students' acceptance of information or theories counter to their folklore or previous beliefs.

The discussion method, like all teaching methods, has advantages and disadvantages, listed next. When considering using the discussion method, it's important to think about these advantages and disadvantages and their relationship to your particular teaching objectives.

Advantages of the discussion method:

1. Two heads are better than one—more ideas, resources, and feedback are generated.
2. It provides students practice in expressing themselves clearly and accurately.
3. It helps students gain skill in defending and supporting their views.
4. Discussions expose students to a variety of ideas, beliefs, and information different from their own.
5. There are motivational effects—students enjoy the activity and feedback discussion provides.

Disadvantages of the discussion method:

1. It takes considerable time.
2. Successful discussion requires that teachers and students possess discussion skills.

Remember, that from a transactional perspective, this strategy views the students as active agents in the learning process. With the discussion strategy, teachers must be willing to relinquish control and realize that students can share in the teaching responsibilities. Their experiences, examples, and knowledge may offer insights of the material to the teacher and other students. For example, in the course of the discussion, a student may offer a personal example of a certain concept that the teacher could not. This example, in turn, may help another student to internalize the information that may have otherwise been misunderstood.

ADVANTAGES AND DISADVANTAGES
OF THE SMALL GROUP METHOD

The advantages and disadvantages of the small group teaching method are similar to those of the discussion method and are listed next. When considering use of the small group as a teaching method, keep these advantages and disadvantages in mind. Consider your students and your objectives, making sure that the method is appropriate to both.

Advantages of the small group method:

1. It enhances student motivation and fosters positive attitudes toward the sub-ject matter; students enjoy working together in small groups.
2. It develops students' problem-solving and decision-making skills.
3. It enables students to share their ideas with other students for critiquing and comparison.

Disadvantages of the small group method:

1. It is time consuming.
2. Students need an understanding of small group communication processes.

ADVANTAGES AND DISADVANTAGES OF STORYTELLING AND COMMUNICATIVE READING

All stories are full of bias and uniqueness; they mix fact with meaning. This is the root of their power. Stories allow us to see something familiar through new eyes. We become in that moment a guest in someone else's life, and together with them sit at the feet of their teacher. The meaning we may draw from someone's story may be different from the meaning they themselves have drawn. No matter. Facts bring us to knowledge, but stories lead to wisdom. (Remen, 1996, p. xxviii)

Storytelling and communicative reading are powerful teaching tools for several reasons. In their text, *The Power of Story,* Collins and Cooper (1997) suggest that stories, whether in the form of telling or reading, are advantageous because they

- enhance imagination and visualization
- enhance students' appreciation of the beauty and rhythm of language
- increase vocabulary
- enhance speaking and listening skills
- enhance writing and reading skills
- enhance creative and critical thinking skills
- help students realize the importance of literature as a mirror of human experience
- help students understand their cultural heritage and those of others
- nourish students' intuitive sides

As with any teaching method, there are disadvantages to storytelling and communicative reading as teaching strategies. Perhaps the major disadvantage is that it can be time consuming to find the right materials for your particular stu-dents and your objectives. In addition, students often need guidance in terms of re-lating the story to the content you are teaching.

In the next four chapters, we discuss each of these teaching methods in depth. As you read these chapters, remember to consider the advantages and dis-advantages of each method.

CHAPTER FIVE

SHARING INFORMATION

Objectives

After reading this chapter, you should be able to:

- Identify the variables that affect information processing in the classroom.
- Understand the importance of clarity.
- State the four principles of information exchange and explain how they relate to lecturing.
- Identify communication barriers that often arise when lecturing.
- Understand the causes of teacher communication apprehension.
- Prepare a lecture using the five steps of lecture preparation.
- Use visual aids effectively.
- Present a minilecture in a microteaching situation.

Recall from the Unit II overview on Instructional Strategies that you should consider yourself as teacher, the lesson objectives, the students, and the environment before selecting a particular teaching method. Before proceeding with this chapter and the ones that follow, refer to the advantages and disadvantages provided in the unit overview for each of these strategies. For example, although lecture is often very useful in conveying new or complex information very efficiently, it is not always the best strategy to use in the classroom. The tips provided in the unit overview further address the issues to consider when making choices about teaching.

THE LECTURE

Teachers are often called on to give information. No teacher escapes giving directions, specifying procedures, providing demonstrations, making assignments, and reviewing. Although we focus on the lecture as sharing information, remember that the suggestions made concerning the lecture relate to other forms of information sharing as well.

> The robins sang and sang and sang,
> but teacher you went right on.
> The last bell sounded the end of the day,

but teacher you went right on.
The geranium on the window sill just died,
but teacher you went right on. (Cullum, 1971, p. 56)

Too often, this poem describes students' reactions to lecturing. However, this doesn't have to be the case. When you use the lecture method, it doesn't excuse you from responsibility for getting students involved during the lecture. Rhetorical questions, handouts to be completed as the lecture progresses, previewing the lesson, and continually referring to the reading assignment are all means of enhancing student involvement in the lecture. As you read about how to effectively construct and use a lecture, keep in mind that the lecture is a communicative event and the give-and-take of communicative messages is a transactional process.

Lecturing is, essentially, sharing information. The major purpose is to secure clear understanding of the concepts you present. Before discussing the best method of constructing a lecture to help ensure that you enable clear understanding, variables affecting information processing as well as principles of information exchange are examined.

VARIABLES AFFECTING INFORMATION PROCESSING

Students acquire and process information symbolically through language, their perceptions of you and the classroom situation, and their perceptions and communication with self. Several variables affect this symbolic interaction process in the classroom—sensory limitations, perception differences, emotional states, needs, values, and beliefs. We examine student variables, message variables, and some principles of information exchange, and communication apprehension.

Student Variables

All of us have *sensory limitations*. We may have a hearing or sight problem. However, even if we don't have an extreme problem, we all differ in how well we use our senses in the learning process. In addition, any time we as teachers use a strategy that eliminates use of one or more senses by students to receive messages, we are limiting their learning ability even further. Simply lecturing on how to dissect a frog is not nearly as effective as combining that lecture with student dissection of the frog.

Our *emotional states* affect how well we are able to process information. It's extremely difficult to acquire and process any information when we are tired, depressed, anxious, or experiencing some kind of conflict or personal problem. The more supportive you can make the climate in your classroom, the less tense and anxious students will be and the easier it will be for them to acquire the information you present.

As Maslow has told us for years, when lower-level needs (such as safety) are not met, students cannot fulfill higher-level needs. Maslow classified human needs into five hierarchical categories. An adaptation of his hierarchy for educational settings is shown in Figure 5.1. For example, many schools and districts now offer breakfast programs to ensure that all students enter the learning environment free from the physical need for food.

Finally, students' *attitudes* and *beliefs* can affect their information processing. How students feel about themselves affects the ways in which they process information. How the student feels about you as a teacher can affect information processing. If a student does not like you or the topic covered, she will probably not respond well to the information you present.

Learning style refers to the way in which a learner learns and processes information. According to Dunn, Dunn, and Price (1979, p. 53), "learning style is the way in which responses are made because of individual psychological differences." Keefe (1982) defines learning style as "cognitive, affective, and physiological traits that serve as relatively stable indicators of how learners perceive, interact with and respond to the learning environment" (p. 44). For example, Sinatra (1986) reviewed a large body of research that indicates that the learning style of the gifted and talented can be described as independent, internally controlled, self-motivated, persistent, perceptually strong, task committed, and nonconforming. These learners prefer learning through independent studies and projects rather than through lecture or discussion.

As Dunn, Beaudry, and Klavas (1989) indicate, no learning style is better or worse than another. What is important, however, is the fact that the closer the match between a student's style and the teacher's, then the higher the student's grade point average. When students are permitted to learn difficult academic information or skills through their identified learning style preferences, they tend to achieve statistically higher test and aptitude scores than when instruction is dissonant with their preferences.

Teachers need to identify their students' learning styles. There are numerous commercially published instruments that measure one or many aspects of learning style. However, Cornett (1983) suggests that even without formal instruments, it is possible to obtain assessment information from observations of students or discussing with students their own views by asking "How, when, where and what do you learn best?" Another technique is to ask students to write or tell about a learning or study situation in which they were either productive or nonproductive and analyze the situation.

Cornett (1983, pp. 15–18) presents an informal learning style inventory that you might want to complete in order to understand your own learning style (see Box 5.1). You may also want to consider having your students complete this inventory as you begin to make decisions on how to instruct them.

After completing this inventory, perhaps you will discover things about your learning and teaching styles that you had not realized before. If your cognitive profile lies more to the left, then you probably are more left-brain oriented; if it lies to the right, then you are likely to be more right-brain oriented. If your affective profile lies to the left, you are probably more systematic, structured, and organized. If your affective profile is more to the right, you are probably more flexible, group-oriented,

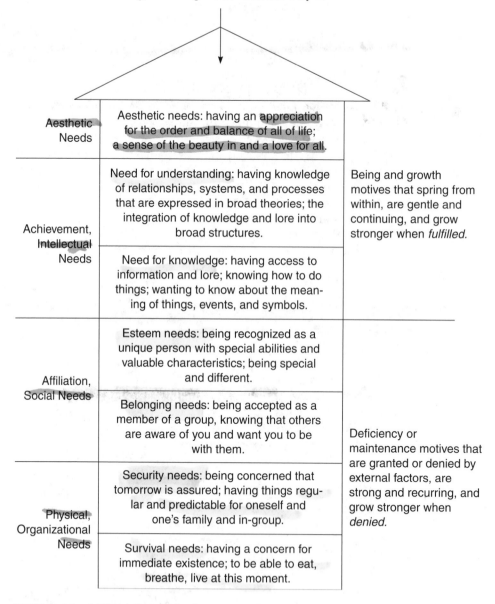

Self-actualization, displaying the needs of a fully functioning student or human being; becoming the self that one truly is.

Aesthetic Needs	Aesthetic needs: having an appreciation for the order and balance of all of life; a sense of the beauty in and a love for all.	Being and growth motives that spring from within, are gentle and continuing, and grow stronger when *fulfilled.*
Achievement, Intellectual Needs	Need for understanding: having knowledge of relationships, systems, and processes that are expressed in broad theories; the integration of knowledge and lore into broad structures.	
	Need for knowledge: having access to information and lore; knowing how to do things; wanting to know about the meaning of things, events, and symbols.	
Affiliation, Social Needs	Esteem needs: being recognized as a unique person with special abilities and valuable characteristics; being special and different.	
	Belonging needs: being accepted as a member of a group, knowing that others are aware of you and want you to be with them.	Deficiency or maintenance motives that are granted or denied by external factors, are strong and recurring, and grow stronger when *denied.*
Physical, Organizational Needs	Security needs: being concerned that tomorrow is assured; having things regular and predictable for oneself and one's family and in-group.	
	Survival needs: having a concern for immediate existence; to be able to eat, breathe, live at this moment.	

FIGURE 5.1   A Hierarchy of Needs.

This hierarchy of needs is based on a formulation by Maslow (1954) as modified by Root (1970).

From N. L. Gage and D. C. Berliner, *Educational Psychology* (Chicago: Rand McNally, 1974) 286. Copyright © 1975 by Houghton Mifflin Company. Used with permission.

■ ■ ■ ■ ■

BOX 5.1
INFORMAL LEARNING STYLE INVENTORY

DIRECTIONS
1. For the sections dealing with cognitive and affective styles, put an X on the line at a point where you think you fall with regard to the polar concepts expressed by the two words. For the section dealing with physical aspects of learning style, check your preferences and describe the environment in which you learn best.
2. After completing the inventory draw a line connecting the Xs. This, along with your preferences, will give you a rough profile of your learning and teaching style.

COGNITIVE STYLE (CONCERNED WITH PROCESSING, ENCODING, STORAGE, AND RETRIEVAL OF INFORMATION)

sequential...random
serial ....simultaneous
focusing...scanning
separating..integrating
parts...whole
discriminate..generalize
sharpening..leveling
abstract...concrete
compartmentalization...........................differentiation
narrow categories ....broad categories
analyze by describing ....draw relationships based on functions and themes
reflective ....impulsive
deductive..inductive
convergent..divergent
analytic..global
splitter ....lumper
logical ....metamorphic
words..images
time-oriented...nontemporal
digital ....spatial
details and facts. ....generalizations
careful...quick
literal ....figurative
outline ....summarize
surface approach ....deep approach
memorize..associate/understand
verbal communication...........................nonverbal communication
implications...analogies

(continued)

BOX 5.1   CONTINUED

AFFECTIVE STYLE (CONCERNED WITH ATTENTION, MOTIVATION, AND PERSONALITY)

objective	subjective
practical	theoretical
reality	fantasy
subject-oriented	people-oriented
realistic	imaginative
intellectual	creative
close-minded	open-minded
conformist	individualist
concentration	distraction
reserved	outgoing
thinker	intuiter
rigid	flexible
Groucho humor (puns; satire)	Harpo humor (slapstick)
competitive	cooperative
structured	unstructured
intrinsically motivated	extrinsically motivated
persistent	gives up easily
cautious	risk-taking
intolerant of ambiguity	tolerant of ambiguity
internal locus of control	external locus of control
leader	follower
pessimistic	optimistic
future-oriented	present-oriented
does not like pressure	likes pressure
likes working alone	likes working in a group

PHYSICAL STYLE (CONCERNED WITH PERCEPTUAL MODES, ENERGY LEVEL, TIME PREFERENCES, AND ENVIRONMENT)

DIRECTIONS

1. Check your preferences.

Receiving Information		Expressing Yourself	
visual (reading and viewing)	____	visual (writing, drawing, etc.)	____
auditory (listening)	____	oral (speaking)	____
kinesthetic (feeling and doing)	____	kinesthetic (art, demonstrating, or showing)	____
smell	____		
taste	____		

2. Describe the environment in which you learn best (lighting, furniture, room arrangement, noise level, time of day, etc.).

From Cornett (1983, pp. 15–18).

and creative. Perhaps you will discover a balance of right and left. What is important is to "know thyself." But remember, this is only a rough indicator.

It is important to note that cultural differences affect learning styles. Although several ways to examine learning styles exist, the following five are most relevant to the intercultural classroom. Cultures differ on four major dimensions that relate to learning styles (Hofstede, 1991, pp. 10–11):

1. *Individualism* as a characteristic of a culture opposes *collectivism*. Individualist cultures assume that: any person looks primarily after her own interests and the interests of her immediate family (husband, wife, and children). Collectivist cultures assume that any person through birth and possible later events belongs to one or more tight "in-groups," from which he cannot detach himself. The "in-group" (whether extended family, clan, or organization) protects the interests of its members, but in turn expects their permanent loyalty. A collectivist society is tightly integrated; an individualist society is loosely integrated.

2. *Power distance* as a characteristic of a culture defines the extent to which the less powerful persons in a society accept inequality in power and consider it normal. Inequality exists within any culture, but the degree to which it is tolerated varies between one culture and another.

3. *Uncertainty avoidance* as a characteristic of a culture defines the extent to which people within a culture are made nervous by situations that they perceive as unstructured, unclear, or unpredictable, situations that they therefore try to avoid by maintaining strict codes of behavior and a belief in absolute truths. Cultures exhibiting strong uncertainty avoidance are active, aggressive, emotional, compulsive, security-seeking, and intolerant; cultures with a weak uncertainty avoidance are contemplative, less aggressive, unemotional, relaxed, accepting of personal risks, and relatively tolerant.

4. *Masculinity* as a characteristic of a culture opposes *feminity*. The two differ in the social roles associated with the biological fact of the existence of two sexes, and in particular in the social roles attributed to men. The cultures labelled as *masculine* strive for maximal distinction between what men are expected to do and what women are expected to do. They expect men to be assertive, ambitious and competitive, to strive for material success, and to respect whatever is big, strong, and fast. They expect women to serve and to care for the non-material quality of life, for children, and for the weak. *Feminine* cultures, on the other hand, define relatively overlapping social roles for the sexes, in which, in particular, men need not be ambitious or competitive but may go for a different quality of life than material success; men may respect whatever is small, weak, and slow. In both masculine and feminine cultures, the dominant values within political and work organizations are those of men. So, in masculine cultures these political values stress material success and assertiveness; in feminine cultures they stress other types of quality of life, interpersonal relationships, and concern for the weak.

Hall (1977) suggests one other important item—high context versus low context cultures. High context cultures prefer to use messages in which most of the meaning is either implied by the physical setting or is presumed to be part of each individual's internalized values, beliefs, and norms. Low context cultures use messages in which the majority of the information is in the explicit code. In short, high context cultures emphasize the nonverbal code; low context cultures emphasize the verbal code.

Given this general background, let's move on to how learning style relates to cultural differences. The first type of learning style is a preference for groups versus individual learning. In European American cultures, education typically emphasizes individual learning. Each student strives for her individual grade or praise. In many collectivist cultures, group learning is expected. For example, children of Hawaiian ancestry

> come under the guidance of their older siblings very early in life. Parents interact with their children as a group, not so much as individuals. As a result of this kind of upbringing, children learn to learn best from siblings and peers in group situations, not from one adult, as is typical in European American cultures as well as in the school setting. (Cushner & Brislin, 1996, p. 340)

Another difference is out-of-context versus in-context learning. Out-of-context learning requires students to learn in a setting different from that in which the learning is applied. For example, you are learning about intercultural communication from this textbook and this class. Hopefully, someday, you will have the opportunity to apply what you have learned in an intercultural setting.

Students can also learn in real-life settings. Some cultures emphasize this type of learning, particularly those without long histories of written language. As Cushner and Brislin (1996) explain:

> Hunting and gathering societies, in which young males accompany the adults on hunting expeditions from a relatively early age, offer an example of in-context learning. The child learns through active involvement and participation with the adult teacher in the hunting process, with his contributions being of some value to the task at hand, not by passively observing procedures and techniques for future application. He is immediately rewarded when he masters the required skills and completes a kill, not by internalizing the procedure and reproducing it in symbol form (either orally or in writing) upon command. (p. 339)

Gay (1978) indicates that two cognitive patterns are evident from research on ethnic learning styles. The *analytic style* is detail specific, impersonal, requires sustained attention, and uses an elaborate syntactic code. This style seems to be characteristic of European and Jewish Americans. The *relational style* employs self-centered orientations, determines word meanings by situational contexts, focuses on global characteristics of stimuli, uses a descriptive mode of abstracting information from stimuli, and uses a restricted syntactic code. This style seems to be characteristic of Mexican Americans, Asian Americans, African Americans, and some Native Americans.

A third difference in learning style is field dependent versus field independent. In a field dependent learning style, people tend to "take elements or background variables from the environment into account...[and] to perceive the event holistically, including the emotionality and the feelings associated with the entire event (Lieberman, 1994, p. 179). By contrast, field independent learners are analytical and use strategies to isolate elements of the field (Brown, 1987). To put it simply, some people see the forest; some see the trees. Field dependent style is prevalent in group-oriented, high context, and collectivist societies. Field independent styles predominate in low context, highly competitive, and highly industrialized societies (Lieberman, 1994).

Tolerance for ambiguity is related to learning style. Some cultures have more tolerance for ambiguity than others. Tolerance (or intolerance) of ambiguity is related to open-mindedness about differences or contradictions. Cultures with a low tolerance for ambiguity tend to emphasize bipolar languages. As Lieberman (1994) suggests, the English language emphasizes bipolarity. In a problem-solving situation, bipolar language might be: "This is either right or wrong, black or white, good or bad, yes or no, correct or incorrect" (p. 179). Thus, as Samovar and Porter (1995, p. 252) state

> Therefore, tolerance for ambiguity is tied to the degree of bipolarity in the structure and meaning of a culture's language. In the scientifically oriented, competitive American culture, tolerance for ambiguity is not perceived positively in the average classroom. On the other hand, in cultures where bipolarity is de-emphasized, there is a much higher tolerance for ambiguity. Cultures such as that of India are high in tolerance of ambiguity, as exemplified by Nemi Jain who states, "One must know that one's judgements are true only partially and can by no means be regarded as true in absolute terms."

Finally, some cultures value reflectivity (a slow, deliberative seeking of answers), whereas others value impulsivity (quick guesses). For example, in American society, students are rewarded for risk-taking and creativity, for trial and error methods of learning. Often, low context cultures value impulsivity. High context cultures, such as China, value reflectivity. An individual is expected to consider multiple variables before making a decision, because a problem resulting from a decision reached in haste can result in a loss of face.

Kleinfeld (1994) indicates that "the concept of learning styles is useful when it reminds the teacher to create rich and interesting classrooms where children can learn in many different ways" (p. 156). She provides an example of how this might be done. In a remote Eskimo village a teacher tried to introduce the concepts of "calories" and "energy formation" through a lecture. But the expressions on the children's faces indicated they were bored. So, the teacher later asked the children to attend a steam bath, an important event in the village's culture. As they observed what happened to the water when it was gas, solid, and liquid, they asked questions such as, "What happens to the steam when it goes out of the steam bath when someone opens the door?" Kleinfeld points out that the teacher adapted the science lesson to the cultural setting and the learning styles of the children.

Message Variables

Message variables—both verbal and nonverbal—that increase attention will also increase the information processed. The organization of the message—the order in which points are presented—affects processing as well as recall. Points presented first or last in a lecture are better remembered and understood. Concrete language is better remembered and processed than abstract language. In addition, intense language facilitates information processing because it increases, to a certain extent, the students' attention levels. Finally, a two-sided rather than a one-sided message creates greater retention with comprehension, because attention and perceptions are increased by the novelty and contrast produced by this message strategy.

One of the major message variables a teacher needs to be concerned with is teacher clarity. Remember the adage that the difference between knowing and teaching is communication (Hurt, Scott, & McCroskey, 1978)? Teacher clarity is the key to this distinction. That is, a teacher may be an expert in the field, but if she cannot communicate that knowledge in a clear and effective way, learning is not achieved. Clarity, then, is the teacher's ability to present knowledge in a way that students understand. Cawyer (1994) explains that, "when viewed in relationship to 'teacher knowledge,' clarity may be seen as a connecting element between content and pedagogy since it represents an instructor's capacity to transfer the cognitive dimension of teaching into visible instructional behaviors" (p. 30). Teachers should, therefore, have an appreciation for the principles of teacher clarity before attempting to construct a message for their students.

According to Civikly (1992a, p. 139), "The struggle encountered with the teacher clarity construct begins at the definitional level; specifically, what is teacher clarity and how do I know it when I see and hear it?" Several researchers have responded to the problems of definition and abstractness by developing low inference descriptors of teacher clarity. The behaviors that describe teacher clarity are provided in Box 5.2. You can use this list of behaviors to monitor your own teacher clarity as you begin your teaching endeavors.

Many scholars have studied the construct of teacher clarity. Teacher clarity has been linked to student achievement and satisfaction (Frey, Leonard, & Beatty, 1975; Hines, Cruickshank, & Kennedy, 1985). French-Lazovik (1974) found that students judge a teacher's effectiveness, in large part, on clarity behaviors. And according to Gloeckner (1983), teacher clarity can be enhanced through training.

More recently, scholars have suggested that teacher clarity should be reexamined and elaborated (Civikly, 1992a; Simonds, 1997a). Although those who have generated lists to describe clarity have tried to address many concerns, two issues have been neglected in their attempts. The first concern is that teacher clarity comprises more than simply content clarity, and the second is that teacher clarity can be viewed as a relational construct.

First, teacher clarity is more than simply message or content clarity. Current instruments reveal many references to the clarity of the content material or subject matter of the course. For example, the Hines, Cruickshank, and Kennedy (1985) *Clarity Observation Instrument* includes eighteen clarity behavior items that refer to content messages in three categories: explains content of material; stresses important aspects of content; and responds to perceived deficiencies in understanding content material. Teacher clarity is more than simply carefully presenting the subject matter or content of the course. Rather, clarity must be incorporated as a goal

---

BOX 5.2
TEACHER CLARITY BEHAVIORS

1. Orient and prepare students for what is to be taught.
2. Communicate content so that students understand.
3. Provide illustrations and examples.
4. Demonstrate.
5. Use a variety of teaching materials.
6. Teach things in a related, step-by-step manner.
7. Repeat and stress directions and difficult points.
8. Adjust teaching to the learner and topic.
9. Cause students to organize learning in meaningful ways.
10. Provide practice.
11. Provide standards and rules for satisfactory performance.
12. Provide students with feedback or knowledge of how well they are doing.
13. Use concrete examples of concept.
14. Give multiple examples.
15. Point out practical applications.
16. Stress important points.
17. Repeat difficult ideas.

From Cruickshank (1985) and Murray (1985).

---

of general classroom understanding. Simonds (1997a) addresses this issue by presenting an instrument that measures not only content clarity but process clarity as well. Process clarity includes information that relates to various classroom expectations, such as standards for performance, feedback of how well students are doing, explanations of evaluation procedures, practical relevance, and tasks, among others (see Table 5.1).

A second concern is the issue of clarity as a relational construct. Past research has focused on teacher clarity within a process–product paradigm where the construct is examined in its relationship to student outcomes. For example, if a teacher is "clear," students will learn. Civikly (1992a) extends the construct to include message clarity and student clarification techniques. She argues the thesis that clarity is a relational variable and highlights the central role of communication in the process of teaching and of learning. Teacher clarity is a communication variable that may affect the relational climate of the classroom. Studies of the student's role in processing teacher information and of the teacher's clarification strategies indicate that students are part of the instructional clarity process (Darling, 1989; Kendrick, 1987; Kendrick & Darling, 1990; Simonds, 1997a; West & Pearson, 1994). For example, if a teacher is unclear about a classroom expectation, students will use some type of clarification tactic in order to reduce uncertainty. Students may ask questions, observe other students asking questions, or test the

TABLE 5.1   Teacher Clarity Report

My instructor	Very Often	Often	Sometimes	Almost Never	Never
is clear when presenting content.	____	____	____	____	____
uses examples when presenting content.	____	____	____	____	____
relates examples to the concept being discussed.	____	____	____	____	____
uses the board, transparencies, or other visual aids during class.	____	____	____	____	____
gives previews of material to be covered.	____	____	____	____	____
gives summaries when presenting content.	____	____	____	____	____
stresses important points.	____	____	____	____	____
stays on topic.	____	____	____	____	____
clearly explains the objectives for the content being presented.	____	____	____	____	____
defines major/new concepts.	____	____	____	____	____
communicates classroom processes and expectations clearly.	____	____	____	____	____
describes assignments and how they should be done.	____	____	____	____	____
asks if we know what to do and how to do it.	____	____	____	____	____
prepares us for the tasks we will be doing next.	____	____	____	____	____
points out practical applications for coursework.	____	____	____	____	____
prepares students for exams.	____	____	____	____	____
explains how we should prepare for an exam.	____	____	____	____	____
provides students with feedback of how well they are doing.	____	____	____	____	____
provides rules and standards for satisfactory performance.	____	____	____	____	____
communicates classroom policies and consequences for violation.	____	____	____	____	____

Note: The first ten items are content messages, whereas the last ten items are process items.
From "Teacher Clarity Report," from Simonds, C. J. (Summer 1997). *Communication Research Reports 14*(3), 279–290.

expectation in the form of a challenge. Kendrick (1987) developed a conceptual framework for studying student comprehension problems. According to Kendrick, student clarification tactics include requests for help, requests for additional information, requests for specific information, and checks on one's understanding of a point (content). Kendrick and Darling (1990) further found that students ask questions about relevance of material and course assignments (process).

Pearson and West (1991) explored student questions in college classrooms. They report that students ask questions concerning clarification and procedure an average of three times per hour of instruction. More recently, West and Pearson (1994) examined the relationship between student questions and teacher comments in college classrooms. Their analysis produced six categories of student questions: classroom procedures, general content inquiry, clarification, confirmation, general teacher inquiry, and unknown or other. Again, these findings are consistent with the notion that students ask questions about classroom processes as well as content material. That is, students not only have questions about subject matter but also about tasks, relevance, evaluation, and procedures. The way a teacher responds to clarification tactics helps to define the relational climate of the classroom. Simonds (1997a) examined the relationship between teacher clarity and student challenges. She found that the higher a teacher scored on teacher clarity, the fewer student challenges she faced with regard to evaluation procedures, practical relevance, procedural rules, and power plays.

Teachers and students share in the responsibilities and the ability to clarify content. These studies demonstrate the principle that teacher clarity is the result of an interaction that takes place between teacher explanation and student clarification tactics. Because students are concerned about both content material and classroom processes, teachers must be able to identify the appropriate explanation to address student concerns.

In the next section, we discuss principles of information exchange in the form of teacher lectures. However, it must be noted that these principles should be used as a function of overall classroom understanding.

Principles of Information Exchange

In an attempt to make "learning from being told" easier for our students, the following principles of information exchange are recommended.

  1. Create a *need to know* in your students. If you ask your instructor on the first day of class what will be expected—how many papers, tests, and so forth—you'll listen to the answer. You'll feel a "need to know." Similarly, your students must have the same feeling if they are to listen to your lecture.

  2. Make your information *relevant*. This may involve your relating the new information to already familiar information. If your instructor speaks to your class about persuasion theory, the information may not relate to your experience. However, if your instructor relates the information about persuasion theory to advertising and explains how you are affected by persuasive techniques in advertising, you will be more interested in the information.

3. Information is more likely to be understood if it is *well organized, repeated,* and has *emotional impact.*

When presenting information, organization is very important. If you are describing a process, for example, you must begin at the beginning and follow through each step until you reach the end of the process. If you skip around, your students will become confused and information will be lost.

Repetition is also important in retention of information. You should determine the four or five most important ideas in your lecture and use repetitions to drive home your point.

Think about this past week. What event stands out in your memory? Was it when you forgot your speech halfway through it? Perhaps it was a date, a class presentation, or an exam. No doubt it was an event filled with emotional impact. Information that contains such impact is more memorable than straight facts. In your lecturing you should make use of memorable examples, illustrations, and anecdotes to help ensure your students' retention of your key ideas.

4. Retention and understanding are reduced if you *overload* your students with too much information. Most students can handle five to nine "bits" of information comfortably. Thus, only a few main points should be covered in a single lecture. You can reduce information overload by chunking similar information together, previewing the information you'll present, using internal summaries, and narrowing your topic.

COMMUNICATION BARRIERS
TO EFFECTIVE LECTURING

If you decide the lecture method is the most appropriate method for your particular objective, you should be aware of some general communication barriers to effective lecturing. Although there are several, the most common have been outlined by Hart (1973 and are presented) in Box 5.3. You will want to refer to this information as you prepare your own classroom lectures. One particular barrier to effective lecturing may be that you, the teacher, are highly communicatively apprehensive. The following section addresses this concern.

Communication Apprehension

Definition.   Practically speaking, communication apprehension is a serious concern for educators. What exactly is communication apprehension and how extensive is it? The teacher with high communication apprehension is one who attaches high levels of punishment to the communication encounter (McCroskey & Richmond, 1991). The individual is fearful of communication and will go to great

BOX 5.3
BARRIERS TO EFFECTIVE LECTURING

1. *There is too much or not enough information presented.* If you continually solicit feedback from your students, you'll be in a position to determine when information overload (and hence learner frustration) or information underload (and hence learner boredom) exists. Erring in either direction brings about parallel but different educational problems.

2. *Information is presented too factually or too inferentially.* The ideal lecturer is probably neither a fact-spewing computer nor an inference-making guru—she is a scholar who extends knowledge by means of hard data or intelligently conceived hypotheses.

3. *Information is too concrete or too abstract.* Being the active, searching creatures they are, students will demand of a lecturer some capacity to satisfy both their concrete and abstract information needs in some fashion. If you carefully mix and match your material, you should be able to satisfy both demands of students.

4. *Information is too general or too specific.* By carefully and consciously moving from the general to the specific and back again, you can introduce variety and can improve your students' chances of seeing both the forest and the trees.

5. *Communication is feedback-poor or feedback-rich.* Because lecturing is, by nature, a one-way information transmission system you must often be creative in finding ways to assess the teaching potential of your lecturing. Testing, of course, can and does tell *what* information is lost, but unfortunately it does not tell *why* it is lost. Better methods of getting at *whys* might be one or more of the following:

   a. *Selective feedback*—monitor the reaction of one or two representative members of the class and use these responses to guide ongoing changes in your lecture.

   b. *Overt feedback*—many lecturers use the "if you don't understand something, sing out" technique. This is probably the most desirable type of feedback, but an instructor who uses such a technique had better mean it. Students won't tolerate being asked for feedback and then having their wrists slapped when the instructor is affronted by its content.

   c. *Delayed feedback*—setting up a feedback committee (which makes daily or weekly reports to the lecturer) is often a practical device. If the feedback group is representative of the class and insightful, it can be very helpful to you despite the delay in the feedback.

   d. *Indirect feedback*—asking a fellow instructor to attend and critique your lectures can often be helpful, because he is in a position to know what to look for. Obviously, peer group evaluations can sometimes be threatening but so too can bad teacher ratings!

   e. *Self-feedback*—with the advent of audio- and videotaping equipment, the lecturer has a new ally. By reviewing your own lecture in such a fashion, many important insights can be derived if you make a conscious effort to keep bias at a minimum. Although either of these devices can provide you with helpful, corrective information, combining both techniques will create an even more ideal set of feedback circumstances. In addition, teachers need to monitor students' nonverbal feedback throughout the lecture. Too often teachers

(continued)

BOX 5.3   Continued

lecture, assuming they are being understood. Monitoring student nonverbal feedback and adjusting accordingly (clarifying, slowing down or speeding up the pace, providing an example) will add to the teaching potential of the lecture.

6. *Information is presented too rapidly or too slowly.* Most studies indicate that normal conversational delivery is best suited to covering most material with clarity and efficiency. Both excessively rapid and inordinately slow delivery of a lecture decrease students' comprehension.

7. *Information is presented too soon or too late.* Fortunately, the "too soon–too late" problems are easier to solve than most. With careful preparation of the lecture and with the knowledge of a few elementary communication principles, many such problems can be avoided. For example, by remembering that listeners find it easier to move from the simple to the complex, from the concrete to the abstract, or from the immediate to the futuristic, you can often avoid moving into material too quickly. Likewise, knowing that listeners have a need for pattern, chronology, and completeness should remind you that information must be "processed" or "wrapped-up" before students will be able to retain it.

8. *Information is presented with too much or too little intensity.* A monotone voice and few gestures or movements can make the lecture dull. However, too much intensity in voice or movement can be distracting. Varying the intensity appropriately is most effective.

From Hart (1973, pp. 10–14).

lengths to avoid communication situations, and when by chance or necessity he is placed in them, the teacher feels uncomfortable, tense, embarrassed, and shy. Thus, lecturing becomes a problem for a preservice teacher.

Causes of Communication Apprehension.   The specific causes of communication apprehension are not known. Four explanations have been posited: genetic predisposition, skills acquisition, modeling, and reinforcement (Daly & Friedrich, 1981).

The *genetic predisposition explanation* for communication apprehension holds that certain genetic components such as sociability, physical appearance, body shape, and coordination and motor abilities may contribute to the development of communication apprehension. However, as is true with many research findings concerning inherited characteristics, the environment can either enhance or decrease the hereditary predisposition toward communication apprehension.

One may also develop communication apprehension because she fails to acquire the necessary *skills for effective social interaction* at the same rate as her peers. The person with high communication apprehension is slow to develop such necessary social skills as reciprocity, language use, referential communication skills, sensitivity to verbal and nonverbal social cues, interaction management skills, and the use of verbal reinforcers. A vicious cycle emerges: as the apprehensive individual continues to fall behind her less apprehensive (more skillful) peers, she develops more communication apprehension because of her lack of skills.

A third explanation for the development of communication apprehension involves *modeling.* If we as teachers are communication apprehensive, students may observe our behavior and then imitate that behavior.

The explanation most often set forth for the development of communication apprehension relates to the theory of *reinforcement.* If an individual receives positive reinforcement, he finds communication a desirable, rewarding experience. He will develop little if any communication apprehension. If, however, the individual has been taught to be "seen but not heard"—if he has not been reinforced for communicating—he will find communication an unrewarding, undesirable experience, and communication apprehension may be high.

As individuals progress through life, communication apprehension is self-fulfilling. As you recall from Chapter 2, a self-fulfilling prophecy is a prophecy that comes true because we expect it to come true. Individuals with high apprehension fear they won't succeed in social interactions. Consequently, they avoid interaction, and the avoidance results in the loss of valuable practice time in communicating. As a result, when the individual is placed in an interaction, she performs more poorly than others. This failure then reinforces the individual's apprehension. In short, the individual expects to fail, shapes her environment so that she does fail, and is more convinced than ever that communication is punishing.

Obviously, no single explanation—genetic predisposition, reinforcement, skills acquisition, or modeling—is probably sufficient to explain why an individual develops communication apprehension. Instead, all four explanations work together to explain the development of communication apprehension.

Teacher Communication Apprehension.   Approximately one in three teachers at the lower elementary level suffers from communication apprehension (McCroskey & Richmond, 1991). Teachers who are communication apprehensive may gravitate to lower grades because teaching younger children may be less threatening to them.

Although little research has been conducted on the effect of communication apprehension on teaching effectiveness, one fact seems clear: teachers with communication apprehension prefer instructional systems that reduce the amount of student–teacher and student–student communication (McCroskey & Richmond, 1991). Research does suggest that teachers may have an impact on the development of communication apprehension. Based on their findings that students increase in communication apprehension as they progress through elementary school, McCroskey, Andersen, Richmond, and Wheeless (1981) tested two hypotheses:

1. That there is a higher proportion of teachers with high communication apprehension in the lower elementary grades (K–4) than at other grade levels.
2. That there is a higher proportion of teachers with high communication apprehension in the lower elementary grades (K–4) than there are teachers with low communication apprehension in those grades (p. 30).

Both hypotheses were confirmed. Thus, the researchers concluded that highly communication-apprehensive teachers may have an effect on the development of communication apprehension in their students.

Because teacher communication apprehension may have an impact on the way an instructor prepares and delivers a lecture, the concept of communication apprehension and its causes were discussed here. In Chapter 6, we discuss communication apprehension from the student's perspective. Chapter 6 addresses leading classroom discussion and how student levels of communication apprehension may affect their abilities or willingness to participate in such discussions. In addition, Chapter 6 also addresses treatments for communication apprehension that teachers can use when faced with the anxiety associated with planning and delivering lectures.

PREPARING A LECTURE

Perhaps the most important considerations as you prepare your lectures are the teaching objectives you want to accomplish. Everything you do in your lectures should relate to the objectives. As you go through the preparation process, continually ask yourself, "How will this help me meet my teaching objectives?"

There are five steps in lecture preparation: (1) choose a topic; (2) narrow the topic; (3) gather supporting materials; (4) organize the lecture; and (5) practice the lecture. We discuss each of these in detail.

Choose a Topic

The first step in lecture preparation is to choose a topic. What information do you want your students to know? This step is fairly complex. In deciding what you want your students to know, several factors must be considered. First, you need to consider yourself. What do you know about the topic? Can you rely exclusively on your own knowledge or will you need to utilize the thoughts and research of others?

Your students must also be considered—their age and educational level are particularly important. Is the topic of real relevance to them? What knowledge do they already possess concerning the topic? What attitudes, past experiences, and unique characteristics do they have that might influence how the topic should be approached?

The classroom environment is another important factor. Are the physical environment and the psychological environment of the classroom conducive to covering the topic? Is there enough time? Will visual aids be necessary to stimulate attention to and to clarify the topic?

Narrow the Topic

The next step in lecture preparation is to narrow your topic. You need to narrow your lecture topic until you have a simple sentence that states clearly and concisely what you wish to accomplish with your students (thesis statement). This funneling process is graphically illustrated in Figure 5.2.

As you narrow your topic to a thesis statement remember that you must consider the same factors you considered when choosing your topic initially—yourself, your students, and the classroom environment. For example, you considered what you wanted your students to know in general about the topic. As you narrow the topic, you must ask yourself such questions as, "What do I want my students to know specifically about this topic?" "Are they at an age level at which they can understand this particular aspect of the topic?" "What do they already know and how can I use this prior knowledge in my lecture?" and "What material have I already taught them and how can I use this material in this lecture?"

Gather Supporting Materials

The third step in lecture preparation is gathering supporting materials that will make the ideas you're presenting "come alive." Supporting materials can be verbal or nonverbal. They are the materials that provide proof and explanation of what you say.

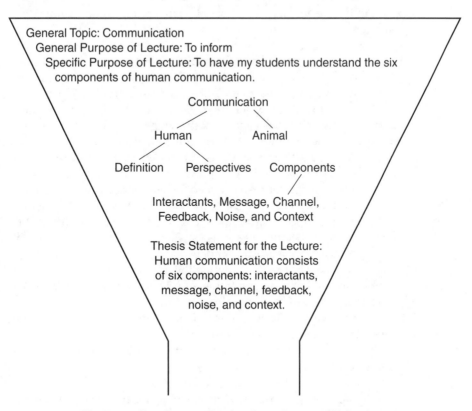

FIGURE 5.2   The Funneling Process: Narrowing a Lecture Topic.

As in every step of lecture preparation, you must consider yourself, your students, and the classroom environment when choosing supporting materials. (Remember the systems perspective.) What supporting materials do you have available already? For example, what personal experiences do you have that you can use as supporting materials? Based on your experiences with your students, what kinds of supporting material do they find particularly enjoyable and helpful? Finally, what constraints does the classroom environment place on you? Perhaps a limited budget prohibits the use of film, for example.

In addition to these considerations, you need to keep the basic purpose of the lecture—to create clear understanding—in the forefront. When choosing supporting materials, consider whether they help clarify your ideas and enhance student attention. Clarification devices are numerous. Table 5.2 presents a brief explanation of the most common types of verbal supporting materials used for clarification.

A nonverbal form of supporting material is the visual aid. Visual aids can make your ideas more concrete by presenting a pictorial or graphic representation of the idea being explained. Visual aids can also help maintain your students' attention. However, these two purposes—clarification and maintaining attention—will be accomplished only if the visual aids you use are appropriate to the subject matter and the students. In addition, all visual aids should conform to the following standards.

1. They should be large enough for all students—even those in the back of the lecture hall—to see. If you feel a need to ask your students, "Can you see this?" you know you've violated the first principle of the effective use of a visual aid!
2. In addition to being large enough, visual aids should be simple rather than detailed and should use heavy, dark drawings or printing that can be seen easily.
3. Speak to your students, not to your visual aid. A mistake teachers often make, particularly when they use a blackboard, is to talk to the blackboard as they write or draw on it. This makes it difficult for students to hear you. In addition, you cannot read the feedback students send when your back is to them or when you are focusing on your aid rather than on them.
4. Make sure you know why you are using the visual aid. It should be an integral part of the lecture. Don't use a visual aid unless there is a purpose for it.
5. Do not pass the visual aid among your students. This is distracting. When students take time out to examine the aid, they break contact with what you are saying at that moment. If they don't take time to look at the aid, choosing to listen to you instead, the aid is useless.
6. Practice with the aid. Anything that can go wrong will go wrong! Be prepared for any eventuality. Most teachers have had the harrowing experience of planning a film that takes 45 minutes, only to arrive in class to find the projector doesn't work.

Many things can be used as a visual aid including posters, overhead transparencies, people, models, charts, videos, and computer generated programs. Each of

TABLE 5.2   **Verbal Supporting Materials: Clarification Devices**

Clarification Device	Function/Example
Example	Expository or descriptive passage used to make ideas, process, and so forth, clear.
1. Illustration	Detailed narrative example.
A. Hypothetical	Tells what *could* have happened.
	An important concept in communication is self-fulfilling prophecies. If we define a situation as real, it becomes real in its consequences. Suppose you are a student in a mathematics class. You have taken other mathematics courses and have not done well. You define yourself as a poor student in this particular class. As a result of that definition, you rarely participate in class, you appear nervous, you cut class several times during the semester and therefore miss content. As a result, you flunk the exam. The instructor calls you into her office and explains that you will have to do better if you want to pass the mathematics course. Your prophecy—that you're a poor student in math—has been fulfilled.
B. Factual	Tells what *did* happen.
	Rosenthal and Jacobson's work has shown that an expectation a teacher has for a child can lead to a self-fulfilling prophecy in that child. Children were randomly labeled as "bloomers." Teachers were told which students were "bloomers" and which students were not. Eight months later, children who had been labeled "bloomers" did indeed bloom. They received higher test scores than students who were not designated as "bloomers." Teachers' expectations that students would do well led to self-fulfilling prophecies in the "bloomers."
2. Instance	An undetailed example—presents numerous examples of the same phenomenon. An important axiom of communication is that meanings are in people, not in words. How cold is cold? To some people, cold is 20° above zero; to others it is 20° below zero. How tall is tall? When you think of a large university, how many students do you envision? One writer tells us that the simple words, "I love you," can mean anything from, "I desire you sexually" to "I hate you." Think of such words as *democracy, cheap, dog,* and *happy.* Write down a brief definition of each. Now compare your meaning with the one of the person sitting next to you. How similar are they?
Statistics	Uses quantification in order to make a complex situation clear, to substantiate a claim, or make an abstract idea concrete.
	Communication apprehension is a common problem. Research indicates that one out of every five students is highly apprehensive about communication, and another 20 percent are moderately apprehensive about communicating.
Testimony	Uses the opinions or conclusions of others—can act as proof or add impressiveness to an idea.
	Because meanings are in people, not in words, we should strive to make our words as explicit as possible. As Mark Twain so aptly indicated, "The difference between the right word and the almost right word is the difference between lightning and the lightning bug."
Definition	Presents a meaning for a word—particularly important when the word is abstract or technical in nature.
	Interpersonal communication is the process of establishing, maintaining, and terminating relationships.

(continued)

TABLE 5.2   Continued

Clarification Device	Function/Example
Contrast	Points out the differences between two phenomenon, one of which is familiar to the students.
	In contrast to the public speaking situation in which communication is very structured, interpersonal communication is a relatively unstructured communication context. In the public context, communication roles are very formalized. This is not true in the interpersonal realm. No one is designated as "speaker" and "receiver." Rather, both people are expected to assume those roles.
Comparison	Points out the similarities between something that is familiar to students and something that is not.
	Communication, like life, is a process. It is ever-changing. Just as we cannot repeat part of our lives, neither can we repeat a communication event. Time has passed and so, even if we say the same words, they are not really the same. Likewise, communication, like life, is irreversible.
Restatement/Repetition	Restatement is the reiteration of an idea in different words—repetition, in the same words. Both restatement and repetition are used to drive home an idea.
	Let me remind you. We communicate—not by what we are, but by what listeners understand. We communicate—not by what we intend to say, but by what listeners see, hear, and are willing to accept. We communicate—not by what we say, but by what listeners hear.

Adapted from Waldo W. Braden, "Beyond the Campus Gate," in *Principles of Speech Communication,* 7th ed., p. 121, by A. Monroe and D. Ehninger (Eds.), (Glenview, IL: Scott, Foresman, 1975). Copyright © 1975 by Addison Wesley. Adapted by permission of Addison Wesley Educational Publishers, Inc.

these aids has guidelines to consider for effective use in the classroom. Design and display rules should be considered. In this next section we discuss the unique considerations for using technology such as video and computer generated programs in the classroom. For video to be effective, certain guidelines must be considered.

1. To obtain the best results from the video, carefully plan how you will use it in your classroom.
2. Consider how you will introduce the video. You might start with a warm-up activity to prepare students for the content of the video.
3. You may want to provide an outline of the video's contents for students to follow along or provide one after the video presentation for students to use as a study guide for evaluation purposes. This allows the students to watch the video more closely rather than feeling compelled to take notes.
4. Decide how you will follow up on the material provided in the video. You might prepare discussion questions according to the guidelines in Chapter 6 to stimulate talk about the video. You may also want to select and prepare additional activities that help to reinforce the material in the video.

5. Videos are not intended to be a sole source on any subject. They should be used in conjunction with other instructional strategies such as lecture, group discussion, activities, and so on.

Many modern classrooms are now equipped with the facilities to use computer generated software programs (PowerPoint, Persuasion, or Astound) as a way of organizing and presenting a lecture. In addition, classrooms now have Internet connections to access the World Wide Web. However, there are a few pedagogical and presentational issues to consider when using such technology. First, technological advances "are resulting in pressure being placed on instructors to become technologically literate" (Hunt & Lippert, 1999, p. 65). To support faculty in their use of technology in the classroom, many educational institutions have computer labs with staff ready to assist in this area. Second, technology should be used as an aid to instruction, not as the instruction itself. In other words, teachers should not make a decision to lecture merely because they have the technology to do so. Rather, the technology should be used to supplement other forms of instruction, including the lecture. Researchers have found that students, especially students whose native language is not English, tend to react favorably to instructors' use of technology in the classroom (Atkins-Sayre, Hopkins, Mohundro, & Sayre, 1998; Downing & Garmon, 2001; Sammons, 1995) when it is used appropriately.

Instructors who have access to technology should consider the same principles of design for using presentational software as they would for any other visual aid (review the suggestions provided earlier in this chapter). Other design principles unique to computer generated slides includes heavy contrast in color (light with dark background), large font sizes (at least 20 point), and limiting each slide to one idea or concept. Slides can also be used to organize the main points of a lecture, and when classroom computer access is limited, slides can be converted easily to overhead transparencies. For more information on using presentation media effectively, instructors can consult texts such as *Looking Good in Presentations* (Joss, 1999), which are written specifically for these purposes. Finally, research has shown that the effective use of technology in the classroom helps teachers teach and students learn (Balli & Diggs, 1996; Hunt & Lippert, 1999). What more reason do we need to become more technologically literate?

Organize the Lecture

Most teachers agree that an organized lecture is better than an unorganized lecture. In her review of research on direct instruction, Anderson (1989) reports that several studies indicate the importance of organization to an effective lesson. Brophy and Good (1986) summarize principles for lesson organization:

> Achievement is maximized when teachers not only actively present material, but structure it by beginning with overviews, advance organizers, or review of objectives; outlining the content and signaling transitions between lesson parts; calling attention to main ideas; summarizing subparts of the lesson as it proceeds; and

reviewing main ideas at the end. Organizing concepts and analogies helps learners link the new to the already familiar. Overviews and outlines help them to develop learning sets to use: rule-example-rule patterns and internal summaries tie specific information items to integrative concepts. Summary reviews integrate and reinforce the learning of major points. (p. 362)

A lecture has a general organization of introduction, body, and conclusion. The body can be organized according to several patterns. First let's examine purposes and types of introductions and conclusions.

The introduction of your lecture should accomplish the following three purposes.

1. *Establish student–teacher rapport.* One of the most important variables in the teaching–learning process is the relationship between the teacher and students. Students feel better about themselves and the learning situation when they feel their relationship with their instructor is a positive one. Students will be more willing to listen if you establish rapport in your introduction.
2. *Gain student attention.* If students are not attending to what's being said, they cannot learn it. Thus, the introduction must "grab" them and make them want to listen to the rest of the lecture.
3. *Set the scene.* The introduction should preview what you'll cover in your lecture. If you have three main points, enumerate each of those for students. Indicate to them what your objectives are—what they will be expected to know from having heard the lecture. In addition, students should know why what you have to say is important—why they need to know the content you'll cover.

Several different types of introductions can accomplish these three purposes. You might use a quotation, an anecdote, a series of rhetorical questions, examples, a startling statement of fact, or an opinion. Whichever method you choose, make sure it is relevant to your students and the lecture material.

The conclusion to the lecture should accomplish two purposes:

1. *Give an overview.* Too often we confuse coverage of content with learning. Student exposure to the subject and student learning of the subject are not synonymous. Students need to be reminded of what it was they were to learn from the lecture. This is easily done by summarizing your main points.
2. *Provide a sense of closure.* Avoid false endings. It is frustrating for students to believe that you're finished and then have you add "just one more point."

In addition to a summary, you might also want to conclude your lecture with a quotation, an example, or any of the methods of introduction discussed earlier. One good technique is to refer back to your introduction. This helps tie your lecture together, making it a complete package. Suppose you began a lecture on perception showing the transparency of the young–old woman (Figure 4.1, Chapter 4) and asking students, "How old is the woman shown here?" You then explain the process of perception, why we don't all perceive people and events identically, techniques to make us more accurate perceivers, and so forth. In the conclusion to the lecture you might show the transparency again as you summarize the major points: "We began this lecture with this picture. You now know the process you went through in perceiving the woman (enumerate them), why we didn't all agree on her age (enumerate those reasons), and what you can do to eliminate problems in perception (enumerate those)."

The main points of the body of your lecture can be arranged according to several patterns. The most often used organizational patterns are presented in Table 5.3. Examples of each are also provided. The important thing to remember about organizing the body of your lecture is that it should relate to the central idea of the lecture and the instructional objectives.

PRACTICE THE LECTURE

In your first few attempts at presenting new content, you will want to be sure that the information is addressed in such a way that your students will not only listen but also understand. This might require that you practice the presentation to ensure

TABLE 5.3   Organizational Patterns for the Body of the Lecture

Type	Definition	Example
Chronological	A time sequence	In preparing a lecture, five sequential steps must be followed: choose a topic, narrow the topic, gather supporting materials, organize the lecture, deliver the lecture.
Spatial	Space relationships—moving systematically from east to west, front to back, center to outside, and so forth	Proxemic behavior differs across cultures. A "comfortable" distance between people as they converse differs. We'll examine this phenomenon in the United States and Latin America. We'll then "fly across the ocean" and examine conversational distances of northern Europeans and southern Europeans. Finally, we'll examine the proxemic behaviors of Asians and Arabs.
Causal	Enumerating causes and moving to effects or enumerating effects and moving to causes	We all structure our own reality because we all perceive differently. Our perceptions differ because of differing environments, differing stimuli, differing sensory receptors, and differing internal states.
Problem–Solution	Describe the problem and present a solution	Researchers tell us that one of the major problems for people in the 1990s is developing and maintaining warm, personal relationships. The only way for us to solve this problem is to learn how to communicate effectively.
Topical	Topic provides its own organizational structure	Human communication consists of six components: interactants, message, channel, feedback, noise, and context.

that it is dynamic and meaningful. If you happen to have access to a trial audience that is similar in age to your students, you can ask them to give you feedback about your presentation. Did they understand the content, what questions would they ask, was it interesting, what other possible examples could be used that relate to this age group? Sometimes, a colleague who has taught the same age group would be willing to provide similar feedback. Having gone through a process such as this will give you the confidence you need to deliver content that is both interesting and appropriate to an intended audience.

DELIVER THE LECTURE

You're now ready to present your lecture. As we indicated earlier, a teacher's delivery can have a great impact on students' reactions to a lecture. If you are enthusiastic about your lecture material, that enthusiasm will come through in your delivery. An animated, enthusiastic delivery can greatly increase your students' desire to listen to you and, thus, enhance their learning.

Most classroom lectures are delivered extemporaneously, in other words, using brief notes so that you can maintain eye contact and a sense of connection with your students. This type of delivery is particularly effective for the lecture because it leaves you free to change your delivery in response to your students' reactions. You can rephrase and repeat ideas as necessary. In addition, your tone will be more conversational, because you must think about your ideas as you phrase them.

Effective delivery takes careful planning and practice. Following are some principles that should be useful to you.

1. *Think—really think—about what you're saying.* Speak ideas rather than simply reciting words.

2. *Communicate.* Think of your lecture as a dialogue, not a soliloquy. Talk with your students, not at them. This involves being direct and conversational and looking at your audience. Remember that it is not a group of empty chairs, but living students. Don't simply look at them—really see them and relate to them.

3. *Support and reinforce your ideas with your body, face, and voice.* Vocal aspects of which you should be aware are pitch, intensity, rate, and quality. Pitch is the highness or lowness of your voice. Studies indicate that a varied pitch is more effective for speaking than is a monotone. Your own experience no doubt supports this belief. A teacher who speaks in a monotone soon begins to make us weary. In addition, a monotone diminishes student comprehension and retention of what is said. To be an effective lecturer, then, you'll need to vary your pitch. Remember, however, that the variance in your pitch should be meaningful—should emphasize the thoughts you are communicating.

Vocal intensity refers to the loudness of your voice. A voice that is too loud or too soft is distracting. You should use loudness, just as you use pitch, to emphasize important thoughts. Remember too that a decrease in loudness can be just as effective for emphasis as can an increase in loudness. The important point here is that variety in intensity is important and you should strive for it.

Most beginning lecturers speak too fast. Their speech rate—the timing and pacing of their vocal delivery—is seldom varied. One way to vary the rate of your speech is through the use of the pause. Pauses "punctuate" a speaker's thoughts just as commas, periods, and semicolons punctuate written discourse.

Oral punctuation—the pause—helps students accurately interpret the messages you send. Pauses also allow students time to reflect on what they have heard and how the previous statements relate to one another. Finally, pauses provide emphasis that will aid in student retention as well as comprehension.

As a lecturer, don't be afraid to use the pause as a means of providing yourself time to gather your thoughts. If you need to reflect on where you are, do so. Remember that pauses seem much longer to you than they do to your students. Don't feel a need to fill your pauses with "uhs" or "ahs." Such vocalized pauses are very distracting.

Voice quality is the special sound of your voice. Obviously, a pleasant voice quality is more effective than a nasal, shrill, hoarse, or breathy quality. One way to make your voice quality pleasant is through sharp, precise articulation. A lecturer who mumbles or has a "mushy" quality is difficult to understand. Because your goal as a lecturer is to present information clearly, articulation problems such as those just mentioned must be avoided.

Slovenly pronunciation, like slovenly articulation, must also be avoided. If your pronunciation is not clear or correct, students may misunderstand you—again reducing their comprehension.

In addition to vocal factors in delivery, you should also be aware of the visual factors of effective delivery. Your interest in your topic can be communicated by your posture, gestures, and facial expressions. Stand erect, poised, and relaxed. You'll look better and feel better. It is also easier to move from that position in order to emphasize ideas or signal variations in thought.

Gestures should flow from your thoughts. Don't force them. Most of us use gestures naturally in our conversations. Patterned or mechanical gestures distract from, rather than complement what you're saying. The key here is to be natural.

Facial expressions also communicate much about your interest in the topic presented. A deadpan expression does not enhance your presentation. As we've suggested before, look at your audience. Eye contact and animated facial expressions are very important for generating interest and enthusiasm in your students. If you fail to look at your students, they, no doubt, will suspect you are unconcerned or ill at ease. If you don't have visual contact with your students, there is no way you can adjust to their feedback.

4. *Adapt to your students.* Watch for cues indicating that you need to change some aspect of your delivery—pace, volume, pitch, gestures, and so forth.

An interesting study examined the way in which students signal a lack of comprehension. In lecture classes students often ignored the problem of lack of comprehension. In fact, ignoring was found to be more prevalent in the lecture than in discussion or small group formats. Indicating confusion (with either a quizzical look or some short expression such as "Huh?") and asking for elaboration were used less in the lecture than in the other two formats (Kendrick & Darling, 1990).

5. Those of you who are beginning teachers should *practice your delivery.* Practice "on your feet" and aloud. If possible, you should practice in the room in which you'll actually present the lecture. You might want to practice before a mirror in order to get an idea of the visual image you present or you may want to get some friends to listen to you. The advantage to the latter is that they can comment on how they view you. You might videotape your lecture. Or, if videotaping is not possible, at least audiotape your lecture.

Maintaining Attention

Perhaps your most difficult task as a lecturer is to maintain the attention of your students. If students don't attend to what is being presented in the lecture, they cannot learn it. Several factors can help you hold the attention of your audience. We examine seven of the most common factors.

If you are to maintain attention, you must *make your lecture topic and supporting materials relevant.* When we outlined principles of information exchange, we mentioned the fact that you need to "create a need to know" in your students. One of the best ways to create a need to know is to make your information relevant. Two factors will aid you in making information relevant: proximity and reality. Elements that are close to students in time and space are more relevant than elements that are far removed from their experience. Whenever possible, make use of incidents that occur at your school or in your community. Use examples that are recent. Rather than talking in general abstract terms, refer to the immediate, the concrete, and the actual. For example, if you are lecturing on the strategies used by politicians in their campaigns, use examples from local campaigns or from well-known national figures rather than using hypothetical or historical examples.

It's long been known that active learning is more effective than passive learning. One means of involving students is to *insert questions into the lecture.* Berliner (1968) noted that questions can serve the following functions in a lecture:

1. *Emphasis.* You can call special attention to important points by asking a question.
2. *Practice.* A response to a question enables the student to practice her newly acquired knowledge. The old adage, practice makes perfect, seems to be borne out in educational research.
3. *Self-Awareness.* Students can be made aware that they do not understand the material. Often students are robotlike in a lecture—sitting quietly and taking notes. They often do not realize they don't comprehend the material until they study it later. Questions can stimulate their thinking while they're in the lecture, when it's still possible to get clarification from the instructor.
4. *Diversion.* Much like a coffee break at work, questions inserted into a lecture can represent a form of stimulus variation. As we discuss later, stimulus variation can be an aid to attention and, thus, to learning.

5. *Review.* Questions scattered throughout the lecture can require students to review previous material presented in the lecture in order to answer the questions. If questions are structured so that such a review is necessary, students are exposed to the lecture material more than once. This increased exposure should enhance learning.

In addition to inserting questions into the lecture, attention can be enhanced by *your enthusiasm and activity during the lecture.* If you are excited about lecturing, you can generate excitement in your students. Don't lecture because you have to say something; lecture because you have something to say! Enthusiasm of the instructor has been correlated with student achievement. Students learn more from lectures delivered dynamically and enthusiastically.

Variety in movement and gesturing by a lecturer is also correlated positively with student achievement. This may be so because activity generates enthusiasm. At any rate, if you're to be effective as a lecturer, research indicates you need to use a variety of vocal and facial expressions, gestures, and movement in your delivery.

A fifth major means of maintaining attention is a *combination of the familiar and the novel.* Familiarity, in the extreme, may breed contempt, but it is necessary to a certain degree. New material needs to be related to something familiar if learning is to occur. However, things that are new or unusual catch our eye. We're all interested in new experiences, new ideas, new products. The unusual is also attention getting. Someone once said, when a dog bites a man, that is not news, but when a man bites a dog, that is news!

Suspense and conflict can create interest and maintain attention. When the outcome of an event is uncertain, the uncertainty increases our attention. Soap operas always end each day with a conflict situation or a suspenseful event. However, we can get bored with soap operas when the conflict is never resolved or the suspense unending. Likewise, students will give up listening if you make the information too mysterious or if there seems little hope of resolving the conflict.

Fresh, sparkling, appropriate humor is excellent as an attention-maintaining device. Humor can help students enjoy their learning experience by providing a change of pace, relieving tensions, or promoting good student–teacher relationships. Remember that to be effective, humor must be brief, fresh, relevant, and in good taste.

The saying "variety is the spice of life" may be trite, but in the case of lecturing, it's true. A monotonous sentence structure, clichés, lack of movement, or the constant use of a single communication channel soon bores students. Whatever you as a lecturer can change fairly often without creating distractions from the subject matter will no doubt help students maintain their attention.

EVALUATING YOUR LECTURE SKILLS

In Appendix A, we discuss teacher evaluation in depth. However, suffice it to say here that evaluation of your lecture skills by you, colleagues, and students can increase your teaching expertise. A sample lecture evaluation form follows. After presenting a lecture, ask your students to complete the form. In addition, videotape one of your lectures. View the tape with a colleague. Using the evaluation form, discuss your lecture, and ways to improve it, with your colleague.

IN SUM

Lecturing has been described as "the process whereby the notes of the professor become the notes of the student without going through the minds of either" (Walker & McKeachie, 1967, pp. 13–14). If you consider the principles of information exchange, clarity, and intercultural concerns as you go through the steps of lecture preparation discussed in this chapter—choose a topic, narrow the topic, gather supporting materials, organize the lecture, and deliver the lecture—you should be able to make your lecture a communicative transaction with your students. Not only will your notes go through your mind but your students' minds as well!

ACTIVITIES

5.1   Getting to know your students is important; it's impossible for you to effectively teach students you don't know. The following examples suggest the types of questions you might ask your students on a questionnaire. These questions are only suggestions. It's likely you'll want to add others depending on the age level of your students. Indicate to your students that all information is confidential and they may choose to skip any questions they would rather not answer.

1. How old are you?
2. What are your parent's/guardian's occupations?
3. How many children are in your family?
4. Name a hobby or activity you enjoy.
5. What are your favorite academic subjects? Your least favorite?
6. Who are your best friends?
7. List three adjectives that describe you.
8. If you had one wish, what would it be?
9. What books, magazines, and newspapers do you read?
10. Do you have a job? If so, how many hours a week do you work? Describe your job.
11. In what extracurricular activities are you involved?
12. What is your major goal for this year?

5.2   Analyze a lecture you recently presented or attended. Was the lecture method appropriate? Why or why not?

5.3   This activity is the first in a series. The remainder of the activities will prepare you for the culminating activity—microteaching (teaching a short lesson to a

Lecture Evaluation Form

Lecturer's Name _____

Topic _____

Please mark an "x" in the space that best represents your evaluation of the lecture.

	Poor	Adequate	Good	Excellent
Enthusiasm				
Speaks expressively or emphatically	___	___	___	___
Moves about while lecturing	___	___	___	___
Gestures with hands and arms	___	___	___	___
Shows facial expressions	___	___	___	___
Uses humor	___	___	___	___
Clarity				
Uses concrete examples of concepts	___	___	___	___
Gives multiple examples	___	___	___	___
Points out practical applications	___	___	___	___
Stresses important points	___	___	___	___
Repeats difficult ideas	___	___	___	___
Interaction				
Addresses students by name	___	___	___	___
Encourages questions and comments	___	___	___	___
Talks with students after class	___	___	___	___
Praises students for good ideas	___	___	___	___
Asks questions of class	___	___	___	___
Task Orientation				
Advises students regarding exams	___	___	___	___
Provides sample exam questions	___	___	___	___
States course objectives	___	___	___	___
Rapport				
Is friendly, easy to talk to	___	___	___	___
Shows concern for student progress	___	___	___	___
Offers to help students with problems	___	___	___	___
Tolerates other viewpoints	___	___	___	___
Organization				
Puts outline of lecture on board	___	___	___	___
Uses headings and subheadings	___	___	___	___
Gives preliminary overview of lecture	___	___	___	___
Signals transition to new topic	___	___	___	___
Explains how each topic fits in	___	___	___	___
Suggestions for improving the lecture				

Adapted from H. Murray, "Classroom Teaching Behaviors Related to College Teaching Effectiveness" in *Using Research to Improve Teaching*, ed. J. Donald and A. Sullivan (San Francisco: Jossey-Bass, 1985) 25. Copyright © 1985 by Jossey-Bass. Adapted by permission.

small group of students). Choose a topic for a lecture. Analyze yourself, the student group to whom you will present the lecture, and the classroom environment in which the lecture will be given.

5.4   Using the topic you chose, narrow the topic to a thesis statement. You should plan for a fifteen-minute microteaching session. Thus, your thesis statement must be narrow enough so that you can adequately cover it in fifteen minutes.

5.5   Examine your thesis statement. What supporting materials will you use to develop this thesis statement? Describe them.

5.6   Organize your lecture using any of the organizational patterns discussed, then outline your lecture. Your outline should follow this form.

Thesis statement:

Organizational pattern chosen for the body of the lecture:

Reason you choose this pattern:

Outline your lecture in correct outline form.

5.7   Present your lecture. Using the evaluation form in this chapter, evaluate your lecture.

FURTHER READING

Bonwell, C. (1992, February). "Suggestions for improving lectures." *The Teaching Professor, 6,* 3.

Suggestions for helping teachers create interesting lectures are presented in this article.

Civikly, J. (1992). "Clarity: Teachers and students making sense of instruction." *Communication Education, 41,* 138–152.

This article provides an excellent review of the literature addressing the issue of clarity in classroom communication.

King, A. (1992). "Comparison of self-questioning, summarizing, and notetaking–review as strategies for learning from lectures," *American Educational Research Journal, 29,* 303–323.

This article is well worth reading. It contains a good review of the literature as well as an extremely interesting study.

Magnan, R. (1990). *147 practical tips for teaching professors.* Madison, WI: Magna.

This book contains tips for beginning a class, lecturing, discussion, group projects, motivation, and evaluation.

Murray, J., & Murray, J. (1992). "How do I lecture thee?" *College Teaching, 40,* 109–113.

A well-written article describing a systematic approach to lecture preparation.

Weiner, M., & Neff, R. A. (Eds.). (1990). *Teaching college: Readings for the new instructor.* Madison, WI: Magna.

This text contains several good readings dealing with improving lectures.

CHAPTER SIX

LEADING CLASSROOM DISCUSSIONS

Objectives

After reading this chapter, you should be able to:

- List the types of discussions.
- Explain the experiential learning process.
- List the characteristics of the discussion method.
- Write a sequence of questions using Bloom's *Taxonomy*.
- Use question strategies that promote student involvement.
- Use response strategies that promote student involvement.
- Explain how student communication apprehension might affect willingness to engage in discussion.
- Evaluate your discussion skills.

Dr. Cooper shares the following about leading classroom discussions:

> I have a love–hate relationship with the discussion method of teaching. It's noisy, messy, and sometimes unnerving. It's always hard work, but exciting. I can't always predict exactly where the discussion will lead, nor am I always sure how to keep the discussion on track. Yet I want my students to participate actively in the teaching–learning process—ask more questions of me, themselves, and one another—and think critically and creatively. I am left with my frustrations about the method and my love of its outcomes. Most teachers I talk with share my feelings. Like me, many of them also love the challenge and the excitement of the discussion method.

In this chapter we suggest ways to plan the discussion and examine characteristics of the discussion method placing special emphasis on question asking skills and response styles. Ways to evaluate your discussion skills are presented. Before reading this chapter on leading classroom discussions, please refer to the suggestions for choosing this strategy as well as the advantages and disadvantages provided in the unit overview.

PLANNING THE DISCUSSION

Even though it is possible to identify a general structure for all discussions, there are different types of discussions. Hyman (1987) discusses five types:

1. *Explaining*—analyzes the causes, reasons, procedures, or methods for what has occurred. For example, (1) "Why have terrorist activities increased in the past twenty years?" and (2) "How did Japan become an electronics giant since 1945?"
2. *Problem solving*—seeks to answer a conflict or problem facing the group or the larger community outside the classroom. For example, (1) "How can we decrease sexism—male and female—in our school?" and (2) "How can the federal government win its battle against illegal drugs?"
3. *Debriefing*—reflects on the facts, meanings, and implications of a shared activity such as a trip to the Statue of Liberty, a view of the play or film *Death of a Salesman*, participation in a mock 4-H convention, or hearing a guest speaker from NASA on "Space Travel in the Next Century." For example, "Let's now discuss our trip to the Statue of Liberty. What did we see and what does it all mean?"
4. *Predicting*—predicts the probable consequences of a given situation, condition, or policy. For example, (1) "If the greenhouse effect on our planet continues, what will happen to plant and animal life as we know it today?" and (2) "What are the implications for humankind now that medicine has increased the average length of life to about sixty-five years?"
5. *Policy deciding*—sets policy on how the group should act or recommends policy for the larger community outside the classroom. For example, (1) "Should we *as a class* participate in our town's protest parade next Tuesday against the state government building a dam here on Silver Creek?" and (2) "Should the U.S. government ban cigarette smoking in the entire country?"

A discussion, like a lecture, should have an introduction, a body, and a conclusion.

The Introduction

The introduction of the discussion should create attention in the students. It should motivate them to want to discuss the topic or idea. In addition, it should clarify the purpose of the discussion. In other words, it should preview the main points to be covered. Also, it should create a need to know in students by explaining the importance and relevance of the topic to them.

The Body

Planning the body of the discussion is somewhat different from planning the body of a lecture. The emphasis for the teacher should not be "What am I going to say?" but rather "What questions can I ask that will enable my students to meet the objectives?" Thus, although the body of the discussion may follow one of the general organizational patterns in Chapter 5, the pattern will be developed by your (and your students') use of questions and responses rather than by your explanations, examples, and so forth. In other words, you and your students share in the development of the body of the discussion.

The Conclusion

The main purpose of the conclusion is to tie the entire discussion together. Often students leave a discussion session saying things such as, "That was interesting, but I'm not exactly sure what I was supposed to get out of it." As a teacher, you need to summarize the major ideas developed in the discussion. You might also preview how the knowledge learned will relate to topics to be discussed in upcoming lessons.

CHARACTERISTICS OF THE DISCUSSION METHOD

The discussion method is characterized by (1) experiential learning, (2) an emphasis on students, (3) a focus on critical thinking, (4) the use of questions, and (5) responses to questions. Let's examine each of these.

Experiential Learning

One of the major characteristics of the discussion method of teaching is that it is based on experiential learning. The underlying assumption of experiential learning is that we learn best when we are actively involved in the learning process—when we "discover" knowledge through active participation. Johnson and Johnson (1991, p. 41) diagram the experiential learning process as shown in Figure 6.1.

Using the discussion method, a student's concrete, personal experiences are followed by observation, reflection, and analysis of these experiences. This process leads to formulation of abstract concepts and generalizations, which, in turn, leads to hypotheses to be discussed and tested in future experiences. This process occurs in the discussion as a whole, as well as in each individual student's mind.

Emphasis on Students

The second characteristic of the discussion method, and one that flows directly from the experiential learning characteristic, is the emphasis on students. Students are the focus of this method. It is their experiences that serve as the basis for the discussion. Although you—the teacher—must have a specific goal in mind and a general framework for reaching the goal, student input determines the specific direction the discussion takes.

Focus on Critical Thinking

Much has been written recently about the importance of teaching critical thinking skills. One can hardly pick up an education-related journal or magazine without coming across an article on the topic. A growing consensus reflected in these

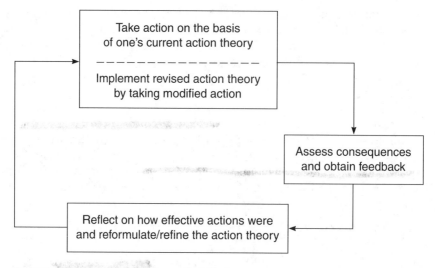

FIGURE 6.1   Experiential Learning Cycle.

From D. Johnson and E. Johnson, *Joining Together: Group Theory and Group Skills,* 4th ed. Copyright © 1991 by Allyn and Bacon. Reprinted by permission.

writings is that, although "the basics" are extremely necessary, students must also be competent thinkers (see, for example, Marzanno, Brant, Hughes, Jones, Presseisen, Rankin, & Shuor, 1988). Too often, testing and accountability drive the educational system so that the main message communicated to students is that they should provide "the right answer." Paul (1986) contends that the right answer should not be the end product of education, but rather that an inquiring mind should show the following:

> A passionate drive for clarity, accuracy, and fair-mindedness, a fervor for getting to the bottom of things, to the deepest root issues, for listening sympathetically to opposite points of view, a compelling drive to seek out evidence, an intense aversion to contradiction, sloppy thinking, inconsistent application of standards, a devotion to truth as against self-interest—these are essential components of the rational person. (p. 1)

Use of Questions

The discussion method involves a questioning strategy. In advance of the discussion, you must prepare carefully sequenced questions in order to organize the discussion. In addition, you must be flexible and adapt your questioning strategy to the needs of the students as the discussion evolves. Student responses must be integrated into the discussion and student questions should be elicited.

You may be asking yourself, "What's so important about questions?" Questioning is, perhaps, the single most influential teaching practice because teacher questions promote student involvement and are central to the analysis and synthesis of ideas (Dillon, 1988a, 1988b, 1990).

Research indicates that between 66 and 80 percent of the average school day is taken up with questioning—primarily teacher questions—and that this has held true since 1912 (West & Pearson, 1994). In fact, Pearson and West (1991) found an average of three student questions in each hour of instruction and these were often questions of clarity and procedure. In 1994, these researchers indicated that only 108 students' questions were asked in thirty hours of classroom time. Karabenic and Sharma (1994) report that few student questions are asked in a fifty- to seventy-five-minute period—an average of six. We not only know that a lot of questions are asked during the school day but we also know the pattern of interaction these questions elicit. The basic interaction pattern is

Solicitation (SOL) by the teacher
Response (RES) by the student
Reaction (REA) by the teacher

In other words, the teacher asks a question, the student answers the question, and the teacher reacts to the student's answer (Cazden, 1988; Mehan, 1979).

Because meaning is derived from social interaction, it seems reasonable that students need to be active in the interaction process. The more active students are in the process, through questioning and discussion, the clearer the meanings they derive (Garside, 1996).

When we vary question levels, probe, rephrase, prompt, wait for student responses, ask process questions ("How did you get that answer?"), and stress student's understanding of meaning, we promote critical thinking. We challenge students to think, not simply to parrot back to us what we've taught or what they've read in the textbook.

Most educators agree that questioning skills are very important, but teachers in training receive little instruction in either the theory or the art of questioning (Collins, 1993). So, where do we begin? The best place is to return to Bloom's *Taxonomy.* Your questions, depending on how they are phrased, can require different levels of thinking. Table 6.1 indicates the levels and examples and typical question terms for each level.

I started the discussion with the question, "What do teachers want from children in school?" After some initial hesitation, the group responded that teachers want children to learn, to do well, to get good grades, and to go on to college. The children were repeating all the cliché answers that they had heard from their parents and their teachers for so long. As I stated my questions more clearly, however, asking what the teachers want from children every day, they said that the teachers want answers. In response to, "Answers to what?" the children said answers, both oral and written, to all kinds of questions that teachers pose. Because I was pursuing a particular course, I asked the children to discuss the kinds of answers teachers wanted. Did the teachers want any particular kind of answer? After a few hesitations and a few false starts, one of the children answered, "Yes, what the

TABLE 6.1 Levels of Cognitive Skills You Can Require of Your Students with Your In-Discussion Questions (Based on Bloom's *Cognitive Domain of the Taxonomy of Educational Objectives***)**

Level	Key Words	Typical Question Terms
A. Knowledge: Questions that require simple recall of previously learned material Example: What are the components of Berlo's communication model?	Remember	1. Name 2. List, tell 3. Define 4. Who? When? What? 5. Yes or no questions: "Was…?" "Is…?" 6. How many? How much? 7. Describe, label, match, select
B. Comprehension: Questions that require students to restate or reorganize material in a literal manner to show that they understand the essential meaning Example: Explain Berlo's model in your own words.	Understand	1. Give an example 2. What is the speaker's most important idea? 3. What will the consequences probably be? 4. What caused this? 5. Compare (What things are the same?) 6. Contrast (What things are different?) 7. Paraphrase, rephrase, translate, summarize, defend
C. Application: Questions that require students to use previously learned material to solve problems in new situations Example: A Democrat and a Republican are discussing foreign policy. Where in Berlo's model of communication would you predict their communication will break down?	Solve the problem	1. Solve 2. Apply the principle (concept) to… 3. Compute, prepare, produce, relate, modify, classify
D. Analysis: Questions that require students to break an idea into its component parts for logical analysis Example: Here are four models of the communication process. How are the components of these models similar? How do they differ?	Logical order	1. What reasons does the author give for his conclusions? 2. What does the author seem to believe? 3. What words indicate bias or emotion? 4. Does the evidence given support the conclusion? 5. Break down, differentiate, distinguish

TABLE 6.1   Continued

Level	Key Words	Typical Question Terms
E. **Synthesis:** Questions that require students to combine their ideas into a statement, plan, product, and so forth, that is new for them Example: Diagram your own model of communication.	Create	1. Develop a model 2. Combine those parts 3. Write a speech 4. Create, combine, design, diagram, document, propose, write
F. **Evaluation:** Questions that require students to judge something based on some criteria Example: Which of the three models presented in class do you think depicts the communication process most accurately?	Judge	1. Evaluate that idea in terms of… 2. For what reasons do you favor…? 3. Appraise, criticize, justify, assess

teacher wants is right answers." When I followed with, "Do you mean that the questions asked are questions that can be answered by a right answer?" there was general agreement that they were. I then asked them, "Can teachers ask questions that do not have right and wrong answers but that still can have important answers?" This question threw the students completely off balance and they were unable to recover for the rest of the discussion. Despite much talk, no satisfactory response emerged. Because I was in a teaching situation and because we were in school, the students' orientation was almost totally to right and wrong answers. One boy, however, said, "Do you mean questions we give our opinions on?" When I asked him to continue, he said, "Well, do teachers ever ask questions that call for the opinions of the students in the class?" He thought for a while, and the others thought for a while, and they decided that what they thought—their opinions, their ideas, their judgments, and their observations—was rarely asked for in class. (Glasser, 1969, p. 51)

As indicated in the preceding quotation, research findings consistently show that most teacher questions occur on the knowledge (recall) level. Gall (1970) found that 60 percent of questions asked by teachers were recall level, 20 percent were procedural, and only 20 percent required students to think at higher levels of Bloom's *Taxonomy*. In a later study, Gall (1984) found that 80 percent of the questions asked in classrooms required students to do something other than think. If one of our goals as teachers is to help students develop their cognitive abilities, we need to ask them questions that require higher-level cognitive processes than mere recall. In addition,

not mere recall

higher-order questions require more student talk to answer, so student participation increases. This is the first step in changing the typical SOL-RES-REA cycle of classroom communication. Finally, we need to ask higher-order questions because such questions appear to have a positive effect on achievement. Deethardt (1974) and Redfield and Rousseau (1981) cite research indicating that a teacher's asking of higher-order questions has been linked to greater student achievement.

When you are structuring your classroom questions, remember that there's nothing inherently wrong with the lower-level questions of Bloom's *Taxonomy*. We need them to help guide students' thinking patterns and to help eliminate understanding problems. Notice the questioning sequence in the following example and the role of lower-level questions in creating the sequence (Duke, 1971, p. 470).

Knowledge: When was *Lyrical Ballads* published?

Comprehension: Compare a poem by Wordsworth with one by Coleridge. What differences to you find? What similarities?

Application: Does this particular poem show the characteristics of poetry as indicated by Wordsworth and Coleridge in the "Preface" to *Lyrical Ballads*? If so, how? If not, what are the differences?

Analysis: What would some journalists and writers of the nineteenth century attack in *Lyrical Ballads*?

Synthesis: From studying Wordsworth's poetry, what conclusions can you make about his beliefs?

Evaluation: Do you feel that the concepts of romanticism as expressed by Wordsworth and Coleridge are still affecting our modern literature? Explain.

Although the *Taxonomy* is helpful in determining the level of cognitive process you are requiring of your students, it is not without limitations. Several important types of questions are omitted. For example, the *Taxonomy* does not include questions that cue students on an initially weak response, in other words, the probing question. Questions such as "Why?" "Could you elaborate?" "Can you think of any other examples?" and "Doesn't that contradict what you said previously?" are all examples of probing questions.

Probing questions are important. A positive relationship exists between the frequency of teacher probing questions and the amount of student oral participation. In addition, a positive relationship exists between a teacher's probing and pupil achievement. Finally, probing questions are important in fostering critical thinking (Kurfill, 1988).

Also missing from the *Taxonomy* are questions that stimulate a discussion atmosphere. For example, a question such as "Johnny, do you agree with _____?" encourages students to question one another—an idea we'll return to later in this chapter.

In Box 6.1, Davis (1993) suggests teachers develop an inventory of questions in order to balance the kinds of questions asked. As you begin to develop questions for your own classroom discussions, you may want to refer to this inventory as a model.

weak? . are probing Questions

Improving Classroom Questions

Let It Live

Never kill a question;
it is a fragile thing.
A good question deserves to live.
One doesn't so much answer it as converse with it,
or, better yet, one lives with it.
Great questions are the permanent
and blessed guests of the mind.
But the greatest questions of all
are those which build bridges to the heart,
addressing the whole person

No answer should be designed to kill the question.
When one is too dogmatic, or too sure,

BOX 6.1
INVENTORY OF QUESTIONS

- *Exploratory questions* probe facts and basic knowledge: "What research evidence supports the theory of a cancer-prone personality?"
- *Challenge questions* examine assumptions, conclusions, and interpretations: "How else might we account for the findings of this experiment?"
- *Relational questions* ask for comparisons of themes, ideas, or issues: "What premises of *Plessy v. Ferguson* did the Supreme Court throw out in deciding *Brown v. Board of Education*?"
- *Diagnostic questions* probe motives or causes: "Why did Jo assume a new identity?"
- *Action questions* call for a conclusion or action: "In response to a sit-in at California Hall, what should the chancellor do?"
- *Cause-and-effect questions* ask for causal relationships between ideas, actions, or events: "If the government stopped farm subsidies for wheat, what would happen to the price of bread?"
- *Extension questions* expand the discussion: "How does this comment relate to what we have previously said?"
- *Hypothetical questions* pose a change in the facts or issues, "Suppose Gregg had been rich instead of poor; would the outcome have been the same?"
- *Priority questions* seek to identify the most important issue: "From all that we have talked about, what is the most important cause of the decline of American competitiveness?"
- *Summary questions* elicit syntheses: "What themes or lessons have emerged from today's class?"

From Davis (1993, pp. 83–84).

one shows disrespect for truth
and the question which points toward it.
Beyond my answer there is always more,
more light waiting to break in,
and waves of inexhaustible meaning
ready to break against wisdom's widening shore.
Wherever there is a question, let it live! (Frost, 1974, p. 31)

Your success in the discussion method of teaching will depend greatly on your ability to let questions "live." Listed in Box 6.2 are several guidelines to help you develop and improve your questioning skills. These guidelines will be extremely useful to you throughout your teaching career. You will want to reflect on them each time you decide to use the discussion method. As seasoned instructors, your authors still reflect on these guidelines to help keep students at the center of instructional discussions. *Need to reference the material 1st*

Response Styles. Much research suggests that how we respond to students will stifle or enhance the discussion process. For example, students who perceived the greatest amount of support for their discussion efforts were more motivated and active in the learning process (Karabenick & Sharma, 1994; see also, Aitken & Neer, 1993; Andersen & Nussbaum, 1990; Austin & MacRone, 1994; Nadler & Nadler, 1990). Listed in Box 6.3 are several pragmatic suggestions to help you respond appropriately to your students and thus encourage their participation. As with all the boxes provided in this text, you will want to visit these suggestions early and often throughout your teaching career.

In general, start discussions with a structure move. That is, set the knowledge base for the question. What do students need to know in order to answer the question? This is where you reference the material of the lesson so that students can elaborate with their own ideas and experiences. Next, solicit a student response by asking the question. Remembering Bloom's *Taxonomy*, ask questions that require higher levels of thinking. Limit knowledge level questions so that students do not feel that they are being quizzed. Try to ask questions that don't necessarily have a correct or incorrect answer. Rather, ask questions that require students to provide opinions, experiences, and so forth. *Wait.* Once a student has responded, *react* positively to the student's response. The nature of this reaction will determine the future success or failure of the discussion. One of the authors, Dr. Simonds, shares this story:

> I remember a professor who asked us to read an article and come to class prepared to talk about it. He asked a question and a student answered. The professor responded, "No, you're wrong." The discussion halted and the professor continued to lecture about why the student was wrong. We never had another discussion in that class.

Once you've reacted positively to a student's response, allow other students to either react to the student's response or to provide a response of their own. This process should continue until you believe that all students have had an opportu-

■ ■ ■ ■ ■
BOX 6.2
GUIDELINES FOR QUESTIONS *— Useful to mark ? Live*

- *Have a commitment to questions.* Developing questioning skills is difficult. In order to really master the art, you have to be willing to give the time and effort required.
- *Write out a sequence of "major" questions.* Begin with knowledge level questions and progress to evaluation level questions. This practice will help you keep the class progressing systematically toward the objective.
- *Have a clear purpose.* Why are you asking the question? What's the response you want? Pupils demonstrate increased achievement when clear-cut goals are communicated.
- *Phrase questions clearly.* Because questions define the kind of answer possible and affect several characteristics of the answer given, it behooves the teacher to phrase questions clearly. If students are unfamiliar with the words in the question, they cannot answer it even if they know the information being requested. In addition, teachers should ask only one question at a time. When teachers ask several questions in succession without waiting for a student response, student learning is negatively affected. (Gall & Rhody, 1987)
- *Know your subject matter.* When you do, you can direct your energies to observing and directing students' mental processes rather than having to focus on your notes. Davidson and Ambrose (1995) term this "peripheral vision." Peripheral vision is the ability to keep track of a discussion in terms of a whole variety of process issues, such as when to provide more direct guidance, when to offer encouragement, and when to reinforce with words and actions. Closely related to peripheral vision is a sense of timing—knowing when to ask a question, when to offer a summary, or when to bridge from something said earlier, as well as when to keep silent.
- *Keep all students on-task.* Because only one student answers a question at a given moment, there is the chance that other students may get off-task. Off-task behavior is associated with decreased learning (Berliner & Fisher, 1985). One option that is useful in keeping students on-task is the *overhead technique:* ask a question, pause, recognize, or call on a student. Some researchers suggest that this technique increases the chances that all students will be considering the answer, because no one knows who will be asked to respond.
- *Don't answer your own questions.* When students learn you'll answer your own questions if they simply wait long enough, they'll wait you out. Wait for students to answer. Silence seems very frustrating to teachers, yet it is not only desirable but also necessary:

> There will be some silence in any class,
> Sometimes it may be just dead silence
> with nothing happening.
> This is a terrifying thing;
> one can only ask the spirit to brood over it,
> creating again,
> repeating the first miracle,
> turning nothing into something.

(continued)

BOX 6.2   CONTINUED

> But there are other silences,
> the silence of reflection,
> of confession, or reaffirmation,
> or, the silence of recognition,
> affection, opposition,
> or even the silence of struggle
> and decision.... (Frost 1974, p. 72)

- *Seat students in a semicircle.* Remember our discussion of seating arrangements in Chapter 4. The semicircle or horseshoe (U-shaped) arrangement encourages participation.

- *Ask probing questions* in order to

  - *initiate a discussion, change the subject, or modify the direction:*

    What reaction are you having to this information?
    What are you feeling at this moment?
    How would you try to prevent a situation like this?
    How does this approach apply in other situations?
    Have we considered this idea: _____?

  - *lead a member toward a particular statement or generate a logical sequence of steps toward a conclusion:*

    Are there factors that lead to one explanation rather than another?
    Given what you just said, what do you think the next step might be?
    What do you think are the implications of that statement?
    How can you relate this to what Debbie said?

  - *clarify a statement, help a member make a succinct statement, establish whether listening was accurate, or permit a member to amplify statements:*

    Let me be sure I understand what you said; could you repeat it?
    You seem to be saying _____. Right?
    By that do you mean _____?
    Can you say a little more about that?

  - *probe for more information, generate a more extensive response, or turn the discussion back to a member or the group:*

    How do you feel when that happens to you?
    Can you give a specific example?
    I wonder why that happens....
    Can you extend your analysis just a bit?
    Why do you say that?
    Has this happened to you personally?
    Have others of you had similar experiences? (Fisch, 1992, p. 5)

- *Guide the flow of the discussion* by asking questions in order to

  - *suggest that the discussion might be wandering:*

    What specific issues are we considering now?

  - *encourage consideration of the personal significance of a discussion and to relate it to members' individual frames of reference:*

    How does this relate to you personally?
    Have you ever been in this kind of situation yourself?

- *avoid working over the same issues without fruitful results and to assess the group's position, if any:*
  On what issues do you think we are in substantial agreement?
- *elicit a response when a conclusion or consensus is near, but no one is willing to state it, or to suggest that it's time to move on:*
  Can we add anything new that bears on this matter?
- *suggest that a group is not ready to act:*
  How do you feel about thinking this over and reconsidering it the next time we get together?
- *get a student to take the initiative if the group is experiencing a momentary lull:*
  Are there other aspects that you wish to discuss?
  Do you wish to explore the idea of _____? (Fisch, 1992, p. 6)
- *Finally, respond in a way that fosters the discussion process.*

nity to share with regard to the original question, or until the discussion gets off track, whichever comes first. Once this process is complete for the first question, move on to the next line of questioning.

THE ROLE OF THE STUDENT

Thus far we've discussed the role of the teacher in classroom discussion. However, students need to understand their role in the discussion process.

Deemer (1986, p. 4) suggests teachers distribute a list of participation principles to students:

- I am critical of ideas, not people. I challenge and refute the ideas, but I do not indicate that I personally reject them.
- I focus on coming to the best decision possible, not on winning.
- I encourage everyone to participate.
- I listen to everyone's ideas even if I don't agree.
- I restate what someone has said if it is not clear to me.
- I first bring out all ideas and facts supporting all sides, and then I try to put them together in a way that makes sense.
- I try to understand all sides of the issue.
- I change my mind when the evidence clearly indicates that I should do so.

Tiberius (1990) also recommends several strategies students should follow in order to make discussions productive:

- Seek the best answer rather than trying to convince other people.
- Try not to let your previous ideas or prejudices interfere with your freedom of thinking.

BOX 6.3
RESPONDING TO QUESTIONS

1. *Respond to student answers positively and constructively.*
   a. Distribute questions so that all, including nonvolunteers, are included. Encouraging student–student interaction by involving a balance of volunteering and nonvolunteering students forces the focus to shift from the teacher to the students. In this way, the discussion process contributes to students' "ownership" of their learning.
   b. Build on contributions. Use student responses to build other questions and draw out further information: "Good point. How do you think that relates to our discussion of theme earlier today?"
   c. Reflect questions directed to you back to the class—"That's an interesting question. Can anyone help us out?" or "I'm not sure. Does anyone have an idea?"

2. *Accept and develop students' feelings.* Feelings are real. Demonstrate verbally and nonverbally that you are receiving the message and that you are interested in it. Make sure you understand what they're saying and ask any questions necessary to assist them in communicating their specific feelings. Too often we as teachers are concerned with the student's ideas, but not with the student:

To learn is to live,	Why do we fragment,
to be,	dissect, destroy
to grow	the learner
in the light of new knowledge.	in the learning? (Frost, 1974, p. 86)

   Gauge when to pursue students' feelings and when to take no action. Here, you as the professional must make the decision based on your knowledge of the student.

3. *Praise rather than criticize.* It is easy to be critical but you accomplish much more by enhancing the student's self-concept than by destroying it with criticism. When students are not succeeding, it is time you reevaluated your objectives in terms of the pupil and the methods, strategies, and activities you have provided. It is time to be critical of your program rather than of the students.

4. *Encourage.* When you encourage, you are demonstrating your belief in the student and her ability. Nothing is achieved when you communicate to a student that she couldn't possibly succeed in a task.

5. *Use active listening.* How many times do we hear and not listen? Listening to our students provides us a wealth of information not found in the permanent records. By really "tuning in" to our students, we obtain the vital data that will enable us to instruct them as individuals.

6. *Encourage student input.* First, don't talk most of the time. From our own experience, we have found this is a most difficult task to accomplish. When you have grown accustomed to information giving, the initial frustrations in monitoring yourself and reducing the amount of teacher talk are great. Second, redirect questions to students, rather than simply answering questions directed toward you. Third, comments such as "What do the rest of you think about that?" or "Does anyone have something they'd like to add?" encourage student input.

7. *Metacommunicate.* Communicate about your communication. Make sure that you and the student both understand what's being said. Verify what you hear, in other words, "If I understand you correctly, you're suggesting that...."

8. *Accept student mistakes.* Accept the mistakes without reprimanding, but focus on why the student made the mistake. For example, you might say something such as, "OK, Jamie, let's think about this. Let's examine what you said in relation to what you read in the text and see why your answer is incorrect."

9. *Use a variety of responses.* Beginning teachers often ask, "What do I do if no one answers my question or if the answer given is wrong?" Too often beginning teachers give a one word response such as "Good" or "Right" if a student's answer is correct. To stimulate questions, it's important to use a variety of response techniques. The following list suggests a variety of responses for various situations.

   a. When the student's answer is correct

      1. Praise the student.
      2. Restate the correct response as given by the student.
      3. Modify the answer if necessary while maintaining the student's original idea.
      4. Apply the student's answer to some situation
      5. Compare the student's response to something in the text, something already discussed, or some similar, concurrent event.
      6. Summarize the response to draw a conclusion or to make a point.
      7. Call on another student to agree, disagree, or build on the original answer.

   b. When the student's answer is incorrect

      1. Support the student's answer while saying the response is incorrect, as in, "Good try, John, but that's not the correct answer."
      2. Rephrase the question.
      3. Provide additional information for the student's use.
      4. Probe the student's response for a route to the correct answer.
      5. Consider the following:

         "What do you mean by _____?"

         "Can you give me an example of _____?"

         "How does that relate to the problem or issue?"

         "All of your answer depends on the idea that _____?"

         "Why did you base your answer on this rather than _____?"

         "What are your reasons for saying this?"

         "Can you be more specific?"

         "Let me see if I understood you. Do you mean _____?"

         "Could you explain your answer further?"

         "Can you rephrase you answer?"

         "What I heard you say was _____? Is that what you meant?"

         "Pattie, do you agree with the answer Bruce just gave?"

         "Let me rephrase the question. Now, what do you think?" (Eleser, Longman, & Steib, 1996, p. 3)

(continued)

BOX 6.3   CONTINUED

    c. When the student's response is "I don't know"
1. Urge the student to try to answer.
2. Restate the question.
3. Rephrase the question.
4. Redirect the question to another student.
5. Ask the student what part of the question is unclear or if she can answer part of the question.

10. *Encourage quiet students.*
- Pose casual questions that don't call for a detailed response: "What are some reasons why people may not vote?" "What do you remember most from the reading?" or "Which of the articles did you find most difficult?"
- Assign a small specific task to a quiet student: "Carrie, would you find out for next class session what Chile's GNP was last year?"
- Reward infrequent contributors with a smile.
- Bolster students' self-confidence by writing their comments on the board.
- Stand or sit next to someone who has not contributed; your proximity may draw a hesitant student into the discussion. (Davis, 1993, pp. 78–79)

11. *Discourage students who monopolize the discussion.*
- If only the dominant students raise their hands, restate your desire for greater student participation: "I'd like to hear from others in the class."
- Avoid making eye contact with the talkative.
- If one student has been dominating the discussion, ask other students whether they agree or disagree with that student.
- Explain that the discussion has become too one-sided and ask the monopolizer to help by remaining silent: "Larry, since we must move on, would you briefly summarize your remarks, and then we'll hear the reactions of other group members."
- Assign a specific role to the dominant student that limits participation (for example, periodic summarizer).
- Acknowledge the time constraints: "Jon, I notice that our time is running out. Let's set a thirty-second limit on everybody's comments from now on."
- If the monopolizer is a serious problem, speak to him or her after class or during office hours. Tell the student that you value his or her participation and wish more students contributed. If this student's comments are good, say so; but point out that learning results from give-and-take and that everyone benefits from hearing a range of opinions and views. (Davis, 1993, p. 79)

12. *Provide wait time.* Wait time is the amount of time the teacher waits for a response after asking a question. Frequently, teachers have a pattern of rapid-fire questioning. Generally, teachers wait no more than one second for a student response and, after the student does respond, teachers begin their reaction or pose the next question in less than one second. When students are asked a question, they must go through a series of steps before responding. They must attend to the question, decipher its meaning, generate a covert response, and generate an overt response. To expect students to do this in one to three seconds is unrealistic. Wait time is of two types (Rowe, 1987):

> *Wait time 1:* How long do you think you wait after you ask a question for students to begin an answer?
>
> *Wait time 2:* After students give you an answer, how long do you wait for further explanation or elaboration?

Rowe (1986) reports that if teachers increase the average length of wait time after asking a question and after hearing a student response, the changes in student use of language and logic, as well as student and teacher attitudes and expectations, are pronounced.

Increased wait time increases student responses, speculative thinking, number of questions asked by students, student–student interactions, variety of students volunteering in discussions, student confidence, and student achievement. In addition, disciplinary problems and failure on the part of students to respond decrease. Perhaps most interesting is the effect on certain students, particularly minority students. When wait time increased, these students did more talking relevant to the task, and took a more active part in discussions.

Increased wait time also has an effect on teachers. When teachers increase their wait times, the level of their questions is more cognitively advanced and greater continuity in the development of ideas exists. Rowe (1987) lists several responses that can interfere with wait time as well as communicate unwanted messages to students:

1. *"Think!"* Too often we rush into a statement such as this before three seconds has elapsed. This probably communicates our exasperation and is of very little help to students.
2. *Mimicry.* In the elaboration process, teachers often repeat some or all of a student's answer, frequently beginning before the desirable wait time. The implicit message in this is that there is no payoff for listening to each other or trying to evaluate what other students say, because the teacher's reaction will indicate which answers are acceptable and which are not.
3. *"Yes…but…and…though"* constructions. When we respond with these constructions, students feel as if the discussion is "going nowhere." These constructions signal that the speaker is not receiving and exploring the new ideas but, rather, is concerned with countering them.
4. *"Isn't it?"* and *"Right?"* These responses produce compliance, at least on the surface.
5. *"Don't you think that…?"* This phrase sounds, at first hearing, like a question. However, such a construction makes it very difficult to disagree because the implicit answer is "yes."

- Speak whenever you wish (if you are not interrupting someone else, of course), even though your idea may seem incomplete.
- Practice listening by trying to formulate in your own words the point that the previous speaker made before adding your own contribution.
- Avoid disrupting the flow of thought by introducing new issues; instead wait until the present topic reaches its natural end; if you wish to introduce a new topic, warn the group that what you are about to say will address a new

topic and that you are willing to wait to introduce it until people are finished commenting on the current topic.

- Stick to the subject and talk briefly.
- Avoid long stories, anecdotes, or examples.
- Give encouragement and approval to others.
- Seek out differences of opinion; they enrich the discussion.
- Be sympathetic and understanding of other people's views.

In Chapter 5, we discussed how teacher communication apprehension might affect the lecture process. Because student communication apprehension may affect student participation in the discussion method, it is important to address at this point.

Student Communication Apprehension

The presence of highly apprehensive students can baffle even the best teacher. There's nothing more disheartening than a student who has something worthwhile to contribute but, because of communication apprehension, is both unwilling and fearful of sharing that knowledge with others.

The low communication-apprehensive student presents quite a different picture. He is generally perceived as a high interactor, mature, independent, self-assured, assertive, competitive, talkative, determined, enjoys people, is chosen for leadership, decisive, open-minded, tolerant of ambiguous or uncertain situations, has a high need to achieve, sees himself as being in control of his own life, seeks occupations requiring a large amount of communication, and has high self-esteem.

Research (Allen & Bourhis, 1996; Ericson & Gardner, 1992; Hawkins & Stewart, 1991; Neer, 1992; O'Mara, Allen, Long, & Judd, 1996) indicates that highly communication-apprehensive students interact less frequently. In addition, highly apprehensive students

1. Do not assume positions of leadership in groups.
2. Do not volunteer to participate in classroom question and answer sessions.
3. Drop classes requiring a large amount of communication.
4. Are perceived by teachers as having less likelihood of success in almost every subject area regardless of intelligence, effort, or academic ability.
5. Have low self-esteem.
6. Express a preference for seating arrangements that inhibit communication interaction.
7. Have lower grade point averages (GPAs) and score lower on student achievement tests than low communication-apprehensive students.
8. Are more likely to drop out of school.
9. Generally avoid classroom discussions.

From the previous research findings, a picture of the highly communication-apprehensive student can be drawn. Generally, this student is withdrawn; has a hard time with self-expression; is quiet, reserved, dissatisfied, easily annoyed, and strongly affected by emotions; lacks leadership; is a follower; is submissive; has a low task orientation; is restrained; avoids people and participation in groups; dislikes interaction; is shy; is an ineffective speaker; has little success in groups; is indecisive, tense, frustrated, and closed-minded; has a low tolerance for ambiguous or uncertain situations, low need to achieve, and low self-esteem; chooses occupations requiring little communication; and sees others as controlling his life.

In general, a review of the communication apprehension research indicates that students with high levels of communication apprehension from the elementary to college levels are less academically successful than students with low levels of communication apprehension, as measured by final grades, GPAs, and standardized achievement tests (see, for example, Chesebro, McCroskey, Atwater, Behrenfuss, Cawelt, Gaudino, & Hodges, 1992; Comadena & Prusank, 1988; Rosenfeld, Grant, & McCroskey, 1995). In addition, teachers expect students with high levels of communication apprehension to be less academically and socially successful (Watson & Monroe, 1990).

Identifying the Highly Communication-Apprehensive Student

The first step in identifying the highly communication-apprehensive student is observation. Reexamine the characteristics of this type of student. If you have a student who exhibits several of these characteristics, she may be a highly communication-apprehensive person. You might also use an independent observer, such as your principal, speech therapist, or another teacher, to share their observations of your students with you.

You can also administer the Shyness Scale (SS) (Table 6.2) to your students. The scale can be administered orally if students are in the lower elementary grades. The SS can indicate which students will be highly verbal. Although little research has been conducted examining overly talkative children, they can be very frustrating to the classroom teacher. In addition, teachers must be careful when "toning down" the overly talkative student in order to avoid causing communication apprehension in this student (McCroskey & Richmond, 1991).

Not every student who is quiet will be communication apprehensive. Some quiet students may lack certain communication skills, feel alienated from society, or be from a different ethnic or cultural background. To identify whether a quiet child is communication apprehensive, you can administer the Personal Report of Communication Fear (PRCF). This questionnaire can be administered verbally to young children.

Treating the Highly Communication-Apprehensive Student

Although clinical approaches to reducing communication apprehension (systematic desensitization, cognitive modification, skills training, and visualization)

TABLE 6.2 Shyness Scale (SS)

The following fourteen statements refer to talking with other people. If the statement describes you well, circle "YES." If it describes you somewhat, circle "yes." If you are not sure whether it describes you or not, or if you do not understand the statement, circle "?". If the statement is a poor description of you, circle "no." If the statement does not describe you at all, circle "NO." There are no right or wrong answers. Answer quickly; record your first impression.

1. I am a shy person.
   YES   yes   ?   no   NO

2. Other people think I talk a lot.
   YES   yes   ?   no   NO

3. I am a very talkative person.
   YES   yes   ?   no   NO

4. Other people think I am shy.
   YES   yes   ?   no   NO

5. I talk a lot.
   YES   yes   ?   no   NO

6. I tend to be very quiet and listen in class.
   YES   yes   ?   no   NO

7. I don't talk much.
   YES   yes   ?   no   NO

8. I talk more than most people.
   YES   yes   ?   no   NO

9. I am a quiet person.
   YES   yes   ?   no   NO

10. I talk more in a small group (3-to-6) than others do.
    YES   yes   ?   no   NO

11. Most people talk more than I do.
    YES   yes   ?   no   NO

12. Other people think I am very quiet.
    YES   yes   ?   no   NO

13. I talk more in class than most people do.
    YES   yes   ?   no   NO

14. Most people are more shy than I am.
    YES   yes   ?   no   NO

Scoring:

   YES = 1; yes = 2; ? = 3; no = 4; NO = 5.

   To obtain your SS score, complete the following steps:

Step 1. Add the scores for items 1, 4, 6, 7, 9, 11, and 12.

Step 2. Add the scores for items 2, 3, 5, 8, 10, 13, and 14.

Step 3. Complete the following formula: Shyness Score = 42 (minus) total from Step 1 (plus) total from Step 2.

   Your score should be between 14 and 70.

   Scores above 52 indicate a high level of shyness. Scores below 32 indicate a low level of shyness. Scores between 32 and 52 indicate an average level of shyness.

Interpretation

If you scored above 52, it is likely that you are shy and perhaps do not talk a lot. The higher your score, the more shyness you experience, and the less likely you are to be talkative. This suggests that you are quieter than most people. A high score does not necessarily mean that you are afraid to talk, but only that you prefer to be quiet in many circumstances when others would prefer to talk.

   If you scored below 32, it is likely that you are not shy and probably talk a lot. The lower your score, the less shy you feel, and the more likely you are to be talkative. This suggests that you are more talkative than most people. A low score means that your own oral activity will dominate the activity of quiet children. You will need to be particularly careful not to be verbally aggressive or to expect your children to become as talkative as you are.

   Scores within the moderate range (32 to 52) indicate that some situations might cause you to be shy. In other words, in some cases you might be quiet, and in other cases you might be verbally active.

   Your score on the SS should give a fairly good indication of your normal oral activity level. If your score is incongruent with your own perceptions of your behavior, however, do not necessarily accept it at face value. Talk to someone whom you trust and who knows you well to see if your acquaintance thinks that the scale is accurate. If you teach above the kindergarten to fourth-grade level, discuss shyness with your students to see if their perceptions of you confirm your score.

From J. McCroskey and V. Richmond, *Quiet Children and the Classroom Teacher* (Bloomington, IN: ERIC, 1991) 27–30. Used by permission of the Natural Communication Association.

have been found to reduce apprehension, such methods are rarely at the classroom teacher's disposal (see, for example, Ayres, Hopf, & Ayres, 1994; Whitworth & Cochran, 1996). Reinforcement—a method in which individuals are conditioned to talk more by a series of reinforcing events—has also been found to reduce apprehension and is more readily available to the classroom teacher.

One of the best ways to help the communication-apprehensive student is to provide a friendly, nonthreatening classroom climate (see Tables 6.3 and 6.4) (Cooper & Galvin, 1982; Ellis, 1995). On the first day, make clear to students exactly what is expected of them. Set ground rules that foster communication (for example, "you don't 'cut down' another student's comment"). Engage in some "get-acquainted" exercises (Friedrich & Cooper, 1990). For example, you might use an exercise in which you and your students share your full name and the significance of it.

Don't grade on oral participation. Although taking a speech course has been shown to reduce the average student's communication apprehension, the same is not true for the student with high communication apprehension.

Vary the task assignments for students with high and low communication apprehension. Booth-Butterfield's (1986) research suggests that students with high communication apprehension need more structured tasks than students with low communication apprehension. The more concrete the assignment for highly communication-apprehensive students, the better their performance will be.

In addition, some research suggests that students may benefit from working in small group or interpersonal settings with acquaintances (Booth-Butterfield, 1988). Also, communication apprehension is reduced when (1) student perceptions of dissimilarity are reduced; (2) a noncritical, attentive classroom atmosphere is produced and maintained; (3) students present short, rather than long, speeches; and (4) performance criteria are few (Beatty, 1988).

When talking to highly communication-apprehensive students about getting help for their apprehension, teachers should attempt to be private and personal, provide positive feedback before negative feedback, be specific rather than general about what needs to be worked on, and note that they are encouraging other students to seek help also (Proctor, Douglas, Garera-Izquierdo, & Wartman, 1994).

Finally, recent studies have examined communication apprehension and culture (see, for example, Bolls & Tan, 1996; Klopf, 1984; McCroskey & Richmond, 1990; Olaniran & Roach, 1994; Olaniran & Stewart, 1996; Richmond & Andriate, 1984). One general caution these studies suggest is that what appears to be communication apprehension in American culture may not actually be communication apprehension when seen in students from other cultures. For example, Klopf (1991) suggests, "With a low inclination to talk, the [Japanese] student relies more on nonverbal behavior to communicate feelings...the student will be rated low as a friendly, attentive, contentious, animated, impression-leaving communicator..." (p. 137). In general, Asians exhibit relatively low verbal output, cautious and indirect speech, periods of silence, low expressiveness, and lack of eye contact (Barnlund, 1975; Chou, 1979; Elliott, Scott, Jensen, & McDonough, 1981; Hall, 1977; Kendon, 1967; Kindaichi, 1975; Nakane, 1970; Schneider & Jordan, 1981), whereas

TABLE 6.3   Personal Report of Communication Apprehension (PRCA-24)

Because we know that many teachers, as well as students, have high levels of communication apprehension, it is important for you to determine your own level of communication apprehension. In order to do this, complete the following Personal Report of Communication Apprehension (McCroskey & Richmond, 1991, pp. 31–33).

Directions

This instrument is composed of 24 statements concerning feelings about communicating with other people. Please indicate the degree to which each statement applies to you by marking whether you (1) Strongly Agree, (2) Agree, (3) Are Undecided, (4) Disagree, or (5) Strongly Disagree. There are no right or wrong answers. Answer quickly; record your first impression.

_____ 1. I dislike participating in group discussions.

_____ 2. Generally, I am comfortable while participating in group discussions.

_____ 3. I am tense and nervous while participating in group discussions.

_____ 4. I like to get involved in group discussions.

_____ 5. Engaging in a group discussion with new people makes me tense and nervous.

_____ 6. I am calm and relaxed when I am called upon to express an opinion at a meeting.

_____ 7. Generally, I am nervous when I have to participate in a meeting.

_____ 8. Usually, I am calm and relaxed while participating in meetings.

_____ 9. I am calm and relaxed when I am called upon to express an opinion at a meeting.

_____ 10. I am afraid to express myself at meetings.

_____ 11. Communicating at meetings usually makes me feel uncomfortable.

_____ 12. I am relaxed when answering questions at a meeting.

_____ 13. While participating in a conversation with a new acquaintance, I feel very nervous.

_____ 14. I have no fear of speaking up in conversations.

_____ 15. Ordinarily, I am very tense and nervous in conversations.

_____ 16. Ordinarily, I am very calm and relaxed in conversations.

_____ 17. While conversing with a new acquaintance, I feel very relaxed.

_____ 18. I'm afraid to speak up in conversations.

_____ 19. I have no fear of giving a speech.

_____ 20. Certain parts of my body feel tense and rigid while giving a speech.

_____ 21. I feel relaxed while giving a speech.

_____ 22. My thoughts become confused and jumbled when I am giving a speech.

_____ 23. I face the prospect of giving a speech with confidence.

_____ 24. While giving a speech, I get so nervous I forget facts I really know.

The PRCA-24 permits computation of one total score and four subscores. The subscores are related to communication apprehension in each of four common communication contexts: group discussions, meetings, interpersonal conversations, and public speaking. To compute your scores, add or subtract your scores for each item as indicated below.

1. Group Discussions
   18 (plus) scores for items 2, 4, and 6;
   (minus) scores for items 1, 3, and 5.

                                                              Subtotal _____

TABLE 6.3   Continued

2. Meetings
   18 (plus) scores for items 8, 9, and 12;
   (minus) scores for items 7, 10, and 11.

   Subtotal _____

3. Interpersonal Conversations
   18 (plus) scores for items 14, 16, and 17;
   (minus) scores for items 13, 15, and 18.

   Subtotal _____

4. Public Speaking
   18 (plus) scores for items 19, 21, and 23;
   (minus) scores for items 20, 22, and 24.

   Subtotal _____
   Total _____

   Scores on the four contexts (Group Discussions, Meetings, Interpersonal Conversations, and Public Speaking) can range from a low of 6 to a high of 30. Any score above 18 indicates some degree of apprehension. If your score is above 18 for the Public Speaking Context, you are like the overwhelming majority of Americans.

   To obtain your total score for the PRCA-24, add your four subscores together. Your score should range between 24 and 120. If your score is below 24 or above 120, you have made a mistake in computing the score.

From J. McCroskey and V. Richmond, *Quiet Children and the Classroom Teacher* (Bloomington, IN: ERIC, 1991) 27–30. Used by permission of the National Communication Association.

persons in the United States tend to exhibit high verbal output, self-assertion, verbal and nonverbal expressiveness, and frequent, sustained eye contact (Barnlund, 1975; Elliott, Scott, Jensen, & McDonough, 1981; Hall, 1977; Kindaichi, 1975; Suzuki, 1973).

EVALUATING YOUR DISCUSSION SKILLS

If we want to improve our discussion skills, we need to honestly evaluate ourselves. Several types of evaluation are available. First, make your own informal evaluation of the discussion. Did everyone contribute to the discussion? How much did the teacher dominate the session? What was the quality of students' comments? What questions worked especially well? How satisfied did the group seem about the progress that was made? Did students learn something new about the topic (Davis, 1993, p. 72)?

Second, ask your students to make an informal evaluation of your discussion skills (see Table 6.5). Third, videotape one of your lessons. View the tape and complete the evaluation form that follows. Have a colleague view the tape with you and also complete the form. Discuss.

TABLE 6.4   Personal Report of Communication Fear (PRCF)

Directions

The following 14 statements concern feelings about communicating with other people. Please indicate the degree to which each statement applies to you by circling your response. Mark "YES" if you strongly agree, "yes" if you agree, "?" if you are unsure, "no" if you disagree, or "NO" if you strongly disagree. There are no right or wrong answers. Answer quickly; record your first impression.

1. Talking with someone new scares me.

   YES   yes   ?   no   NO

2. I look forward to talking in class.

   YES   yes   ?   no   NO

3. I like standing up and talking to a group of people.

   YES   yes   ?   no   NO

4. I like to talk when the whole class listens.

   YES   yes   ?   no   NO

5. Standing up to talk in front of other people scares me.

   YES   yes   ?   no   NO

6. I like talking to teachers.

   YES   yes   ?   no   NO

7. I am scared to talk to people.

   YES   yes   ?   no   NO

8. I like it when it is my turn to talk in class.

   YES   yes   ?   no   NO

9. I like to talk to new people.

   YES   yes   ?   no   NO

10. When someone asks me a question, it scares me.

   YES   yes   ?   no   NO

11. There are a lot of people I am scared to talk to.

   YES   yes   ?   no   NO

12. I like to talk to people I haven't met before.

   YES   yes   ?   no   NO

13. I like it when I don't have to talk.

   YES   yes   ?   no   NO

14. Talking to teachers scares me.

   YES   yes   ?   no   NO

Scoring

YES = 1, yes = 2, ? = 3, no = 4, NO = 5.

To obtain the score for the PRCF, complete the following steps:

Step 1. Add the scores for the following items: 2, 3, 4, 6, 8, 9, and 12.

Step 2. Add the scores for the following items: 1, 5, 7, 10, 11, 13, and 14.

Step 3. Compute the following: 42 (plus) total of Step 1 (minus) total of Step 2.

Your score should be between 14 and 70.

The normal range of scores on the PRCF is between 28 and 47. Students who score above 47 are most likely communication-apprehensive. These are the children who need very careful, special attention. Those who score below 28, on the other hand, are very low in communication apprehension. These children are likely to be highly verbal, and they often will be the students who are most disruptive in the classroom. They are also those who most likely will do well in a traditional instructional system. In addition, they are frequently well liked by other students and, unless they are particularly disruptive, well liked by their teachers.

From J. McCroskey and V. Richmond, *Quiet Children and the Classroom Teacher* (Bloomington, IN: ERIC, 1991) 27–30. Used by permission of the National Communication Association.

TABLE 6.5   Evaluating Your Discussion Skills

I. Introduction to the lesson

    A. Attention gaining strategy was

        Successful _____ _____ _____ _____ _____ Unsuccessful

    B. Motivating strategy was

        Successful _____ _____ _____ _____ _____ Unsuccessful

    C. Preview was

        Successful _____ _____ _____ _____ _____ Unsuccessful

    Comments:

II. Questioning strategy

    A. Most questions were asked on the _____ level.

    B. Any probing questions asked?

    C. Did students ask questions of me? Of one another?

    Comments:

    Generally, my questioning behavior was

        Effective _____ _____ _____ _____ _____ Ineffective

III. Wait time

    A. Appropriate to question level

        Usually _____ _____ _____ _____ _____ Never

IV. Response style

    A. What did I do to create a supportive, responsive climate?

    B. What types of responses did I get?

    Comments:

    Generally, my responses were

        Effective _____ _____ _____ _____ _____ Ineffective

V. Conclusion

    A. Summary was

        Successful _____ _____ _____ _____ _____ Unsuccessful

    Comments:

IN SUM

In this chapter we have examined the discussion method of teaching. We have stressed not only the mechanics of this method, but the attitude toward teaching necessary to use this method effectively. Gerhard Frost summarizes that attitude:

Deliver Us!

From classrooms
that creak and squeak
rule-ridden and constrictive
defensive and rigid,
reflecting the neuroses
of adults

rather than the needs of children;
from prison-houses
of artificiality and anxiety,
where nothing breathes,
Good Lord,
deliver us!
(Frost, 1974, p. 71)

Much research suggests that when students interact with one another in a cooperative way, achievement increases, student attitudes toward learning and teachers are more positive, and self-esteem and motivation increase. Discussion that encourages students to work together to solve problems and to talk through ideas fosters positive results (Johnson & Johnson, 1991).

If you follow the guidelines presented in this chapter, two phenomena will occur in your classroom.

1. **Student participation will increase.** You'll foster a positive attitude toward discussion.
2. **Students will become questioning beings.** Postman and Weingartner (1969) suggest, "Children enter school as question marks and leave as periods" (p. 3). They'll remain question marks in an atmosphere that fosters their curiosity and creativity—in a classroom in which questions are encouraged.

One teacher describes the effect of following guidelines such as those presented here:

Since I changed my method of questioning, I've found that my students have changed their attitudes toward learning. This change, very subtle at first, is now quite startling. Students pay attention. They listen to each other and give answers that show they're thinking about what they're going to say. The quality of their questions has also improved. They seem to have a better understanding of concepts and are showing improvement on tests and written work.

Since I have become used to this new style, the amount of material I cover seems to be about the same now as it was in the past, although I must admit that when I was learning to use good questioning techniques, the process did take longer. (Schumaker, 1986, p. 37)

Perhaps the determinant of commitment to the discussion method is your self-concept as a teacher. You must feel comfortable enough to relinquish your control as the *teacher* and become a *learning facilitator.* When you encourage students to question you, themselves, and other students, everyone becomes a teacher. If you are a person who has a low tolerance for ambiguity and a high need for control, the discussion method is probably not for you.

ACTIVITIES

6.1   Consider your teaching field. Considering the advantages, disadvantages, appropriateness, and inappropriateness of the discussion method, list three topics for which the discussion method would be appropriate and explain why.

6.2   Read the following case study (Amidon & Hunter, 1966, pp. 114–116). In a small group, discuss how the cycle of experiential learning is exemplified.

> "You've all had time to finish the story assigned for today," said Ms. Garber to one of her fourth-grade reading groups, "so let's take some time to discuss it."
>
> "I wish I was Whitey and lived on a ranch. He was lucky."
>
> "Yeah. He was a real cowboy, and he was only the same age as us."
>
> "What do you mean by 'real' cowboy?" asked Ms. Garber.
>
> "Well, he had his own horse, and he wore cowboy clothes."
>
> "And he worked like the cowboys do. He roped cattle and he rode around the ranch."
>
> "He didn't rope cattle like at a roundup. All he did was use his rope to pull a calf out of the mud."
>
> "Do you think that would be part of the job of a cowboy?" Ms. Garber inquired.
>
> "Sure."
>
> "I saw a show on TV where the rustlers got the cattle. But they didn't take the meat like in this story and leave the hides. They took the cattle with them."
>
> "Yeah, I saw a show like that. The bad guys were rustlers."
>
> "How did the rustlers look in this story?" asked Ms. Garber.
>
> "Well, they were just ordinary. They didn't look like bad guys."
>
> "Would you read the part of the story that tells about that, Sandy?" Ms. Garber requested.
>
> Sandy found the place and read, "They didn't look like the bad men Whitey had imagined. They weren't wearing guns, and they didn't talk big to the sheriff. They wore overalls, like homesteaders. One even had on a straw hat and plow shoes. Whitey was mighty disgusted with them."
>
> "Why was Whitey disgusted with them?" was the next question.
>
> "Because they looked like ordinary people instead of like bad men."
>
> "Why would that matter?" pursued Ms. Garber.
>
> "Well, it would have been more fun for Whitey if they looked like the bad guys we see on TV. He probably read some stories about rustlers and then he was disappointed."
>
> "So it might have been more exciting to him if the rustlers had guns in their holsters and if they sounded tough. Probably most thieves just look like ordinary people, though," commented Ms. Garber. "How can you figure out how much reward money Whitey received for his part in catching the rustlers?"

"You have to divide six into fifty, because there was fifty dollars and it had to be shared by six people."

"How much did that amount to, then?"

"About eight dollars and something—so Whitey couldn't buy a saddle."

"I've got eight dollars saved up for a bike."

"Where did you get the money to save?" asked Ms. Garber.

"Well, I get a quarter for an allowance, and if I do some extra things for my mother sometimes I get paid."

"This summer we sold lemonade and we made some money. But we spent it."

"Do you think Whitey's uncle might give him any more calves of his own, so that he could try again to earn some money?" inquired Ms. Garber.

"He doesn't need the money anymore. Because the cattlemen gave him a saddle."

"Yeah, but the story said he had old boots and an old hat, so he could still have things to buy."

"Or he could save up to buy his own ranch when he's grown up."

"Why do you think," Ms. Garber went on, "that Whitey's uncle said not to bother the rustlers on the way out to the range?"

"Well, they had to catch them with the meat—otherwise they couldn't really prove that they were the thieves."

"Yeah—they had to catch them with the goods."

"What does that mean—the 'goods'?" Ms. Garber asked.

"The things you steal are the goods."

"What do you think the sheriff meant when he said, 'We'll put these men to soak in the cooler for a spell'?" asked Ms. Garber.

"The cooler's the jail. He was going to put them in jail."

"What's the reason for having jails?" was Ms. Garber's next question.

"If you do something bad you can go to jail. Like these rustlers took cattle that wasn't theirs, so they had to be locked up."

"You have to have a jail to keep the bad people away from the other people."

"I know somebody who went to jail. A man on our street took some money from the place where he worked, so they sent him to jail."

"All right. That's all the time we have today," said Ms. Garber. "For your seat work tomorrow I'm going to assign you to groups so that you can make up a script for a TV show about a cowboy or cowgirl on a ranch. For homework tonight you can think of ideas for your script. Now let's quietly take our chairs back to our places."

6.3 Choose a discussion topic and prepare an introduction for a discussion. Also, prepare a conclusion.

6.4 Tape a classroom discussion (at least fifteen minutes) in which you are involved. Classify the questions asked according to

1. Student-initiated or teacher-initiated
2. Level according to Bloom's *Taxonomy*

What do your findings tell you about classroom discussion?

6.5 Using the topic you chose, develop the body of your discussion by preparing a sequence of questions. Begin with the knowledge level and progress to the evaluation level.

6.6   Are you a thinking teacher? Thinking teachers encourage students to think by asking students to relate the subject matter to their own lives and experiences; asking questions at the higher levels of Bloom's *Taxonomy*; encouraging students to think of alternatives; stressing how to think rather than what to think; and encouraging students to critique each other's thinking. Complete the following checklist. Discuss your answers with those of another classmate.
In my classroom I

	Often	Sometimes	Never
1. Encourage students to question the text material	_____	_____	_____
2. Ask students to give reasons for their answers	_____	_____	_____
3. Encourage students to question one another	_____	_____	_____
4. Stress how to think rather than what to think	_____	_____	_____
5. Ask students to relate subject matter to their own experiences	_____	_____	_____
6. Use higher-order questions rather than only knowledge or comprehension level questions	_____	_____	_____
7. Ask students to work collaboratively	_____	_____	_____

FURTHER READING

Billingsley, R. (1993, February). "Fostering diversity: Teaching by discussion." *The Teaching Professor, 7,* 3–4.

Fourteen tips for fostering diversity through the discussion method are presented.

Hunkins, F. (1994). *Teaching thinking through effective questioning* (2nd ed.). Norwood, MA: Christopher Gordon.

Hunkins provides a wealth of specific ideas for involving students in the questioning process.

Overholser, J. (1992). "Socrates in the classroom." *College Teaching, 40,* 14–19.

The eight-step Socratic method is described as a way to challenge students and encourage the active and critical evaluation of their beliefs.

Palmerton, P. (1992, August). "Thinking skills or teaching thinking?" *Journal of Applied Communication Research,* 335–341; Powell, R. (1992, August). "Critical thinking and speech communication: Our teaching strategies are warranted—NOT." *Journal of Applied Communication Research, 22,* 342–347.

Both articles examine speech communication pedagogy, raising questions about how critical thinking is currently taught and suggesting alternative methods.

CHAPTER SEVEN

SMALL GROUP COMMUNICATION

Objectives

After reading this chapter and completing the activities, you should be able to:

- Define small group.
- Discuss the teacher's role in small group communication instruction.
- Define collaborative learning.
- Discuss the students' role in small group communication.
- Describe group development.
- Teach a lesson using the small group method.

> *No man is an Island, intire of itselfe; every man is a peece of the continent, a part of the main: if a Clod bee washed away by the Sea, Europe is the lesse, as well as if a Promonttorie were, as well as if a Mannor of thy friends or of thine owne were: any man's death diminishes me, because I am involved in Mankinds: And therefore never send to know for whom the bell tolls; It tolls for thee.*
>
> —John Donne

Much of our lives is spent in groups—family, peer, and professional groups. We are socialized and obtain our identity through our communication within groups. Much of what we learn about ourselves is learned through interaction in groups. We see our image of self mirrored by others in the small groups to which we belong. Because of the pervasiveness of groups in our lives, it's important that teachers provide their students with experiences in small group communication. The more opportunities we provide students to "try out" behavior in small groups and to internalize the mirrored reactions of others to these behaviors, the more effective communicators our students can be.

In addition, research suggests that small group work can enhance higher cognitive levels of analysis on the part of students (see research reviewed in Dougherty, Bowen, Berger, Rees, Mellon, & Pulliam, 1995; Smagorinsky & Fly, 1993). Small group work also helps students gain in the acquisition of content knowledge and persistence (continuing study of the content area) as well as motivation (Bruffee, 1993; Tinto, 1993). Before proceeding with this chapter, please refer to the advantages and disadvantages of using small group communication as a teaching strategy provided in the unit overview.

DEFINITION OF A SMALL GROUP

Numerous definitions of "small group" exist. Most of these definitions stress the interactional nature of small groups: persons who communicate with one another often over a span of time and who are few enough that each person is able to communicate with all others, not indirectly, but face-to-face.

After reviewing theories of small group communication, Rosenfeld (1973) developed a general model of the small group process that presents the relationship among the basic components of a small group. This model is presented in Figure 7.1.

According to the model, small group processes occur across time and also change across time. Thus, small group processes are dynamic, and the relationships among the components are constantly changing. *Group composition* consists of the members in the group—their attitudes, personalities, self-concepts, needs, and perceptions. Included also are group interaction variables, such as size and compatibility. *Group structural variables* are communication and attraction networks in the group. *Operating variables* are the roles, norms, and operating procedures of the group. The group—composition, structural, and operating variables—exists within a framework consisting of four more variables: task, outcomes, group atmosphere,

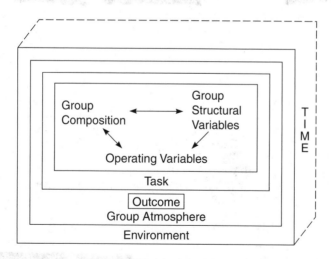

FIGURE 7.1   Rosenfeld's Model of the Small Group Process.

From Rosenfeld, Lawrence, *Human Interaction in the Small Group Setting*, 1973, p. 7. Reprinted by permission of Prentice Hall, Upper Saddle River, New Jersey.

and environment. The *task* is the primary purpose of the group, the reason for the group's existence. The *outcome* is what the group accomplishes (quality, quantity, appropriateness, and efficiency of outcomes) and the group's satisfaction with the outcomes. This outcome, regardless of whether it's positive or negative, affects subsequent group interactions. *Group atmosphere* is the emotional climate of the group. The *environment* is both physical and social. It places limitations on the group that can either facilitate or hamper task accomplishment.

Note that Rosenfeld (1973) takes a transactional approach to examining groups. The model indicates that every component interacts with every other component. In addition, the perceptions and meanings of group members are considered important to the functioning of the group.

TEACHER CONCERNS

As we discussed previously, active learning has numerous positive outcomes. Yet, despite these, small group work can be disastrous if the teacher does not "set the stage" for this work very carefully. The remainder of this section will focus on the teacher's concerns and issues in using small group instruction.

Teacher Roles

When using small groups as an instructional strategy, the teacher needs to understand that her role becomes one of an academic counselor and consultant (Joyce & Weil, 1986). After initially presenting the small group task, the teacher "responds to, rather than directly orchestrates, student activity" (Darling, 1990, p. 274). Darling also notes, what is "key here is the idea of collaborative learning—the 'heart and soul' of small group instruction" (p. 274).

Collaborative Learning

I was brought up in a traditional school setting, in which the roles of the teacher and students were clearly defined. The teacher bawled into our ears for fifty minutes, perhaps on the fox-hunting outfits in *Silas Marner*, and we took notes. Or the teacher demanded a 485-word essay—no fewer words—on "roadside beauty," and we students obliged. Later, when I began to teach, I did exactly the same thing. It was "teach as I was taught": the lessons were ground out, the desks were evenly spaced, a feet-on-the-floor atmosphere was maintained at all times.... About this time, I came upon the gospel of James Moffett. I was appalled. The man advocated a student-centered language arts curriculum, one in which students generated the ideas to be used in the classroom; one in which students taught each other through cross-teaching techniques; one in which the emphasis was on student cooperation and collaboration. The man was obviously a kook. Wouldn't my kids hoot and take advantage of the ensuing chaos? Wouldn't they tear each other up much worse than in their daily battles on the playground and in the halls? Terms like cooperation and collaboration weren't part of their vocabulary. And as for their teaching each other, wouldn't it be a case of the blind leading the blind? They didn't know a comma from a semiquaver. (Whitworth, 1988, p. 13)

In the preceding quotation, Richard Whitworth describes his trepidation about using collaborative learning. His description will be familiar to many teachers who "teach as they were taught." However, collaborative learning, the grouping and pairing of students for the purpose of achieving an academic goal, has been widely researched and advocated throughout the educational literature.

The collaborative learning method has been characterized as "a form of indirect teaching in which the teacher sets the problem and organizes students to work it out collaboratively" (Bruffee, 1984, p. 637). One of the basic features of collaborative learning is student talk. In fact, students are supposed to talk with one another as they work through various classroom activities and projects. Students assimilate their ideas and information through their talk. Thus, collaborative learning is a deliberate attempt to take advantage of differing viewpoints and perspectives through interaction of individuals and their ideas in a reciprocal or alternating action (Sills, 1988, p. 21). Merely putting students into groups, however, does not mean that collaborative learning is taking place. Specifically, "students put into groups are only students grouped and are not collaborators, unless a task that demands learning unifies the group activity" (Weiner, 1986, p. 55). They need guidance. As Golub indicates, the role of the teacher changes from "information giver" to "guide on the side" (1988, p. 5). The teacher is a facilitator whose role involves questioning, suggesting, and directing the discussion.

In sum, as Bruffee (1980) so aptly describes,

> The basic idea of collaborative learning is that we gain certain kinds of knowledge best through a process of communication with our peers. What we learn best in this way is knowledge involving judgment. We can sit by ourselves and learn irregular French verbs, benzene rings, the parts of an internal combustion engine, or the rhetorical devices which are useful in eloquent or effective prose. But when we want to know how to use this discrete knowledge—to speak French, to combine organic compounds, to find out why an engine won't start and then to fix it, or actually to write eloquent prose—we have to learn quite differently.... The best way to learn to make judgments is to practice making them in collaboration with other people who are at about the same stage of development as we are. (p. 103)

Johnson and Johnson (1991, p. 243) outline four elements necessary for effective collaborative learning:

1. *Positive interdependence.* There must be a clear structure to ensure that the group works together. In other words, the group must understand exactly what it is to accomplish.
2. *Face-to-face interaction.* The Johnsons refer to this as "eye-to-eye and k-to-k (knee-to-knee)." Students must sit looking at and facing one another.
3. *Individual responsibility.* Although the entire group learns collectively, each student must be responsible for some task. Too often, if this is not the case, one or more students may "go along for the ride," but not really contribute.

being relating to

4. *Appropriate interpersonal skills.* The teacher should not assume that students know how to communicate in groups. Students need to be taught interpersonal skills such as paraphrasing, clarifying, listening, responding, agreeing, disagreeing, and so forth.

The values of collaborative learning are well established (see research in Bruffee, 1993; Dougherty et al., 1995; Qin, Johnson, & Johnson, 1995; Tinto, 1993). Collaborative learning promotes higher mastery, retention, and transfer of concepts. It promotes a higher quality of reasoning strategies than do competitive and individualistic structures. It promotes healthier cognitive, social, and physical development and higher levels of self-esteem. It results in more positive student–student relationships that are characterized by mutual liking; positive attitudes toward one another; and mutual feelings of obligation, support, acceptance, and respect.

In addition, the "socialness" of the collaborative learning method may be its most important value. The group process is the life process. As Resnick and Klopfer (1988) suggest

> Most important of all, the social setting may let students know that all the elements of critical thought—interpretation, questioning, trying possibilities, demanding rational justifications—are socially valued. The social setting may help to shape a disposition to engage in thinking. There is not much research on how intellectual dispositions are socialized, but we do know how other traits such as aggressiveness, independence, or gender identification develop. By analogy with these traits, we can expect intellectual dispositions to arise from long-term participation in social communities that establish expectations for certain kinds of behavior. Through participation in communities, students would come to expect thinking all the time, to view themselves as able, even obligated, to engage in critical analysis and problem solving. (p. 9)

The teacher may find that the collaborative learning method is not "neat and tidy" either in practice or in ease of assessing its outcomes. It is somewhat chaotic. However, as Berthoff (1981) suggests, the learning is well worth the chaos:

> Now, chaos is scary: the meanings that can emerge from it, which can be discerned taking shape within it, can be discovered only if students who are learning to write can learn to tolerate ambiguity. It is to our teacherly advantage that the mind doesn't like chaos; on the other hand, we have to be alert to the fact that meanings can be arrived at too quickly, the possibility of other meanings being too abruptly foreclosed." (pp. 70–71)

Classroom Climate

In addition to clearly understanding the teacher role and collaborative learning, the teacher also needs to create a supportive classroom climate. As we have discussed throughout this text, students are more likely to participate when a climate of respect and trust has been established in the classroom.

TASKS

Defining the Task

The real key to effective use of small instructional groups in the classroom is the planning and organizing of the task. Simply telling students to "get together and solve this problem," or "work in groups to complete the assignments," or "get together in small groups and discuss *Ethan Frome*," will make their learning experience frustrating at best! You must take considerable time to "set the scene." Any unfamiliar terms or concepts should be defined and clarified. The goal of the small group task should be clear to students as well as the time allotted for them to complete the task. As groups work, you will need to observe them and provide immediate corrective feedback of student errors and positive reinforcement for "on-task" behavior. In short, teachers structure, guide, encourage, inform, and evaluate small groups all along the way to the conclusion of the task. Allen, Brown, and Sprague (1991) suggest

> For example, if the teacher observes that a small group of students, working cooperatively on a play-reading assignment, is floundering in its discussion of the play's meaning, the teacher should provide additional information regarding the author or the period in which the play was written. In independent or group study projects, teachers often must provide information regarding available resources, methods of gathering data, and intellectual methodologies. When students stumble in their learning tasks, teachers must provide information to enable them to regain their balance. (p. 286)

When groups have completed the task, you must process the experience; that is, answer the question students always ask: "What were we supposed to get out of this?" The class as a whole should discuss the major themes and subtopics their individual groups discussed. This material should be related to previous topics and readings, and implications of the new material for students should be identified.

Types of Tasks

A wide variety of tasks for small groups exist. In his text, *Learning in Groups,* Jaques (1992) outlines several. As you examine the list in Box 7.1, think of ways you could use some of them in your own classroom.

Perhaps small groups are most often used as problem-solving task groups. Students are given a problem, and the task is to solve it. For example, you might divide your math class into "families." Each family is provided a monthly income and a list of fixed expenses such as lodging, car payment, department store credit charges, and so on. Each family must determine how the remainder of their monthly income is to be spent—how much should be budgeted for recreation, food, clothing, and so forth.

BOX 7.1
TYPES OF TASKS

- Argue with the instructor or students
- Discuss presentation
- Discuss misunderstandings
- Draw up a list of similarities and differences
- List items from experience
- List items from observation in the group
- List items from reading
- Mark their own or each other's essays
- Set criteria for marking essays
- Generate ideas
- Make categories
- Clarify a problem, solve it, and evaluate it
- Enact
- Discuss critically
- Diagnose
- Argue relative merits
- Share anxieties
- Share essay plans
- Share study methods
- Watch videos
- Read and evaluate text
- Report back on the previous session

From Jaques, 1992, pp. 77–78.

Before attempting to solve a problem, either real or hypothetical, students should be familiar with problem-solving patterns. For example, students could be taught the following problem-solving pattern:

1. Identify the problem—its limits and specific nature.
2. Analyze the problem—its causes and consequences.
3. Set up standards for possible solutions. What criteria would a good, workable solution have to meet?
4. Suggest possible solutions.
5. Choose the best solution. Which one of the solutions suggested in step 4 meet the most criteria outlined in step 3?

In a problem-solving task group the members are requested to come to an agreement on a decision concerning the case study. This agreement can be reached in several ways—majority vote, minority vote, consensus, compromise, or an expert's decision.

general
agreement

Majority vote assumes that although 51 percent of the group members agree on the decision, dissenting (minority) views have been heard. Minority vote can occur when a subgroup determines the decision. Perhaps the entire group has difficulty meeting, and so members agree to abide by the decision of those members who do meet. The main problem here is that the total group may not really be committed to the decision, and conflicts remain unresolved. Decision by consensus occurs when all group members support the decision. Every student must feel he has had a chance to influence the decision. Although this type of decision making requires the most time, it has the strongest commitment of group members. Decision by compromise occurs when group members cannot agree on a decision.

Another common task for small groups is research. Students can be divided into small groups and asked to research a topic area. Research groups enable students to develop research skills and critical thinking. For example, a social studies teacher might want students to study Mexico. Small research groups could be formed, one to research the history of Mexico, one to research the geography, one to research relations between Mexico and the United States, and so forth. Each group could then report its findings to the class.

Small groups can also be used in debate. Students are presented with a current issue being debated in their city, county, nation, or even internationally. A teacher assigns small groups to research the issue, discuss the issue in their groups, and finally, based on the research and discussion, have each member prepare a short speech that articulates a position. Each student is then placed with a partner who holds the same position. In teams of two, students debate one another using the following format:

Constructive Speeches	Affirmative Speaker 1	5 minutes
	Negative Speaker 1	5 minutes
	Affirmative Speaker 2	5 minutes
	Negative Speaker 2	5 minutes
Rebuttal Speeches	Negative Speaker 1	2 minutes
	Affirmative Speaker 1	2 minutes
	Negative Speaker 2	2 minutes
	Affirmative Speaker 2	2 minutes

Students not debating vote for the side they think won the debate. Small groups could decide which two members of their group will debate, or all students could have a turn at debating. Class discussions following the debates should focus on the issues and arguments presented, helping students to think critically. Small groups can also be used with other experimental learning methods—the case study, role plays, and games or simulations.

The case study method has been described as an "active, discussion-oriented learning mode, disciplined by case problems drawn from the complexity of real life" (Christensen & Hansen, 1987, p. 16). More specifically, a case is a partial, historical, clinical study of a situation that has confronted a practicing administrator or managerial group. Presented in narrative form to encourage student involvement, it provides data—substantive and process-oriented—essential for an analysis of a specific situation, for the framing of alternative action programs, and for their implementation recognizing the complexity and ambiguity of the practical world (Christensen & Hansen, 1987, p. 27).

The major goals of the case method are to teach students to solve problems and to select important factors necessary to solve the problem from a tangle of less important factors. As McKeachie (1986) suggests

> Teachers attempting to help students learn complex discriminations and principles in problem solving need to choose initial cases in which the differences are clear and extreme before moving to more subtle, complex cases. (p. 173)

Small groups may be used in role play situations as a means of learning to solve problems and relate to others. Group members are presented with a true-to-life situation and asked to assume roles and act out the situation. Observations are made by other class members. These observations are then compared to the reactions and observations of the role players.

Role plays enable students to experience the learning objectives rather than simply reading and studying them. Role plays, to be effective, must be carefully planned and executed. Following are several ideas to keep in mind when using role plays:

1. Role plays are more than entertainment. Although students enjoy role plays, they should never lose sight of their major purpose—to act out real-life situations and analyze their own behavior and that of others.
2. Role plays are most effective when the classroom climate is supportive. To begin, you might have students role play in small groups rather than in front of the class. As students become more comfortable with this instructional technique, they can role play in front of the entire class.
3. Role plays have no scripts. In other words, the situation and characters are clearly defined for students, but students create the words and actions.
4. Role plays, to be effective, require observers. Assign some students to act as observers who will describe what they observed in relation to the objective of the role play. For example, what did they observe that contributed to the effectiveness of the communication in the role play?
5. Role plays should always be followed by an evaluation session. Both observers and participants should take part in the evaluation session. Questions such as the following should be discussed:
   a. What happened during the role play?
   b. What helped make the communication effective or ineffective?
   c. How did the participants feel during the role play?
   d. What did we learn that we can apply to similar situations?

You might present your class with a simulation, a game, or a simulation game task that could involve several small groups. A simulation models reality, whereas a game is an activity in which participants agree to abide by a set of rules. A simulation game, then, is an activity that models reality, and the participants agree to "follow the rules." A simulation game often portrays adult society. Thus, students are encouraged to make responsible decisions in complex situations they may well come across in later life. If your goal as an educator is to prepare students for life in society, simulation games may be one of the most effective means of accomplishing your goal.

Many commercial simulation games are available. However, these may not fit the particular needs of your class. Simulation games are relatively easy to construct. The guidelines presented in Table 7.1 should help you in constructing your own games, simulations, or simulation games (Sharon & Sharon, 1965, pp. 201–205).

Whenever case studies, role plays, games, or simulations are used, the debriefing by the teacher becomes extremely important. During the debriefing process, as students analyze, draw conclusions, and discuss implications, the real learning of the activity occurs. Covert (1978) suggests an *edit* system for debriefing. Students *experience* the game, simulation, or role play; *describe* what happened to them during the activity; *infer* from the descriptions what general principles, theories, or hypotheses might be developed about communication; and then *transfer* these principles to a usable form in their own lives.

Weaver (1974) suggests that debriefing consider four areas: the awareness created of concepts and principles; the expressions of feeling brought out in the activities; the details of what happened during the interaction; and the success or failure of the exercise as a whole. Whatever method of debriefing you choose, the emphasis should be on what students learned and how that learning can be related to course objectives and content. As Nyquist and Wulff (1990) indicate, "The job of the instructor, then, is to choose a structure for debriefing and to develop the questions that will assist in the debriefing process. When reasonable, debriefing should also address the strengths, limitations, and overall usefulness of the activity to provide feedback for future use" (p. 354).

STUDENT CONCERNS

Often students are hesitant about working in small groups. Perhaps past experience has suggested that small groups don't often work well or efficiently. Perhaps they have never been taught about the processes that affect group productivity. Whatever the case, students will need information and guidance about the task, the expected outcome, the procedures to be followed, as well as their role in the whole process. Thus, as Nyquist and Wulff (1990) suggest

> Active participation in small groups requires interpersonal skills that all students may not possess. Each person within a group brings to the task a variety of personality variables that create interpersonal relationships and affect the levels of participation, the satisfaction, and ultimately, the outcomes of the group. It behooves the instructor, then, to think about the kinds of roles that emerge within small groups and ways to help groups to function with those roles. Instructors may want to talk

TABLE 7.1   Guidelines for Constructing Games and Simulations

	Typical Questions to Be Answered
1. Objectives	
a. list your educational objectives	**a.** What do you want the participants to learn? Skills, information, feelings, concepts, system constraints, system process?
b. translate educational objectives into behavioral ones	**b.** What kind of behavior should participants perform in order to demonstrate that they achieved the educational objective?
2. Real-life situation	What is the most specific description you can give of the situation to be modeled?
3. General model of the game	What roles, if any, are to be represented? (Some games have none.) Are the roles to be individuals, groups, institutions, nations?
a. determine the roles needed	
4. Interactions	
a. determine the game structure	**a.** Who deals with whom? Can everyone interact with everyone else? If not, what are the restrictions?
b. determine the game's procedures	**b.** In what way are the parties to interact? Do they buy and sell, fight, debate, cooperate, compete? What exactly are they to do with each other?
c. consider the kind of learning desired when determining 4a and 4b	**c.** Does the game intend to teach information, skills, feelings, processes? If information, then some type of classifying scheme should be included, or the teaching of a skill for using the information. If a concept is to be learned, then the game should allow for the application of the concept in different situations. If the game emphasizes feelings, then getting points for satisfaction or frustration should be emphasized. If skills are important, opportunities for practice will be needed.
5. Resources	
a. determine the media of interaction	**a.** What means or sources of power are appropriate for the roles through which the participants can express themselves and conduct their affairs? Are the resources money, shares, votes, troops, knowledge, and so forth?
b. determine the quantity of resources	**b.** How much of these resources is to be allocated to each role at the start of the game? Have you considered the inequalities found in reality when determining the allocation?
6. Schedule of events	In what order do players make their moves? Is the sequence of moves clear to all participants? How is the game to start? Who makes the first move and what will this be?
a. determine a sequence for performing the game's activities	
7. Rules	
a. determine the rules governing the interaction in the game	**a.** What laws or other limitations govern the real-life situation represented in the game?

TABLE 7.1   Continued

	Typical Questions to Be Answered
	b. How can the laws affecting the real-life system be translated into rules of the game? **c.** Are there any specific acts that players may not perform? **d.** Are the rules simple and few in number so they can be easily learned and observed and not inhibit the game's progress?

8. Scoring Criteria
   a. determine how a team or individual can win
 	
   b. determine the way players learn of their success or failure
	a. Does the game have an internal winner, such as: the most satisfied person, the first to reach a given goal, the one who gets his way, the nation which conquers the most territory, the candidate who gets the most votes? Are the criteria for winning clearly related to the players' resources?
	 b. Do players receive information about their position during each round, at the end of each round, or only once at the end of the game? How will timing of this information affect their conduct in the game?

9. Materials	What equipment is needed to facilitate the functioning of the game? Does the game require a playing board, role profiles, a scenario, a data bank, score cards, information cards, dice, spinners, special signs, toys?
10. Write and design the materials and game components listed above	**a.** Write an outline of the scenario (if one is included in the materials). **b.** Write role profiles. Prepare one index card for each profile and list on the card where each player is located and what she does in each stage of the game. Group cards according to their first appearance in the game sequence. On separate sheets of paper list all the ideas you want to transmit, to be discussed or investigated during the game. Divide these ideas among the role profiles, keeping in mind when the players will be exchanging ideas during the game. Expand each role profile to more life-like proportions. For example, you might include information about family background, economic background, character, feelings, attitudes, strivings and goals, friends, enemies, affiliations.
11. Write instructions for the game leader and participants	The instructions should include a description of the materials included in the game, its objectives, the roles for participating, and procedures for playing the game. Also, directions should be offered on how to use the game with different numbers of players, the physical facilities required, and how to lengthen or shorten the game according to the level of the students. Suggestions should be made to the game leader as to how she can ensure that the game proceeds smoothly. Write instructions for players, if necessary. Include the game's objectives, preparations for the game, procedures, and any special rules.
12. Test the game and rewrite items as necessary	

to students about the various task, maintenance, and personal roles that group members might assume and about the stages through which a group will progress as a result of those roles. It is also helpful to clarify for students what the use of small groups requires from them in terms of preparation, participation, and debriefing. (p. 347)

Two variables are important for students' understanding of effective small group discussion: roles and group development.

Roles

Roles may be formal or informal. Formal roles are assigned and identify a position, such as "president," "chair," or "secretary." Formal roles are independent of any person filling the role. The role of president has certain duties regardless of the person in that role. Thus, formal roles do not emerge naturally from communication transactions.

In most classrooms the roles of small groups are informal. Informal roles emphasize functions, not positions. For example, a group member may act as a leader without having been formally appointed as "the leader." Leadership, simply put, is the ability to influence others (Gamble & Gamble, 1999). Leadership can be either a positive or negative influence. In other words, a positive leader is someone who facilitates task accomplishment, whereas a negative leader inhibits group productivity. In this respect, any and all group members can become leaders. Whether their contribution is a positive or negative one "depends on individual skills, on personal objectives, and on commitment to the group" (p. 293). Some groups will assign the role of leader, whereas other groups will let that person emerge. It is important to note that there is a difference between being appointed as leader by other members of the group and exhibiting leadership. A positive leader will facilitate group meetings, keep the discussion on track, and make sure that all group members contribute to the discussion and tasks. Leadership must be exhibited by one or more members of the group to successfully accomplish group goals.

The duties expected from a group member playing an informal role are implicitly defined by the communication transactions among group members. In other words, the group members don't tell an individual what to do in order to be a good leader. Rather, members show their approval or disapproval as the person acts as a leader.

Informal roles are generally of three types: task, maintenance, and disruptive. Examining the role types in relationship to their communication function, Rothwell (1995) tells us:

> *Task roles* move the group toward the attainment of its goal. The central communicative function of task roles is to extract the maximum productivity from the group. *Maintenance roles* focus on the social dimension of the group. The central communicative function of maintenance roles is to gain and maintain the cohesiveness of the group. Self-centered or *disruptive roles* serve individual needs or goals (Me oriented)

while impeding attainment of group goals. Individuals who play these roles often warrant the tag "difficult group member." The central communicative function of self-centered, disruptive roles is to focus attention on the individual. This focus on the individual can diminish group productivity and cohesiveness. Competent communicators avoid these roles. (p. 129)

Table 7.2 provides samples of each of the three informal roles types. As you read these samples, remember that a student may fulfill many of these roles during a small group interaction. A competent small group communicator

1. *Demonstrates flexibility.* This person plays a variety of maintenance and task roles, and adapts to the needs of the group. Fighting for roles is perceived to be more prestigious and desirable—may leave vital group needs unattended.
2. *Avoids disruptive roles.* This person shows a commitment to group effectiveness, not self-centeredness at the expense of group success.
3. *Is experimental.* This person tries different roles in different groups, and doesn't get locked into playing the same role in all groups. (Rothwell, 1995, p. 133)

Group Development

Although there are several theories of group development, Fisher's (1970) theory will be used here because it focuses on verbal interaction. In addition, it is a clear way to explain to students what to expect in terms of communication in small groups. Four phases, each with a characteristic interaction pattern, emerged from Fisher's analysis of groups:

1. *The orientation phase* is primarily concerned with social interaction—with getting acquainted, clarifying and tentatively expressing attitudes. There's a great deal of agreement during this phase as people work toward interpersonal understandings of one another. Opinions are expressed in tentative and qualified terms.
2. *The conflict phase* is filled with dissent and dispute. Statements are less ambiguous than in the orientation stage. Polarization occurs as coalitions of group members advocating similar views appear.
3. *Emergence* is characterized by cooperation. People become less polarized. Favorable comments are followed by more favorable comments until a group decision emerges. Unfavorable comments become more ambiguous.
4. In the *reinforcement phase*, dissent is almost nonexistent. The group is concerned with affirming its unity as each member reinforces the decision. The ambiguity so prevalent in phase three tends to disappear. This is the "pat ourselves on the back" phase.

Any small task group will progress through these stages. It's helpful for you to become aware of these phases so you can gauge how groups in the classroom are progressing toward task completion.

TABLE 7.2   Sample of Informal Roles in Groups

Task Roles

1. *Initiator–Contributor:* Offers lots of ideas and suggestions; proposes solutions and new directions.
2. *Information Seeker:* Requests clarification; solicits evidence; asks for suggestions and ideas from others.
3. *Opinion Seeker:* Requests viewpoints from others; looks for agreement and disagreement.
4. *Information Giver:* Acts as a resource person for the group; provides relevant and significant information based on expertise or personal experience.
5. *Clarifier–Elaborator:* Explains, expands, and extends the ideas of others; provides examples and alternatives.
6. *Coordinator:* Draws together ideas of others; shows relationships between facts and ideas; promotes teamwork and cooperation.
7. *Secretary–Recorder:* Serves group memory functions; takes minutes of meetings; keeps group's records and history.
8. *Director:* Keeps group on track; guides discussion; reminds group of goal; regulates group activities.
9. *Devil's Advocate:* Challenges prevailing point of view for the sake of argument in order to test and critically evaluate the strength of ideas, solutions, or decisions.

Maintenance Roles

1. *Supporter–Encourager:* Bolsters the spirits and goodwill of the group; provides warmth, praise, and acceptance of others; includes reticent members in discussion.
2. *Harmonizer–Tension Reliever:* Maintains the peace; reduces tension through humor and by reconciling differences between members.
3. *Gatekeeper–Expediter:* Controls channels of communication and flow of information; encourages evenness of participation; promotes open discussion.
4. *Feeling Expresser:* Monitors feelings and moods of the group; suggests discussion breaks when mood turns ugly or energy levels flag.

Self-Centered or Disruptive Roles

1. *Stagehog:* Seeks recognition and attention by monopolizing conversation; prevents others from expressing their opinions fully; wants the spotlight.
2. *Isolate:* Deserts the group; withdraws from participation; acts indifferent, aloof, uninvolved; resists efforts to include him in group decision making.
3. *Clown:* Engages in horseplay; thrives on practical jokes and comic routines; diverts members' attention away from serious discussion of ideas and issues; steps beyond the boundaries of mere tension reliever.
4. *Blocker:* Thwarts progress of group; does not cooperate; opposes much of what group attempts to accomplish; incessantly reintroduces dead issues; makes negative remarks to members.
5. *Fighter–Controller:* Tries to dominate group; competes with members; abuses those who disagree; picks quarrels with members; interrupts to interject own opinions into discussion.
6. *Zealot:* Tries to convert members to a pet cause or idea; delivers sermons to group on state of the world; exhibits fanaticism.
7. *Cynic:* Displays sour outlook (a person who "smells flowers [and] looks around for a coffin"—H. L. Mencken); engages in fault finding; focuses on negatives; predicts failure of group. (Rothwell, 1995, pp. 129–131)

OBSERVING AND EVALUATING
SMALL GROUPS

If students are to learn effectively from small group interaction, they must increase their small group interaction skills. One of the best ways to help students increase these skills is to have them evaluate themselves and their group, and to observe and evaluate other groups.

Through observation and evaluation, students can reduce their errors, build on their strong points, and correct weak points. Following every small group experience, students should discuss their own experience in the group. Each of the components of the small group should be analyzed—the group composition, the structural and operating variables, task, outcome, group atmosphere, and environment. You might ask students to evaluate their experience in a small group on an evaluation form such as the one shown in Table 7.3.

In addition to evaluating your students, you will also want to evaluate your ability to use small groups as a teaching strategy. To do that, you could use the evaluation form in Table 7.4. Ask your students to complete it.

IN SUM

In this chapter we have set forth the concerns that teachers and students have in small group communication. The types of tasks, group development issues, and issues in observing and evaluating small group communication were also discussed.

ACTIVITIES

7.1   Your instructor will place you into groups of five members. As a group, analyze your classroom in terms of Rosenfeld's model.

Group composition:

Structural variables:

Operating variables:

Task:

Outcome:

Group atmosphere:

Environment:

7.2   Think about your group in this classroom. In terms of the activity (7.1) your group has completed, answer the following questions.

1. What task roles did you assume? Under what conditions did you assume them? How successful were you in aiding the group in completing its task?

TABLE 7.3   Small Group Evaluation Form

Instructions: Circle the number that best indicates your response to the following questions about the discussion in which you participated.

1. *Adequacy of Communication:* To what extent did you feel members understood one another's statements and positions?

0	1	2	3	4	5	6	7	8	9	10

Much talking past each   Communicated directly with
other, misunderstanding   each other, understanding well

2. *Opportunity to Speak:* To what extent did you feel free to speak?

0	1	2	3	4	5	6	7	8	9	10

Never had a chance to speak   All the opportunity to talk I wanted

3. *Climate of Acceptance:* How well did members support one another, show acceptance of individuals?

0	1	2	3	4	5	6	7	8	9	10

Highly critical and punishing   Supportive and receptive

4. *Interpersonal Relations:* How pleasant and concerned were interpersonal relations?

0	1	2	3	4	5	6	7	8	9	10

Quarrelsome, status   Pleasant, empathic,
differences emphasized   concerned with persons

5. *Leadership:* How adequate was the leader (or leadership) of the group?

0	1	2	3	4	5	6	7	8	9	10

Too weak ( ) or   Shared, group-centered,
dominating ( )   and sufficient

6. *Satisfaction with Role:* How satisfied were you with your personal participation in the discussion?

0	1	2	3	4	5	6	7	8	9	10

Very dissatisfied   Very satisfied

7. *Quality of Product:* How satisfied were you with the decisions, solutions, or understandings that came out of this discussion?

0	1	2	3	4	5	6	7	8	9	10

Very dissatisfied   Very satisfied

8. *Overall:* How do you rate the discussion as a whole, apart from any specific aspect of it?

0	1	2	3	4	5	6	7	8	9	10

Awful, waste of time   Superb, time well spent

TABLE 7.4 **Small Group Teaching Evaluation**

	Never		Usually		Always
1. The teacher clearly defined the objective of the small group task.	1	2	3	4	5
2. The teacher encouraged our group.	1	2	3	4	5
3. The teacher allowed us enough time to complete the task.	1	2	3	4	5
4. The group task stimulated my interest.	1	2	3	4	5
5. The teacher's debriefing was clear.	1	2	3	4	5
6. The teacher created a classroom environment conducive to small group work.	1	2	3	4	5

2. What socioemotional roles did you assume? Under what conditions did you assume them? How successful were you in these socioemotional roles?

3. Discuss your answers to questions 1 and 2 with your group members. Did they perceive you in a similar manner? If not, why?

7.3 Read the following case study (Amidon & Hunter, 1966, pp. 36–38) and analyze why it is likely that this class will learn to be open and spontaneous.

Mr. Leavitt was finishing up the committee assignments in his seventh-grade class.

"Now let's see—Joe will be in George's group."

"Do we have to have him again?" and "Aw, gee" came from the classroom.

"Well, I gather that some people have objections to working with you, Joe," said Mr. Leavitt.

"I don't care. I don't want to work with any of them anyway. I'd rather work by myself," responded Joe.

"Let's see if we can't talk a bit about this. I'd like to hear what some of the reasons are for not wanting to work with Joe," Mr. Leavitt requested.

"Well, he's always butting in when anyone else talks. And he thinks he's the only one who has any good ideas."

"Yeah, and if you don't agree with him he tells you you're dumb and you don't know anything"

"If he can't have his own way, he spoils things for everyone. No wonder we don't want to work with him."

"I guess you're saying," said Mr, Leavitt, "that working with people in groups can cause difficulty. People don't always agree with one another, and some committee members want their own way. And people sometimes think that their ideas are better than other people's ideas. In order for a group to work together, though, people have to listen to each other and sometimes change their own ideas or even give up their own ideas."

"Right! And Joe never gives up his own ideas."

Mr. Leavitt continued. "Why is it that people usually think the ideas they have are good ones? And have you noticed that some people give in more easily than others?"

"Yeah—my brother never gives in. What a pest!"

"Well, I think that people think their own ideas are good just because they're theirs. Like you usually think your country is best, or your town."

"Well, I stick up for my ideas because I really think they're good," said Joe. "Otherwise I wouldn't suggest them. And you know, Mr. Leavitt, you've told me many times that I contribute some of the best suggestions in class. Some people really have more ideas or better ideas than other people, and if they're better then they should stick up for them."

"I guess we've all noticed that some people put up more of a fight for what they want to say than others," said Mr. Leavitt. "And certainly we've all noticed that some people talk much more than other people do. We know that in a democracy everyone should be allowed to contribute, while at the same time considering the rights of others. In our groups we want to practice democracy—give everyone a chance to contribute, and utilize as many ideas and skills as we can. Does anyone have any suggestions for ways of working out the kind of problem we have been talking about here in class?"

"Well, what's the use of giving Joe a chance, he doesn't even want to change."

"Maybe we could try some role playing—you know, like we did last week about the kids picking on the other kids who can't play baseball too good. I liked that."

"All right," said Mr. Leavitt. "Any suggestions for situations?"

"Well, we could have the kids who are really on the committee with Joe go up and start to work together. Joe could play the chairman, and somebody else could play Joe."

"What do you say, Joe?" asked Mr. Leavitt.

"Well, I'll do it, but I'd still rather work alone," replied Joe.

"I think it might be good to give this a try, and then we'll decide," said Mr. Leavitt. "Who would like to be…?"

7.4   In a microteaching situation, teach using the small group approach. Divide the class into groups. Choose a task for the groups to complete. How effective were you in using this approach? Did you feel comfortable? Did your groups find the experience worthwhile? What changes would you make if you used this approach again?

FURTHER READING

Several excellent books are available that focus on small group communication. The following three provide basic information about small group processes, decision-making groups, and using small groups in the classroom.

Barker, L., Whalers, K., & Kibler, R. (1987). *Group in process: An introduction to small group communication* (3rd ed.). Englewood Cliffs, NJ: Prentice Hall.

Bormann, E., & Bormann, N. (1988). *Effective small group communication* (4th ed.). Edina, MN: Burgess.

Cohen, E. (1986). *Designing groupwork: Strategies for the heterogeneous classroom.* Wolfeboro, NH: Teachers CP.

Silverman, R., Welty, B., & Lyon, S. (1994). *Case studies for teacher problem solving.* Hightstown, NJ: McGraw-Hill.

The cases included in this text are based on real-life scenarios and are well written and compelling.

Slavin, R. (1989, December–1990, January). "Research on cooperative learning: Consensus and controversy." *Educational Leadership, 47,* 52–54.

This is an excellent synthesis of sixty studies that contrast achievement outcomes in cooperative learning with results of learning via more traditional methods of instruction.

Smagorinsky, P., & Fly, P. (1993). "The social environment of the classroom: A Vygotskian perspective on small group process." *Communication Education, 42,* 159–171.

The authors explore the successes and failures of small group work.

Tubbs, S. (1988). *A systems approach to small group interaction* (3rd ed.). New York: Random House.

CHAPTER EIGHT

COMMUNICATIVE READING AND STORYTELLING

Objectives

After reading this chapter, you should be able to:

- Define the components of communicative reading.
- Prepare a selection for communicative reading.
- Present the selection.
- Discuss the value of storytelling.
- Use storytelling techniques to tell a story.

> *After supper she (the Widow Douglas) got her book and learned me about Moses and the Bullrushers, and I was in a sweat to find out all about him.*
> —Mark Twain

No teacher should pass up the opportunity to read and tell stories to students. Reading aloud and storytelling can be used to introduce a unit of instruction, to help explain a concept, to motivate students, and to simply provide enjoyment and appreciation of literature. Here is a fond remembrance of one of your authors.

> One of my favorite teachers was Mrs. Nicholson, my fourth-grade teacher. Every day after lunch she would either read to us or tell us a story. How I looked forward to that time each day! In addition, during our lessons, it was not uncommon for Mrs. Nicholson to use a story to demonstrate some factual information or to read us a passage from a book or newspaper relevant to the topic under discussion. I remember Mrs. Nicholson was always ready to hear our stories as well. Often she would ask us to share our own experiences that related to the concept she was teaching. She also encouraged us to bring in materials we could read to the class. Both of these teaching tools—communicative reading and storytelling—made learning fun as well as relevant.

In this chapter we explore communicative reading and storytelling. Both of these teaching tools can be used to make your teaching creative and stimulating.

WHAT IS COMMUNICATIVE READING?

Reading aloud—communicative reading—involves more than simply vocalizing words. "It requires an appreciation of one's material as a work of literary art and the ability to communicate that work of art through voice and body. It demands full intellectual and emotional response from the interpreter, and a control and channeling of the understanding and emotion to elicit the appropriate response from the audience" (Lee & Galati, 1977, p. 3). Communicative reading is reading aloud to communicate meaning to an audience. You want your audience to "see," in their minds, the images and ideas you create orally. To accomplish this, you need to be aware of three important characteristics of the material being read. First, you need to understand the content of the material. You cannot communicate the message of the material if you do not understand it. Second, you need to understand the emotional quality of the selection—the "feelings" in the selection. Finally, you need to be aware of aesthetic entirety, or the manner in which the parts work together to create the whole.

As the transactional perspective suggests, you do not read in a vacuum. Your students are an integral part of the communicative reading process. When we share literature with others, we want them to understand and enjoy the selection. Thus, a triadic relationship exists among the communicative reader (you), the literary selection, and the audience (your students). This relationship can be diagrammed as a triangle and, like all communicative relationships, is dynamic (Figure 8.1). Each component influences and is influenced by every other component.

Components of Communicative Reading

We discuss each of the three components important in communicative reading—the communicative reader, the literary selection, and the audience—separately. Remember, however, that this separation is for analysis only. In actuality, the components

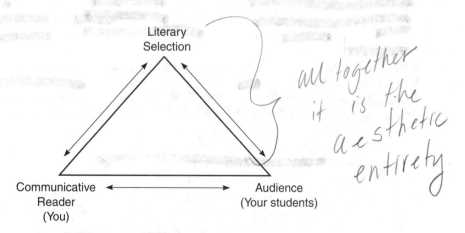

all together it is the aesthetic entirety

FIGURE 8.1   The Three Interactive Components of the Communicative Reading Relationship.

cannot be separated; they work together to create the "aesthetic entirety" discussed earlier. In addition to these three components, some techniques of oral presentation are discussed.

The Communicative Reader.   Think back to our discussion of self-concept in Chapter 2. We indicated that we each reveal ourselves every time we communicate. The literature you choose to share with your students reveals a lot about you—your feelings, beliefs, and attitudes. It's important to choose material that you enjoy. Beginning public speakers are often told to choose a topic of interest to them. The same can be said of communicative reading. If you're not truly interested in the material, your students won't be either. Have a genuine desire to communicate with your students. Never read to your students simply to "fill up time." Communicative reading should be used because it can help students with motivation, learning, or attitudes.

Consider your skills as an oral communicator. Consider your voice, gestures and bodily movements, eye contact, facial expressions, and so forth. Do you have any habits that might be distracting? Many things can distract your students from what you're reading, such as the time of day, noises outside as well as inside the classroom, and their internal states. You may not be able to control these factors, but you can eliminate the elements in yourself that could be distracting. Remember, the focus of your students should be on the thought, emotions, and attitudes of the selection, not on you as a reader.

The Literary Selection.   You have a variety of literature from which to choose—poetry, prose fiction, non-fiction prose, and drama. Regardless of the type of literature, several guidelines should be followed when choosing literature for communicative reading.

Perhaps the first consideration when choosing literature is whether or not it's worth your time and effort. Does it have literary merit? Does it have unity and harmony of theme and style? Does it have sufficient variety and contrast to hold interest? Is the plot clear? Are the characters well developed? Does it have aesthetic qualities?

Having determined that the selection has sufficient literary merit to warrant your time and effort, your next consideration should be its appropriateness. Is it appropriate for your students? Will the selection hold their interest? Is it appropriate for their age level? Can they understand and appreciate it on the first reading?

Is the selection appropriate for the classroom situation? What are the physical limitations, such as time allotted for a particular subject or unit? Similarly, is the selection appropriate for your educational purpose? For example, suppose you want to instill an appreciation for poetry in your students by reading some poetry to them. It will be very important to choose poetry that they will enjoy. Although you may find *Beowulf* extremely exciting, it's probably not the best poem to choose for instilling an appreciation of poetry, at least not initially.

Finally, is the selection appropriate for reading aloud? Some selections are too complex for your students to understand when hearing them read aloud. They may contain too many words the students don't understand. The style could be too complex. For a variety of reasons, some literature is simply not appropriate for oral presentation.

The Audience—Your Students

> It's June, and it's over
> The quizzes, the tests—
> they passed them all.
> But I never found time to get to know them. (Cullum, 1978, p. 60)

Too often we fail to really get to know our students. If we want to be effective communicative readers, we must know our audience—their attitudes, beliefs, likes, and dislikes. Only when we really know our students can we accurately determine what selections are appropriate for them.

In addition to analyzing your students prior to the actual oral reading, you'll need to analyze them as you are reading and adapt accordingly. For example, if students are straining to hear you, you'll need to talk louder. If the oral reading is to be successful, it will be necessary to monitor the reactions of your students. This will be difficult if you never look up from your material!

Finally, postanalysis is important. Ask for reactions from your students. Did they enjoy the reading? What did they learn? Ask them questions to determine if you fulfilled your purpose.

PREPARING THE SELECTION

Now that you've chosen a selection that is suitable for you and your students, it's time to prepare the selection for reading.

Understanding the Selection

Preparation of the selection begins with a thorough understanding of it. What is the mood of the selection? What conflict exists? Who are the characters? What is the point of view of the selection? What is the theme? Does knowledge of the author's background or other works by the author help you to understand the selection? What images are created? What literary techniques, such as alliteration, metaphor, metonymy, hyperbole, or onomatopoeia are used? Put yourself into the selection by considering such questions as, "How would I feel?" "What would I say?" and "What would my reactions be?"

Cutting the Selection

Sometimes you will find a selection that fits your purposes perfectly except that it is too long. If this is the case, the selection must be cut. Cutting a selection must not impair its purpose, attitude, atmosphere, or total impact. What to cut:

1. When possible, cut whole incidents that are not essential to understanding the portion you will read.

2. Cut out characters who are not essential to the part you will read.
3. Cut any description unnecessary to the setting of the mood.
4. Cut any repetition unless it is necessary for emphasis, or for some other obvious reason.
5. Cut the "he saids" and descriptions of action or manner of speaking: "Gary looked up shyly." Imply the action with voice, movement, gestures, or facial expressions.
6. Cut profanity or any element that may offend your audience.

Determining How the Selection Should Be Read

When you've completed any necessary cutting, you're ready to determine "how" the selection should be read. You'll use your voice and body to communicate the meaning of the selection. Voice changes can be used to communicate anger or joy. Posture and facial expression can help create a mood. Movement and gesture can help create a character.

Read the poem "Pam," which follows. In order to create images in your audience's mind you need to recall the smells and sounds of summer, the sights of a street you may have skipped along at age nine, the joy of your own childhood play pretending, the taste of a lollipop.

When you recall such things, your voice, facial expressions, gestures, movement, and so forth will reflect the images in your own mind. As a result, you will be better able to communicate these images to your audience.

Marking the Script

As a communicative reader, you should develop a system of marking the selection to indicate how you plan to read the material. Following are a few suggestions.

1. A diagonal line to indicate a pause—the more lines between the words, the longer the pause.
2. A curved line connecting words that should be read without stopping.
3. Italics to indicate words to be stressed.
4. Broken underlining to demonstrate a faster pace.
5. A dash to indicate the continuation of a thought from one line to another.
6. Notations to designate movement, gesture, facial expression, and others.

Examine the following selection by Beth Cooper (1956). Notice how the marking system is used.

Pam

Her ponytail bounces—
As moccasined feet/
Hop skip

And jump skip [make voice reflect movement]
The leaf shaded street.
Clad in checkered blue shorts—
And a white midriff top/
A band aided hand—
Flaunts an iced lollipop. [raise hand up as if holding a lollipop]
She has sun-blessed complexion.
She has eyes trusting grey.
She has a pert nose—
And curved mouth/
Enchantingly gay.
She lives play pretending—
This bewitched elf of mine/
For the whole world
Is *magic/*
When a lady/
Is nine.

Introducing the Selection

In order to prepare your students for the communicative reading, you'll need to introduce the material you plan to read. The introduction to communicative reading has the same functions as any introduction. These are to (1) gain the attention of the audience; (2) tell the author and title of the selection; and (3) establish a favorable atmosphere for the performance.

DELIVERING THE SELECTION

You've done your job as a communicative reader of literature well so far. Now you arrive at the actual moment of sharing your material with your students. Perhaps the most important concept to remember is that you should interpret the material and not "act it out." It is fine to use gestures, movement, and voice variation as long as they do not distract from the reading itself. Anything that calls attention to the reader rather than to the reading should be avoided.

Facial expressions can be very effective in communicative reading. You can indicate that you expect a humorous response by a sly grin or twinkle in the eye, for example. The mood of the selection, be it sadness, joy, or confusion, can be communicated effectively through facial expressions representing these emotions.

Be direct. Although you are reading to your students, you need to maintain a great deal of eye contact with them. Eye contact allows you to gauge how your students are receiving the reading, and enables you to make any necessary adjustments. Obviously, there may be some selections, or parts of selections, that don't need direct eye contact. If seclusion or privacy is being communicated, for example, indirect eye contact is probably more effective than direct eye contact. Once again, the selection determines how much eye contact is necessary. However, more selections will profit from direct than indirect eye contact.

Don't leave your students "hanging." We've all been in the situation of being unsure when a speaker has finished. Such experiences are frustrating. When you finish your reading, make a definite concluding movement so the listeners will know the reading is over. For example, pause and close your book.

Evaluating Communicative Reading

Using the form in Table 8.1, you can evaluate your communicative reading. You might also use this form to gather feedback about your communicative reading skills from your students.

STORYTELLING

> One dollar and eighty-seven cents. That was all. And sixty cents of it was in pennies. Pennies saved one and two at a time by bull-dozing the grocer and the vegetable man and the butcher until one's cheeks burned with the silent imputation of parsimony that such close dealing implied. Three times Della counted it. One dollar and eighty-seven cents. And the next day would be Christmas.

So begins O. Henry's story *The Gift of the Magi* (1982, p. 1). As a child I was mesmerized every time my mother read or told me this story. The story remains a

TABLE 8.1   Evaluating Communicative Reading

Name _____

Type of Literature _____

Title of Selection _____

Author _____

	Excellent				Poor
1. Introduction	5	4	3	2	1
2. Appropriateness of vocal responsiveness	5	4	3	2	1
3. Appropriateness of physical responsiveness	5	4	3	2	1
4. Communication of mood, emotion, and thought	5	4	3	2	1
5. Appropriateness of selection	5	4	3	2	1
6. Clarity of ideas expressed	5	4	3	2	1
7. General effectiveness	5	4	3	2	1

Comments:

Total Score _____(out of possible 35)

favorite of mine. Perhaps it appeals to me because I am a romantic. Perhaps it appeals to me because I have always coveted beautiful, long thick hair, and so I can understand the sacrifice Della makes. Perhaps I love this story simply because it is a wonderful story.

We may not all be as eloquent storytellers as O. Henry, but we are all, nonetheless, storytellers. We tell stories every day. The parent asks the child, "What did you do in school today?" Husbands and wives ask each other, "How was work today?" The college student calls home, "You'll never guess what happened!" The point is, humans are storytelling animals. We tell stories to make sense of our lives, to share our experiences, and to share ourselves.

Fisher (1984) indicates that the essential nature of human beings is that they are the storytelling animal—the "homo narran." Other writers concur. For example, Heilbrun (1989) says we live our lives through our text. In other words, we are the stories we tell. These stories create a "witchery"—even making the mundane significant. It is through stories that we become "in cahoots" with one another (Coles, 1989). We "make sense" of our environment (Kramer & Berman, 2001) and bring peace to our mind (Kirkwood, 2000).

Storytellers Ellin Greene and Laura Simms asked children, "What would happen if there were no stories in the world?" The children gave some very perceptive answers as recorded in the *Chicago Journal*, May 26, 1982:

"People would die of seriousness."

"When you went to bed at night it would be boring, because your head would be blank."

"There wouldn't be a world, because stories make the world."

Each of us lives by stories. The stories we "buy into" shape us, give our lives meaning and direction. It is not, however, merely the content of these stories that is important. Perhaps more important is the process of storytelling—the dynamic learning experience that the occasion of storytelling makes possible. This no doubt occurs because the process of storytelling is one human reaching out to another in a direct and positive manner.

Jack McGuire (1988) makes a strong argument for the educational value of storytelling:

> Within the necessarily artificial climate of a classroom environment, storytelling is alive, intimate, and personally responsible in a way that the majority of contemporary educational processes are not. In fact, it can be easily claimed that no other educational process comes as naturally to our species. Throughout humankind's preliterate history, storytelling remained the preeminent instructional strategy. By casting information into story form, ancient instructors accomplished several purposes: they rendered that information more entertaining and memorable (for themselves as well as their pupils); they made that information more relevant to their pupils' lives, because it was already grounded in a recognizably human context; and they expressed themselves not simply as experts but as creative, living beings, which helped their pupils to understand, trust, and emulate them more effectively. (p. 6)

Several researchers have examined the positive effect of using storytelling as a teaching strategy (see Collins & Cooper, 1997), and teachers are increasingly using this strategy. Why? No doubt the reasons relate to the value of storytelling.

Citing a decline of language skills over the past two generations, child psychologists and educators are actively championing storytelling as an ideal method of influencing a child to associate listening with pleasure, of increasing a child's attention span and retention capacity, of broadening a child's vocabulary, and of introducing a child to the symbolic use of language (see research cited in Collins & Cooper, 1997). The specific educational and social benefits of storytelling from the child's point of view are numerous and well documented. In addition to increasing a child's vocabulary, concentration, and ability to think symbolically and metaphorically, storytelling's benefits also include

- building children's sensitivity to various forms of syntax, diction, and rhetoric
- helping children to recognize patterns in language and in human experience
- stimulating children's overall powers of creativity
- providing children with problem-solving and decision-making exercises
- strengthening children's capacity to form objective, rational, and practical evaluations
- helping children to develop skills in dialogue and cooperative interpersonal behavior
- familiarizing children with the symbols, artifacts, and traditions that are part of their cultural heritage

In addition, storytelling introduces us to the symbols, artifacts, and traditions that characterize our culture and the cultural heritages of others. Stories are one of the best tools for cultural understanding. As Kepler and her associates (1996) suggest

> Reading a story is like traveling to another culture. It offers us the opportunity to experience what the world is like for other persons, even if fictional. As we read about the lives of others, we are immersed in their perspectives and the rich details of their existence. (p. 182)

In some cultures storytelling was the major teaching tool. Because traditional cultures were not literate, they needed an efficient way to store and transmit cultural values. Their method was storytelling. Stories were not only for entertainment but they also could be used to model ideal values and behavior, define the place and purpose of people in the cosmos, and provide language models.

Even today some cultures still use storytelling as a major teaching tool. One of our Native American friends tells the story of growing up with her grandmother. Whenever the friend did something she shouldn't, her grandmother would tell her a story. The point of the story was always what happened to those who engaged in the behavior in which our friend engaged. Such learning stories are common among Native Americans and can communicate values of the Native American culture. In our families, much of the history and values are communicated through story.

Storytelling is among the oldest forms of communication. It exists in every culture. Storytelling has a commonality among all human beings, in all places, at all times. Storytelling is powerful. Michael Patterson (1999) provides a vivid description:

> Storytelling is the most powerful activity we can engage in to empower communities, because storytelling is how new empowering ideas are shared. Success stories are the best sales method there is. "War stories" are the most useful part of any training, because they animate the tools. Who would not listen closely, when it's time to get the "low down" on the higher ups? In Japanese art there's a term for the "space between"—the white space on this page, for example, the context for the text. Stories deal with and structure this "space between" in the human psyche, and give meaning and context to most of what we do. (p. 3)

Perhaps most important, storytelling is fun. Storytelling is not a spectator sport. The listener and teller are united in the building of the story. The listener may engage in one or more types of participation: ritual, coactive, bantering, predictive, and eye contact. In addition, it is not only the teacher who tells stories. Students should be encouraged to tell stories also. One of the authors asked her students at the Chinese University of Hong Kong to tell a folktale from their culture. They then discussed how cultural stories can help us to understand another's culture and to analyze cultural universals.

IN DEFENSE OF TELLING STORIES

I tell a lot of stories. Stories are nails that I hammer into the wall. On those nails I can hang up the whole, usually highly abstract, conceptual stuff of a philosophy course. If there are no nails in the wall, all the stuff falls down and will be forgotten. But if there are stories, illustrations, visualizations, they will not be forgotten; and contained in the stories there are the problems and the concepts. Years later students will remember the stories and because of the stories, still understand the concepts.

—Jacob Amstutz, philosophy professor emeritus,
University of Guelph (*Teaching Forum*, 1987)

STORYTELLING TECHNIQUES

Choosing a Story

When choosing a story, look for one that has

- simple, yet colorful language (repetitions, rhymes, catch phrases)
- simple, well-rounded plot
- limited number of well-delineated characters
- single theme, clearly defined
- suspense
- fast tempo and excitement

TABLE 8.2   Steps in Learning a Story

1. Read the story over several times.
2. Close the book and try to see the sequence of the story in your mind.
3. Read the story again, this time for the words that will add color to your telling (descriptive, concrete words that describe shape, color, design, etc.).
4. Repeat the same process of visualizing the story in your mind.
5. Now write out, draw, or outline the story (whatever suits you).
6. Retell the story in your own words, out loud so you can hear whether it pleases the ear.
7. Tell the story to a friend, or record it.
8. Retell the story until you are pleased with your "performance."

Most important, tell a story you *really* like. If you choose a story you like, your ability to remember it and tell it convincingly are enhanced.

Learning a Story

Beginning storytellers often try to memorize a story word for word. This is neither necessary nor desirable (unless there is a repeated phrase or rhyme that is central to the story). Memorizing a story leaves no room for your individual additions and nuances. What should be remembered is the sequence of events and images created in your mind. Table 8.2 presents the steps in learning a story.

Tips for Telling

You've prepared well. It's now time to tell your story to an audience—your students. Following the guidelines in Table 8.3 will greatly enhance your chances for success (Collins & Cooper, 1997).

Evaluating Your Storytelling Skills

As with any teaching method you use, you'll want feedback concerning how you did. Ask your students to complete a form such as the one presented in Table 8.4. Analyze their responses and determine your strengths and weaknesses as a storyteller.

IN SUM

On the mornings you tell us about the night before,
you're like one of us.
The dress you bought,
or a movie you saw,
or a strange sound you heard.

TABLE 8.3   Guidelines for Storytelling

- *Rapport* is everything! Eye contact is essential. Each listener should feel that the story is being told just for him.
- *Image!* The tale teller must create vivid images for herself if she wants listeners to see them too. See the pictures and people you are describing. Encourage your audience to imagine with all five of their senses.
- Use *vocal variety;* predictability is death. Be sure to vary tone, rhythm, pitch, volume, and intensity. Use silences and pauses that will give your listeners time to imagine.
- Whenever possible, give the telling a *sense of occasion.* Use ritual (light a candle, share an object, close your eyes for a moment) to transform an environment into a private place for storytelling.
- Capture your audience with a *well-baited hook.* Make them eager to hear the story before you begin the telling.
- Leave your listeners with a *"button."* Give your story a sense of closure.
- Relish the *language.* Find the characteristic words that give this story its special flavor. Enjoy the alliterations, the onomatopoeia, and the other devices of language.
- Be *selective.* The artist knows how little is needed to tell a story well. Choose words, characters, and events carefully.
- *Enthusiasm* is a key ingredient for effective storytelling. As Winifred Ward, a well-known teacher of storytelling, said, "Tell it with zest!"

> You're a good storyteller, teacher, honest!
> And that's when I never have to be excused. (Cullum, 1971, p. 18)

Communicative reading and storytelling can have a positive influence in the classroom. They offer ways to "connect" with students. As a result, they can enhance learning.

Storyteller's Creed

> I believe that imagination is stronger than knowledge.
> That myth is more potent than history.
> That dreams are more powerful than facts.
> That hope always triumphs over experience.
> That laughter is the only cure for grief.
> And I believe that love is stronger than death. (Fulghum, 1988, p. viii)

ACTIVITIES

8.1   Think back over your school experiences to an occasion when an instructor used communicative reading. For what purpose was it used? Did you enjoy it?

TABLE 8.4   Evaluating Storytelling Skills

Name of storyteller: _____ Date: _____

Name of evaluator: _____

1. Specifically, what did you like about this story?

   _____

   _____

   _____

2. Did the storyteller use language, voice, gestures, and body movement to help you create a mental image of the characters, setting, and time?

   _____

   _____

   _____

   _____

3. List five things you think the storyteller did that made the story enjoyable to the listener.

   a. _____

   b. _____

   c. _____

   d. _____

   e. _____

4. List five suggestions to improve this storyteller's performance.

   a. _____

   b. _____

   c. _____

   d. _____

   e. _____

Why or why not? What effect did the use of communicative reading have on your motivation to learn? Your feelings for the class? For the instructor?

1. What types of literature do you like best—poetry, prose, drama? Jot down some of your favorite literary selections and authors.
2. Analyze your strengths and weaknesses as an oral reader.

8.2   Choose a concept you would be likely to teach. Choose the grade level you'll teach. Choose a teaching method—lecture, discussion, or use of small groups. Return to the literary selections you listed in activity 8.1. Choose one of these to introduce or develop the concept. Analyze the selection by answering the following questions:

> Is the selection worth your time and effort? Why?
> Is the selection appropriate for the grade level? Why?
> Is the selection appropriate for your purpose and situation? Why?
> Is the selection appropriate for oral presentation? Why?

8.3   Return to the selection you chose in the previous activity. Will it be appropriate for the students you'll teach? Why or why not?

8.4   Below is a selection by Beth Cooper (1965). Analyze the selection until you are sure you understand it. Then cut the selection. Compare your cutting with that of another classmate. Discuss why you cut the selection in the way you did.

I Was Sure to Follow

My gimlet eye zeroed in on Rob and Bill sneaking around the corner of the house. "Hey, you guys!" I called cheerily all in a breath, "Me and Pink git to go help fetch the cow 'cause Mama said we could!"

The boys stopped, disgusted. They hated Me and Pink, Rob and Bill did, and there was no doubt about it.

Bill narrowed his eyes and hissed, "Geez, you cry babies make me wanta throw up! Why don'tcha ever mind yer own beeswax!"

"Yeah," Rob growled, "Me and Bill, we can't never do nothin' or go nowhere but what yer right on our heels. An' one of these days yer gonna be plenty sorry!"

Both boys glowered at Me and Pink so fiercely that if looks could kill we would have met our demise right then and there. But we weren't worried. We'd heard that threatening lingo too many times before. Besides, we held the winning ace in the hole—my Mother had said we could go.

Me and Pink were six years old that summer and I will call us that now as I did then although I had been told a thousand times to say "Pink and I." I was a fat little girl in a cotton sunsuit with my hair chopped off above the lobes of my ears. Pink, whose given name was David Eugene, was a cousin visiting all the way from the City of Angels, Los Angeles, California.

Pink was a whole inch shorter than I, and skinny, and he smelled little boy good, like castile soap and sunshine. Everybody called him Pink because he was crazy about what he called pink bean soup, a concoction of navy beans cooked with tomatoes and ham hock that was standard fare those hard time years. Pink ingested barrels of the stuff.

Pink's hair was bleached white from the sun and it stuck up in back like Alfalfa's in "Our Gang" comedies. He had at least half a million freckles and he was my favorite cousin. I loved him even though he was dizzy as a June bug. I knew for a fact he was loony. Else he never could have stood to leave his home in Los Angeles, right next door you might say, to movie stars like Mickey Rooney and Judy Garland and be content to spend the summer in a dusty backwoods village in North Missouri. The very idea was beyond me! But when I asked him about it, Pink thought a bit, spit on his thumb, crossed his heart and hoped to die and said, "Well, hell! I like it here in Missouri a damn sight better than California any day of the damn week!" Pink swore an awful lot but I noticed he never did within the hearing of the mothers.

Rob was Pink's brother and Bill was another cousin and they were four years older than Me and Pink. Being that much advanced in age, the two of them fairly radiated *savoir-faire*. They did wicked, secret things Me and Pink were always trying to copy. Such as rolling cornsilk cigarettes in newspaper which they smoked in a rickety tree house high up among concealing leaves. Naturally Me and Pink thought they were the living end while they considered us to be a disaster.

The cow we were to fetch was named Josephine and she was beautiful. Her coat was white with brown spots and her soft velvety ears and great liquid eyes captured our trembling hearts. Me and Pink usually got to ride her home, spraddled across her broad back that tickled our knobby knees digging into her sides, while Rob and Bill prodded her along. "Git on, Josephine! Hi! Hi! Git along now!" But Josephine, having a mind all her own, never planned to hurry—she preferred to munch her way home.

This most lovely of bovines, Josephine, belonged to Bill's parents and it was at their home the entire family—aunts, uncles and cousins of all sizes—had gathered to honor the visiting Californians.

In winter Josephine dwelt luxuriously in a snug shed down the slope back of the house. But in summer she was pastured at the end of a country lane near the edge of town and it was Bill's chore to milk her and drive her to pasture in the morning and back again at night. These excursions were highlights of the day to Me and Pink and we looked forward to tagging along.

I would like to make it clear right here and now that Rob and Bill never once begged us to go with them. And this time they ran down the road slapping their thighs and galloping like horses. They were Tom Mix and Gene Autry riding to head the rustlers off at the pass and they yelled, "HYAH! HYAH!" hoping Me and Pink would give up the chase just this one time and stay at home.

Pink scoffed derisively at their retreating backsides, "Hells bells! Lookit 'em go!" he said. "They oughta know they ain't never gonna git rid of us that damn easy!"

It was late in the afternoon and just plain hot. You could see heat waves shimmering in the distance but Me and Pink didn't mind. We were used to it.

We were unusually carefree because we had somehow managed to stay out of trouble all the day long. Which was a star-spangled miracle in itself for Pink was a wizard at getting us into spankable mischief and exactly like Mary's little lamb "everywhere cousin Pink went I was sure to follow."

We ambled along and scuffled our bare feet in the dust. We picked dandelions pregnant with scraggly seed and scattered it upon the lawns of rich and poor alike, happily ensuring a bumper crop of dandelions the following spring.

It being supper time there drifted upon the air the delicious aroma of someone frying potatoes in bacon fat. Since Me and Pink were nearly always hungry it made our stomachs churn and we broke into a run to catch up with Rob and Bill at the pasture gate.

For some reason Rob and Bill had undergone a miraculous change of heart that Me and Pink would have been hard put to believe had we stopped to think about it. Acting with splendid politeness they held open the wooden gate and graciously ushered us through. Then they pulled the gate closed behind them and dropped a board into a slot shutting us securely inside Josephine's pasture.

Bill grinned, winked slyly at Rob and singsonged, "Won'tcha step into my parlor said the spider to the fly?" And the two of them snickered at a private joke Me and Pink couldn't be expected to understand.

There was always the devil of a time catching Josephine. She was a young heifer and loved to tease. She would lope about the pasture staying out of reach and playing the coquette until she grew weary of the game. Then, suddenly shy, she would butt her head against us and want to be scratched behind her ears.

But Me and Pink, taking advantage of Rob and Bill's expansive attitude, were in no mood for Josephine's shenanigans.

"C'mon, Pink!" I cried. "Let's you and me go lookin' for toads," and we grabbed up some sticks and ran over to a farm pond and started poking in the mud. My daddy had showed us how to stroke a toad on its head to make it "sing." Daddy said it was the male or the female, one or the other, that "sang." I never did remember which sex could be induced to perform this remarkable feat but sometimes they would give a kind of creaky bumble and sometimes not.

To tantalize me Pink hummed "La Cucaracha" under his breath. For days I had implored him to teach me the words and he'd always refused. But suddenly, out of the kindness of his heart, he declared he'd do it. I could barely believe my ears!

"Now lissen close," he said. "These're Spanish words and you gotta git 'em just right. They go like this—'La Kook a raw cha, la kook a raw cha—'"

Happily oblivious to everything around us Me and Pink didn't notice that Rob and Bill had corralled Josephine and led her to where we squatted on the brink of the pond.

"Say, Bill," Rob cooed confidently, "I betcha these two little brats would like a nice swim on such a hot day, don't you?"

"Maybe they would at that!" Bill agreed.

Now Me and Pink were not stupid and we recognized instantly the danger of our position. We tried to scramble away but it was too late.

Dispassionately, like the cold-blooded fiends we always knew them to be, Rob and Bill pushed us into that indescribable mess.

It might well have been the shock of our lives up to that point! Never in a hundred years would we have ventured into that filth on our own.

The summer had been one of severe drought with not so much as a single drop of rain failing for weeks and weeks so that there was little more to the pond than a layer of stagnant water over festering mud, the whole covered with scrabby green scum that stank something terrible. And it was into this horrid putrification Me and Pink flew headfirst, sprawling on all fours.

We struggled soggily out of the muck in slow motion like spawning prehistoric fledglings, wiping slime from our eyes and sputtering it from our nostrils. We were completely swaddled in a cocoon of ooze. Too stunned to merely cry, we crawled up the clay banks of the pond dripping gore, clambered over the pasture gate slipping and clutching at the boards and headed for home squalling loud enough to be heard a mile away.

Pink was so furious he was in a fit. He screamed, "Damn ya sonzabitches! I'll gitcha fer this! I'll gitcha if it's the last thing I ever do!"

Awe stricken, gasping and hilarious, Rob and Bill watched our humiliating escape, observing the scheme to get even with Me and Pink for dogging their every step culminating in a howling, no pun intended, success.

Never being ones to suffer in silence, Me and Pink shrieked louder as we neared our destination to bring the mothers and aunts rushing to see what we had got into this time.

I suppose everyone has at least one excitable aunt and ours was Aunt Ola. She didn't let us down but began her usual screechy "Hoo! Hoo! Hoo!" in a reedy voice like a moonstruck owl which added to the bedlam considerably.

Pink controlled himself enough to sob the explanation for our contaminated condition. "Those damn guys, Rob and Bill, they pushed us in the damn pond!" I heard him say the taboo word and I quaked in my bones for Pink. "He's sure gonna catch it now!" I thought. But nobody else seemed to hear which was a good thing I guess.

Me and Pink stunk so bad everyone gagged and held their noses while we were shepherded around to the back of the house where our mothers filled galvanized washtubs with water and collected old towels for a bath in the yard. The foul likes of us wouldn't be allowed to sully our aunt's pristine bathroom!

My mother and Pink's were mad as old wet geese! Looking for all the world like medieval witches, they gingerly snipped our ruined clothes off with sewing shears and burned them right before our astonished eyes, meanwhile muttering all sorts of evil incantations against Rob and Bill. Pink suggested a day or two of Chinese water torture would be fitting punishment and they agreed which lifted our spirits a good deal. But as it turned out Rob and Bill didn't even get a whipping. Those two boys were smart. They didn't show up until the worst of the mothers' wrath was spent so all they ever got was a harsh scolding. Which didn't disappoint Rob and Bill so that you could notice it but made Me and Pink pretty sad.

It took a lot of scrubbing and three changings of water to get us clean. But at last we were clothed in soft pajamas and hysterical Aunt Ola, who could nonetheless be counted on in an emergency, rubbed our legs and arms with her homemade rose scented glycerol lotion that stung in the scratches but soon left us feeling pampered and soothed. And all the while she was doing it she babbled—"I-declare-I-wouldn't-be-a-bit-surprised-if-the-both-of-you-don't-come-down-with-typhoid-fever-or-somethin'-dreadful-bein'-dunked-in-a-nasty-old-pesthole-like-that-those-boys-need-the-tarnation-whipped-out-of-them-you-poor-little-darlings—" etc. etc. Me and Pink could tell she was getting all worked up to hoot again.

At supper Aunt Ola hovered over us protectively, clucking like a mother hen with newly hatched chicks while her manner toward Rob and Bill was "decidedly chilly with no appreciable change in sight." So the ordeal hadn't been such a total loss, after all.

Me and Pink were so tired we didn't protest when we were sent to bed soon after dark. The night was smotheringly warm and we were allowed to spread sweet smelling quilts on the floor where it might be a bit cooler. Not a single wisp of breeze stiffed the ruffled curtains. And from where I lay I could see the Big Dipper high in God's Heaven, timeless and reassuring. Somewhere beyond the inky Missouri night lurked a bright dawning, impatient to herald another adventuresome day just for Me and Pink. In spite of preceding events of the day, my world was definitely intact.

Still, I was restless. Something nagged at my consciousness like an unfinished melody. There was some meaning to the day I didn't quite understand. Suddenly into my six year old brain flashed a revelation—a spark of truth! Rob and Bill did not always desire the company of Me and Pink! "I reckon," I mused to myself drowsily, "we better not tag after them all of the time." And so, having determined that bit of wisdom, I clutched my shredded ego to my breast along with an equally tattered one-eyed teddy bear and slept.

The next morning, as I recall, Me and Pink were taking turnabout in Bill's tire swing and I was letting the old cat die. No, that is not exactly true. Actually I was Dale Evans and my weary horse staggered and slowed as I desperately sought Roy Rogers to warn that a misguided posse was hot on his trail. "I ben thinkin', Roy—er, Pink," I said, "an' I ain't ganna always tag along after Rob and Bill to fetch the cow."

I glanced at Pink to see how such a novel idea would appeal to him but Pink was not there. John Wayne was, though. Tall, silent, strong. His steely eyes scanned the menacing horizon. A hard hand drifted down and casually caressed his holstered gun, making sure it was there should he have need of it. Deliberate and calm he spat into a mound of dust at his feet. He hitched up his pants. At last he spoke. "Me neither, Ma'am!" he drawled feelingly. "Not e-ver-y damn time!"

So I have to surmise that Pink had learned the same lesson as I—that lesson being that my presence, charming and stimulating though it might be, is not indispensable to other people's happiness or peace of mind. It has stood me in good stead. Through the years I've discovered that no matter how close the relationship, whether between husband and wife or parent and child or friend and friend, each person needs time to be alone. Time to plan and to dream. Time in which to come to know the most cantankerous, complex person of all, oneself.

Looking back, I believe I learned almost everything really important those childhood years. Some lessons I've had to relearn time and again but valuable things like how to give and accept love and how to get along with my fellow travelers on this spinning orb, these things I learned in the bosom of that large, wonderful, loving family. I was a fortunate child.

All of the old ones are gone, the aunts and uncles, the mothers and fathers, and Me and Pink are the older generation now. Isn't that strange?

Bill is gone, too. Destined to never become older than twenty-one years of age—he died in a bomber over Germany in World War II. And Rob, no less a casualty of that terrible holocaust, wanders the face of the earth a homeless creature, with not wife nor child nor brother knowing his whereabouts for months at a time.

Yes, I remember them all and I loved them fiercely. Or to be more exact, I love them. For as long as I live, every one of them lives, too, in my heart.

8.5   Mark the selection you've chosen using the system suggested or one of your own invention.

8.6   Read the following poem by Beth Cooper (1960) and write an introduction to it. Share your introduction with the class. Discuss how the different introductions could affect students' perception and reception of the poem.

The Spaces in Between

This house of mine has a Person—
You can't see it, but it's there—

It fills this house to bursting
And its heartbeat is everywhere.
You shrug a bit and laugh and say,
"My sense is not so keen.

I only see the walls and doors
And spaces in between."
Yes, there are doors and window sills
And walls that can be seen.
But the soul of this house dwells within
Those spaces in between!
And there you have the answer
It's not the things you see
That makes my pulse leap with joy
And means so much to me.
Rather, it's the laughter that
Rings out within these walls,
And the love that's here and happiness
And, the sadness that befalls
At times to every house. And so it is that all
These unseen things combine to mean
That the being of this house
Lives in the spaces in-between.
Yes, this house has a soul.
Don't glance with such chagrin,
For the soul of this house is composed
of all of those who dwell herein.

8.7   Now write an introduction to the selection you chose in activity 8.2.

8.8   Think about the events of today. What incident(s) stands out in your mind? What makes it (them) memorable?

8.9   Choose a story to tell. It may be one you have read or heard. It may be a personal story. Why is this story a good one to tell? Tell the story you chose to your classmates.

8.10   You have completed several activities focusing on how you view yourself as a teacher. Reexamine your answers. With which teaching methods do you feel most comfortable? (If you have never taught, with which methods do you think you would feel most comfortable?) Explain your answer. Are you willing to try other teaching methods? Why or why not?

FURTHER READING

Collins, R., & Cooper, P. (1997). *The power of story.* Scottsdale, AZ: Gorsuch Scarisbrick.

This text provides a rationale for using storytelling in the classroom, storytelling techniques, and storytelling activities. It also contains interviews with children, teachers, and professional storytellers.

Lee, C., & Gura, T. (1992). *Oral interpretation* (8th ed.). Dallas: Houghton Mifflin.

A "classic" in the field of oral interpretation—discusses basic principles of oral interpretations and the interpretation of various literary genres.

Pelias, R. (1998). *Performance studies: The interpretation of aesthetic texts.* New York: St. Martin's Press.

The underlying premise of this text is that all human communication can be viewed as performance.

Remen, R. N. (1996). *Kitchen table wisdom: Stories that heal.* New York: Putnam.

The author, a physician, describes how stories heal us.

Rosenfeld, L. (Ed.). (1993, October). When teaching 'works': Stories of communication education. *Communication Education, special edition, 42.*

This issue presents 13 "docustories" about "when teaching works" and four critical responses to the docustories.

Stucky, N. (1996). Performing oral history: Storytelling and pedagogy. *Communication Education, 44,* 1–14.

Stucky's article describes a class project in collecting and performing oral history interviews. Students enhance their understanding of another person's experience.

Witherall, C., & Noddings, N. (Eds.). (1991). *Stories lives tell: Narrative and dialogue in education.* New York: Teachers College Press.

The authors included in this edited volume believe that narratives are the primary tools in the work of educators, and that narrative and dialogue can serve as a model for teaching and learning across disciplines, professions, and cultures.

Organizations

The National Association for the Preservation and Perpetuation of Storytelling.

A membership organization that sponsors conferences, workshops, the *National Storytelling Magazine,* and a newsletter, and provides members with technical assistance in becoming or finding a storyteller. For more information contact: NAPPS, P.O. Box 309, Jonesborough, TN 37659. www.storynet.org

COMMUNICATION IMPACT

Our communication counts. It influences our students and our students' communication influences us. That's the transactional nature of communication we have been talking about throughout this text. *process*

However, as we have also discussed, much of the communication that occurs in our classrooms is not focused on content. Remember that each message has two components, the content and the relational. Although the content message is extremely important, much of the influence we have on students, and they on us, is a result of the relational message.

In his book, *Random Thoughts: The Humanity of Teaching,* Louis Schmier (1995) makes this point eloquently:

> What I am trying to foster is courage, risk-taking, taking the plunge. I'm trying to bolster self-confidence and encourage growth. I am trying to promote knowledge of some principles. I am trying to develop critical thinking. I am trying to support the application of such skills, and I am trying to emphasize emotion or attitude. The competence demonstrated by a student should not be only a grasp of the subject, but the emergence of a greater self-assurance and self-confidence that would do him or her in good standing in the rest of the class, in other classes, and hopefully throughout life.
>
> So many students come into most classes with a bunch of hidden, non-academic, non-intellectual factors that limit or prevent their success. Singularly or in combination, these factors cause anxiety, apathy, and/or chaos for many students. I just held an open evaluation in my classes. Do you know that few students doubted my authority or knowledge? Instead, they talked about whether I was fair, did I care about them as human beings, were they capable, did they have potential. The first reactions students exhibit in the class are not about whether the professor knows his or her stuff or not, not whether this is going to be a good course or not. They are about "Will the professor understand me?" "Does the professor care?" "In what ways can the professor connect this stuff to me and my issues?" And those issues, not necessarily conscious ones, are self-esteem, self-confidence, need for validation, and need for affirmation.
>
> All I'm saying is that the emotions are there. If we truly care for the students, then we, as teachers, need to be more aware and less afraid of that dimension of

our students *and* of *ourselves*. We must be more honest and more authentic in what we're doing. The purpose for recognizing, naming, and addressing tensions and emotions that exist within both the students and professors in the classroom is to help us become more comfortable with the spirit of inquiry and the joy of learning, become more aware of our intellectual powers. If a student believes he or she is mediocre, that is the best he or she will strive to become and will ever be. Fear and apathy have a debilitating impact on performance. The state of mind can affect the state of learning. It is manifest in the unquestioned self-descriptions of "I'm shy" or "I'm a listener" or "I can't write" or "I can't talk." And it's all too easy to let immediate "can'ts" evolve into prolonged "won'ts" that mire into eternal "don'ts." (p. 168)

What does this mean for us as communicators? It means, as the next two chapters suggest, that we need to be attuned to our ethical behavior, our strategies for classroom management, and our use of power in the classroom. We also need to be aware of factors that affect how classroom interaction is perceived, such as ethnicity and sexism.

CHAPTER NINE

INFLUENCE

Objectives

After reading this chapter, you should be able to:

- Discuss the relationship between ethics and the role of the teacher.
- List the guidelines for ethical decision making.
- Identify the issues that have a potential for social influence in the classroom.
- Discuss strategies for classroom management.
- Discuss the relationship between power and compliance in the classroom.
- Identify behavior alteration techniques and compliance–resistance strategies.
- Discuss the causes of conflict in the classroom.
- Critically reflect on the research regarding social influence issues.
- Identify student challenge behaviors.
- Discuss the ways to handle disruptive students.

At his retirement dinner, a former professor of communication relayed to his audience that his one desire was to gather all the students from his first ten years of teaching into one large auditorium, stand out in the middle of the auditorium among them, and say... "I'm sorry!" Unfortunately, like this retiring professor, it is not until we have influenced many lives that we as educators realize the potential of our social influence. The classroom involves various forms of social influence. As teachers, we have great influence over our students—the knowledge they acquire, the skills they master, and their attitudes toward self, others, and learning. By the very nature of who we are, the way we communicate, and the teaching methods we employ, we wield a form of social influence toward a desired end. Richmond and Roach (1992) suggest that social influence is by definition inherent in the role of a teacher. In order to have a lasting impact on student learning, teachers must facilitate academic growth while, at the same time, creating an environment conducive to learning. That is, we must establish and maintain positive teacher–student relationships if we hope to have a positive influence on learning. Because the classroom is a place of social influence, it is important to consider the ethical responsibilities that accompany such a dynamic.

ETHICAL CONSIDERATIONS

In recent years there has been an increased interest in ethical issues. Educators should not only be concerned with their own ethical practices but also with instilling ethical awareness and practices in their students. The question is, "What standard of ethics do we practice and teach?" Before the answer to that question is addressed, let's first discuss the nature of ethics and the relationship of ethics and the teacher. Next, we discuss those ethical standards, and then close this section with a discussion of student ethical obligations.

Ethics Defined

According to Andersen (1990), ethics is "the systematic study of value concepts such as *good, bad,* and *right,* and the application of such terms to actions, to intentions, and as descriptors of character" (p. 460). In this sense, ethics is concerned with how one ought to teach and what constitutes a good teacher, and is concerned with values such as power, fairness, honesty, trustworthiness, and knowledge.

In 1999, the National Communication Association's (NCA) governance board addressed the task of developing a code of ethics for scholars and teachers in the communication field (see Box 9.1). This credo addresses the distinction between ethics and ethical communication. You may refer to this credo as you encounter the ethical dilemmas associated with your role as a teacher (Morreale & Andersen, 1999).

Ethics and the Teacher

Ethical issues are inherent in the teaching profession and, more specifically, in the classroom. Teachers must always be aware of questions concerning clarity of course requirements, evaluating students, grading standards, favoritism, enforcement of rules, and effects of bias or prejudice (Andersen, 1990). These ethical issues cannot be overlooked or avoided. Andersen (1990) elaborates that "many elements of classroom management (protecting students from harassment, limiting intrusions and disruptions, accommodating a range of opinions and points of view, encouraging active participation, avoiding ridiculing or embarrassing students for 'wrong answers') are important ethical goals" (p. 461). There are also ethical dilemmas when considering relationships with colleagues, administrators, parents, and the community. For example, important decisions will be made with regard to reviewing colleagues for merit raises, conducting research, student or parent favoritism, professional conduct, social pressure, professional preparation, and finally, individual conscience. Audi (1994) explains the ethical role of the teacher in saying, "One is never *just* a teacher. One is always—even if not consciously—an advocate of a point of view, a critic of certain positions, an exemplar of someone trying to communicate, a purveyor of images, a practitioner of behavioral standards, a person dealing with, and indeed responsible for, others in common tasks" (p. 35).

■ ■ ■ ■ ■ ▬▬▬▬▬▬▬▬▬▬▬▬▬▬▬▬▬▬▬▬▬▬▬▬

BOX 9.1
NCA CREDO FOR ETHICAL COMMUNICATION

Questions of right and wrong arise whenever people communicate. Ethical communication is fundamental to responsible thinking, decision making, and the development of relationships and communities within and across contexts, cultures, channels, and media. Moreover, ethical communication enhances human worth and dignity by fostering truthfulness, fairness, responsibility, personal integrity, and respect for self and others. We believe that unethical communication threatens the quality of all communication and consequently the well-being of individuals and the society in which we live. Therefore we, the members of the National Communication Association, endorse and are committed to practicing the following principles of ethical communication:

- We advocate truthfulness, accuracy, honesty, and reason as essential to the integrity of communication.
- We endorse freedom of expression, diversity of perspective, and tolerance of dissent to achieve the informed and responsible decision making fundamental to a civil society.
- We strive to understand and respect other communicators before evaluating and responding to their messages.
- We promote access to communication resources and opportunities as necessary to fulfill human potential and contribute to the well-being of families, communities, and society.
- We promote communication climates of caring and mutual understanding that respect the unique needs and characteristics of individual communicators.
- We condemn communication that degrades individuals and humanity through distortion, intimidation, coercion, and violence, and through the expression of intolerance and hatred.
- We are committed to the courageous expression of personal convictions in pursuit of fairness and justice.
- We advocate sharing information, opinions, and feelings when facing significant choices while also respecting privacy and confidentiality.
- We accept responsibility for the short- and long-term consequences for our own communication and expect the same of others.

From Morreale & Andersen, 1999.

In Box 9.2, several examples of potential ethical classroom dilemmas are presented that were born out of real-life situations. As you enter the teaching field, you may want to refer to these dilemmas and reflect on how you would handle each situation using the NCA credo or ethical standards provided in this chapter.

Why should we as teachers be concerned with ethics in the classroom? Because for many hours of a student's day, we are held responsible for what happens to them. Let's examine two examples of ethical issues that teachers deal with on a

■ ■ ■ ■ ■ ■

BOX 9.2
POTENTIAL CLASSROOM ETHICAL DILEMMAS

- The daughter of your best friend of many years is a student in your class. Several students have reported to you that they have seen her bullying other students. You know that if you sanction the student or report it to her parents, that it will most likely affect your relationship with them. What will you do?
- In your first year of teaching, you notice that a student is cheating on an exam. You promptly report this to the principal and are chastised for not creating a classroom climate conducive to "test-taking." After taking this into consideration and making proper adjustments (providing multiple copies of the exam, separating students, etc.), you see another student cheating on the next exam. What will you do?
- You notice several bruises on a student who comes from a very influential family in your community. What is your obligation?
- You overhear a couple of students making sexual or racial slurs in the back of the classroom. You're not sure if anyone else heard the comments. What should you do?
- During a discussion on classroom ethics, a student raises his hand and says he would like to post a list of the "Ten Commandments" on the wall to remind everyone in the class how to behave. You want to promote openness and tolerance of ideas. How will you respond?

regular basis that might affect student learning or well-being. In the course of your teaching career, you will most likely be faced with the issue of cheating or plagiarism. It is interesting to note that the word *plagiarism* comes from the Latin word *plagiarius,* which means kidnapper. Thus, plagiarism occurs when someone presents another person's ideas or words as her own (Gibaldi, 1999). Whether intentional or unintentional, it is the ethical responsibility of a teacher to report and deal with plagiarism or cheating when it occurs. Keep in mind that most educational institutions have formal written policies on such matters and it is incumbent on each teacher to enforce them. Another growing concern for educators with ethical implications is bullying. Bullying can be either physical or emotional and when it occurs between students will certainly have an impact on a student's learning and well-being. Most people can remember instances of bullying in their own lives that are quite vivid and universally painful (Beane, 2000), but it is important to note that "bullying is not normal, natural, or acceptable" (p. 1). In other words, it is a teacher's ethical responsibility to deal with instances of bullying in or out of the classroom. Beane (2000, p. 43–44) provides several suggestions for dealing with these conflicting situations:

1. Cool down. Make sure there is some time between the incident and any discussion of it.

2. Describe the conflict. Teachers should be sure not to take a position during this step.
3. Describe what caused the conflict. Again, no blaming allowed.
4. Describe the feelings raised by the conflict.
5. Listen. Refer back to the chapter on effective listening skills in this text.
6. Brainstorm solutions. Make sure all ideas are presented and that none are ridiculed.
7. Keep trying out solutions.

Another suggestion that we would like to offer is to have students develop a classroom credo of ethical behavior including any consequences for violation. Teachers can prompt students by providing a list of suggestions from the NCA credo (truthfulness, tolerance of ideas, respect for others, etc.) and then have students add their own ideas to the list. In this way, students take ownership of their own behavior.

Other ethical issues of concern include sexual harassment, sexism, and racism in the classroom. These issues are addressed in more detail in Chapter 10.

Andersen (1990) advises that ethical dimensions must be addressed in the classroom because "omission of the topic increases the likelihood of attacks on the teacher for failing to deal with value issues" (p. 467). If this is the case, then how do we as teachers decide what ethical standards to practice and teach? There are many ways to deal with ethical issues.

Ethical Standards

When thinking of the ethical guidelines that serve to resolve certain issues, one might assume that we rely on *religious* or *moral* criteria, but there are various standards that can be employed. Although there is little agreement on which standard to use, there are many strategies to consider (only a few of which will be highlighted here). First, there is the method of *audience analysis* for determining ethical guidelines. That is, one should consider the ethical position of the group to which the standards will apply (Andersen, 1990). For example, a teacher should consider the gender, culture, values, and background of the students in the class. One might also consider the *political system* of the group as the basis for ethical reasoning (Andersen, 1990; Johannesen, 1990). For example, are the standards being applied to a democracy or a dictatorship? However, one might consider that *human nature* should be respected when making ethical decisions (Johannesen, 1990). This perspective allows for the analysis of individual differences and perspectives within an overall political structure. The *dialogical perspective,* first articulated by Buber (1970), suggests that one should listen to all sides of an issue while remaining committed to one ethical decision. There is also a *situational perspective* that promotes the idea that rules cannot be applied to ethical decisions because the situational element will determine one's standards (Johannesen, 1990; Rogge, 1959). One could also rely on the judicial system or the *legal perspective* for determining ethical guidelines (Johannesen, 1990). Finally, there is a *personal code* of ethics that can be applied after systematically reflecting on various approaches (Andersen, 1990). There are many standards that guide the ethical decisions teachers make in the classroom. It is only when we become aware of these that we can begin to apply them to our own teaching practices and inform our students of the same.

Student Ethical Obligations

The previous discussion highlighted the role of the teacher and ethical decision making in the classroom. But teachers are not the only ones held responsible for ethical behavior. Reed and Hallock (1996) share the following standards for student ethical obligations (see Table 9.1).

To summarize, we as educators have a responsibility to reflect on our own ethical practices and to help our students to become aware of their own ethical behavior as it relates to the climate of the classroom. There are numerous inherent features of the classroom that require ethical decision making such as teacher–student relationships, evaluation procedures, and classroom management issues. Infante (1995) suggests that we have an ethical obligation to teach students to understand and control verbal aggression. These and other issues have an impact on the climate of the classroom and have the potential to influence learning. As such, it is our ethical responsibility to address them.

ISSUES OF INFLUENCE

Some scholars have studied the impact of teacher influence in the classroom (e.g., McCroskey & Richmond, 1983; Richmond & McCroskey, 1984; Richmond & Roach, 1992), whereas others have examined forms of mutual influence in which the teacher influences students, students influence the teacher, and students affect one another (e.g., Simonds, 1997b; Staton, 1990). Whether you agree that the classroom is a place of teacher influence or mutual influence, it is important to explore the issues that have the potential to impact student learning.

Classroom Management

One of the greatest fears reported by teachers is a feeling of being "out of control" (Cooper, 1985). Whether instructors are novices or seasoned, they can be haunted by a fear of being unprepared and, consequently, unable to manage the climate of the classroom. Classroom management can be described as actions that create, implement, and maintain a classroom climate that supports learning.

Creating a Supportive Climate

Most scholars believe that classroom management actions should be proactive rather than reactive and that decisions regarding these actions should be done in advance of entering the classroom. These advance choices about the social climate

TABLE 9.1 Encouraging Ethical Behavior in Class

As a student in this class, your ethical obligations are to

1. Engage in the free pursuit of learning by:
   - Seeking help and clarification when needed.
   - Respecting fellow students', professor's, and guests' opinions without disparaging and dismissing them.
   - Seeing beyond "personality issues" with others to appreciate their contributions to the learning environment.

2. Model ethical scholarly standards by:
   - Avoiding plagiarizing and all other breaches of academic honesty.
   - Avoiding any seeming approval, acceptance, or encouragement of fellow students' academic dishonesty and bringing any such instances to the attention of the professor and/or university officials.
   - Engaging in discussions with other students and professors about ethical issues in academics.

3. Acknowledge, accept, and expect just assessment of your learning by:
   - Understanding the professor's methods and rationale for your assessment and asking for clarification if you don't understand.
   - Engaging in accurate, just, objective self-assessments of your own work.
   - Engaging in constructive, value-neutral discussion with the professor about discrepancies between your self-assessment and the professor's assessment of your work.
   - Refraining from comparing assessments and grades with classmates' so as not to diminish classmates' self-esteem.

4. Avoid harassment, discrimination, and exploitation by:
   - Getting to know classmates and the professor as individuals rather than applying prejudices and stereotypes.
   - Contributing your full effort in team and collaborative projects.
   - Respectfully voicing your expectations of full participation in team and collaborative projects to fellow students.
   - Not discouraging, in any way, a member's full participation in a collaborative project.
   - Being careful not to make racist, sexist, and other types of discriminatory remarks during class.
   - Being careful not to monopolize class discussion time so that others do not have a chance to participate or are intimidated about participating.

From "Encouraging Ethical Behavior in Class," by JoyLynn H. Reed and Daniel E. Hallock, in *The Teaching Professor* (January 1996), Magna Publications. Used by permission.

have important implications for student behavior, learning, and discipline. According to Evertson and Harris (1992), effective management enhances instruction and time on-task by setting and conveying both procedural and academic expectations. Orenstein (1994) supports the notion that planning and preparation are the most effective ways to prevent problems and to provide a suitable climate for learning. He notes that "orderly classrooms are brought about by teachers' efforts to manage behavior in ways that reduce the occurrence and effects of student disruption"

(p. 594). Krasnow (1992) found that teachers who use management programs report less time spent on conflict resolution and fewer distracting behaviors.

Some of the most important research on classroom management was done by Kounin (1970) as he studied how a teacher's handling of misbehavior influences other students who witness it but are not themselves participants. He called this the "ripple effect." Kounin concluded that it was not so much how effective teachers handled misbehavior that influenced other students as much as how they prevented problems from happening in the first place. Kounin described the most effective teachers as possessing the skills necessary to elicit high levels of work involvement and low levels of misbehavior. These strategies include *withitness*—communicating awareness of student behavior; *overlapping*—doing more than one thing at once; *smoothness and momentum*—moving in and out of activities smoothly and with appropriately paced and sequenced instruction; and *group alerting*—keeping all students attentive in a whole-group focus.

According to research studies, an approach to classroom management includes, but is not limited to, the following:

1. Organization of instruction and support activities.
2. Housekeeping procedures and behavior rules.
3. Techniques for conflict resolution. (Brophy, 1983)
4. Setting the tone in the first class.
5. Demonstrating mastery of subject.
6. Demonstrating enthusiasm for subject.
7. Reviewing skills.
8. Assigning work carefully.
9. Developing fair tests.
10. Monitoring student involvement.
11. Being aware of barriers to learning. (Brodsky, 1991)

Implementing a Supportive Climate

Once teachers have planned a management system, they must consider how they will implement that system at the beginning of the school year. According to Evertson (1987), "The first day of school has special significance for both teachers and students. It is at this time that rules, routines, and expectation are established. Students' first impressions about their classrooms, their teachers, and what standards are expected can have a lasting effect on their attitudes and on the ways they will engage in classroom tasks" (p. 34). Evertson and Emmer (1982, p. 153) summarize advice about implementing a classroom management approach. Teachers should begin their year by

1. Preparing and planning classroom rules and procedures in advance.
2. Communicating their expectations clearly.
3. Establishing routines, procedures, and expectations for appropriate performance.

4. Systematically monitoring student work and behavior.
5. Providing feedback about academic performance and behavior.

Because the first day is so significant, it is important to provide students with information that will form positive first impressions and have a lasting impact. According to Friedrich and Cooper (1999), there are three categories of information that students wish to acquire on the first day of class: course coverage, course rules, and teacher personality. In providing this information, instructors should discuss assignments, rules, expected behaviors, and issues related to grades. Friedrich and Cooper (1999) add that "more important than the specific choice a teacher makes on such issues is the fact that the teacher makes and consistently enforces a choice" (p. 288). Gordon (1974) also recommends discussion of rules at the beginning of the school year. He recommends that teachers not only communicate these rules but that they explain how these rules can benefit students. In doing so, teachers should describe the rule, explain why the rule is important, and describe the consequences of violating the rule.

Maintaining a Supportive Climate

Teachers must not only plan and implement their management system, but they must also maintain it as well. Rule violation is an important issue to consider in the overall scheme of classroom management. As the school year progresses, it is important to maintain classroom rules and procedures continually and consistently. There is a major program of research devoted to the issue of rule violation or misbehavior. Within this research program, issues of power, compliance gaining, and conflict have been addressed.

Power and Compliance

Barraclough and Stewart (1992) define power as the potential or capacity to influence the behavior of some other person or persons. A great deal of research in the communication field has focused on power in an attempt to determine the strategies teachers use to gain student on-task compliance. Borrowing from the work of French and Raven (1959), McCroskey and Richmond (1983) described five bases of teacher power: coercive, reward, legitimate, expert, and referent. This began a series of studies called "Power in the Classroom" that explored the patterns and influences of teacher power. This line of research has linked instructor power and compliance gaining to factors such as student cognitive learning, affective learning, and learning motivation (e.g., Kearney, Plax, Richmond, & McCroskey, 1984; Kearney, Plax, Richmond, & McCroskey, 1985; McCroskey & Richmond, 1983; McCroskey, Richmond, Plax, & Kearney, 1985; Plax, Kearney, McCroskey & Richmond, 1986; Richmond, 1990; Richmond & McCroskey, 1984; Richmond, McCroskey, Kearney, & Plax, 1987).

McCroskey et al. (1985) examined the types of behavior alteration techniques teachers and students perceive that teachers use in effective classroom management. The result was a twenty-two-item list of behavior alteration techniques (BAT)

TABLE 9.2   Behavior Alteration Techniques (BATs)

Technique	Sample Messages
1. Immediate Reward from Behavior	You will enjoy it. It will make you happy. Because it's fun. You'll find it rewarding or interesting. It's a good experience.
2. Deferred Reward from Behavior	It will help you later on in life. It will prepare you for college (or high school, job, etc.). It will prepare you for your achievement tests. It will help you with upcoming assignments.
3. Reward from Teacher	I will give you a reward if you do. I will make it beneficial to you. I will give you a good grade (or recess, extra credit) if you do. I will make you my special assistant.
4. Reward from Others	Others will respect you if you do. Others will be proud of you. Your friends will like you if you do. Your parents will be pleased.
5. Self-Esteem	You will feel good about yourself if you do. You are the best person to do it. You are good at it. You always do such a good job. Because you're capable!
6. Punishment from Behavior	You will lose if you don't. You will be hurt if you don't. It's your loss. You'll feel bad if you don't.
7. Punishment from Teacher	I will punish you if you don't. I will make it miserable for you. I'll give you an "F" if you don't. If you don't do it now, it will be homework tonight.
8. Punishment from Others	No one will like you. Your friends will make fun of you. Your parents will punish you if you don't. Your classmates will reject you.
9. Guilt	If you don't, others will be hurt. You'll make others unhappy if you don't. Your parents will feel bad if you don't. Others will be punished if you don't.
10. Teacher–Student Relationship: Positive	I will like you better if you do. I will respect you. I will think more highly of you. I will appreciate you more if you do. I will be proud of you.
11. Teacher–Student Relationship: Negative	I will dislike you if you don't. I will lose respect for you. I will think less of you if you don't. I won't be proud of you. I'll be disappointed in you.
12. Legitimate–Higher Authority	Do it, I'm just telling you what I was told. It is a rule, I have to do it and I will have to give you an "F" if you don't.
13. Legitimate–Teacher Authority	Because I told you to. You don't have a choice. You're here to work! I'm the teacher, you're the student. I'm in charge, not you. Don't ask, just do it.
14. Personal (Student) Responsibility	It is your obligation. It is your turn. Everyone has to do her share. It's your job. Everyone has to pull her own weight.
15. Responsibility to Class	Your group needs it done. The class depends on you. All your friends are counting on you. Don't let your group down. You'll ruin it for the rest of the class (team).
16. Normative Rules	We voted, and the majority rules. All of your friends are doing it. Everyone else has to do it. The rest of the class is doing it. It's part of growing up.

TABLE 9.2   Continued

Technique	Sample Messages
17. Debt	You owe me one. Pay your debt. You promised to do it. I did it the last time. You said you'd try this time.
18. Altruism	If you do this, it will help others. Others will benefit if you do. It will make others happy if you do. I'm not asking you to do it for yourself; do it for the good of the class.
19. Peer Modeling	Your friends do it. Classmates you respect do it. The friends you admire do it. All your friends are doing it.
20. Teacher Modeling	This is the way I always do it. When I was your age, I did it. People who are like me do it. I had to do this when I was in school. Teachers you respect do it.
21. Expert Teacher	From my experience, it is a good idea. From what I have learned, it is what you should do. This has always worked for me. Trust me—I know what I'm doing. I had to do this before I became a teacher.
22. Teacher Feedback	Because I need to know how well you understand this. To see how well I've taught you. To see how well you can do it. It will help me know your problem areas.

From "Power in the Classroom V: Behavior Alteration Techniques, Communication Training, and Learning," by J. C. McCroskey, V. P. Richmond, T. G. Plax, and P. Kearney, *Communication Education 34* (1985), p. 217. Used by permission of the National Communication Association.

and representative behavior alteration messages (BAM), shown in Table 9.2. Student behavior can be either active or passive (Kearney & Plax, 1987), and teacher alteration messages can be either prosocial or antisocial (Sorensen, Plax, & Kearney, 1989).

In addition to examining the behaviors teachers use to gain compliance, researchers have also examined the compliance–resistance behaviors of students. This research indicates that students are more likely to resist teachers who employ antisocial, as opposed to prosocial, techniques. College students report greater likelihood of resisting nonimmediate (those perceived as cold, distant, and unfriendly) as opposed to immediate teachers (those perceived as warm, relaxed, and approachable). Table 9.3 lists nineteen compliance–resistance techniques and the messages students might use.

In a follow-up study these same researchers suggest that students blame either the teacher or themselves for problems that arise in the classroom. Interestingly, if teachers were perceived as warm, approachable, and friendly, students "blamed" themselves for the problem. If teachers were perceived as cold, aloof, and distant, students "blamed" the teacher.

More recently, Golish and Olson (2000) found that a teacher's use of reward power was related to students' use of prosocial BATs. Conversely, the use of coercive power by the teacher was related to the use of antisocial BATs by students. Finally, yet another link is made between immediacy (discussed in Chapter 2) and

TABLE 9.3   Compliance–Resistance Techniques and Messages

1. **TEACHER ADVICE:**
   Prepare yourself better so you give better lectures.
   Be more expressive; everything will work out to your advantage.
   You should relate more with students before trying to give any advice.
   If you open up, we'll tend to be more willing to do what you want.

2. **TEACHER BLAME:**
   The teacher is boring.
   The teacher makes me feel uneasy.
   It is boring; I don't get anything out of it.
   Your teaching methods do not motivate me.
   You don't seem prepared yourself.
   If you weren't so boring, I would do what you want.

3. **AVOIDANCE:**
   I would drop the class.
   I won't participate as much.
   I won't go to class.
   I might keep the class but quit attending.
   I'll sit in the back of the room.

4. **RELUCTANT COMPLIANCE:**
   I'll do only enough work to get by.
   Although I will comply with the teacher's demands, I would do so unwillingly.
   I'll come prepared but not interested at all.
   I will be unwilling to do this but will probably comply.
   Grudgingly, I'll come prepared.

5. **ACTIVE RESISTANCE:**
   I won't come prepared at all.
   I'll leave my book at home.
   I'll keep coming to class unprepared.
   I would not go along with the teacher.
   I'll never come prepared.
   I'll continue to come unprepared to get on the teacher's nerves.

6. **DECEPTION:**
   I'll act like I'm prepared for class even though I may not be.
   I may be prepared, but I'll play dumb for spite.
   I'll make up lies about why I'm not performing well in class.
   I will cheat off someone else.
   I might tell the teacher I will make an effort to comply but will not.
   I'll pretend to be prepared, but instead, borrow from others in class.

7. **DIRECT COMMUNICATION:**
   I'll go to the teacher's office and try to talk to her.
   After class, I'll explain my behavior.
   I'll tell the teacher of his communication problem.

TABLE 9.3 Continued

I will talk to the instructor and tell her the way she is perceived by the class.
I'll talk to the teacher and explain how I feel.

8. **DISRUPTION:**

I will be noisy in class.
I'll disrupt the class by leaving to get needed materials.
I'll talk to friends in class while the teacher is lecturing.
I'll ask questions in a monotone voice without interest.
I'll be a wiseguy in class.

9. **EXCUSES:**

I don't feel well.
I don't understand the topic.
I will keep giving excuses.
I can remember things without writing stuff down.
I forgot and I'm sorry.
The class is so easy I don't need to stay caught up.
My car broke down.

10. **IGNORING THE TEACHER:**

I probably won't say anything; just do what I have done before.
I'll ignore the teacher's requests, but come to class.
I will simply let the teacher's request go in one ear and out the other.
I will just ignore the remark and keep up the same habit.

11. **PRIORITIES:**

I have other homework so I can't prepare well for this one.
I have kids and they take up my time.
I'm too busy.
This class is not as important as my others.
This class doesn't have anything to do with my major.
Due to a heavy class load, I just don't have the time.
I only took this class for general education requirements.

12. **CHALLENGE THE TEACHER'S BASIS OF POWER:**

I will ask the teacher if others in class were asked to do the same.
No one else is doing it, so why should I have to?
Do you really take this class seriously?
How does the teacher know what will be good or bad for me?
Why will this help or hurt me?
If this is such a good idea, why don't you prove it?

13. **RALLY STUDENT SUPPORT:**

I will talk to other students to see if they feel the same (there is safety in numbers).
I'll try to get the class to rally around the teacher's unprofessional style or unrealistic demands.
I will tell my classmates not to go to class.
I might get other students to go along with me in not doing what the teacher wants.
I'll get the rest of the class to support my behavior that the teacher is trying to change.

(continued)

TABLE 9.3   Continued

14. **APPEAL TO POWERFUL OTHERS:**

I might complain to the department head that this instructor is incompetent and can't motivate the class.

I will make a complaint to the Dean of the school about the teacher's practices.

I will talk to my advisor.

I will speak to the department head.

I'll threaten to go to the Dean.

15. **MODELING TEACHER BEHAVIOR:**

I would participate more if you were more enthusiastic about what you're doing.

You aren't enjoying it, so how can I?

If the teacher is not going to make the effort to teach in an interesting way, I will not make an effort to listen.

With the effort the instructor puts forth, why should I prepare for class?

You don't do it, so why should I?

16. **MODELING TEACHER AFFECT:**

You don't seem to care about this class, why should I?

You don't care.

The teacher doesn't care about students, so why should I care about what the teacher wants?

The teacher doesn't seem to care except when there are problems.

You have no concern for this class.

17. **HOSTILE DEFENSIVE:**

I'm old enough to know how I can do in this class.

Tell the teacher what she can do with this class!

Tell the teacher that my behavior is my business.

Right or wrong, that's the way I am.

I'm surprised you even noticed I'm in your class.

Lead your own life!

18. **STUDENT REBUTTAL:**

I don't need this grade anyway.

I'm doing fine right now without changing my behavior.

We'll see when the test comes up.

I have my own way of doing things.

I know what works; I don't need your advice.

19. **REVENGE:**

I'll express my dissatisfaction with the teacher and the course on evaluations at the end of the term.

I won't recommend this teacher or class to others.

I'll steal or hide the teacher's lecture notes and tests.

I'll tear assigned articles out of books or journals in the library.

I'll write a letter to put in the teacher's file.

From "Compliance-Resistance in the College Classroom," by N. F. Burroughs, P. Kearney, and T. Plax, *Communication Education 38* (July 1989), pp. 221–223. Used by permission of the National Communication Association.

another important communication variable as Golish and Olson also found that teachers who are friendly encourage students to demonstrate their knowledge and take responsibility for their own learning.

Recently, compliance gaining in the classroom has been investigated from a multicultural perspective. Lee, Levine, and Cambra (1997) found that students from a collectivist society were less likely to resist teacher influence than students from an individualistic society. They report that students from a collectivist view "should be more concerned with appropriate and polite behavior and should be more likely to see a teacher as an authority figure who ought to be obeyed" (p. 34). This suggests that the power research reflects the assumptions of individualism and that teachers should take into account the cultural background of students before reacting to certain student behaviors. Not only can a student's behavior vary according to cultural boundaries, but the behaviors of teachers with differing backgrounds may vary as well.

Although previous research with U.S. teachers shows a preference for reward-based, prosocial BATs, Lu (1997) found that Chinese teachers said they were more likely to use punishment-oriented, antisocial BATs. Lu explains that Chinese teachers emphasized authority, morality, and modeling in their use of BATs and BAMs. The *authoritarian* teacher is always the symbol of respect and authority and the source of knowledge and wisdom. Authoritarian teachers have complete control over the classroom and should be obeyed at all times. The authoritarian classroom is a very formal place where students must raise their hands and stand at attention before speaking. Also, a student who comes to class late must get the teacher's permission to enter the classroom (Lu, 1997). The *moralist* teacher often informs students of the rules of moral conduct and reasons for such conduct. These teachers are not only responsible for intellectual education but for cultivating a strong sense of societal and filial responsibilities. Students have a debt to their government and their families for the cost of their education. They must honor and bring glory to their families and to society. Finally, Lu (1997) describes *modeling* teachers as "gardeners" who teach students by example as if "raising seedlings." Students should follow the example of their teacher, their peers, or their group (the whole class). The modeling teacher will often use the collective as an example mainly for the purpose of correcting an individual student's behavior. Modeling teachers tend to demand uniformity and conformity of student behaviors. This line of research allows us to make the claim that teacher influence and student resistance is a culturally bound phenomenon.

Power and compliance are important issues for all teachers to consider in the overall scheme of their classroom management system. These are also issues which may lead to classroom conflicts.

Conflict

The classroom is a very complex place where great sensitivity is required to deal with conflicts that arise. According to Civikly (1992b), there are two inherent features of the classroom that encourage conflict: the structure of power differences between teacher and students and a focus on evaluation and grading. Gordon (1974) suggests that there are three conditions that create conflict between teacher and students: (1) when there are no clear-cut rules or policies; (2) when rules and policies are difficult to understand or interpret; and (3) when rules appear unfair or unreasonable. Still other causes of conflict may include student competition, the demand for individual attention, differences in perception, or even teacher misbehavior. Kearney, Plax, and Burroughs (1991) suggest that teachers who deliver boring lectures, stray from the subject matter, employ unfair testing procedures, present confusing lectures, and return student work late may invoke conflicts with students.

According to Hocker and Wilmot (1991), "Conflict is an express struggle between at least two interdependent parties who perceive incompatible goals, scarce rewards, and interference from the other party in achieving their goals" (p. 12). Conflict is normally viewed as negative. Conflict can, however, be positive in the classroom when it prompts the teacher and students to alter behavior in such a manner that the learning environment is enhanced (Hocker, 1986; Jamieson & Thomas, 1974; Johnson & Johnson, 1985; Kreidler, 1984; Powell, 1990; Williams & Winkworth, 1974). According to Hocker (1986), "The goals of any productive conflict are to solve the immediate problem represented in the conflict and to enhance the interpersonal relationship to the extent that such is needed to continue working together. If the problem is solved but the relationship worsens, the conflict is not settled" (p. 74). Although these are the goals of productive conflict, research suggests that students typically recall conflict with teachers as unproductive and destructive (Branon, 1972). Wilmot (1976) reports that students feel angry, frustrated, misunderstood, and revengeful. If this is the case, then perhaps we as educators should reexamine the way that we have been investigating and handling issues of power, compliance, and conflict in the classroom.

Critical Reflection

Recently, the "Power in the Classroom" research has been called into question. Burleson and Waltman (1993) report that fifty years of observational research on teachers' use of discipline strategies suggests that teachers rely heavily on negative and antisocial strategies to correct student behavior, whereas other researchers have determined that teachers report a greater use of prosocial strategies (Kearney et al., 1985; Richmond et al., 1987; Roach, 1991). These findings suggest that what teachers say they do is quite different from what they actually do. Waltman (1995) further questions the validity of the checklist of strategies (BATs) that teachers report using. Because positive and prosocial behaviors may be seen as socially desirable, they may be falsely reported with greater likelihood. That is, teachers may desire to be prosocial, but their actual practices may in reality reflect something altogether different.

These questions bring up the need for critical reflection of the research in effective classroom management. Because theory and research help us as educators to make informed decisions on the practices we employ, it is imperative that we begin to ask questions about the nature of the research being reported. Sprague (1992) advocates such critical reflection as she comments that instructional communication research, and power research specifically, has been narrow in focus because researchers have failed to ask a number of important questions. Sprague says that we must consider the social implications of the questions we ask and consider whether "our current approach to scholarship [has] a liberating or dehumanizing effect on students and teachers" (p. 5). Critical reflection of scholarly research allows us to ask questions about what should be, focus on ethical standards and social change, and rationally investigate alternative descriptions of what is taking place in the classroom. In doing so, Sprague (1992) offers six questions that should be asked:

1. Why do schools exist?
2. What do teachers do?
3. What is the nature of development?
4. What is knowledge and how is curriculum established?
5. How does language function in education?
6. How does power function in the classroom?

This last question deals specifically with the power research. Sprague (1992) argues that the research is "a one-dimensional view of power, that is, a view limited to the conscious intent of A to get B to do something that B would not do otherwise" (p. 15). Sprague maintains that communication should play a central role in the *creation* of knowledge and that students should not be kept in a passive role. Sprague argues that power should be negotiated among teachers and students and that the classroom is a place of mutual rather than specifically teacher influence.

Alternative Perspective

As stated previously, the power research examines issues involving teacher control or influence and offers suggestions for methods of controlling student behavior. More recently, Simonds (1995) provides an alternative for studying challenges in the classroom. Rather than looking at issues of teacher influence, Simonds explores the nature of teacher–student interactions from a relational perspective where classroom expectations are negotiated, transactional, and mutually influenced.

Consistent with the transactional perspective of this text, Simonds describes the classroom as a unique culture where the teacher is the only one who knows, in advance, what the expectations of that particular classroom are. Because the teacher, as such, is the only "native," students must identify the teacher's expectations and speculate about the strategies necessary to meet these expectations successfully. Students are likely to face uncertainty about the rules, norms, and expectations of the classroom and may attempt to reduce uncertainty in a variety of ways. They can observe the culture to determine expectations, ask questions, or test the rules or norms in the form of a challenge. Simonds (1997b) states that challenge behavior occurs when a student behaves contrary to implicit or explicit classroom expectations. Such behaviors can be motivated by a lack of classroom understanding or the "cultural" expectations of the class. For example, if a teacher does not communicate a certain expectation (or if the expectation is implicit), the student may want to know what will happen if she behaves a certain way. However, if the teacher does communicate an explicit expectation, the student may want to know if the teacher will follow through with the consequences for violation. In this sense, challenge behavior is a strategy that students use to share ownership of the classroom culture. It may be motivated by uncertainty and is manifested by behaviors that are contrary to teacher expectations. To test whether challenge behavior was motivated by student uncertainty, Simonds (1995) examined the relationship between teacher clarity and the frequency of student challenges and found that as a teacher's clarity increased, student challenges decreased.

Simonds (1997b) notes that challenge behavior, if addressed appropriately, can serve to foster a supportive relational climate. For example, if a student is uncertain about a classroom rule and challenges that rule, then the resulting communication between the teacher and the student can enhance their relationship and the climate of the class. Teachers need to be able to identify student challenges so that they can adapt their communication practices accordingly—that is, provide the information the student needs to know.

Simonds (1997b) describes four types of challenge behavior and provides an instrument with which teachers can identify the frequency of challenges in their classrooms (see Table 9.4). *Evaluation* challenges occur when students question the nature of testing procedures or grades received. *Procedural* challenges occur when students test the rules and norms, whether implicit or explicit, in the classroom. *Practicality* challenges occur when students question the relevance of the course or certain tasks. *Power* challenges occur when students try to influence the behavior of the teacher or other students in the class.

Several challenge behavior scenarios are provided in Box 9.3. You will want to refer to these as you may encounter them in your own class. In considering how you would approach these situations in advance, you will be taking the first steps in your own classroom management efforts.

The challenge behavior research examines the role of the student, as well as the teacher, in the influence process. Simonds (1997b) would argue that communication between teachers and students plays a vital role in the culture of the classroom. Research from both the teacher influence and mutual influence perspectives provides educators with insight for managing classrooms. For example, scholars (e.g., Barraclough et al., 1992; Kearney et al., 1984; and McCroskey et al., 1983) from the power research perspective would suggest to teachers that they use prosocial statements to gain student compliance; whereas Simonds (1997b) would direct teachers to clearly communicate classroom expectations prior to the need for a student challenge. We close this chapter with a few more practical suggestions.

PRACTICAL SUGGESTIONS

Handling Minor Misbehaviors

It's important to remember that you need not intervene every time a problem arises in your classroom. Some problems are minor. For example, if one student briefly whispers to another, there's no reason to call attention to it. When behavior continues or threatens to spread to other students, you can no longer ignore it.

TABLE 9.4   Critical Incidents Frequency Report

Complete the following information based on the course you attended just prior to the one you are currently in. **All responses will remain anonymous. Please answer as honestly as possible.** In this section you are asked to recall how often you have observed students in your class engaging in the following behaviors. Choose only one answer for each behavior.

Generally, students…	very often	often	sometimes	almost never	never
are absent excessively.	___	___	___	___	___
beg for higher grades in class.	___	___	___	___	___
question instructor's knowledge of content.	___	___	___	___	___
question the relevance of tasks to everyday life.	___	___	___	___	___
want to receive full credit for late work.	___	___	___	___	___
compare scores with other students.	___	___	___	___	___
attempt to control when a task will be done.	___	___	___	___	___
question the importance of subject matter.	___	___	___	___	___
offer "off the wall" examples in class discussion.	___	___	___	___	___
question fairness of grading.	___	___	___	___	___
don't want to participate.	___	___	___	___	___
complain that theories do not apply to real life.	___	___	___	___	___
come to class late.	___	___	___	___	___
question grades on assignments.	___	___	___	___	___
attempt to embarrass the instructor.	___	___	___	___	___
question why the class should be required.	___	___	___	___	___
talk during class.	___	___	___	___	___
argue over test questions.	___	___	___	___	___
interrupt instructor to reinforce their own opinion.	___	___	___	___	___
question relevance of concepts being discussed.	___	___	___	___	___

"Critical Incidents Frequency Report," from Simonds, C. J. (Fall 1997). *Communication Research Reports, 14*(4) 481–492. Used by permission.

■ ■ ■ ■ ■ ■

BOX 9.3
CHALLENGE BEHAVIOR SCENARIOS

- John comments on the difficulty of an exam as he turns it in. Later, as you are going over the exam, John persists in questioning the validity of specific items.
- You are explaining an upcoming assignment. Sherry raises her hand to say, "I don't understand why we have to do this. How will I ever be able to use this in the real world?"
- Jim began the semester by coming to class late occasionally. As the semester progressed, his tardiness began to disrupt the class. Sometimes he would come in as late as fifteen minutes after class started.
- As you are lecturing, Sally interrupts to state an opinion that is contrary to the position in the textbook. You diplomatically points out that there is little evidence to support Sally's view and continue the lecture. A few minutes later, Sally interrupts again to reiterate her original opinion.
- After you return presentation grades to your students, you notice that some of them are comparing scores. After class, Bill comes up to you to discuss his grade. Bill believes he should have received a higher score because he did as well as Cathy did and Cathy received a better grade than he did.
- You are lecturing when Pam asks, "How does this information relate to our lives? I mean, is this really important?"
- While you are lecturing, you notice that Chris and Tom are discussing matters irrelevant to class. After several nonverbal hints, you have to stop the lecture and ask them to please stop talking. A few days later, you notice Chris and Tom engaged in another conversation while a student is giving a presentation.
- During a class activity, you notice that Robert is not participating. When asked to participate, Robert says, "I don't feel like it." As the activity progresses, you notice that Robert has drawn other students away from the activity.

Good and Brophy (1987) suggest that minor misbehavior is fairly easy to eliminate by any one or a combination of the following:

1. *Eye contact.* If eye contact can be established, it usually is enough by itself to return attention to the task at hand. To make sure the message is received, the teacher may want to add a head nod or other gesture such as looking at the book the student is supposed to be reading.

Eye contact becomes doubly effective for stopping minor problems when the teacher regularly scans the room. Because students will know that the teacher regularly scans the room, they will tend to look at the teacher when they are misbehaving (to see if they are being watched). This makes it easier for the teacher to intervene through eye contact. Teachers who do not scan the room properly will have difficulty using eye contact in these situations, because they usually will have to wait longer before students look at them.

2. *Touch and gesture.* When the students are close by, the teacher does not need to wait until eye contact can be established. Instead, the teacher can use a simple touch or gesture to get their attention. This is especially effective in small group situations. A light tap, perhaps followed by a gesture toward the book, will get the message across without any need for verbalization.

Gestures and physical signals are also helpful in dealing with events going on in different parts of the room. If eye contact can be established, the teacher may be able to communicate messages by shaking the head, placing a finger to the lips, or pointing. These gestures should be used when possible, because they are less disruptive than leaving the group or speaking to students across the room. In general, touch and gesture are most useful in the early grades, where much teaching is done in small groups and where distraction is a frequent problem. Touching would be unwise with some adolescents who resent any attempt by a teacher to touch them.

3. *Physical closeness.* When the teacher is checking seat work or moving about the room, he can often eliminate minor student behavior problems simply by moving close to the students involved. If the students know what they are supposed to be doing, the physical presence of the teacher will motivate them to get busy. This technique is especially useful with older elementary students.

4. *Asking for responses.* During lessons or group activities, the simplest method of returning students' attention may be to ask them a question or call for a response. This request automatically compels attention, and it does so without mentioning the misbehavior.

Handling Disruptive Students

Sometimes punishment is unavoidable. You, however, not the principal, should do the punishing. Sending a student to the principal may work on a short-term basis, but sooner or later you must "come to grips" with behavior problems in your classroom. You must take responsibility for them. Deferring to someone else should be a last resort.

When punishment becomes necessary, communicate to the student that you are punishing him only because he has left you no other alternative. Your actions and paralanguage should communicate concern for the student as well as regret that punishment must be used. In other words, it should be clear to the student that he has no one to blame but himself. His own behavior is the cause for the punishment.

When punishing, several guidelines are important. Make the reasons for the punishment clear, as well as the type of punishment. Don't make threats or punishments you can't "make good." In addition, "make the punishment fit the crime." In other words, the punishment should be related to, and proportional to, the offense. If a student plagiarizes, she should receive no credit for that particular paper, but should not fail the course.

Curwin and Mendler (1988) suggest that teachers need to think in terms of consequences rather than punishment. Consequences are simple, direct, related to the rule that's been broken, and instructive. They also preserve a student's dignity. Punishment, however, is not related to a natural extension of the rule and tends to generate anxiety, resentment, and hostility in the student. Following are some examples of the difference between consequences and punishments:

Rule: All trash must be thrown in the basket.

Consequence	*Punishment*
Pick your trash up off the floor.	Apologize to the teacher in front of the whole class.

Rule: Tests and homework must be completed by yourselves unless group work is assigned. There is no copying other students' work.

Consequence	*Punishment*
Do the test or homework again under supervision.	Write 100 times "I will not copy other students' work."

Rule: No talking when someone else is talking. If you want to speak, wait until the current speaker has finished.

Consequence	*Punishment*
Wait five minutes before speaking.	Sit in the hall for the entire period.

Rule: You must be in your seat by five minutes after the bell.

Consequence	*Punishment*
You are responsible to get any information or make up any work that you missed by being late.	Miss entire class sitting in the principal's office, then make up work.

Whenever conflict arises, control your anger. Pause before you react to the disruptive behavior. Think for a moment so you don't overreact and designate a punishment you can't enforce. In addition, the momentary pause may give the student time to "settle down"—to get over his anger or resentment.

IN SUM

As teachers, we have great influence in the education environment. Because social influence is an inherent part of teaching, it is important to consider the ethical responsibilities that educators must practice and teach. Many features of the classroom require ethical decision making, such as teacher–student relationships, evaluation procedures, and classroom management issues. These and other issues have an impact on the climate of the classroom and have the potential to influence learning. Through critical reflection, we can make informed judgments of how to incorporate theory and research into our own classroom practices.

ACTIVITIES

9.1 In triads, role play the following communication interactions. Two people should role play and one should observe. Discuss what occurs.

Teacher–Administrator: The principal has called you in to discuss a student in your class. The student has complained that your grading practices are unfair. The student in question has caused considerable problems for you in the past. You don't particularly like the student.

Parent–Teacher: A student in your class consistently performs poorly. You think the student should be retained a second year. You have called the parent in to discuss this possibility.

Teacher–Teacher: You are in the faculty lounge. The school year is just beginning, and you are reading your class lists. Another teacher begins to discuss one of the students on your list—one who was "academically slow" and a "behavior problem" for the teacher the year before.

9.2   Create and evaluate your own ethical dilemmas. In groups, create an ethical dilemma that might take place in a classroom or school setting. Some topics might include questions of course requirements, evaluating students, favoritism, enforcement of rules, protecting students from harassment, limiting disruptions, accommodating a range of opinions, and encouraging active participation. Once the dilemmas are created, each group should share them with the class and discuss possible ethical standards to employ in deciding how to handle each dilemma (refer to this section in your text).

FURTHER READING

Downs, J. (1992). Dealing with hostile and oppositional students. *College Teaching, 40,* 106–108.

   Downs outlines eight "Steps toward Harmony."

Johannesen, R. L. (1990). *Ethics in human communication.* Prospect Heights, IL: Waveland Press.

   The author includes a more thorough discussion of the standards for evaluating ethical decision making.

O'Hair, M., & Balse, J. (1992). Power and politics in the classroom: Implications for teacher education. *Action in Teacher Education, 14,* 10–17.

   The authors present an overview of five types of power and their effects in the classroom, and outline four implications for teacher education.

Richmond, V., & McCroskey, J. (1992). *Power in the classroom: Communication, control and concern.* Edina, MN: Burgess.

   This text presents a status report on what instruction communication specialists understand about power in the classroom.

Additional Resource

Nyquist, J., Wulff, D., & Quigley, B. (1983). *Encounters with teaching.* Annandale, VA: Speech Communication Association.

   This video presents teacher–student interactions that beginning teachers find difficult to manage. The video is to be used as an impetus to class discussion on topics ranging from student challenges of evaluation procedures to minority issues. An instructor's guide accompanies the video and helps to facilitate discussion.

CHAPTER TEN

COMMUNICATION CONCERNS

Objectives

After reading this chapter you should be able to:

- Define sexism.
- Describe the extent of sexism in the classroom.
- Describe the effects of sexism on classroom interaction.
- Describe the effect of racism and ethnicity in the classroom.

The teaching–learning process is primarily a communication process that relies largely on the interactive behaviors of students and teachers. Any variable that prohibits effective communication can adversely affect the learning process.

In this chapter we discuss two communication concerns—sexism, and racism and ethnicity.

SEXISM IN THE CLASSROOM

As Wood (2001) tells us, "schools teach us, who is important and who is not; who influenced the directions of history, science and literature, and social organization …and contribute in major ways to the process of gendering individuals" (p. 221). And despite several decades of research suggesting problems in our educational system in terms of gender bias, the dominant mode in education remains geared to males. The system stresses objectivity, separateness, competitiveness, and hierarchical structure (Palmer, 1998; Simonds & Cooper, 2001).

Schools teach us in a variety of ways—through curriculum, educational materials, and classroom interaction. We examine each of these in relation to gender bias, discuss progress made in each area, and consider areas still needing improvement. Before we begin, it's extremely important to remember that although the focus has been on females in recent years, sex discrimination in education affects males as well (Sadker & Sadker, 1994; Sommers, 2000). Research suggests that

- from grade school to high school, boys receive lower marks on their report cards

- more boys than girls drop out and repeat grades
- more boys than girls get suspended from school
- boys are designated as learning disabled and labeled emotionally disturbed more often than girls
- boys are four times as likely to commit suicide as girls (Chethik, 1994, p. 5)

Other investigations confirm these findings. For example, in 1992, the American Association of University Women Educational Foundation commissioned a comprehensive review of 1,331 studies of gender and educational practices. The result was a report entitled "How Schools Shortchange Girls" ("Sexism in the Schoolhouse," 1992) in which evidence was amassed to show that female students continue to receive less attention, less encouragement, and less serious regard than their male peers. This new report focused on emerging gaps in areas, such as technology, that threatened to disadvantage girls as they confronted the demands of the twenty-first century. For example, the report suggested that technology was the new "boys' club" in public schools. Whereas boys programmed and problem solved with computers, girls used computers for word processing. In *Gender Gaps: Where Schools Still Fail Our Children* (1998) the foundation documented the progress and failure of schools in providing a fair and equitable education since 1992. Synthesizing 1,000 research studies, *Gender Gaps* reviewed issues of historic concern for girls—math and science enrollment, high-stakes standardized testing, extracurricular activities, and health and development risks—and new areas, such as technology and school-to-work programs. The report indicates that from 1992 to 1994, girls' enrollments in advance placement (AP) and honors calculus and chemistry improved relative to boys. And the 1997 addition of a writing skills section on the PSAT raised girls' scores and narrowed the gender gap from 4.5 to 2.7 points. Yet, despite the progress in certain areas, the report indicated that gender gaps remained:

- High school girls and boys took similar numbers of science courses, but boys were more likely than girls to take all three core science courses (biology, chemistry, and physics) before they graduated.
- Girls took fewer computer science and computer design courses.
- Boys took fewer English courses.
- Girls enrolled in AP classes in larger numbers, but fewer girls than boys received the high scores on AP tests needed for college credit.
- Girls clustered in traditionally female occupations in school-to-work and vocational education programs.
- Girls continued to experience risks to their health and development, such as sexual harassment and abuse, pregnancy, substance abuse, and delinquency.
- Boys repeated grades and dropped out of school at a higher rate, but girls who were held back were more likely to drop out.
- Girls continued to consider a narrower set of careers than boys did.

In March 2000, the National Center for Education Statistics (the primary federal entity for collecting, analyzing, and reporting data related to education in the United States) released *Trends in Educational Equity of Girls and Women* (U.S. Department of Education, 2000). The report suggests

- Females consistently outperform males in reading and writing.
- There are no more gender differences favoring male students in mathematics and science.
- Achievement gaps appear more closely related to attitudes than to course taking.
- Females are just as likely as males to use computers at home and school (some researchers note that females are more likely to use computers recreationally to pursue hobbies and e-mail friends whereas males use the computer to further professional endeavors (Cyber Dialogue, 1999).
- Females and males tend to participate in different types of extracurricular activities. Females are more likely than their male peers to participate in music or other performing arts, belong to academic clubs, work on the school newspaper or yearbook, or participate in the student council or government. Males are more likely than females to play on athletic teams.
- Male and female bachelor's degree recipients tend to choose different majors. Female recipients are much less likely than men to major in the sciences, computer science, and engineering. Males are much less likely than females to major in education, health, and psychology. These choices could have long-term consequences in the labor market. The fields men choose tend to lead to higher paying jobs than the fields women choose. The National Committee on Pay Equity suggests that a woman has to work a full year plus a little more than three months (to April 8) to earn what a man earns in just twelve months (Stewart, 1999). In 1997, women earned median pay of $24,973, 74.1 percent of men's pay (Stewart, 1999).
- Women have made substantial progress at the graduate level overall, but they still earn fewer than half of the degrees in many fields. Women's progress toward earning an equal share of first professional degrees has been notable. In 1970, 5 percent of the law degrees, 8 percent of medical degrees, and 1 percent of dentistry degrees were awarded to women. In 1996, the corresponding percentages were 44, 41, and 36.

Curriculum Material

In the 1970s researchers examining the most heavily used elementary textbooks in first through sixth grades reported disturbing results (Weitzman & Rizzo, 1975). For example, in social studies textbooks, only 33 percent of the illustrations included females. In one series designed to teach reading, 102 stories were about boys and 35 were about girls. Mliner (1977) examined elementary and junior high school math and science texts. In these textbooks, females were pictured as Indian dolls or witches or as participating in activities such as skipping rope and buying balloons. Males were pictured as sailors, kings, bakers, circus performers, band members, and balloon sellers. Males were pictured fifteen times for every one female pictured. More recently, Purcell and Stewart (1990) and Tetenbaum and Pearson (1989) found that sex stereotypes such as these persist. Although many changes have been made since that time, comparing three decades of science material, Nilsen (1987) found that artists were still drawing three times as many pictures of males as females. In addition, in the majority of books examined in this study, the word *man* was used to describe people in general, and few books depicted women in scientific careers. Such discrepancies present negative images of females and reinforce gender stereotypes. Thus, although more females may be taking math and science classes, some curriculum materials still tend to reinforce traditional gender stereotypes.

Discrepancies also exist in the number of male and female authors included in textbooks. In an early survey of English literature anthologies, the seventeen books examined included selections by 147 male authors and only twenty-five female authors (Arlow & Froschel, 1976). Carlson (1989) reports that a survey of high-school-level anthologies still revealed a preponderance of male authors. One anthology, for example, included more than ninety selections by male authors and only eight by female authors. Most anthologies dealing with speech communication feature more speeches by men (Campbell, 1991; Vonnegut, 1992), and some history textbooks devote only about 2 percent of their pages to women (Sadker & Sadker, 1994) whereas some art textbooks discuss male artists rather than female artists (Sadker & Sadker, 1994).

Generally, gender stereotypes may be found in all types of textbooks (Carter & Spitzack, 1989; Cawyer et al., 1994; Ferree & Hall, 1990; Kramarae, Schultz, & O'Barr, 1984). Hurd and Brabeck (1997) conducted a content analysis of the presentation of women in sixty-nine college textbooks published between 1970 and 1990; Stone (1996) examined twenty-five introductory sociology texts to determine patterns of race–ethnic coverage; Hogben and Waterman (1997) conducted a content analysis of diversity issues covered in twenty-eight introductory psychology texts. The results of all these studies indicated that women and ethnic groups were underrepresented.

A recent investigation of public speaking textbooks (Hanson, 1999) found that the mean number of pages devoted to discussing gender issues was 7.26. Sixteen of the seventeen texts analyzed pictured men in power positions more frequently than women and all texts pictured men more frequently in all photographs.

Feiner and Morgan (1987) analyzed twenty-one major introductory economic texts and found that the number of pages that even make a passing reference to economic topics of special interest to women and minorities is extremely small. The number of pages referring to women or minorities ranged from 2 to 22. The average number of pages per book is 800. As Feiner and Roberts (1990) write

> The almost total silence of the texts on the economic status of minorities speaks louder than words: The student cannot help but absorb the message that these are matters of relative unimportance. (p. 179)

With the adoption of nonsexist guidelines during the past decade, many textbook publishers have made substantial progress. Harwood (1992) notes that "a cursory look through any high school Spanish or French book will, for the most part, reveal an equal number of illustrations of men and women and a fair depiction of their roles" (p. 16). Nevertheless, some authors have made relatively few changes to increase the visibility of females and to decrease the stereotyping of males and females. For example, the "nonbiased" material is often added to the center or end of a textbook without any attempt to integrate it into the overall format of the book. Peterson (1994) quotes one student as saying, "You'll see women's pictures all put in one chapter—'great women in history'—rather than throughout the book" (p. 2D). And Harwood (1992) describes a popular high school Latin textbook that rarely uses the word *she* in practice sentences and depicts more than two-thirds of the characters in the reading lessons as male.

In addition to textbooks, educators are being encouraged to use other books to supplement the basic curriculum. The image of males and females in literature—from a child's first picture book to adult best-sellers—can influence the way in which males and females see themselves and, thus, can influence their communication.

In many ways, children's literature reflects and reinforces gender stereotypes. Numerical disparities and stereotyped behavior patterns and characteristics reflected in children's literature may help teach girls to undervalue themselves and teach boys to believe that they must always strive to be stereotypically masculine.

Although the situation continues to improve, females are not included in children's books in numbers that reflect their presence in the general population. Four studies have examined how gender is treated in books that have won the Caldecott Medal or the Newbery Award (Cooper, 1989; Cooper, 1993b; Kolbe & LaVoie, 1981; Weitzman, Eifler, Hokada, & Ross, 1972). The Caldecott Medal is given by the Children's Service Committee of the American Library Association for the most distinguished picture book of the year. The Newbery Award is given by the American Library Association for the best book for school-age children. From 1967 to 1972, the ratio of male characters to female characters in Caldecott Medal books was 11:1. From 1972 to 1979, the ratio of male characters to female characters in Newbery Award books was 1.8:1. Interestingly, from 1980 to 1987, the ratio of human male characters to human female characters in Caldecott Medal books was 2:1, and the ratio in Newbery Award winners was 6:1. From 1967 to 1987, only fourteen books (out of a total of ninety-seven) depicted women working outside the home.

Although numerical disparities seem to be decreasing in children's books, the role models presented for children have not become less stereotyped. The three studies cited previously also examined the stereotyped behavior patterns and characteristics depicted in children's books. The 1967 to 1972 education study showed that when females were illustrated, gender-stereotyped characterizations were reinforced: girls were passive, boys were active; girls followed and served others, boys led and rescued others. Adult men and women in these books also were stereotyped: women were depicted as wives and mothers, whereas men held a variety of occupations. In the years from 1972 to 1987, gender stereotypes were still prevalent. From 1967 to 1972, all eighteen Caldecott Medal books portrayed traditional gender stereotypes; from 1972 to 1979, seventeen out of nineteen did; and from 1980 to 1987, twenty-six out of thirty-one did. Of the twenty-nine Newbery Award books for 1980 to 1987, twenty-two contained traditional gender stereotypes.

Caldecott Medal winners suggest similar patterns. Heinz (1987) examined the occupations of characters in Caldecott Medal–winning books from 1971 to 1984. Males were shown in three times as many occupations as females. Almost half of the females pursuing any type of work were depicted in homemaker roles. Dougherty and Engel (1987) analyzed Caldecott winners and honor books from 1981 to 1985 and found that although numerical disparities decreased considerably, gender-stereotyped images did not.

Gender-stereotyped portrayals do not occur only in Newbery Award and Caldecott Medal books (Peterson & Lach, 1990). In an analysis of nursery rhymes and fairy tales (the first literature to which most children are exposed), Donlan (1972) found three recurring types of female characters: the sweet little old lady, the beautiful young heroine, and the aggressive female. The first two types, sweet little old lady and beautiful heroine, were both depicted as lovable and incompetent. The aggressive females took many forms: witch, domineering housewife (who functions as wife, mother, or stepmother), and shrew (cruel, vain, greedy, and demanding). Donlan concluded that in children's literature, women may be portrayed as ineffectual creatures who need to be dominated by men or as aggressive monsters who must be destroyed by men.

Examining 2,216 children's books published from 1900 to 1984, Grauerholz and Pescosolido (1989) found that males were the dominant characters and females conformed to the passive stereotype. In a random sampling of 1,380 school library books in grades K through 6, female athletes frequently fell victim to gender stereotyping. Boys were shown participating in a variety of individual sports, and girls predominated only in traditionally feminine activities, such as dance. In team sports, thirty-four out of thirty-eight baseball players were male, as were seven out of eight basketball players (Weiller & Higgs, 1989).

Cooper (1987) explored the gender stereotypes in children's books concerning stepfamilies. She examined forty-two books (from 1975 to 1983) available in libraries in the Chicago metropolitan area and found numerous gender stereotypes. Women worked, but in stereotyped jobs, such as receptionists, secretaries, or nurses. When women were employed outside the home, they neglected their children or became aggressive. They were relatively passive and focused primarily on their appearances. Men were depicted as lawyers and doctors who were usually inept at simple household duties. They were caring and sensitive, but only to a point; when problems were not resolved quickly, they became impatient. In updates to this study, Cooper (1994, 2000) found that although images are improving, stepmothers continued to be portrayed in negative ways.

Barton (1984) suggested that the gender stereotyping of male characters in children's literature has been greatly ignored. As a result, this author analyzed more than fifty children's books and found that books depicting sensitive male role models did exist, but not in great numbers. Vaughan–Roberson, Tompkins, Hitchcock, and Oldham (1989) examined sexism in basal readers. The study was conducted to determine if positive female traits (such as nurturing) are attributed to male main characters. Their analysis indicated that, although classically positive female traits appear in some male characters, the overall composite and, to a lesser degree, depiction of individual characters are dominated by masculine stereotypes, such as independence and a willingness to take risks.

Classroom Interaction

Numerous studies have shown that (1) boys get teachers' attention by being straightforward and unreserved, (2) teachers praise boys more often, (3) boys receive more academic help, and (4) teachers are more likely to accept boys' ideas or opinions during classroom discussion (see research reviewed in Condravy, Skirboll, & Taylor, 1998; Simonds & Cooper, 2001; Stewart, Cooper, & Stewart, 2003).

Most of these studies have focused on student participation using a range of methodologies—reviews of anecdotal reports, observational studies focusing on both quantitative and qualitative variables, and surveys of students perceptions. In general these studies support the idea that males and females experience classroom interaction differently.

For example, Karp and Yoels (1976) found that male students accounted for a majority of interactions in classes, 75.4 percent of those occurring in male taught classes and 57 percent in classes taught by female instructors, even though the classes contained nearly equal numbers of female and male students. Krupnick (1985) and her research team reviewed videotapes of twenty-four undergraduate classes and examined the duration of speech. Regardless of the demographics of the classroom, female students never spoke longer than male students. Male students spoke much longer in classrooms where the instructor was male. Female students spoke almost three times as long in classes taught by female instructors than in classes taught by male instructors. Hutchinson and Beadle (1992) observed the interaction of a group of twenty-six students who attended two seminars, one taught by a female and one taught by a male professor. These researchers found that women and men made proportionately equitable numbers of contributions in the female professor's seminar, but in the male professor's seminar, male students spoke more often and for longer periods of time than the women. The female professor achieved gender parity by more closely managing the discussion, designating specific students to speak. The male professor more often allowed students to initiate discussion at will.

This pattern seems to be consistent at all educational levels. Sadker and Sadker (1994) observed teacher–student interactions in 100 fourth, sixth, and eighth grade classrooms. Boys consistently out talked and out participated girls, primarily because teachers allowed boys to call out, responded more positively to boys than to girls when they did call out, called on boys more frequently, and gave them more feedback on their answers.

The research studies on classroom interaction are not unequivocal. Some studies have found that although males may not talk more than females, the communication of males and females focuses on different things. For example, Pearson and West (1991) examined question asking. They audiotaped each of fifteen classes for one hour and discovered that although female and male students did not differ significantly in the frequency of questions that they asked overall, males asked more questions than females in classes taught by males. Constantinople, Cornelius, and Gray (1988) observed forty-eight classes of various disciplines. They found that male students made more follow-up comments and volunteered information more frequently than the women. Male students were more likely to have their comments acknowledged or expanded on than were female students.

Some studies have examined the perceptions of students and instructors. Nadler and Nadler (1990) surveyed 272 undergraduate classes. Males in this study did not report initiating more interactions or receiving more supportive behavior than the women did. Women did not report that they received more dominant behaviors than male students did. Males did indicate that they disagreed with the professor and were more comfortable doing so than did the women. However, this difference was not statistically significant.

In a survey of more than 700 students in thirty-one classes, Crawford and MacLeod (1990) indicated that male students perceived that they had volunteered more often, were called on more frequently even when their hands were not raised, and were responded to more favorably when they asked questions. Female students responded that they did not volunteer as often as male students, did not engage as frequently in class discussion, and did not perceive that their contributions were received as positively as those of the male students.

Auster and MacRone (1994) interviewed 132 students. Their results indicated that male students were significantly more likely than female students to report participating often in class and more likely to feel very comfortable in class. Both male and female students indicated they participated the most when a female professor taught the class.

In a survey of 1,000 students in fifty-one classes, Fassinger (1995) found that male students perceived themselves as more confident and involved in the classroom, whereas female students perceived themselves as more interested in class and others' comments. Females also perceived they were better prepared for class than did their male classmates.

Condravy, Skirboll, and Taylor (1998) reported the results of a faculty survey (187 responses: 110 male, 77 female). Both male and female faculty perceived that (1) male students interrupt more frequently and assume leadership roles more frequently than females and (2) female students seek outside help and are more open to constructive criticism than are male students. Male faculty perceived that female students participate more and volunteered responses more frequently than male students. In contrast, female faculty perceived that male students participated more and volunteered responses more. Female faculty perceived male students more defensive and more confident than did male faculty.

Research has examined not only the perception that students have of themselves and the perception that teachers have of students but also the perceptions students have of their instructors. Rosenfeld and Jarrard (1985) examined how the perceived sexism of college professors affected classroom climate. They found that students who perceived their male teachers to be highly sexist described their classes as less supportive and less innovative than those taught by nonsexist male teachers. In a follow-up study (Rosenfeld & Jarrard, 1985), the researchers examined coping mechanisms used by students in classes taught by sexist and nonsexist teachers. Coping mechanisms used by students in sexist male teachers' classes were passive (not doing what the teacher asked, hiding feelings) when students liked the class. If students did not like the class and perceived the male teacher as sexist, students used a more active coping mechanism: forming alliances against the teacher. Generally, teachers in disliked classes are perceived as more sexist than teachers in liked classes. Also, male teachers are perceived as more sexist than female teachers.

Bachen, McLaughlin, and Garcia (1999) examined how students' stereotypes of gender roles affected how they evaluated their instructors. The researchers concluded that female students' identification with female faculty was strong and probably constituted a measure of educational success for those students. Male students did not rate female faculty differently from male faculty, but their qualitative comments indicated that males were more comfortable with female faculty when the females seemed to be adapting to a more male style in the classroom. Extant research indicates that female instructors are consistently rated as significantly less credible than male instructors (Anderson & Miller, 1997; Centra & Gaubatz, 2000; Hargett, 1999).

Most of the research on sexism and classroom interaction has not directly considered gender. Studies that classify teachers and students according to their gender rather than biological sex may yield more clear-cut findings than simply classifying teachers and students according to biological sex. Several communication researchers have begun to examine this area of classroom communication. For example, teacher-effectiveness research suggests that qualities of effective teaching can be grouped according to stereotypically masculine (for example, self-confident, independent, logical, objective, and aggressive) and stereotypically feminine (for example, warm, gentle, facilitative, and concerned for others) styles (see research reviewed by Wheeless & Potorti, 1987).

Bray and Howard (1980) find that androgynous teachers score higher than stereotypically masculine teachers in both student satisfaction and progress, and higher than stereotypically feminine teachers in terms of pupil progress. Wheeless and Potorti (1987) find that androgynous teachers produce the highest levels of student learning, followed by traditionally feminine, traditionally masculine, and undifferentiated teachers. Similar results are reported by Jordan, McGreal, and Wheeless (1990). In general, students are most positively affected by teachers who show concern for them as individuals but who are also able to show some sense of independence and classroom leadership.

An interesting aspect of gender in the classroom that has only recently begun to be examined is sexual orientation. Russ, Simonds, and Hunt (2002) examined the influence of instructor sexual orientation on perceptions of teacher credibility. The purpose was to determine if college students perceive gay teachers as less credible than straight teachers. In addition, the authors explored the role of teacher credibility in terms of perceived student learning. In order to examine these variables, a male confederate presented a lecture on cultural influences to 154 undergraduate students enrolled in eight separate introductory communication courses. The confederate's sexual orientation was systematically manipulated. Students perceived a gay teacher as significantly less credible than a straight teacher. Students of a gay teacher perceived that they learned considerably less than did students of a straight teacher.

Sexual harassment is also an issue for concern. *Hostile Hallways: The AAUW Survey on Sexual Harassment in America's Schools* [American Association of University Women (AAUW)] represents the first national scientific study of sexual harassment in public schools. Based on the experiences of 1,632 students in grades 8 through 11, the researchers found that 85 percent of the girls and 76 percent of the boys surveyed had experienced sexual harassment. The survey also indicated that although both girls and boys experienced sexual harassment, sexual harassment takes a greater toll on girls; girls who have been harassed are more afraid in school and feel less confident about themselves than boys who have been harassed.

Specific studies bear out these findings. For example, Stepp (2001) surveyed college students and coaches involved in extracurricular speech and debate activities. She found that sexual harassment is widespread and that females are sexually harassed (defined as ranging from generalized sexist remarks or behavior to sexual assault) more than males.

RACE AND ETHNICITY IN THE CLASSROOM

Before we begin a discussion of race and ethnicity, several terms need to be defined. First, *stereotypes.* Stereotypes are generalizations about some group of people that oversimplify the group. When we stereotype, we categorize others based on easily identifiable characteristics. We then assume that certain attributes apply to all or most members of the group. Finally, we assume individual members of the category have the attributes associated with the group.

How do stereotypes affect our communication? When we stereotype we often make errors in our interpretation of another's behavior. Kunta and Sherman-Williams (1993) tell us

> Consider, for example, the unambiguous act of failing a test. Ethnic stereotypes may lead perceivers to attribute such failure to laziness if the actor is Asian but to low ability if the actor is Black. Thus stereotypes will affect judgments of the target's ability even if subjects base these judgments only on the act, because the stereotypes will determine the meaning of the act. (p. 97)

Stereotypes often lead to *prejudice.* Prejudice involves prejudging without knowledge or examination of the available data. When we say things such as, "Well, of course Junmei always gets the highest grade. Asians study all the time," we are communicating our prejudices.

When a negative attitude toward a group is translated into action, *discrimination* results. Discrimination is the process of treating individuals unequally on the basis of characteristics such as sex, age, ethnicity, race, or sexual orientation.

Racism categorizes individuals on the basis of their external physical characteristics, such as skin color, facial structure, eye shape, leading to prejudice and discrimination. Racism is a social construction. In other words, it is an attempt to give social meaning to physical differences. Race is biologically meaningless because biological variations blend from one racial category to another (Rogers & Steinfatt, 1999).

An *ethnic group* is a group of people who share a common culture that is usually based on nationality or language. In the United States the terms used to categorize ethnic groups are as follows (Rogers & Steinfatt, 1999):

Asian American or *Asian*—people who trace their origins to the Asian continent or to the Pacific Islands (for example, Korea, Japan, China, Samoa).

African American or *Black*—people who trace their origins to the sub-Saharan part of Africa. In the United States, *African American* is often the preferred term by black citizens of the United States, whereas black citizens of the Caribbean and Latin America prefer *black*.

Latino—people who trace their origins to Latin America or to Spain. *Chicano* refers to Mexican heritage. *Hispanic* is the term used by the U.S. Census Bureau for all of these individuals.

Native American—the native peoples of the United States.

White, Anglo American, and *European American*—persons of European background other than Spanish.

Cultural Dimensions

Race and ethnicity, like gender, are cultural in nature. In other words, our culture teaches us how to perceive these. In order to understand this, it is important to understand culture. Although there are several approaches to the study of culture, one that is helpful in the educational environment is Hofstede's (1991) work. In his view, four cultural dimensions affect what occurs in the classroom: individualism/ collectivism, power distance, uncertainty avoidance, and masculinity/femininity. The first of these is individualism/collectivism. In an individualistic culture, the focus for an individual is on her/himself and her/his immediate family (spouse, children). Collectivist cultures assume that any person belongs to one or more tight "in groups" from which she/he cannot detach. The "in group" (family, clan, organization) protects the interests of its members and in turn expects their permanent loyalty.

In terms of classroom behavior, in collectivist cultures students expect to learn how to do things for themselves, speak up in class only when called on personally by the teacher, and believe education is a way of gaining prestige within the social environment and of joining a higher status group. Formal harmony is important and neither a teacher nor a student should ever be made to lose face. In contrast, in individualistic cultures, students expect to learn how to learn, will speak up in class in response to a general invitation by the teacher, and believe education is a way of improving economic worth and self-respect based on ability and competence. Confrontation in the classroom is not necessarily avoided. Conflicts can be brought into the open and face-consciousness is weak.

In a collectivist culture the group is emphasized rather than the individual; harmony and circularity are emphasized. This explains why Native American children learn better in an environment that is noncompetitive, holistic, and cooperative. Similarly, an understanding of this dimension explains why Mexican children, because their culture emphasizes cooperation, allow others to share their homework or answers. This demonstrates solidarity, helpfulness, and generosity—all important characteristics of their collectivist culture (see research reviewed in Calloway-Thomas, Cooper, & Blake, 1999).

The second of Hofstede's dimensions, power distance, defines the extent to which the less powerful persons in a society accept inequality in power and consider it normal. In terms of classroom behavior, the power dimension suggests that in small power distance societies, the educational process is student centered. Students initiate communication, outline their own paths to learning, and can contradict the teacher. Thus, in the United States, where the power distance is small, students are encouraged to challenge the teacher and one another. The teacher encourages students to discuss and debate issues, to learn how to solve problems, and to create their own answers to the questions posed. Students prefer to learn through personal discovery and problem solving rather than through memorizing facts presented to them by an authority figure.

In contrast, in large power distance societies, the educational process is teacher centered. The teacher initiates all communication, outlines the paths of learning students should follow, and is never publicly criticized or contradicted. The emphasis is on the personal "wisdom" of the teacher. Thus, in Asian societies, the power difference between teacher and student is large. A Chinese student would never consider arguing with a teacher. The Asian student's role is to accept and respect the wisdom of the teacher. Asking questions is seen as a challenge to the teacher's authority or as an admission of the student's ignorance (Wallach & Metcalf, 1995).

Uncertainty avoidance is the third of Hofstede's dimensions. It defines the extent to which people within a culture are made nervous by situations that they perceive as unclear, unstructured, or unpredictable. Therefore, they try to avoid these situations by adhering to a strict code of behavior and a belief in absolute truth.

In terms of the classroom, in a weak uncertainty avoidance society, students feel comfortable in unstructured learning situations (vague objectives, no timetable, and broad assignments) and are rewarded for innovative approaches to problem solving. Teachers can say, "I don't know," interpret intellectual disagreements as stimulating, and ask parents for advice concerning their children. As you might suspect, in strong uncertainty avoidance societies, students feel most comfortable in structured learning situations (precise objectives, strict timetables, and detailed assignments) and are rewarded for accuracy in problem solving. Teachers are expected to know all the answers, interpret intellectual disagreement as personal disloyalty, and consider themselves experts who do not need parents' ideas.

Students in weak uncertainty avoidance cultures, such as the United States, Great Britain, Ireland, and India, tend to be competitive, need fewer instructions, and see conflict as stimulating. Students in strong uncertainty avoidance cultures, such as France, Chile, Spain, Portugal, and Japan, tend to prefer clear instructions, avoid conflict, and dislike competition.

The final dimension is masculinity/femininity. Cultures labeled as masculine strive for maximal distinction between what men and women are expected to do. Men are expected to be assertive, ambitious, and competitive; to strive for material success; and to respect whatever is big, fast, and strong. Women are expected to care for nonmaterial quality of life, children, and the weak, and to serve others. Feminist cultures define overlapping roles for the sexes. Thus, men do not have to be competitive and women do not have to do all the care giving. In feminine cultures, quality of life, interpersonal relationships, and concern for the weak are stressed as compared to masculine cultures in which material success and assertiveness are stressed.

In terms of the classroom, in masculine societies, academic performance is rewarded. Teachers openly praise good students because academic achievement is highly regarded and competition is fostered. Teachers use the best students as the norm. In contrast, in feminine societies, the students' social adaptations are rewarded. Teachers avoid openly praising students because academic achievement is less important than successful interpersonal relationships, and cooperation among students is fostered. Teachers use average students as the norm.

These cultural dimensions help to explain differences in how students learn and the problems that can arise in the classroom when the teacher and student come from cultures that differ on these dimensions. The way a student studies a problem differs across cultures. For example, Euro-American students tend to be topic centered. Their accounts of events focus on a single topic or closely related topics and are ordered in a linear fashion and lead to a resolution (Au, 1993). African American students often use a topic-associating style in which the student presents "a series of episodes linked to some person or theme. These links are implicit in the account and are not stated" (Au, 1996).

What happens when a teacher is topic centered and a student is topic associated? Stefani (1997) suggests that when the instructor is not familiar with the topic-associating style, he may inadvertently mistime questions or not allow a student to finish her thought because the teacher does not understand how each episode is connected to the other.

These differences in cultural dimensions also affect classroom interaction. As the Rosenthal and Jacobson (1968) "Pygmalion" study suggests, a teacher's expectations for students affects how he communicates with students. In addition, if teachers communicate with different frequency based on a student's group membership, such as race or ethnicity, this difference in access to feedback or accessibility of the instructor can lead to differences in the quality of education. A teacher who interacts less with a student has less information about the student's performance, skill, knowledge, and progress. This lack of interaction might cause reduced levels of immediacy and less learning (Morreale & Jones, 1997; Neuliep, 1995).

In their quantitative summary of fifteen studies concerned with the impact of student race on classroom interaction, Cooper and Allen (1998) coded interactions for positive, negative, and quantity. Positive interaction consisted of the teacher affirming or exhibiting other behavior that provided a desirable reinforcement to the student such as recognizing a student, acknowledging a correct answer, or commending a good question. Negative interaction dealt with teacher interaction involving criticism, ignoring the student, or in some other way providing nonsupportive information. Quantity provided an estimate of the frequency of the interaction a teacher had with a student. Their results indicated that race did indeed have an impact in the classroom. Specifically, African American/Latin students participate in less total classroom interaction with instructors and experience greater proportions of negative interactions and fewer positive interactions than Euro-American students. According to these results, teachers interact with students differently based on race.

Rubin (1998) established that students rate Asian American instructors as less credible and less intelligible than Caucasian instructors. African American instructors have also faced prejudice in the classroom. For example, Hendrix (1998) found that students at a predominantly white university believed that their African American teachers were challenged more often than their white teachers in terms of classroom authority and teaching credentials.

Strategies for Change

Teachers are the primary agents for implementing change in the gender, ethnic, and racial stereotypes. The government publication *Taking the Sexism Out of Education* (1978) emphasizes the role of the teacher: "Teachers' behavior is probably the most critical factor in determining whether what happens in the classroom will encourage the development of flexibility or the retention of old stereotyping practices" (cited in Koblinsky & Sugawara, 1984, p. 365).

Several authors have suggested the importance of developing teacher education programs that emphasize gender and ethnic issues in the educational environment. Sadker and Sadker (1981), surveying twenty-four leading teacher education textbooks, report the following:

- None of the texts provide future teachers with curricular resources or instructional strategies to counteract sexism in the classroom.
- Twenty-three of the twenty-four texts give less than 1 percent of space to sexism in education.
- One-third of the texts fail to mention sexism at all. Most guilty of this are math and science education texts.
- An average of five times as much content space is allocated to males as to females in the education texts analyzed.

- In the science methods texts, an average of seven times more space is allocated to males than to females.
- Continued stereotyping is evident in language arts texts. For example, the Sadkers note one text that indicates girls will read boys' books, but boys will not read girls' books; the text concludes, therefore, libraries should buy two boys' books for every girls' book purchased.

Jones (1989) suggests these findings have not changed significantly and that teacher education programs need to emphasize gender issues because teachers still channel students into gender-stereotyped activities as early as the preschool level. She cites a 1986 research study by Kelly, who estimated in an analysis of gender differences in teacher–pupil interactions that teachers spend, on the average, 56 percent of their time with males and 44 percent with females. Over the duration of a student's school career (about 15,000 hours), males would average 1,800 more hours with teachers than females. When that attention is divided among thirty students, the average girl would end up with sixty fewer hours of individual attention than the average boy. Jones suggests that such a discrepancy should be taken very seriously by the teaching profession.

The same might be said of race and ethnicity. For example, Hanson (1999) examined photographs included in public speaking texts in terms of ethnicity of the person pictured. The most frequently appearing ethnicity in all texts was Caucasian, followed by (in order of next most to least) African Americans, Asian Americans, Hispanics, International students, and Native Americans.

Some authors have suggested that teachers consider a feminist perspective in their teaching. A feminist educational perspective begins with the assumption that all students have equal abilities that need to be nurtured and challenged. Differential treatment of students is acceptable only if it is designed to maximize learning and opportunities for everyone. Wood (1989) says that a feminist perspective on teaching and learning is effective because feminism

- is inclusive so that topics representative of both sexes' experiences and concerns are addressed
- values diversity so that multiple ways of knowing are accepted and valued
- values human relationships so that teaching becomes interactive rather than authoritative
- values personal experience so that thoughtful consideration of how ideas and knowledge relate to personal experience is encouraged
- emphasizes empowerment, not power, so that students have control over their own learning
- seeks to create change so that learners perceive themselves as agents of change (pp. 4–5)

Such an approach to education means that the teacher places an emphasis on individual learning styles, variety in teaching strategies, student–student interactions, collaborative learning, and requesting and reacting to student feedback on course content and pedagogy.

Banks (1998) suggests that we need an *equity pedagogy*. Equity pedagogy exists when teachers use techniques and teaching methods that facilitate the academic achievement of students from diverse racial and ethnic groups and from all social classes. Using teaching techniques that cater to the learning and cultural styles of diverse groups and using the techniques of cooperative learning are some of the ways that teachers have found to be effective in teaching students from diverse racial, ethnic, and language groups.

Vernay (1990), synthesizing recommendations from several researchers, suggests that both policy and curriculum/teaching issues must be considered. Policy considerations include the following:

- Issuing policy statements concerning race, ethnicity, religion, and gender that cover broad school and district philosophy, as well as adhering to hiring practices and the treatment of bias-motivated incidents.
- Maintaining racial and cultural diversity among members of the administration, faculty, and staff.
- Providing services for victims of bias-motivated violence.
- Reporting and monitoring trends in racial attitudes.
- Establishing committees on human relations that include students, faculty, and staff.

Vernay suggests the following curriculum and teaching considerations:

- Use the arts to encourage critical thinking about social issues.
- Check textbooks and other resources for bias.
- Reflect the cultural diversity of the school in teaching strategies.
- Affirm racial and cultural differences with regular and special activities, not only during a special time, such as Black History Month, Women's History Month, Chinese New Year, and so on, but throughout the school year.

As teachers, we need to examine our own *ethnocentrism*. The concept of ethnocentrism comes from two Greek words: *ethos*, people or nation; and *ketron*, center. Sumner (1906/1940) divided the concept of ethnocentrism into two parts: the belief that one's culture is superior to all others and the consequent belief that other groups are inferior. Thus, ethnocentrism is being centered on one's own culture—believing it to be the center of the universe. And because other cultures are judged by our own cultural values, we tend to judge other cultures as inferior to our own. We are all ethnocentric to some degree. The problem is not that we feel proud of our culture, but that we sometimes draw conclusions that another culture is inferior to our own. Thus, ethnocentrism is a hindrance to intercultural communication because it prevents us from understanding other cultures. Teachers need to be diligent in terms of understanding their own ethnocentrism and the problems it could cause in the teaching/learning process.

A final concept particularly useful for teachers is *mindfulness*—the state of "alert and lively awareness" (Langer, 1989, p. 140). Teachers should cultivate this sense of awareness and avoid what Langer refers to as mindlessness—a state of reduced attention. Langer outlines three characteristics of mindfulness. The first is the creation of new categories. According to Langer, we need to create more, not fewer, categories. If we have a category "foreigner" and we treat all people in this category the same, we begin to treat the category in which we place a person (in this case, "foreigner") as his identity. If, however, we make more distinctions within this category (create new categories), we stop treating the person as a category.

In addition to new categories, mindfulness involves openness to new information and awareness of more than one perspective. These two characteristics of mindfulness are related to the idea that we need to focus on the process of communication, not the outcome. Langer explains

> An outcome orientation in social situations can induce mindlessness. If we think we know how to handle a situation, we don't feel a need to pay attention. If we respond to the situation as very familiar (as a result, for example, of over-learning), we notice only minimal cues necessary to carry out the proper scenarios. If, on the other hand, the situation is strange, we might be so preoccupied with the thought of failure ("What if I make a fool of myself?"), that we miss nuances of our own and others' behavior. In this sense, we are mindless with respect to the immediate situation, although we may be thinking quite actively about outcome-related issues. (p. 34)

Thus, focusing on the process of communication (i.e., how we communicate) forces us to be mindful of our behavior in the situations in which we find ourselves. If teachers are mindful, they will be able to communicate with each student as an individual rather than as a category.

In terms of classroom interaction, teachers can promote nonstereotyped interaction among students by integrating teams, lines, seating arrangements, and instructional groups. They can assign classroom tasks on a nonstereotypical basis. For example, girls can help carry chairs and boys can be class secretaries. One of the most extensive lists of behaviors for nonsexist teaching is presented by Hall and Sandler (1982). Their ideas relate to racism and ethnicity as well. They suggest that communication behaviors, such as using language that does not reinforce limited or stereotyped views of race, gender, and ethnicity, and giving all students an equal amount of time to respond after asking questions, can begin to communicate the expectations that all students are equally competent intellectually.

Language can also be a problem in educational materials and educational interaction. As several researchers suggest, the generic grammatical structure (using *he* instead of *he* and *she*, see Chapter 3 for an explanation of this concept) "cannot fail to suggest to young readers that females are a substandard...form of being" (Burr, Dunn, & Farquhar, 1972, p. 843). Richmond and Gorham (1988), in their study of current generic-referent usage among 1,529 public school children in grades 3 through 12, report that, in general, masculine generic usage is still prevalent. Webb (1986) provides pedagogical strategies for persuading students to use nonsexist language in class-related communication. Teachers should not only act as models by using nonsexist language but also use teaching strategies that encourage their students to do the same.

A report by the American Association of University Women notes

> Examples of name calling that imply homophobia, such as "sissy," "queer," "gay," "lesbo," are common among students at all levels of schooling. The fourth-grade boys who teased a peer by calling him a "woman" were not only giving voice to the sex-role stereotype that women are weaker than and therefore inferior to men; they were also challenging their peer's "masculinity" by ascribing feminine characteristics to him in a derogatory manner. Such attacks often prevent girls, and sometimes boys, from participating in activities and courses that are traditionally viewed as appropriate for the opposite sex.
>
> When schools ignore sexist, racist, homophobic, and violent interactions among students, they are giving tacit approval to such behaviors. Environments where students do not feel accepted are not environments where effective learning can take place. (AAUW, 1992, p. 74)

IN SUM

In light of the research reviewed in this chapter, we need to be very cognizant of the "isms" in our classrooms. After three decades of researching gender related issues, Sadker (2000) suggests that the "'glass wall' continues to keep women from the most lucrative careers and keeps men from entering traditionally female jobs. Men continue to dominate the high pay, high status college majors" (p. 6). Fleming (2000) agrees. Although women seem to be improving in overall proficiency and achievement, are participating more in sports, and are choosing professional career paths, bias still exists in the classroom. This bias is reflected in lower expectations, gender stereotypes, and male focused student–teacher interaction patterns. Sadker (2000) indicates that although bias is less problematic today, "its influence is no less virulent" (p. 80). The same is true of racism and ethnicity. A recent *New York Times* study suggests that although the majority of Americans believe racism and its effects have declined in the United States, real progress has only begun and any amount of racism is problematic and destructive.

ACTIVITIES

10.1 Bring three or four textbooks to class. With a classmate, rate the gender stereotypes in the textbooks using the following categories: (1) numerical differences in the portrayal of males and females, (2) stereotyped behavior patterns and characteristics, and (3) sexist language. How would you rate the gender stereotypes found in your textbooks? Do some textbooks contain more gender stereotypes than others? Are gender stereotypes more prevalent in textbooks for some subjects than for others? What messages are being communicated by the authors of these textbooks? If you were the author of one of these textbooks, what changes would you make to avoid gender stereotypes?

10.2 Choose a popular fairy tale such as *Snow White, Cinderella, Jack and the Beanstalk,* or *Rapunzel.* Identify the gender stereotypes contained in the story. Rewrite the story to eliminate these stereotypes. (For example, a rich princess could save Cinderella from his wicked banker.) What gender stereotypes did the original fairy tale contain? How does your rewritten story avoid these stereotypes? Did you add any new gender stereotypes in your version? How difficult is it to write a children's story that eliminates gender stereotypes?

10.3 Think about the expectancies that are communicated to students in your classrooms. As a teacher, how would you communicate that you wanted your students to conform to traditional gender stereotypes? Have you observed any of these behaviors in classes that you have attended? How would you communicate that you wanted your students to have a more equal role in classroom interaction? Have you observed any of these behaviors in classes you have attended? How have you been affected by these teacher behaviors?

10.4 Choose one of your classes to analyze the communication patterns that occur. Answer the following questions:

- Who initiates the communication contacts?
- Who is criticized by the teacher or other members of the class? For what reasons?
- Who is praised? Why?
- Who dominates the classroom verbally?
- Who dominates the classroom nonverbally?

Analyze your answers in terms of gendered behavior. Are males praised more than females? Do males or females initiate the most communication? Who dominates the classroom? Do you think your observations are influenced by the subject matter? For example, do males tend to dominate engineering classes, while females tend to dominate communication classes? Compare your results with others in your class. What conclusions can you draw about communication patterns in the classroom? How do these communication patterns create and maintain gender stereotypes?

10.5 Try this simple test adapted from one developed by Myra and David Sadker (1994). Name twenty famous American women from history. Now, delete the athletes and entertainers. Are there any names left on your list? List real women, not advertising creations like Aunt Jemima or Betty Crocker. Does your list include any women of color? Expand your list to include women from other countries. Consult resources in your school or community library to construct a full list. What does the difficulty of this task say about the portrayal of women in our educational system?

10.6 To determine how you are perceived by your students, ask them to complete the following questionnaire.

Student Perception Questionnaire

Directions:

Answer each of the following questions. Choose only one answer for each question.

1. Your age _____

2. Sex of student
   (a) Male
   (b) Female

3. Sex of instructor
   (a) Male
   (b) Female

4. Ethnicity
   (a) African American
   (b) Asian American
   (c) Caucasian
   (d) Latino
   (e) Native American
   (f) Other_____

5. How often do you voluntarily answer questions or contribute to class discussions in class?
   (a) Never
   (b) One to three times during the course
   (c) An average of once a week
   (d) An average of two to three times a week
   (e) An average of one or more times a day

6. How often does the teacher call on you or ask you to respond to a question or comment?
   (a) Teacher does not call on anyone
   (b) One to three times during the course
   (c) An average of once a week
   (d) An average of two to three times a week
   (e) Never

7. How does the teacher most frequently call on you?
   (a) By name
   (b) By pointing
   (c) By eye contact—looking directly at me
   (d) Teacher never calls on me

8. How many times have you raised your hand to ask a question or make a comment and found that the teacher did not respond?
   (a) Once or twice during the course
   (b) Three or more times during the course
   (c) I am called on when I raise my hand
   (d) I never raise my hand

9. Why do you think the teacher does not respond when you raise your hand? (Select the one answer that best reflects your opinion.)
   (a) Too many students want to speak
   (b) Others beat me to it
   (c) Teacher does not see or hear me
   (d) Teacher ignores me
   (e) This situation never occurs

10. How many times have you wanted to participate in class by asking a question or making a comment but chosen not to do so?
    (a) Once or twice during the course
    (b) Three or more times during the course
    (c) Nearly every day
    (d) Not at all, because I participate when I want to
    (e) I usually do not want to participate

11. If you have wanted to participate in class by asking a question or making a comment but did not do so, what was your reason for not doing so? (Select the one response that most closely corresponds with your feelings.)
    (a) Felt insecure, inadequate, or uncertain
    (b) Another student asked question or commented first
    (c) Too many students in class
    (d) Disagreed with teacher but chose not to speak out

12. In your opinion, which students most frequently participate in class? (Select the one answer that best represents your opinion.)
    (a) Those who are most knowledgeable or most interested in the subject
    (b) Those who are seeking clarification or want more information
    (c) Those who are trying to show off or get attention
    (d) I have not noticed

13. In your opinion, which students ask the most questions and make the most comments in class?
    (a) Male student(s)
    (b) Female student(s)
    (c) Male and female students equally
    (d) I have not noticed

14. How does the teacher react to the questions you ask in class?
    (a) Encourages me to question or comment again
    (b) Discourages me from commenting or asking a question again
    (c) Neither encourages nor discourages me
    (d) I never participate

15. In your opinion, how does the teacher react to opinions and comments given by other students in the class?
    (a) Respects the opinions of students in this class
    (b) Does not respect the opinions of students in this class
    (c) Embarrasses or "puts down" students for their opinions
    (d) I have not noticed

16. Does the instructor make humorous references that you feel are offensive, embarrassing, or belittling to any individuals or groups?
    (a) Never
    (b) Once or twice
    (c) Occasionally
    (d) Frequently

17. How often do students participate in this class by asking questions or making comments?
    (a) Never
    (b) Rarely
    (c) Occasionally
    (d) Frequently

In addition to using student evaluations, we can ask colleagues to observe our classrooms or we can videotape our classroom interactions to help analyze how we relate to our students on the basis of gender.

10.7 In a microteaching session, complete either part A or B of the Student–Faculty Communication Checklist.

Student–Faculty Communication Checklist

It may be difficult for an instructor to be conscious of the interactional dynamics in the classroom while giving a lecture or guiding a discussion. For this reason, the following techniques are suggested to help faculty analyze the interaction in their classes.

A. Classroom Observation

Having a friend, colleague, or teaching assistant observe some of your classes on a random basis can be helpful. Classroom observation can be used to answer questions such as

1. How many males do you call on to answer questions? How many females?
2. Which students (male or female) participate in class more frequently by answering questions or making comments? Is the number disproportionate enough that you should encourage some students to participate more frequently?
3. Do interruptions occur when an individual is talking? If so, who does the interrupting?
4. Is your verbal response to students positive? Aversive? Encouraging? Is it the same for all students? If not, why? (Valid reasons occur from time to time for reacting or responding to a particular student in a highly specified manner.)
5. Do you tend to face or address one section of the classroom more than others? Do you establish eye contact with certain students more than others? What gestures, postures, or facial expressions do you use, and are they different for men, women, or minority students?

B. Audiotaping of Class Session

Have a student tape record some of your class sessions. Self-analysis of the tapes can provide answers to questions such as

1. Which students do you call by name?
2. What language patterns are you using? Do you regularly use male referencing or the generic "he" or "man"? Are stereotypical assumptions about men and women revealed in your classroom dialogue?
3. Are examples and anecdotes drawn from men's lives only?
4. Can differential patterns of reinforcement be detected from the tapes?

10.8 Complete the Generalized Ethnocentrism Scale.

FURTHER READING

Belenky, M., Clinchy, B., Goldberger, N., & Taruk, J. (1986). *Women's ways of knowing. The development of self, voice, and mind.* New York: Basic Books.

Based on interviews with 135 women, these researchers describe five ways of knowing. Based on these descriptions, a new approach to education is discussed.

Gilligan, C., Lyons, N. P., & Hanmer, T. J. (1990). *Making connections: The relational worlds of adolescent girls at Emma Willard School.* Cambridge, MA: Harvard University Press.

The essays in this volume discuss the views of young women on self, relationships, and morality. The overall theme of each essay

The Neuliep–McCroskey Generalized Ethnocentrism Scale

Can you accurately predict your level of ethnocentrism? Circle the number that most nearly describes your beliefs about each statement.

Scale Item	Strongly Agree	Agree	?	Disagree	Strongly Disagree
1. Most cultures are backward compared to my culture.	5	4	3	2	1
2. My culture should be the role model for other cultures.	5	4	3	2	1
* 3. Lifestyles in other cultures are just as valid as those in my culture.	5	4	3	2	1
4. Other cultures should try to be more like my culture.	5	4	3	2	1
* 5. People in my culture could learn a lot from people in other cultures.	5	4	3	2	1
6. Most people from other cultures just don't know what's good for them.	5	4	3	2	1
7. I have little respect for the values and customs of other cultures.	5	4	3	2	1
8. Most people would be happier if they lived like people in my culture.	5	4	3	2	1
9. People in my culture have just about the best lifestyles of anywhere.	5	4	3	2	1
10. Lifestyles in other cultures are not as valid as those in my culture.	5	4	3	2	1
* 11. I respect the values and customs of other cultures.	5	4	3	2	1
12. I do not cooperate with people who are different.	5	4	3	2	1
13. I do not trust people who are different.	5	4	3	2	1
14. I dislike interacting with people who are different.	5	4	3	2	1
15. Other cultures are smart to look up to my culture.	5	4	3	2	1

From Neuliep, J., and McCroskey, J. (1997). "The Development of a US and Generalized Ethnocentrism Scale," *Communication Research Reports, 14*, 393. Used by permission of the Eastern Communication Association.

*Reversed items.
Scores range from a low of 15 to a high of 75. Scores below 38 indicate relatively low ethnocentrism, while scores above 52 indicate relatively high ethnocentrism.

concerns the crisis of connection in girls' lives during adolescence.

Goldberger, N., Tarule, J., Clinchy, B., and Belenky, M. (1996). *Knowledge difference and power: Essays inspired by "Women's Ways of Knowing."* New York: Basic Books.

This book provides interesting ideas, generated from the text, which caused much controversy when first published.

Gonzalez, A., Houston, M., and Chen, U. (2000). *Our Voices: Essays in Culture, Ethnicity and Communication* (3rd ed.). San Francisco: Roxbury.

These essays examine communication in a variety of settings and from a variety of cultural perspectives.

Grancisco, V. L., & Jensen, M. D. (1994). *Women's voices in our time: Statements by American leaders.* Prospect Heights, IL: Waveland.

A collection of speeches and public statements by American women, this book includes notable women in a variety of fields including the arts (Lillian Hellman, Elizabeth Taylor), politics (Barbara Jordan, Elizabeth Holtzman), journalism (Nina Totenberg), and political activism (Wilma P. Mankiller, Maggie Kuhn). It is an excellent complement to textbooks focusing primarily on men's rhetorical acts.

Stewart, L., Stewart, A., Friedley, S., & Cooper, P. (2003). *Communication between the sexes* (4th ed.). Boston: Allyn & Bacon.

This text discusses the issue of gender in various contexts.

Weis, L., & Fine, M. (Eds.). (1993). *Beyond silenced voices: Class, race, and gender in United States schools.* Albany, NY: State University of New York Press.

Weis and Fine go beyond examining policies, discourse, and practices to call up the voices of young people who have been expelled from the centers of their schools and our culture to speak as interpreters of adolescent culture. These voices include Native American college students, lesbian and gay students, and other young people struggling for identities amid the radically transforming conditions of contemporary society.

APPENDIX A

SYSTEMATIC OBSERVATION

Teaching is more than acquiring a repertoire of teaching techniques.... This does not negate the importance of helping potential teachers acquire a repertoire of teaching skills. This is obviously necessary—but not sufficient. Teachers must learn to discern the state of a classroom or pupil at a given point during an educational interchange. They must select the teaching behavior or patterns which are the most likely to be effective. This is the essence of teaching. (Semmel, 1978, p. 27)

Educational reports and educational literature are contemplating the quality of American education. To say that we live in a time of increasing emphasis on teacher assessment is to state the obvious. In no other era has the emphasis on assessment been greater.

The purposes of teacher assessment are four; these are shown in Table A.1 (Costa, Garmston, & Lambert, 1988, p. 148). Two of these purposes focus on the teacher—improving teacher performance and informing personnel decisions about teachers. The other two focus on the educational institution—improving the institution's performance and informing institutional decisions.

In this appendix, we are primarily concerned with the teacher focus. In this regard, assessment can be either formative or summative. The purpose of formative teacher assessment is to help form or modify the teacher's future instructional behaviors. The purpose of summative assessment concerns decisions based on the teacher's past behavior (tenure, termination, merit pay decisions, etc.).

The issues of teacher assessment are complex. For example, what type of assessment (systematic observation, pencil–paper tests, portfolios, etc.) should be used? Who should be responsible for the assessment? What should be the minimum standard for performance? Will that be the same for all teaching levels and teaching areas? Should the standards be state or national? What should be assessed? Should the findings of educational research be incorporated into assessment policies? Who should control the allocation of funds necessary for assessment? What are the legal issues inherent in assessment?

The focus of this chapter is not on trying to answer these questions about assessment. To do so is beyond the scope of this text. Rather, our focus is on ways to assess teacher communication competencies.

TABLE A.1   Four Purposes of Teacher Assessment

	Individual	Organization
	Improve Teacher Performance	*Improve Organizational Performance*
G A T H E R I N G D A T A	■ Develop formative information about teaching performance. ■ Assess hiring criteria and job specifications. ■ Develop formative information about teacher characteristics and capacities. ■ Identify supervision goals. ■ Identify supervision approaches. ■ Model decision-making processes.	■ Gather data about the effectiveness of the staff development system. ■ Gather data about the congruence between hypothetical and actual curriculum. ■ Measure student access to and variety of teaching methodologies. ■ Identify organizational goals and action plans. ■ Assess school climate/trust level.
	Inform Personnel Decisions	*Inform Organizational Decisions*
M A K I N G D E C I S I O N S	■ Produce summative information related to evaluation criteria. ■ Grant tenure. ■ Award promotions, advancements to leadership roles. ■ Administer disciplinary actions. ■ Dismiss teachers.	■ Design staff development program for subject matter of teachers. ■ Inform teachers well in advance of any systemwide changes in instructional methodologies or policies. ■ Allocate budget resources for staff development, supervision, evaluation. ■ Align curriculum.

Of the twenty subfunctions of a comprehensive evaluation system, only one is for the sole purpose of dismissing teachers. However, many districts may be tempted to allow that motive to overwhelm other design considerations.

WHY COMMUNICATION?

Certainly assessment can focus on numerous classroom and educational variables. However, remember that we began this text with the idea that communication is the crux of education. Elements of communication particularly important to effective teaching have been isolated, and we have discussed them throughout this text. Specific skills have been identified by the Speech Communication Association (Cooper, 1988a). Researchers have written about communication competencies important for teachers (see, for example, McCaleb, 1987). In general, these authors have noted the validity of using observational and behavioral measures to identify the strengths and weaknesses of teachers as communicators and have stressed the value to be gained from systematic and multifaceted evaluations.

WHY SYSTEMATIC OBSERVATION? AN OVERVIEW

Systematic observation systems are classificatory systems used to record

> relevant aspects of classroom behaviors as (or within a negligible time after) they occur, with a minimum of quantification intervening between the observation of a behavior and the recording of it. Typically behaviors are recorded in the form of tallies, checks, or other marks which code them into predefined categories and yield information about which behaviors occurred, or how they occurred, during the period of observation. (Medley & Mitsel, 1963, p. 253)

Systematic observation is an effective way to assess teacher competency. Through the use of systematic observation, you can analyze your communication in the classroom, your response style, types and levels of questions you ask, ways you reinforce student communication, and the general pattern of communication in your classroom. Using the information you receive from the use of various appropriate observation instruments, you can alter your communication if you need to. Systematic observation can answer three basic questions:

1. Is this how I want to teach?
2. Is it the best method of instruction for the goals and objectives of the course?
3. If this is not how I want to teach, how far am I from my goal?

In this chapter we examine types of systems available and spend considerable time on two systems. First, however, we discuss what systematic observation can do for you and your students.

What's in It for Me?

Teachers are often reluctant to use systematic observation because

1. They are unaware of the benefits of using systematic observation techniques.
2. Learning to use a systematic observation technique can be time consuming.
3. The observation instruments do not relate specifically to the evaluation instruments an administrator uses in evaluating a teacher's instructional strategies.

However, numerous studies indicate that teacher use of systematic observation instruments can make positive changes in teacher behavior. For example, teachers become more flexible, more accepting, less critical, and more sensitive to pupil attitudes, and they must actively encourage student-initiated comments after using systematic observation. In addition, the use of systematic observation by teachers has been linked to increased student learning.

Systematic observation is one method by which we can increase our effectiveness. True, systematic observation is time consuming (but then, no one ever said teaching doesn't take time) and may not relate specifically to the evaluation instruments our administrators use to evaluate our teaching. Nevertheless, the use of systematic observation can provide insight into our teaching and help us determine what changes we need to make to be more effective. The more effective we are, the more that effectiveness will be reflected in our classrooms, regardless of the instrument the administrator chooses to use to evaluate our teaching.

What's Available?

Basically there are two types of observation instruments—expert-prepared and teacher-prepared. Expert-prepared instruments are prepared by professionals in the field of observation. Teacher-prepared instruments are prepared by teachers for use in their own classrooms.

EXPERT-PREPARED SYSTEMS

A Verbal Observation System—Flanders

One of the best known and most often used expert-prepared systems is the one developed by Amidon and Flanders (1967). The system divides classroom communication into three major categories: teacher talk, student talk, and noncodable. Each of these major categories is divided into smaller categories. The entire system is presented next.

Teacher Talk: Indirect Influence

1. *Accepts Feeling.* Accepts and clarifies the feeling tone of the student in a nonthreatening manner. Feelings may be positive or negative. Predicting or recalling feelings is included.
2. *Praises or Encourages.* Praises or encourages student action or behavior. Jokes that release tension—but not at the expense of another individual, nodding head, or saying "Um hm?" or "Go on"—are included.
3. *Accepts or Uses Ideas of Students.* Clarifying, building on, or developing ideas suggested by a student. As teacher brings more of own ideas into play, shift to category 5.
4. *Asks Questions.* Asking a question about content or procedure with the intent that a student answer.

Teacher Talk: Direct Influence

5. *Lecturing.* Giving facts or opinions about content or procedures; expressing own ideas, asking rhetorical questions.

6. *Giving Directions.* Directions, commands, or orders with which a student is expected to comply.

7. *Criticizing or Justifying Authority.* Statements intended to change student behavior from nonacceptable to acceptable pattern; bawling someone out; stating why the teacher is taking particular action; extreme self-reference.

Student Talk

8. *Student Talk—Response.* Talk by student in response to teacher. Teacher initiates the contact or solicits student statement.

9. *Student Talk—Initiation.* Talk by students that they initiate. If teacher's "calling on" student is only to indicate who may talk next, observer must decide whether student wanted to talk. If so, use this category.

Noncodable

10. *Silence or Confusion.* Pauses, short periods of silence, and periods of confusion in which communication cannot be understood by the observer.

To use the instrument, the observer (another teacher, for example) sits in the back of the classroom and adjusts to the classroom (about ten to fifteen minutes). The observer then records behavior according to one of the categories every three seconds or as often as behavior changes. The numbers of the categories are recorded in sequence on a sheet like the ones shown in Figures A.1 and A.2 below. The observer should record for ten to fifteen minutes. A complete explanation of the Flanders system is found in Appendix B.

A Nonverbal Observation System— Grant and Hennings

Flanders's system focuses on verbal communication in the classroom. However, the use of a teacher's nonverbal communication seems particularly important to

FIGURE A.1   Teacher-Prepared Form for Data Collection on Level of Questions Asked.

	Knowledge	Comprehension	Application	Analysis	Synthesis	Evaluation
Teacher Questions						
Student Questions						

FIGURE A.2   Teacher-Prepared Form for Data Collection on Type and Frequency of Positive Reinforcement by Teacher.

	3	6	9	12	15
Single Word Sentence					
Humor					
Movement Toward Student					
Gesture Toward Student					
Enthusiastic Vocal Tone					

the classroom situation. It is imperative that your nonverbal behavior enhance instruction. If students are confused because of contradictions between verbal and nonverbal aspects of the classroom, the classroom climate, and thus learning, can be affected.

Grant and Hennings (1971) developed an instrument that focuses on nonverbal teacher behavior. The instrument divides nonverbal communication into four areas:

1. *Conducting*—motions that enable teacher to control student participation and obtain attending behavior.
2. *Acting*—motions that amplify and clarify meanings.
3. *Wielding*—motions in which teacher interacts with objects, materials, or parts of the room.
4. *Personal motions*—motions not related to instruction.

In addition to examining nonverbal communication, the instrument gives you an idea of how your nonverbal communication relates to your verbal communication. A complete explanation and inventory is included in Appendix B.

TEACHER-PREPARED SYSTEMS

Often teachers have a specific behavior they want to examine—such as level and sequence of questions asked, types of reinforcement, or specific nonverbal behaviors such as movement or gesture. Regardless of the specific behavior(s) the teacher wishes to observe, several steps must be followed when developing an observation tool. Gerald Bailey (1981) suggests the following steps:

1. Identify the behaviors that will be observed.
2. Examine a number of expert-prepared instruments to get an idea of the design of observation instruments. The expert-prepared observation forms will assist in determining (1) the type of form to be designed; (2) techniques for identifying behavior; and (3) methods for interpreting and analyzing collected information.
3. Construct the observation form to illustrate one or more of these facets: (1) identification of a specific behavior; (2) the frequency of a behavior; and (3) the sequence of behaviors. Design the directions and format for actual data collection.
4. Audiotape or videotape a classroom session; analyze data in terms of how well the classroom interaction was collected.
5. Revise the observation form on the basis of the findings, record another classroom session, and use this recording to collect data on the revised form. (p. 59)

Suppose you want to know the level of questions you ask in your classroom and the level of questions your students ask. You might devise a form similar to the one in Figure A.1. An observer would simply check the appropriate column each time you or your students asked a question. You could also videotape or audiotape a class period and then tally the results yourself.

Perhaps you are interested in the types and frequency of positive reinforcement you use in the classroom. A form such as the one in Figure A.2 could be used. The observer would place a check after each behavior when it occurred in the designated three-minute interval.

Perhaps you are interested in a more global view of the classroom, rather than any specific behavior. If this is the case, you might adapt for your purposes an observation instrument such as that developed by anthropologist Dell Hymes (1972). Hymes suggests the SPEAKING system:

Situation. Setting and scene in which the communication takes place

Participants. People involved—their roles and relationship

Ends. Goals and outcome of the communication

Acts. Message content, form, sequence

Key. Tone of the communication

Instrumentality. Channel or medium of the communication

Norms. Guidelines for or standards of interaction

Genre. Categories such as lecture, sermon, commercial, and so on.

Consider the following example:

The *situation* is a high school math class. The participants are the students (11 males and 14 females age 16 to 17, and one teacher, Ms. Chan). The goal (*end*) of the lesson is for students to be able to solve algebraic equations.

The *acts* are what the teacher and the students say and do. You would not try to write down every single word or nonverbal cue. You are trying to "get the gist." You probably would want to jot down some notes and then write these in a more formal way soon after the lesson was completed. Remember, you're looking for the general content of what Ms. Chan says about algebraic equations, the students' responses and questions to Ms. Chan and their classmates, and the subsequent responses. In other words, what is the general message content and the sequence? For example, is a teacher question generally followed by a student response or a rephrasing of the question by the teacher? Do student responses ever "spark" further student questions or reactions or does the teacher always answer the questions?

The *key* to the lesson is primarily serious because the teacher wants the students to learn algebraic equations. However, mixed with this serious tone might well be humor. *Instrumentality* considers the medium or channel of the communication. For example, is the communication primarily oral or do students spend a great deal of time writing their answers?

What are the *norms* of this classroom? Do students always raise their hands when they wish to speak? Is the teacher the only giver of information in the classroom? Where does the teacher stand or sit? Is the classroom arranged in a traditional straight row arrangement? Do the students call the teacher by first name or title and last name?

Finally, the *genre* of this particular speech situation should be considered. Is the lesson a lecture? A discussion? A combination of both?

Teacher-made observation systems are not without their shortcomings. The process of constructing them is time consuming. The bias of the creator is difficult to avoid. As a result, reliability and validity are difficult to determine. However, these limitations may be less important than the advantage of using an instrument tailor-made for observing the behaviors on which the teacher wishes to focus. Two teacher-prepared observation systems, the *Teacher Behaviors Inventory* and the *Teacher Communication Rating Scale,* are included in Appendix B.

In Sum

We have presented you with a brief discussion of teacher assessment and an overview of systematic observation and how it can help you analyze your teaching. A variety of instruments exist. Choose the one most appropriate to your needs or develop your own. However, remember that no observation system tells you whether you are a "good" teacher. It merely describes your behavior. What you do with that information is up to you.

INSTRUMENTS FOR SYSTEMATIC OBSERVATION

FLANDERS

As discussed in Appendix A, Amidon and Flanders (1967) developed one of the best and most used systematic observation systems. The authors of this instrument present ground rules to aid the user in categorizing behaviors correctly. These are outlined as follows:

1. When not certain in which of two or more categories a statement belongs, choose the category that is numerically farthest from category 5.
2. If the primary tone of the teacher's behavior has been consistently direct or consistently indirect, do not shift into the opposite classification unless a clear indication of shift is given by the teacher.
3. The effect of a statement on the pupils, and not the teacher's intent, is the crucial criterion for categorizing a statement.
4. If more than one category occurs during the three-second interval, then all categories used in that interval are recorded; therefore, record each change in category. If no change occurs within three seconds, repeat that category.
5. Directions are statements that result (or are expected to result) in observable behavior on the part of children.
6. When the teacher calls on a child by name, the observer ordinarily records a 4.
7. If there is a discernible period of silence (at least three seconds), record one 10 for every three seconds of silence, laughter, board work, and so on.
8. When the teacher repeats a student answer, and the answer is a correct answer, this is recorded as a 2.
9. When the teacher repeats a student idea and communicates only that the idea will be considered or accepted as something to be discussed, a 3 is used.
10. If a student begins talking after another student (without the teacher's talking), a 10 is inserted between the 9s or 8s to indicate a change of student.

Tally Sheet

1. ____	26. ____	51. ____	76. ____	101. ____
2. ____	27. ____	52. ____	77. ____	102. ____
3. ____	28. ____	53. ____	78. ____	103. ____
4. ____	29. ____	54. ____	79. ____	104. ____
5. ____	30. ____	55. ____	80. ____	105. ____
6. ____	31. ____	56. ____	81. ____	106. ____
7. ____	32. ____	57. ____	82. ____	107. ____
8. ____	33. ____	58. ____	83. ____	108. ____
9. ____	34. ____	59. ____	84. ____	109. ____
10. ____	35. ____	60. ____	85. ____	110. ____
11. ____	36. ____	61. ____	86. ____	111. ____
12. ____	37. ____	62. ____	87. ____	112. ____
13. ____	38. ____	63. ____	88. ____	113. ____
14. ____	39. ____	64. ____	89. ____	114. ____
15. ____	40. ____	65. ____	90. ____	115. ____
16. ____	41. ____	66. ____	91. ____	116. ____
17. ____	42. ____	67. ____	92. ____	117. ____
18. ____	43. ____	68. ____	93. ____	118. ____
19. ____	44. ____	69. ____	94. ____	119. ____
20. ____	45. ____	70. ____	95. ____	120. ____
21. ____	46. ____	71. ____	96. ____	121. ____
22. ____	47. ____	72. ____	97. ____	122. ____
23. ____	48. ____	73. ____	98. ____	123. ____
24. ____	49. ____	74. ____	99. ____	124. ____
25. ____	50. ____	75. ____	100. ____	125. ____

11. Statements, such as "Uh huh, yes, yeah, all right, okay," which occur between two 9s are recorded as a 2 (encouragement).
12. A teacher joke, not made at the expense of the children, is a 2.
13. Rhetorical questions are not really questions but are merely part of lecturing techniques and should be categorized as a 5.
14. A narrow question is a signal to expect an 8.
15. An 8 is recorded when several students respond in unison to a narrow question.

The numbers from the coding sheet can then be recorded on a 10 × 10 matrix such as that in Figure B.1.

FIGURE B.1   Flanders Work Matrix

Work Matrix

	1	2	3	4	5	6	7	8	9	10	
1											
2											
3											
4											
5											
6											
7											
8											
9											
10											Matrix Total
TOTAL											
%											

The tallies in Figure B.1 are paired, and then recorded on the matrix. The first number in the pair designates the appropriate horizontal row; the second number in the pair designates the appropriate column. For example, assume the first six categories in your observation were

1. 10
2. 5
3. 5
4. 4
5. 8
6. 4

The first pair (10, 5) would be tallied in row 10, column 5 of the matrix. Pair two (5, 5) would be in row 5, column 5 and so forth. These six tallies would appear as shown in Figure B.2.

FIGURE B.2   Flanders Work Matrix

Work Matrix

	1	2	3	4	5	6	7	8	9	10	
1											
2											
3											
4								I			
5				I	I						
6											
7											
8				I							
9											
10					I						Matrix Total
TOTAL											
%											

Once the tallies in Figure B.2 are entered on the matrix, the sequence, the amount, and the pattern of verbal communication in the classroom can be analyzed. The steps in this analysis are as follows:

1. Check the matrix total in order to estimate the elapsed coding time. Number of tallies multiplied by 3 equals seconds; divided by 60 equals minutes.
2. Check the percent of teacher talk, pupil talk, and silence or confusion, and use this information in combination with…(average of about 68 percent teacher talk, 20 percent pupil talk, and 11 or 12 percent silence or confusion).
3. …[Examine] the balance of teacher response and initiation in contrast with pupil initiation.

   a. Indirect-to-direct ratios; useful for matrices with more than 1,000 tallies

   (1) I/D ratio: 1 + 2 + 3 divided by 6 + 7.
   (2) I/D ratio: 1 + 2 + 3 + 4 divided by 5 + 6 + 7.

     b. TRR (teacher response ratio): teacher tendency to react to ideas and feelings of pupils. 1 + 2 + 3 times 100 divided by 1 + 2 + 3 + 6 + 7. Average is about 42.

     c. TQR (teacher question ratio): teacher tendency to use questions when dealing with content. Category 4 times 100 divided by 4 + 5. Average is 26.

     d. PIR (pupil initiation ratio): proportion of pupil talk judged initiation. Category 9 times 100 divided by 8 + 9. Average is close to 34.

4. Check the initial reaction of the teacher to the termination of pupil talk.

     a. TRR89 (instantaneous teacher response ratio): teacher tendency to praise or integrate pupil ideas or feelings when student terminates. Add cell frequencies in rows 8 and 9, columns 1, 2, and 3 times 100 divided by tallies in rows 8 and 9, columns 1, 2, 3, 6, and 7. Average is about 60.

     b. TQR89 (instantaneous teacher questions ratio): teacher tendency to respond to pupil talk with questions compared to lecture. Add cells (8 − 4) + (9 − 4) times 100 divided by (8 − 4) + (8 − 5) + (9 − 5). Average is about 44.

5. Check the proportions of tallies to be found in the "content cross" and "steady state cells" in order to estimate the rapidity of exchange, tendency toward sustained talk, and content emphasis.

     a. CCR (content cross ratio): concerns categories most concerned with content. Calculate the percent of all tallies that lie within the columns and rows of 4 and 5. Average is close to 55 percent.

     b. SSR (steady state ratio): tendency of teacher and pupil talk to stay in same category. Percentage of all tallies in 10 steady state cells (1 − 1), (2 − 2), and so on. Average is around 50.

     c. PSSR (pupil steady state ratio): tendency of pupils to stay in same category. Frequencies in (8 − 8) + (9 − 9) cells times 100 divided by all pupil talk tallies. Average is around 35 or 40.

GRANT AND HENNINGS

As discussed in Appendix A, the Grant and Hennings (1971) system focuses on nonverbal teaching behavior. The inventory is presented next. Although it is stated in terms of self-analysis, it could be used by another teacher to observe you. It might be useful for you to complete the inventory and then have another teacher observe you, completing the inventory "on the scene" as you teach. You could then compare your view with the observer's.

Part I

What kinds of motions tend to predominate in my nonverbal teaching style?

A. Conducting

How do I control participation, focus attention, and obtain attending behavior?

	Very Typical	Typical	Atypical

1. *To indicate who the participant is, I:*

	Very Typical	Typical	Atypical
smile at the participant	_____	_____	_____
focus my eyes on the participant	_____	_____	_____
orient my body in the direction of the participant	_____	_____	_____
nod at the chosen participant	_____	_____	_____
point at the participant with finger, hand, stick, chalk, microphone, book	_____	_____	_____
walk toward the participant	_____	_____	_____
hand the pointer, chalk, book, microphone to the participant	_____	_____	_____
touch the participant	_____	_____	_____
other: _____	_____	_____	_____

2. *To rate a student's participation, I:*

	Very Typical	Typical	Atypical
use facial expressions: smiling, frowning, grinning, wrinkling my brow, raising my eyebrows	_____	_____	_____
shake my head	_____	_____	_____
shrug my shoulders	_____	_____	_____
clap my hands	_____	_____	_____
make the OK sign with my fingers, forming an "O" by touching thumb to forefinger	_____	_____	_____
put my hands to my face	_____	_____	_____
hold my head	_____	_____	_____
scratch my head	_____	_____	_____
write the correct response on the board or on a chart	_____	_____	_____
pat the student on back	_____	_____	_____
move my hand from respondent to another student who has hand up to respond	_____	_____	_____
other: _____	_____	_____	_____

3. *To respond to a student's participation, I:*

	Very Typical	Typical	Atypical
use facial expressions	_____	_____	_____
shake or nod head	_____	_____	_____

	Very Typical	Typical	Atypical
walk toward or away from the participant	_____	_____	_____
point or wave hand	_____	_____	_____
write something on the board	_____	_____	_____
other: _____	_____	_____	_____

4. *To regulate the speed of classroom interaction, I:*

	Very Typical	Typical	Atypical
beckon to student to continue	_____	_____	_____
wave at student to stop	_____	_____	_____
select motions of different speeds	_____	_____	_____
other: _____	_____	_____	_____

5. *To focus student attention on a significant point in the lesson, I:*

	Very Typical	Typical	Atypical
write the significant point on the board	_____	_____	_____
underline a word or words written on the board	_____	_____	_____
point to each word written on the board	_____	_____	_____
write over each word written on the board, perhaps with colored chalk	_____	_____	_____
point to a related chart, bulletin board display, or picture	_____	_____	_____
point to a location on map or globe	_____	_____	_____
point to the actual object	_____	_____	_____
hold up the actual object	_____	_____	_____
point to a person being discussed	_____	_____	_____
point to a picture or statement projected by an audiovisual device	_____	_____	_____
put words or letters into a pocket chart	_____	_____	_____
attach word cards or pictures to the chalkboard using magnets or masking tape	_____	_____	_____
hold up word card or picture	_____	_____	_____
add the key ingredient to a demonstration I am doing	_____	_____	_____
other: _____	_____	_____	_____

	Very Typical	Typical	Atypical

6. *To get the attention of the total class or portion of the class, I:*

close the door to indicate the lesson is beginning

flick the lights

tap a desk bell

pull down a chart or map

pick up a textbook or lesson plan book or record book

walk to the front and center of the room

survey the class, making eye contact

stand at attention

hold up my hand

play a note on the piano

arrange my chair or stool and sit down

tap fingers or pencil on desk

other: _____

7. *To get the attention of a misbehaving student or group of students, I:*

orient my body toward and focus my eyes on the inattentive student(s)

frown or raise eyebrows at misbehaving student(s)

shake my head at the misbehaving student(s)

snap fingers in direction of misbehaving student(s)

clap hands

walk toward the misbehaving student(s)

touch misbehaving student(s)

sit down near misbehaving student(s)

touch object misbehaving student is touching

other: _____

	Very Typical	Typical	Atypical

B. Acting.   How do I use bodily motion to clarify and amplify meanings?

1. *To emphasize meanings, I:*

	Very Typical	Typical	Atypical
use motion of my head	_____	_____	_____
use facial expressions	_____	_____	_____
use motions of my feet	_____	_____	_____
use motions of my entire body	_____	_____	_____

2. *To illustrate a concept, an object, or a process, I:*

	Very Typical	Typical	Atypical
use motions of my hands	_____	_____	_____
use motions of my head	_____	_____	_____
use facial expressions	_____	_____	_____
use motions of my feet	_____	_____	_____
other: _____	_____	_____	_____

3. *To illustrate even more completely, I use role playing motions to:*

	Very Typical	Typical	Atypical
pretend I am an object	_____	_____	_____
imitate an animal	_____	_____	_____
pretend I am a particular character	_____	_____	_____
pretend I am a puppet character	_____	_____	_____
other: _____	_____	_____	_____

C. Wielding.   In what ways do I manipulate objects, materials, or other parts of the environment when students are not expected to focus on my motions? What kinds of materials do I tend to manipulate?

1. *I tend to manipulate:*

	Very Typical	Typical	Atypical
chalk and chalkboard	_____	_____	_____
books or workbooks	_____	_____	_____
audiovisual equipment	_____	_____	_____
paper, pens, or pencils	_____	_____	_____
flow pens and charting paper	_____	_____	_____
pictures or cards	_____	_____	_____
materials related specifically to the teaching of my discipline	_____	_____	_____
other: _____	_____	_____	_____

	Very Typical	Typical	Atypical

2. *During the lesson, I focus my eyes on:*
written materials
my lesson plans
the teacher's manual
the students' books
reference books
material recorded on chalkboard
numerals of the clock
other: _____

3. *Teacher-oriented wieldings I delegate to students are:*
distribution and collection of
   material
setting up equipment
putting material on board or
   bulletin board
reading questions that other
   students answer
other: _____

4. *I manipulate or wield materials:*
before students come into the room
while students come into the room
while students are performing
   some other task
just before using the material
during the actual use of the material
other: _____

D. Personal Motions.   How do I use motions that are more of a personal nature than they are instructional?

1. *Motions I make that are related to my clothing are:*
adjusting my tie or bow
adjusting my collar
straightening jacket
pulling down sweater or skirt
tucking in blouse, sweater, or shirt
other: _____

	Very Typical	Typical	Atypical
2. *Motions I make in the classroom that are aspects of my own personality are:*			
pushing back hair	_____	_____	_____
pulling on beads, necklace, locket, and so on	_____	_____	_____
adjusting glasses	_____	_____	_____
placing hands in pockets	_____	_____	_____
jiggling coins in pocket	_____	_____	_____
twiddling with ring	_____	_____	_____
curling hair around finger	_____	_____	_____
scratching head, nose, neck, leg	_____	_____	_____
other: _____	_____	_____	_____
3. *My physical motions that might be called mannerisms because I repeatedly make them are:*	_____	_____	_____

Part II

How does my nonverbal activity relate to my verbal activity?

1. To communicate meaning, I use nonverbal motion without any verbal accompaniment.	_____	_____	_____
2. I use nonverbal motion in my classroom to support my verbal remarks.	_____	_____	_____
3. I use nonverbal motion in my classroom to support other nonverbal activity.	_____	_____	_____
4. I use verbal remarks without nonverbal accompaniment.	_____	_____	_____

Part III

How do I carry on classroom activity? I generally:

sit at the teacher's desk	_____	_____	_____
sit on the teacher's desk	_____	_____	_____
sit on a stool	_____	_____	_____

	Very Typical	Typical	Atypical
sit on a student's chair	_____	_____	_____
sit on the floor	_____	_____	_____
lean on the chalkboard	_____	_____	_____
lean on a desk	_____	_____	_____
stand at the front of the room	_____	_____	_____
stand at the side or rear of the room	_____	_____	_____
move up and down the aisles	_____	_____	_____
move from group to group	_____	_____	_____
move from child to child	_____	_____	_____
move across the front of room	_____	_____	_____
move from desk to chalkboard	_____	_____	_____
move around the outside edge of the room	_____	_____	_____
sit at a table with the students	_____	_____	_____
other: _____	_____	_____	_____

Part IV

What are the general characteristics of my nonverbal classroom behavior?

A. Acuity Level. Consider the number of nonverbal clues you tend to generate in a classroom. Are you very active, active, not too active? Plot yourself on the following activity continuum:

very active   active   not too active

├───────────────────────────────┼───────────────────────────────┤

B. Speed of Motion. Consider the nonverbal motions you make in the classroom. Do you tend to move rapidly? Do you tend to move rather slowly? Plot yourself on the following activity continuum:

rapid   medium   slow

├───────────────────────────────┼───────────────────────────────┤

C. Size of Motion.   Consider the nonverbal motions you make. Do you tend to make such large motions as gestures of the hand? Or do you tend to make such small motions as a nod or smile? Plot yourself on the following size continuum:

large   medium   small

|————————————————————————|————————————————————————|

D. Personal Motions.   Consider the personal motions you use in a classroom. Do you use many personal motions? Do you use a minimal number of personal motions? Plot yourself on the following continuum:

many personal motions   few personal motions

|————————————————————————|————————————————————————|

E. Verbal and Nonverbal Orientation.   Consider the nonverbal activity and the verbal activity that you carry on in the classroom. Do you have a nonverbal orientation in your teaching? Do you have a verbal orientation? Plot yourself on the following verbal and nonverbal continuum:

verbal   verbal/nonverbal   nonverbal

|————————————————————————|————————————————————————|

F. Clarity of Communication.   Consider these questions:

- Is my bodily stance communicating what I want it to communicate? Is my manner of sitting communicating what I want to communicate?
- Is my manner of walking communicating what I want it to communicate?
- Is my gesturing communicating what I want to communicate?
- Are my facial expressions communicating what I want to communicate?
- In terms of these questions plot yourself on the following clarity of communication continuum:

motion communicates   motion does not communicate
what is intended   what is intended

|————————————————————————|————————————————————————|

TEACHER BEHAVIORS INVENTORY

Instructions to Student

In this inventory you are asked to assess your instructor's specific classroom behaviors. Your instructor has requested this information for purposes of instructional analysis and improvement. Please try to be both thoughtful and candid in your responses so as to maximize the value of feedback.

Your judgments should reflect that type of teaching you think is best for this particular course and your particular learning style. Try to assess each behavior independently rather than letting your overall impression of the instructor determine each individual rating.

Each section of the inventory begins with a definition of the category of teaching to be assessed in that section. For each specific teaching behavior, please indicate your judgment as to whether your instructor should increase, decrease, or make no change in the frequency with which he exhibits the behavior in question. Please use the following rating scale in making your judgments:

1 = almost never
2 = rarely
3 = sometimes
4 = often
5 = almost always

Clarity: method to explain or clarify concepts and principles

Gives several examples of each concept	1	2	3	4	5
Uses concrete everyday examples to explain concepts and principles	1	2	3	4	5
Fails to define new or unfamiliar terms	1	2	3	4	5
Repeats difficult ideas several times	1	2	3	4	5
Stresses most important points by pausing, speaking slowly, raising voice, and so on	1	2	3	4	5
Uses graphs or diagrams to facilitate explanation	1	2	3	4	5
Points out practical applications of concepts	1	2	3	4	5
Answers students' questions thoroughly	1	2	3	4	5
Suggests ways of memorizing complicated ideas	1	2	3	4	5
Writes key terms on blackboard or overhead screen	1	2	3	4	5
Explains subject matter in familiar colloquial language	1	2	3	4	5

Enthusiasm: use of behavior to solicit student attention and interest

Speaks in a dramatic or expressive way	1	2	3	4	5
Moves about while lecturing	1	2	3	4	5
Gestures with hands or arms	1	2	3	4	5
Exhibits facial gestures or expressions	1	2	3	4	5
Avoids eye contact with students	1	2	3	4	5
Walks up aisles beside students	1	2	3	4	5
Gestures with head or body	1	2	3	4	5
Tells jokes or humorous anecdotes	1	2	3	4	5
Reads lecture verbatim from prepared notes or text	1	2	3	4	5
Smiles or laughs while teaching	1	2	3	4	5
Shows distracting mannerisms	1	2	3	4	5

Interaction: techniques used to foster students' class participation

Encourages students' questions and comments during lectures	1	2	3	4	5
Criticizes students when they make errors	1	2	3	4	5
Praises students for good ideas	1	2	3	4	5
Asks questions of individual students	1	2	3	4	5
Asks questions of class as a whole	1	2	3	4	5
Incorporates students' ideas into lecture	1	2	3	4	5
Presents challenging, thought-provoking ideas	1	2	3	4	5
Uses a variety of media and activities in class	1	2	3	4	5
Asks rhetorical questions	1	2	3	4	5

Organization: ways of organizing or structuring subject matter

Uses headings and subheadings to organize lectures	1	2	3	4	5
Puts outline of lecture on blackboard or overhead screen	1	2	3	4	5
Clearly indicates transition from one topic to the next	1	2	3	4	5
Gives preliminary overview of lecture at beginning of class	1	2	3	4	5
Explains how each topic fits into the course as a whole	1	2	3	4	5
Begins class with a review of topics covered last time	1	2	3	4	5
Periodically summarizes points previously made	1	2	3	4	5

Pacing: rate of information presentation, efficient use of time

Dwells excessively on obvious points	1	2	3	4	5
Digresses from major theme of lecture	1	2	3	4	5
Covers very little material in class sessions	1	2	3	4	5
Asks if students understand before proceeding to next topic	1	2	3	4	5
Sticks to the point in answering students' questions	1	2	3	4	5

Disclosure: explicitness concerning course requirements and grading criteria

Advises students on how to prepare for tests or exams	1	2	3	4	5
Provides sample exam questions	1	2	3	4	5
Tells students exactly what is expected of them on tests, essays, or assignments	1	2	3	4	5
States objectives of each lecture	1	2	3	4	5
Reminds students of test dates or assignment deadlines	1	2	3	4	5
States objectives of course as a whole	1	2	3	4	5

Speech: characteristics of voice relevant to classroom teaching

Stutters, mumbles, or slurs words	1	2	3	4	5
Speaks at appropriate volume	1	2	3	4	5
Speaks clearly	1	2	3	4	5
Speaks at appropriate pace	1	2	3	4	5
Says "um" or "ah"	1	2	3	4	5
Voice lacks proper modulation (speaks in monotone)	1	2	3	4	5

Rapport: quality of interpersonal relations between teacher and students

Addresses individual students by name	1	2	3	4	5
Announces availability for consultation outside of class	1	2	3	4	5
Offers to help students with problems	1	2	3	4	5
Shows tolerance of other points of view	1	2	3	4	5
Talks with students before or after class	1	2	3	4	5

TEACHER COMMUNICATION RATING SCALE

Teacher name _____   Date _____

School _____   Evaluator _____

Grade Level _____   Student Teacher? _____

Certified? _____

This evaluation form follows the Speech Communication Association's newly developed description of teacher communication competencies. It can be used as a basis for observation in evaluating the classroom communication skills of student teachers to determine the presence or absence of these communication skills.

It is suggested that the following criteria for rating each item be followed for consistency in using this instrument.

Let a #1 rating mean.... Behavior did not appear in this observation.

Let a #2 rating mean.... Opportunities for behavior were present, but student did not demonstrate the behavior at the appropriate time.

Let a #3 rating mean.... Behavior demonstrated occasionally.

Let a #4 rating mean.... Behavior demonstrated consistently with average effectiveness.

Let a #5 rating mean.... Behavior demonstrated consistently with obvious skill.

Column #6—Confidence of judgment. In observing a teacher for a short period of time, not all behaviors may be judged with equal confidence. Column #6 asks the rater to give a confidence level for the judgment of the indicated skill.

- Rating of 1 indicates low confidence in judgment. There were low levels of the observed behaviors.
- Rating of 2 indicates average confidence in judgment.
- Rating of 3 indicates high confidence in judgment.

Ratings do not need to be made in the order presented here. In some instances, the rating for a behavior may be done during the observation. In other instances, the rating may need to be done at the completion of the observation to ensure an adequate sample.

I.   Informative Messages

A. Sending

1. Structures informative messages effectively by using devices such as initial partitions, transitions, internal summaries, and concluding summaries.

___	___	___	___	___	___
1-NR	2	3	4	5	6-CJ

2. Amplifies information effectively through the use of verbal and audio-visual supporting materials.

| 1-NR | 2 | 3 | 4 | 5 | 6-CJ |

3. Asks effective questions to assess student understanding of information given in lectures.

| 1-NR | 2 | 3 | 4 | 5 | 6-CJ |

4. Presents information in an animated and interesting way.

| 1-NR | 2 | 3 | 4 | 5 | 6-CJ |

B. Receiving

1. Is able to identify main point of student comment.

| 1-NR | 2 | 3 | 4 | 5 | 6-CJ |

2. Can identify structural patterns or problems of informative messages.

| 1-NR | 2 | 3 | 4 | 5 | 6-CJ |

3. Can evaluate the adequacy of verbal supporting materials.

| 1-NR | 2 | 3 | 4 | 5 | 6-CJ |

4. Can formulate questions that probe for the informative content of messages.

| 1-NR | 2 | 3 | 4 | 5 | 6-CJ |

5. Can distinguish messages that are delivered in an animated manner and those that are not.

| 1-NR | 2 | 3 | 4 | 5 | 6-CJ |

II. Affective Messages. Teacher should demonstrate competence in sending and receiving affective messages (i.e., messages that express or respond to feelings).

A. Sending

1. Expresses positive and negative feelings about self to students.

| 1-NR | 2 | 3 | 4 | 5 | 6-CJ |

2. Expresses positive and negative feelings about students to students.

1-NR	2	3	4	5	6-CJ

3. Expresses opinions about classroom content, events, and real-world occurrences.

1-NR	2	3	4	5	6-CJ

4. Demonstrates interpersonal openness, warmth, and positive regard for students.

1-NR	2	3	4	5	6-CJ

5. Demonstrates energy and enthusiasm when relating to students.

1-NR	2	3	4	5	6-CJ

B. Receiving

1. Recognizes verbal and nonverbal cues concerning student feelings.

1-NR	2	3	4	5	6-CJ

2. Invites students to express feelings.

1-NR	2	3	4	5	6-CJ

3. Is nonjudgmental in responding to student feelings.

1-NR	2	3	4	5	6-CJ

4. Asks open-ended questions in response to student expressions of feelings.

1-NR	2	3	4	5	6-CJ

5. If necessary, offers advice tactfully.

1-NR	2	3	4	5	6-CJ

III. Imaginative Messages. Teacher should demonstrate competence in sending and receiving imaginative messages (i.e., messages that speculate, theorize, or include fantasy).

A. Sending

   1. Uses vivid descriptive language.

1-NR	2	3	4	5	6-CJ

   2. Uses expressive vocal and physical behavior when creating or re-creating examples, stories, or messages from exemplars.

1-NR	2	3	4	5	6-CJ

B. Receiving

   1. Responds to imaginative messages enthusiastically.

1-NR	2	3	4	5	6-CJ

   2. Is nondirective when encouraging student creativity.

1-NR	2	3	4	5	6-CJ

IV. Ritualistic Messages. Teacher should demonstrate competence in sending and receiving ritualistic messages (i.e., messages that serve to maintain and facilitate social interaction).

A. Sending

   1. Demonstrates appropriate behavior in performing everyday speech acts such as greeting, turn-taking, and leave-taking.

1-NR	2	3	4	5	6-CJ

   2. Models appropriate social amenities in ordinary classroom interaction.

1-NR	2	3	4	5	6-CJ

   3. Demonstrates competence when participating in or role-playing interviews, conversations, problem-solving groups, legislative groups, and public ceremonies.

1-NR	2	3	4	5	6-CJ

B. Receiving

    1. Recognizes when students perform everyday speech acts appropriately.

____	____	____	____	____	____
1-NR	2	3	4	5	6-CJ

    2. Recognizes appropriate and inappropriate performances of social amenities.

____	____	____	____	____	____
1-NR	2	3	4	5	6-CJ

    3. Recognizes competence and incompetence when students participate in interviews, conversations, problem-solving groups, legislative groups, and public ceremonies.

____	____	____	____	____	____
1-NR	2	3	4	5	6-CJ

V. Persuasive Messages. Teacher should demonstrate competence in sending and receiving persuasive messages (i.e., messages that seek to convince).

A. Sending

    1. Can differentiate between fact and opinion.

____	____	____	____	____	____
1-NR	2	3	4	5	6-CJ

    2. Can recognize audience factors that may encourage or constrain acceptance of ideas.

____	____	____	____	____	____
1-NR	2	3	4	5	6-CJ

    3. Offers sound reasons and evidence in support of ideas.

____	____	____	____	____	____
1-NR	2	3	4	5	6-CJ

    4. Recognizes underlying assumptions in own arguments.

____	____	____	____	____	____
1-NR	2	3	4	5	6-CJ

    5. Demonstrates a preference for reason-giving over power moves when interacting with students.

____	____	____	____	____	____
1-NR	2	3	4	5	6-CJ

B. Receiving

1. Recognizes own bias in responding to ideas.

| ___ | ___ | ___ | ___ | ___ | ___ |
| 1-NR | 2 | 3 | 4 | 5 | 6-CJ |

2. Questions the adequacy of reasons and evidence given.

| ___ | ___ | ___ | ___ | ___ | ___ |
| 1-NR | 2 | 3 | 4 | 5 | 6-CJ |

3. Evaluates evidence and reasons presented.

| ___ | ___ | ___ | ___ | ___ | ___ |
| 1-NR | 2 | 3 | 4 | 5 | 6-CJ |

4. Recognizes underlying assumptions in arguments of others.

| ___ | ___ | ___ | ___ | ___ | ___ |
| 1-NR | 2 | 3 | 4 | 5 | 6-CJ |

REFERENCES

Aitken, J. E., & Neer, M. R. (1993). College student question-asking: The relationship of classroom communication apprehension and motivation. *Southern States Communication Journal, 59*, 73–81.

Allen, M., & Bourhis, J. (1996). The relationship of communication apprehension to communication behavior: A meta-analysis. *Communication Quarterly, 44*, 214–226.

Allen, M., & Preiss, R. (1990). Using meta-analysis to evaluate curriculum: An examination of selected college textbooks. *Communication Education, 39*, 103–116.

Allen, R., Brown, K., & Sprague, J. (1991). *Communication in the secondary school: A pedagogy.* Scottsdale, AZ: Gorsuch Scarisbrick.

Allen, R., & Reuter, T. (1990). *Teaching assistant strategies: An introduction to college teaching.* Dubuque, IA: Kendall/Hunt.

Allinder, R. M. (1994). The relationship between efficacy and the instructional practices of special education teachers and consultants. *Teacher Education and Special Education, 17*, 86–95.

American Association of University Women (AAUW). (1991). Shortchanging girls, shortchanging America. Washington, DC: Greenberg–Lake Analysis Group.

American Association of University Women (AAUW). (1992). How schools shortchange girls. Washington, DC: AAUW Educational Foundation and National Education Association.

American Association of University Women (AAUW). (1993). Hostile hallways: The AAUW survey on sexual harassment in America's Schools. Washington, DC: AAUW.

American Assocation of University Women. (1998). *Gender Gaps: Where Schools Still Fail Children.* Washington, DC: AAUW Education Foundation and National Education Association.

Amidon, E., & Hunter, E. (1966). *Improving teaching.* New York: Holt, Rinehart & Winston.

Amidon, E. J., & Flanders, N. A. (1967). *The role of the teacher in the classroom: A manual for understanding and improving teacher classroom behavior.* Minneapolis, MN: Association for Productive Teaching.

Amstutz, J. (1987, November). In defense of telling stories. *Teaching Forum.*

Andersen, J. (1979). The relationship between teacher immediacy and teaching effectiveness. In D. Nimmo (Ed.), *Communication yearbook 3* (pp. 543–561). New Brunswick, NJ: Transaction Books.

Andersen, J. (1986). Instructor nonverbal communication: Listening to our silent messages. In J. M. Civikly (Ed.), *Communicating in college classrooms* (pp. 39–47). San Francisco: Jossey-Bass.

Andersen, J., & Powell, R. (1994). Cultural and classroom communication. In L. Samovar & R. Porter (Eds., pp. 322–334). *Intercultural communication: A reader.* Belmont, CA: Wadsworth.

Andersen, J. F., & Nussbaum, J. (1990). Interaction skill in instructional settings. In J. A. Daly, G. W. Friedrich, & A. Vangelisti (Eds.), *Teaching communication: Theory, research, and methods* (pp. 301–316). Hillsdale, NJ: Erlbaum.

Andersen, K. E. (1990). Ethical issues in teaching. In J. Daly, G. Friedrich, & A. Vangelisti (Eds.), *Teaching communication: Theory, research, and methods* (pp. 459–470). Hillsdale, NJ: Erlbaum.

Andersen, P., & Andersen, J. (1982). Nonverbal intimacy in instruction. In L. Barker (Ed.), *Communication in the classroom* (pp. 99–105). Englewood Cliffs, NJ: Prentice Hall.

Anderson, I. (1989). Classroom instruction. In M. Reynolds (Ed.), *Knowledge base for the beginning teacher* (pp. 101–116). New York: Pergamon.

Anderson, J. A. (1988). Cognitive studies and multicultural populations. *Journal of Teacher Education, 39*(1), 2–9.

Anderson, J., & Powell, R. (1988). Cultural influences on educational processes. In L. Samovar & L.

Porter (Eds.), *Intercultural communication: A reader.* (pp. 207–214). Belmont, CA: Wadsworth.

Anderson, K., & Miller, E. (1997). Gender and student evaluations of teaching. *PS: Political Sciences and Politics, 30*(2), 216–219.

Arlow, P., & Froschel, M. (1976). Women in the high school curriculum: A review of U.S. history and English literature texts. In C. Ahlum, J. Fralley, & F. Howe (Eds.), *High school feminist studies* (pp. 11–28). Old Westbury, NY: Feminist Press.

Arnold, A. J. (1983, March). What's new? *Learning, 12,* 10.

Atkins-Sayre, W., Hopkins, S., Mohundro, S., & Sayre, W. (1998, November). *Rewards and liabilities of presentation software as an ancillary tool: Prison or paradise?* Paper presented at the National Communication Association, New York. (ERIC Document Reproduction Service No. ED 430 260)

Au, K. H. (1993). *Literacy instruction in multicultural settings.* New York: Harcourt.

Audi, R. (1994, September–October). On the ethics of teaching and the ideals of learning. *Academe, 80*(5), 26–36.

Auster, C., and MacRone, M. (1994). The classroom as a negotiated social setting: An empirical study of the effects of faculty members' behavior on students' participation. *Teaching Sociology, 22,* 289–300.

Austin, C., & MacRone, M. (1994). The classroom as a negotiated social setting: An empirical study of the effects of faculty members' behavior on students' participation. *Teaching Sociology, 22,* 289–300.

Ayres, J., & Hopf, T. (1993). *Coping with speech anxiety.* Norwood, NJ: Ablex.

Ayres, J., Hopf, T., & Ayres, D. (1994). An examination of whether imaging ability enhances the effectiveness of an intervention designed to reduce speech anxiety. *Communication Education, 43,* 252–258.

Bachen, C., McLaughlin, M., & Garcia, S. (1999). Assessing the role of gender in college students' evaluations of faculty. *Communication Education, 48,* 193–210.

Badini, A., & Rosenthal, R. (1989). Visual cues, student sex, material taught, and the magnitude of teacher expectancy effects. *Communication Education, 38,* 162–166.

Bailey, G. (1981). Teacher self-assessment: A means for improving instruction. Washington, DC: National Education Association.

Balli, S. J., & Diggs, L. L. (1996). Educational technology research section. *Educational Technology, 36*(1), 56–61.

Bandura, A. (1997). *Self-efficacy: The exercise of control.* New York: Freeman.

Banks, J. (1998). Multicultural education: Development, dimensions, and challenges. In M. Bennett (Ed.), *Basic concepts of intercultural communication* (pp. 69–84). Yarmouth, ME: Intercultural Press.

Banks, J. A. (1988). *Multiethnic education: Theory and practice.* Newton, MA: Allyn & Bacon.

Barker, L. L. (1971). *Listening Behavior.* Englewood Cliffs, NJ: Prentice Hall.

Barker, L. L. (Ed.). (1981). *Communication in the classroom.* Englewood Cliffs, NJ: Prentice Hall.

Barna, L. (1988). Stumbling blocks in intercultural communication. In L. Samovar & R. Porter (Eds.), *Intercultural communication: A reader* (pp. 322–330). Belmont, CA: Wadsworth.

Barnlund, D. (1975). *The public and private self in Japan and the United States.* Tokyo: Simul Press.

Barraclough, R. A., & Stewart, R. A. (1992). Power and control: Social science perspectives. In V. P. Richmond & J. C. McCroskey (Eds.), *Power in the classroom: Communication, control, and concern* (pp. 1–18). Hillsdale, NJ: Erlbaum.

Barton, L. (1984). What are boys like in books these days? *Learning, 13,* 130–131.

Basow, S. A. (1992). *Gender: Stereotypes and roles* (3rd ed.). Pacific Grove, CA: Brooks/Cole.

Bassett, R., & Smythe, M. J. (1979). *Communication and instruction.* New York: Harper & Row.

Bate, B. (1988). *Communication between the sexes.* New York: Harper & Row.

Beane, A. L. (2000). *The bully-free classroom: Over 100 tips and strategies for teacher K–8.* Murray, KY: Free Spirit Publishing.

Beatty, M. (1988, January). Situational and predispositional correlates of public speaking anxiety. *Communication Education, 37,* 28–39.

Beatty, M. J., & Behnke, R. R. (1980). Teacher credibility as a function of verbal content and paralinguistic cues. *Communication Quarterly, 28,* 55–59.

Beatty, M. J., & Zahn, C. J. (1990). Are student ratings of communication instructors due to "easy" grading practices?: An analysis of teacher credibility and student-reported performance levels. *Communication Education, 39,* 275–292.

Beebe, S. (1980). *The role of nonverbal communication in education: Research and theoretical perspectives.* Paper presented at the meeting of the Speech Communication Association, New York.

Beebe, S. A., & Butland, M. J. (1993, November). *Implicit communication and learning: Explaining affinity-seeking behaviors in the classroom.* Paper presented at the Speech Communication Association Convention, Miami, FL.

Beilke, J. R., & Yasel, N. (1999). The chilly climate for students with disabilities in higher education. *College Student Journal, 33*(3), 364–371.

Berger, P. L., & Luckman, T. (1966). *The social construction of reality.* New York: Doubleday.

Berliner, D. C. (1968). *The effects of testlike events and note-taking on learning from lecture instruction.* Unpublished doctoral dissertation, Stanford University, Stanford, CA.

Berliner, D. C., & Fisher, C. W. (1985). *Perspectives on instructional time.* New York: Longman.

Berlo, D. (1960). *The process of communication.* New York: Holt, Rinehart & Winston.

Berthoff, A. (1981). *The making of meaning: Metaphors, models, and maxims for writing teachers.* Montclair, NJ: Boynton/Cook.

Birdwhistell, R. L. (1970). *Kinesics and context.* Philadelphia: University of Pennsylvania Press.

Bloom, B. S., Englehart, M., Furst, E., Hill, W., & Krathwohl, D. (1956). *Taxonomy of educational objectives: Cognitive domain.* New York: David McKay.

Bohlken, B. (1991). A hearing aid: Improving classroom listening skills. *The Teaching Professor, 7,* 6–7.

Bolls, P., & Tan, A. (1996). Communication anxiety and teacher communication competence among native American and Caucasian students. *Communication Research Reports, 13,* 205–213.

Bond, M. H. (1991). *Beyond the Chinese face: Insights from psychology.* United Kingdom: Oxford University Press.

Booth-Butterfield, M. (1986, October). Stifle or stimulate? The effects of communication task structure on apprehensive and non-apprehensive students. *Communication Education, 35,* 337–348.

Booth-Butterfield, S. (1988, July). Instructional interventions for reducing situational anxiety and avoidance. *Communication Education, 37,* 214–224.

Borisoff, D. (1990). *Community in a multicultural society: Issues and strategies for the 21st century.* Paper presented at the meeting of the Speech Communication Association of Puerto Rico, San Juan.

Borton, W. (1991). *Empowering teacher and students in a restructuring school: A teacher efficacy interaction model and the effect on reading outcomes.* Paper presented at the American Educational Research Association, Chicago.

Bosworth, K., & Hamilton, S. (Eds.). (1994). Collaborative learning: Underlying processes and effective techniques. *New Directions for Teaching and Learning,* (vol. 59). San Francisco: Jossey-Bass.

Bourhis, J., & Allen, M. (1992). Meta-analysis of the relationship between communication apprehension and cognitive performance. *Communication Education, 41,* 68–76.

Bowman, B. (1989, October). Educating language-minority children: Challenges and opportunities. *Phi Delta Kappan, 71,* 118–120.

Bozik, B. (1989). Teaching students to listen. *Teacher Talk, 7, 2, 7.*

Braithwaite, D. O. (1990). From majority to minority: An analysis of cultural change from able-bodied to disabled. *International Journal of Intercultural Relations, 14,* 465–483.

Braithwaite, D. O. (1991). Just how much did that wheelchair cost? Management of privacy boundaries by persons with disabilities. *Western Journal of Speech Communication, 55,* 254–274.

Braithwaite, D. O. (1996). "I am a person first": Different perspectives on the communication of persons with disabilities. In E. B. Ray (Ed.), *Communication and disenfranchisement: Social health issues and implications* (pp. 257–272). Mahwah, NJ: Erlbaum.

Braithwaite, D. O., & Braithwaite, C. A. (2000). Understanding communication of persons with disabilties as cultural communication. In L. A. Samovar & R. E. Porter (Eds.), *Intercultural communication* (pp. 136–145). Belmont, CA: Wadsworth.

Branon, J. M. (1972). Negative human interaction. *Journal of Counseling Psychology, 19*(1), 81–89.

Braun, C. (1976). Teacher expectation: Sociopsychological dynamics. *Review of Educational Research, 46,* 206.

Bray, J. H., & Howard, G. S. (1980). Interaction of teacher and student sex and sex role orientations and student evaluations of college instruction. *Contemporary Educational Psychology, 5,* 241–248.

Brislin, R. (1993). *Understanding culture's influence on behavior.* San Diego, CA: Harcourt.

Brodsky, S. M. (1991). Behavioral instructional and departmental strategies for retention of college students in science, engineering, or technology programs: How to become an even more effective teacher or departmental administrator. *CASE 15(91).* Albany: New York State Education Department.

Brophy, J. (1987, October). Synthesis of research on strategies for motivating students to learn. *Educational Leadership, 45,* 4–13.

Brophy, J. E. (1983). Classroom organization and management. *Elementary School Journal, 83,* 265–286.

Brophy, J., & Good, T. (1974). *Teacher–student relationships: Causes and consequences.* New York: Holt, Rinehart & Winston.

Brophy, J., & Good, T. (1986). Teacher behavior and student achievement. In M. C. Wittock (Ed.), *Handbook of research on teaching.* New York: Macmillan.

Brown, C., & Keller, P. (1979). *Monologue to dialogue.* Englewood Cliffs, NJ: Prentice Hall.

Brown, H. (1987). *Principles of language learning and teaching* (2nd ed.). Englewood Cliffs, NJ: Prentice Hall.

Brownell, J. (1996). *Listening: Attitudes, principles, and skills.* Boston: Allyn & Bacon.

Bruffee, K. (1980). *A short course in writing* (2nd ed.). Boston: Little, Brown.

Bruffee, K. (1984). Collaborative learning and the conversation of mankind. *College English, 46,* 634–640.

Bruffee, K. (1993). *Collaborative learning: Higher education, interdependence, and the authority of knowledge.* Baltimore, MD: Johns Hopkins University Press.

Bryant, J., Comisky, P., & Zillman, D. (1979). Teachers' humor in the college classroom. *Communication Education, 28,* 110–118.

Buber, M. (1970). *I and thou* (W. Kaufmann, Trans.). New York: Appleton-Century-Crofts.

Buck, S., & Tiene, D. (1989). The impact of physical attractiveness, gender, and teaching philosophy on evaluations. *Journal of Educational Research, 82,* 172–177.

Burleson, B. R., & Waltman, M. S. (1993, May). *Assessing the validity of message behavior check lists: Some conceptual and empirical requirements.* Paper presented at the annual meeting of the International Communication Association, Washington, DC.

Burley, W. W., Hall, B. W., Villeme, M. G., & Brockmeier, L. L. (1991, April). *A path analysis of the mediating role of efficacy in first-year teachers' experiences, reactions, and plans.* Paper presented at the Annual Meeting of the American Educational Research Association, Chicago.

Burr, E., Dunn, S., & Farquhar, N. (1972). Women and the language of inequality. *Social Education, 36,* 841–845.

Burroughs, N., Kearney, P., & Plax, T. (1989). Compliance-resistance in the college classroom. *Communication Education, 38,* 214–229.

Campbell, K. (1991). Hearing women's voices. *Communication Education, 40,* 33–48.

Calloway-Thomas, C., Cooper, P., & Blake, C. (1999). *Intercultural communication: Roots to routes.* Boston: Allyn & Bacon.

Cano, J., Jones, C., & Chism, N. (1991). TA teaching of an increasingly diverse undergraduate population. In J. Nyquist, R. Abbott, D. Wulff, & J. Sprague (Eds.), *Preparing the professorate of tomorrow to teach* (pp. 87–94). Dubuque, IA: Kendall Hunt.

Carlson, M. (1989). Guidelines for a gender-based curriculum in English, grades 7–12. *English Journal, 36,* 30–33.

Carnahan, S. (1994). Preventing school failure and dropout. In R. Simeonsson (Ed.), *Risk, resilience and prevention: Promoting the well-being of all children* (pp. 103–123). Baltimore, MD: Paul H. Brooks.

Carter, K., & Spitzack, C. (Eds.), (1989). *Doing research on women's communication: Perspectives on theory and method.* Norwood, NJ: Ablex.

Cashin, W. (1995, January). *Answering and asking questions.* IDEA Paper no. 31, Center for Faculty Evaluation and Development. Kansas State University, Manhattan, KS.

Cawyer, C. S. (1994). *A cross-disciplinary assessment of teacher communications behaviors in the classroom.* Unpublished doctoral dissertation, University of Oklahoma, Norman.

Cawyer, C., Bystrom, D., Miller, J., Simonds, C., O'Brien, M., & Storey–Martin, J. (1994). Community gender equity: Representation and portrayal of women and men in introductory communication textbooks. *Communication Education, 45,* 325–331.

Cazden, C. B. (1988). *Classroom discourse: The language of teaching and learning.* Portsmouth, NH: Heinemann Educational Books. (ERIC Document Reproduction Service No. ED 288 206)

Centra, J., & Gaubatz, N. (2000). Is there gender bias in student evaluations of teaching? *Journal of Higher Education, 71,* 17.

Chesebro, J., McCroskey, J., Atwater, D., Behrenfuss, R., Cawelt, G., Gaudino, J., & Hodges, H. (1992). Communication apprehension and self-perceived communication competence of at-risk students. *Communication Education, 41,* 345–360.

Chethik, N. (1994, August 28). Boys, too, shortchanged in classroom. *The Cleveland Plain Dealer,* p. 5.

Chisholm, I. (1994). Preparing teachers for multicultural classrooms. *The Journal of Educational Issues of Language Minority Students, 14,* 43–67.

Chism, N., Cano, J., & Pruitt, A. (1989). Teaching in a diverse environment: Knowledge and skills needed by TAs. In J. Nyquist, R. Abbott, & D. Wulff (Eds.), *Teaching assistant training in the 1990's: New directions for teaching and learning* (pp. 23–35). San Franciso: Jossey-Bass.

Chou, P. P. (1979). *An empirical study of Chinese communicative competence in an American cultural setting.* Unpublished master's thesis, Texas Tech University, Lubbock.

Christensen, C. R., & Hansen, A. J. (1987). *Teaching and the case method.* Boston: Harvard Business School.

Christophel, D. (1990). The relationship among teacher immediacy behaviors, student motivation, and learning. *Communication Education, 39,* 323–340.

Christophel, D. (1996). Russian communication orientations: A cross-cultural examination. *Communication Research Reports, 13*(1), 43–51.

Christophel, D., & Gorham, J. (1995). A test-retest analysis of student motivation, teacher immediacy, and perceived sources of motivation and demotivation in college classes. *Communication Education, 44,* 293–306.

Civikly, J. (1982). Self-concept, significant others, and classroom communication. In L. Barker (Ed.), *Communication in the classroom.* Englewood Cliffs, NJ: Prentice Hall.

Civikly, J. M. (1992a). Clarity: Teachers and students making sense of instruction. *Communication Education, 41,* 138–152.

Civikly, J. M. (1992b). *Classroom communication: Principles and practice.* Dubuque, IA: Wm. C. Brown.

Cohen, E. (1987). *Design group work: Strategies for the heterogeneous classroom.* New York: Teachers College Press.

Cohen, J. (1998). *Disability etiquette.* Jackson Heights, NY: EPVA.

Cole, R. (Ed.). (1995). *Educating everybody's children: Diverse teaching strategies for diverse learners.* Alexandria, VA: ASCD.

Coleman, L., & DePaulo, B. (1991). Uncovering the human spirit: Moving beyond disability and "missed" communications. In N. Coupland, H. Giles, & J. M. Wiemann (Eds.), *Miscommunication and problematic talk* (pp. 61–84). Newbury Park, CA: Sage.

Coles, R. (1989). *The call of stories: Teaching and the moral imagination.* Boston: Houghton Mifflin.

Collier, M. J., & Powell, R. (1990). Ethnicity instructional communication and classroom systems. *Communication Quarterly, 4,* 334–349.

Collins, C. (1993). Teacher skills with classroom discussion: Impact on student mastery of subject matter, self-concept, and oral expression skills. *Roeper Review, 43*(1), 45–53.

Collins, R., & Cooper, P. (1997). *The power of story: Teaching through storytelling.* Boston: Allyn & Bacon.

Comadena, M. E., & Prusank, D. T. (1988). Communication apprehension and academic achievement among elementary and middle school students. *Communication Education, 37,* 270–277.

Combs, A. W. (1965). *The professional education of teachers.* Boston: Allyn & Bacon.

Condon, J. (1986). The ethnocentric classroom. In J. M. Civikly (Ed.), *Communicating in college classrooms* (pp. 11–20). San Francisco: Jossey-Bass.

Condravy, J., Skirboll, E., & Taylor, R. (1998). Faculty perceptions of classroom gender dynamics. *Women and Language, 21,* 18–27.

Constantinople, A., Cornelius, R., & Gray, J. (1998). The chilly climate: Fact or artifact? *The Journal of Higher Education, 59,* 527–550.

Cooper, B. I was sure to follow. [Unpublished personal collection.] 1965

Cooper, B. Pam. [Unpublished personal collection.] 1956

Cooper, B. The spaces in between. [Unpublished personal collection.] 1960

Cooper, E., & Allen, M. (1998). A meta-analytic examination of the impact of student race on classroom interaction. *Communication Research Reports, 15,* 151–161.

Cooper, H. (1985). Models of teacher expectation communication. In J. Dusek (Ed.), *Teacher expectancies* (pp. 135–158). Hillsdale, NJ: Erlbaum.

Cooper, H., & Good, T. (1983). *Pygmalion grows up: Studies in the expectation communication process.* New York: Longman.

Cooper, H., & Tom, D. (1984). Teacher expectation research: A review with implications for classroom instruction. *The Elementary School Journal, 85,* 77–89.

Cooper, P. (1987). Sex role stereotypes of stepparents in children's literature. In L. P. Stewart & S. Ting-Toomey (Eds.), *Communication gender, and sex roles in diverse interaction contexts* (pp. 61–82). Norwood, NJ: Ablex.

Cooper, P. (1988a). *Communication competencies for teachers.* Speech Communication Association: Annandale, VA.

Cooper, P. (1988b). *Teacher effectiveness as a function of communicator style.* Speech Communication Association, Annandale, VA.

Cooper, P. (1989). Children's literature: The extent of sexism. In C. Lont & S. Friedley (Eds.), *Beyond boundaries: Sex and gender diversity in education* (pp. 233–250). Fairfax, VA: George Mason University Press.

Cooper, P. (1993b). Women and power in the Caldecott and Newbery winners, 1980–90. In C. Berryman-Fink, D. Ballard-Reisch, & L. Newman (Eds.), *Communication and sex-role socialization* (pp. 7–27). New York: Garland.

Cooper, P. (1994). The image of stepmothers in children's literature 1980–1991. In L. Turner & H. Sterk (Eds.), *Differences that make a difference.* Westport, CT: Bergin & Gravey.

Cooper, P. (2000). Image of stepmothers in children's literature, 1980–2000. Organization for the Study of Communication, Language and Gender Conference, Milwaukee, WI.

Cooper, P., & Galvin, K. (1982). *Improving classroom communication.* Washington, DC: Dingle Association.

Cooper, P., & Galvin, K. (1983). *Improving classroom communication.* Washington, DC: Dingle Associates.

Cooper, P. J., Stewart, L. P., & Gudykunst, W. B. (1982). Relationship with instructor and other variables influencing student evaluations of instruction. *Communication Quarterly, 30,* 308–315.

Cornett, C. (1983). *What you should know about teaching and learning styles.* Bloomington, IN: Phi Delta Kappa Educational Foundation.

Costa, A., Garmston, R., & Lambert, L. (1988). Evaluation of teaching: The cognitive development view. In S. Stanley & W. J. Popham (Eds.), *Teacher evaluation: Six prescriptions for success* (p. 148). Alexandria, VA: ASCD.

Covert, A. (1978). *Communication: People speak, instructor's manual.* New York: McGraw-Hill.

Crawford, M., & MacLeod, M. (1990). Gender in the college classroom: An assessment of the "chilly climate" for women. *Sex Roles, 23,* 101–122.

Cruickshank, D. R. (1985). Applying research on teacher clarity. *Journal of Teacher Education, 36,* 44–48.

Cullum, A. (1971). *The geranium on the window sill just died but teacher you went right on.* New York: Harlin Quist.

Cullum, A. (1978). *Blackboard, blackboard on the wall who is the fairest one of all?* New York: Harlin Quist.

Curwin, R., & Mendler, A. (1988). *Discipline with dignity.* Alexandria, VA: ASCD.

Cushner, K., & Brislin, R. (1996). *Intercultural interactions: A practical guide* (2nd ed.). Thousand Oaks, CA: Sage.

Cyber Dialogue. (1999). The American Internet User Survey (on-line). Available at http://www.cyberdialogue.com/free_data/index.html

Czubaj, C. A. (1996). Maintaining teacher motivation. *Education, 116,* 372–378.

Daly, J. A., & Friedrich, G. (1981). The development of communication apprehension: A retrospective analysis of contributory correlates. *Communication Quarterly, 29,* 243–255.

Daly, J. A., & Kreiser, P. O. (1993). Affinity in the classroom. In V. P. Richmond & J. C. McCroskey (Eds.), *Power in the classroom: Communication, control, and concern* (pp. 121–143). Hillsdale, NJ: Erlbaum.

Darling, A. (1989). Signaling non-comprehensions in the classroom: Toward a descriptive typology. *Communication Education, 38,* 34–40.

Darling, A. (1990). Instructional models. In J. Daly, G. Friedrich, and A. Vangelisti (Eds.), *Teaching communication: Theory, research and methods* (pp. 267–278). Hillsdale, NJ: Erlbaum.

Darling, A., & Civikly, J. (1987). The effect of teacher humor on student perceptions of classroom communicative climate. *Journal of Classroom Interaction, 22,* 24–30.

Davidson, C., & Ambrose, S. (1995). *The new professor's handbook.* Boston: Anker Publishing.

Davis, B. G. (1993). *Tools for teaching.* San Francisco: Jossey-Bass.

Decker, S. (1969). *An empty spoon.* New York: Harper & Row.

Deemer, D. (1986). Structuring controversy in the classroom. In S. F. Schomberg (Ed.), *Strategies for active teaching and learning in university classrooms.* Minneapolis, MN: Office of Educational Development Programs, University of Minnesota.

Deethardt, J. E. (1974). The use of questions in the speech-communication classroom. *Speech Teacher, 23,* 15–20.

DeFleur, M. L., Kearney, P., & Plax, T. G. (1998). *Fundamentals of human communication* (2nd ed.). Fort Worth, TX: Harcourt.

Dillon, J. T. (1988a). *Questioning and teaching.* New York: Teachers College Press.

Dillon, J. T. (1988b). The remedial status of student questioning. *Journal of Curriculum Studies, 20,* 197–210.

Dillon, J. T. (1990). *The practice of questioning.* London: Routledge.

Dodd, C. H. (1995). *Dynamics of intercultural communication* (4th ed.). Madison, WI: Brown & Benchmark.

Dolin, D. J. (1995). *Ain't misbehavin: A study of teacher misbehaviors, related communication behaviors, and student resistance.* Unpublished doctoral dissertation, West Virginia University, Morgantown.

Donlan, D. (1972). The negative image of women in children's literature. *Elementary English, 49,* 604–611.

Dorman, M. (1998). Using e-mail to enhance instruction. *The Journal of School Health, 68*(6), 260–261.

Dougherty, R., Bowen, C., Berger, T., Rees, W., Mellon, E., & Pulliam, E. (1995). Cooperative learning and enhanced communication: Effects on student performance, retention, and attitudes in general chemistry. *Journal of Chemical Education, 72,* 793–797.

Dougherty, W., & Engel, R. (1987). An 80s look for sex equality in Caldecott winners and honor books. *The Reading Teacher, 40,* 394–398.

Downing, J., & Garmon, C. (2001). Teaching students in the basic course how to use presentation software. *Communication Education, 50*(3), 218–229.

Downs, V. C., Javidi, M., & Nussbaum, J. F. (1988). An analysis of teachers' verbal communication within the college classroom: Use of humor, self-disclosure, and narratives. *Communication Education, 37,* 127–141.

Duke, C. (1971). Questions teachers ask: By-pass or through-ways? *The Clearing House, 45,* 468–472.

Dunn, R., Beaudry, J., & Klavas, A. (1989). A survey of research on learning styles. *Educational Leadership, 50,* 58.

Dunn, R., Dunn, K., & Price, G. (1979). Identifying individual learning styles. In O. Kiernan (Ed.), *Student learning styles: Diagnosing and prescribing programs.* Reston, VA: National Association of Secondary School Principals.

Ekman, P., & Friesen, W. V. (1969). The repertoire of nonverbal behavior: Categories, origins, usage, and coding. *Semiotica, 1,* 49–98.

Eleser, C., Longman, D., & Steib, P. (1996, October). A dozen responses to incorrect answers. *The Teaching Professor, 10,* 1.

Elliott, S., Scott, M. D., Jensen, A. D., & McDonough, M. (1981). Perceptions of reticence: A cross-cultural investigation. In D. Nimmo (Ed.), *Communication yearbook* (Vol. 5, pp. 591–602). New Brunswick, NJ: Transaction Books.

Ellis, K. (1995). Apprehension, self-perceived competency, and teacher immediacy in the laboratory-supported public speaking course: Trends and relationships. *Communication Education, 44,* 64–78.

Elsen, A. (1969). The pleasures of teaching. In *The study of education at Stanford: Report to the university, VIII, teaching, research, and the faculty* (pp. 78–87). Stanford, CA: Stanford University.

Ennis, R. (1985). Goals for a critical thinking curriculum. In A. Costa (Ed.), *Developing minds: A resource book for teaching thinking* (p. 54). Alexandria, VA: Association for Supervision and Curriculum Development.

Epperson, S. E. (1988, September 16). Studies link subtle sex bias in schools with women's behavior in the work-place. *Wall Street Journal,* p. 27.

Ericson, P., & Gardner, J. (1992). Two longitudinal studies of communication apprehension and its effects on college students' success. *Communication Quarterly, 40,* 127–137,

Evertson, C. M. (1987). Creating conditions for learning: From research to practice. *Theory into Practice, 26,* 44–50.

Evertson, C. M., & Emmer, E. T. (1982). Effective management at the beginning of the school year in junior high classes. *Journal of Educational Psychology, 74*(4), 485–498.

Evertson, C. M., & Harris, A. H. (1992, April). What we know about managing classrooms. *Educational Leadership,* 74–78.

Fagot, B. I. (1984). Teacher and peer reactions to boys' and girls' play styles. *Sex Roles, 11,* 691–702.

Fassinger, P. (1995). Understanding classroom interaction: Students' and professors' contributions to students' silence. *Journal of Higher Education, 66*(1), 82–97.

Fassinger, P. (1996). Professors and students perceptions of why students participate in class. *Teaching Sociology, 24,* 25–33.

Fayer, J. M., Gorham, J., & McCroskey, J. C. (1993). Teacher immediacy and student learning: A comparison between U.S. mainland and Puerto Rican classrooms. In J. Fayer (Ed.), *Puerto Rican communication studies* (pp. 111–126). Puerto Rico: Fundacion Arquelogica, Anthropologica, Historica de Puerto Rico.

Feiner, S., & Morgan, B. (1987). Women and minorities in introductory economics textbooks: 1974 to 1984. *Journal of Economic Education, 18,* 376–392

Feiner, S., & Roberts, B. (1990). Hidden by the invisible hand: Neoclassical economic theory and the textbook treatment of race and gender. *Gender and Society, 4,* 159–181.

Feitler, F. C. (1971, September). Teacher's desk. Reprinted in K. Goodoll, Tie line. *Psychology Today, 6,* 12.

Feldhusen, J. (1989, March). Synthesis of research on gifted youth. *Educational Leadership, 46,* 6–11.

Ferree, M. M., & Hall, E. J. (1990). Visual images of American society: Gender and race in introductory sociology textbooks. *Gender and Society, 4,* 500–533.

Fisch, L. (1992, November). *The teaching professor.* Madison, WI: Magna Publications.

Fisher, B. A. (1970). Decision emergence: Phases in group decision making. *Speech Monographs, 37,* 53–66.

Fisher, W. R. (1984). Narration as a human paradigm. *Communication Monographs, 51,* 1–22.

Fitch-Hauser, M., Barker, D., & Hughes, A. (1992). Receiver apprehension and listening apprehension: A linear or curvilinear relationship? *The Southern Communication Journal, 57,* 62–77.

Fleming, P. M. (2000). Three decades of education progress (and continuing barriers) for women and girls. *Equity and Excellence in Education, 33,* 74–79.

Fouts, J., & Myers, R. (1992). Classroom environments and middle school students' views of science. *The Journal of Educational Research, 85,* 356–361.

Frankel, C. (1965). *The neglected aspect of foreign affairs.* Washington, DC: Brookings Institute.

French, R. P., & Raven, B. (1959). The bases for social power. In D. Cartwright (Ed.), *Studies in social power* (pp. 150–167). Ann Arbor, MI: Institute for Social Research.

French, R. P., & Raven, B. (1960). The bases of social power. In D. Cartwright & A. Zander (Eds.), *Group dynamics* (pp. 607–623). Evanston, IL: Row, Peterson.

French-Lazovik, G. (1974). Predictability of students' evaluations of college teachers from component ratings. *Journal of Educational Psychology, 66,* 373–385.

Frey, P., Leonard, D., & Beatty, W. (1975). Student ratings of instruction: Validation research. *American Educational Research Journal, 12,* 435–447.

Friedrich, G., & Cooper, P. (1999). First day. In J. Daly, G. Friedrich, & A. Vangelisti (Eds.), *Teaching communication: Theory, research, and methods* (pp. 287–296). Hillsdale, NJ: Erlbaum.

Friedrich, G. W. (1982). Communication in the classroom: Original essays. In L. L. Barker (Ed.), *Teacher as only native.* Englewood Cliffs, NJ: Prentice Hall.

Frost, G. E. (1974). *Bless my growing.* Minneapolis, MN: Augsburg Publishing House.

Fry, P. G. (1994). Equity: A vision for multicultural education. *Equity and Excellence, 25,* 139–144.

Frymier, A., & Houser, M. (2000). The teacher–student relationship as an interpersonal relationship. *Communication Education, 49*(3), 207–220.

Frymier, A. B. (1994a). A model of immediacy in the classroom. *Communication Quarterly, 42*(2), 133–144.

Frymier, A. B. (1994b). The use of affinity-seeking in producing liking and learning in the classroom. *Journal of Applied Communication Research, 22,* 87–105.

Frymier, A., & Shulman, G. (1995). What's in it for me? Increasing content relevance to enhance students' motivation. *Communication Education, 44,* 40–50.

Frymier, A., & Thompson, C. (1992). Perceived teacher affinity-seeking in relation to perceived teacher credibility. *Communication Education, 41,* 388–399.

Fulghum, R. (1988). *All I really need to know I learned in kindergarten.* New York: Villard Books.

Fusani, D. (1994). Extra-class communication: Frequency, immediacy, self-disclosure, and satisfaction in student–faculty interaction outside the classroom. *Journal of Applied Communication Research, 22,* 232–255.

Gabriel, S. L., & Smithson, I. (Eds.). (1990). *Gender in the classroom: Power and pedagogy.* Urbana, IL: University of Illinois Press.

Gage, N. L., & Berliner, D. C. (1975). *Educational Psychology: Study Guide.* Boston: Houghton Mifflin.

Gall, M. (1970). The use of questions in teaching. *Review of Educational Research, 40,* 707–721.

Gall, M. (1984). Synthesis of research on teachers' questioning. *Educational Leadership, 42,* 40–47.

Gall, M., & Rhody, T. (1987). Review of research on questioning techniques. In W. Wilen (Ed.), *Questions, questioning techniques, and effective teaching* (pp. 23–48). Washington, DC: NEA.

Galvin, K. (1985). *Listening by doing.* Lincolnwood, IL: National Textbook Co.

Gamble, T. K., & Gamble, M. (1999). *Communication works* (6th ed.). New York: McGraw-Hill.

Gambrell, L. (1983). The occurrence of think-time during reading comprehension. *Journal of Educational Research, 77,* 77–80.

Garside, C. (1996). Look who's talking: A comparison of lecture and group discussion teaching strategies in developing critical thinking skills. *Communication Education, 45,* 212–227.

Garwood, S. (1983, March). *Learning, 11,* 8.

Gay, G. (1978). Viewing the pluralistic classroom as a cultural microcosm. *Educational Research Quarterly, 2,* 49–55.

Gerritz, K. (1983, February). Dear Ms. McCrea, about that conference next week. *Learning, 11,* 46.

Gibaldi, J. (1999). *MLS handbook for writers of research papers* (5th ed.). New York: Ballantine Books.

Gibb, J. (1961). Defensive communication. *Journal of Communication, 11,* 142–148,

Gibson, J. (1982, June 2). Do looks help children make the grade? *Family Weekly,* 9.

Gill, M. (1994). Accent and stereotypes: Their effect on perceptions of teachers and lecture comprehension. *Journal of Applied Communication, 22,* 348–361.

Glasser, W. (1969). *Schools without failure.* New York: Harper & Row.

Gloeckner, B. (1983). *An investigation into the effectiveness of a preservice teacher clarity training unit in two different experimental settings.* Unpublished doctoral dissertation, Ohio State University, Columbus, OH.

Gold, D., Crombie, G., & Noble, S. (1987). Relations between teachers' judgments of girls' and boys' compliance and intellectual competence. *Sex Roles, 16,* 351–358.

Golish, T. D., & Olson, L. N. (2000). Students' use of power in the classroom: An investigation of student power, teacher power, and teacher immediacy. *Communication Quarterly, 48*(3), 293–310.

Gollnick, D. M., & Chinn, P. C. (1994). *Multicultural education in a pluralistic society.* New York: Merrill.

Golub, J. (1988). Focus on collaborative learning. Urbana, IL: National Council of Teachers of English.

Good, T., & Brophy, J. (1991). *Looking in classrooms* (5th ed.). New York: Harper & Row.

Gordon, T. (1974). *T.E.T.: Teacher effectiveness training.* New York: David McKay.

Gorham, J. (1988). The relationship between verbal teacher immediacy behavior and student learning. *Communication Education, 37,* 47–48.

Gorham, J., & Christophel, D. (1990, January). The relationship of teachers' use of humor in the classroom to immediacy and student learning. *Communication Education, 39,* 46–62.

Gorham, J., & Christophel, D. M. (1992). Students' perceptions of teacher behaviors as motivating and demotivating factors in college classes. *Communication Quarterly, 40,* 237–252.

Gorham, J., Kelley, D. H., & McCroskey, J. C. (1989). The affinity-seeking of classroom teachers: A second perspective. *Communication Quarterly, 37,* 16–26.

Goza, B. (1993). Graffiti needs assessment: Involving students in the first class session. *Journal of Management Education, 17,* 99–106.

Grant, B., & Hennings, D. (1971). *The teacher moves.* New York: Columbia University.

Grauerholz, E., & Pescosolido, B. (1989). Gender presentation in children's literature: 1900–1984. *Gender and Society, 3,* 113–125.

Greene, E., & Simms, L. (1982, May 26). What would happen if there were no stories in the world? *Chicago Journal.*

Guild, P. (1994). The culture/learning style connection. *Educational Leadership, 51,* 16–21.

Guskey, T. R., & Passaro, P. D. (1994). Teacher efficacy: A study of construct dimensions. *American Educational Research Journal, 31,* 627–643.

Hall, E. T. (1977). *Beyond culture.* Garden City, NY: Anchor.

Hall, R., & Sandler, B. (1982). *The classroom climate. A chilly one for women?* Washington, DC: Association of American Colleges Project on the Status and Education of Women.

Hall, R. M., & Sandler, B. R. (1984). *Out of the classroom: A chilly campus climate for women.* Washington, DC: Association of American Colleges Project on the Status and Education of Women.

Haney, W. V. (1967). *Communication and organizational behavior: Text and cases.* Homewood, IL: Richard D. Irwin.

Hanson, T. (1999). Gender sensitivity and diversity in selected basic public speaking texts. *Women and Language, 22*(2), 13–20.

Harari, H., & McDavid, J. (1983, March). *Learning, 11,* 8.

Hargett, J. (1999). Students' perceptions of male and female instructors' level of immediacy and teacher credibility. *Women and Language, 22*(2), 46.

Hart, R. P. (1973). *Lecturing as communication: Problems and potentialities.* West Lafayette, IN: Purdue Research Foundation.

Hart, R., & Williams, D. (1995). Able-bodied instructors and students with physical disabilities: A relationship handicapped by communication. *Communication Education, 44,* 140–154.

Harwood, N. (1992). Writing women into textbooks. *Feminist Teacher, 6*(3), 16–17, 31.

Hawkins, K., & Stewart, R. (1991). Effects of communication apprehension on perceptions of leadership and intragroup attraction in small task-oriented groups. *The Southern Communication Journal, 57,* 1–10.

Heilbrun, C. (1989). *Writing a woman's life.* New York: W. W. Norton.

Heinz, K. (1987). An examination of sex and occupational role presentations of female characters in children's picture books. *Women's Studies in Communication, 11,* 67–78.

Hendrix, K. (1998). Student perceptions of the influence of race on professor credibility. *Journal of Black Studies, 28,* 738–764.

Henry, O. (1982). *The gift of the magi.* Neugebauer Press USA. Distributed by Natick, MA: Alphabet.

Higgins, P. C. (1992). Making disability: Exploring the social transformation of human variation. Springfield, IL: Charles C. Thomas.

Hilliard, A. G. (1989). Teachers and cultural styles in a pluralistic society. *NEA Today.* Washington, DC: National Education Association.

Hines, C. V., Cruickshank, D. R., & Kennedy, J. J. (1985). Teacher clarity and its relationship to student achievement and satisfaction. *American Educational Research Journal, 22,* 87–89.

Hocker, J. L. (1986). Teacher–student confrontations. In J. M. Civikly (Ed.), *Communicating in college classrooms* (pp. 71–82). San Francisco: Jossey-Bass.

Hocker, J. L., & Wilmot, W. (1991). *Interpersonal conflict* (3rd ed.). Dubuque, IA: William C. Brown.

Hofstede, G. (1984). *Cultural differences in teaching and learning.* Verperweg, Netherlands: Institute for Research on Intercultural Cooperation.

Hofstede, G. (1991). Culture and organizations: Software of the mind. London: McGraw-Hill.

Hogben, M., & Waterman, C. (1997). Are all of your students represented in their textbooks? A content analysis of coverage of diversity issues in introductory psychology textbooks. *Teaching Psychology, 24,* 95–100.

Holladay, S. J. (1984). *Student and teacher perception of teacher self-disclosure.* Unpublished master's thesis. University of Oklahoma, Norman, OK.

Hunt, S. K., & Lippert, L. (1999). Instructor training for implementing technology and media in the speech communication classroom. *Journal of the Illinois Speech and Theatre Association, (DL),* 65–72.

Hurd, T., & Brabeck, M. (1997). Presentation of women and Gilligan's ethic of care in college textbooks: 1970–1990. An examination of bias. *Teaching of Psychology, 24,* 159–167.

Hurt, H. T., Scott, M. D., & McCroskey, J. C. (1978). *Communication in the classroom.* Reading, MA: Addison-Wesley.

Hutchinson, L., & Beadle, M. (1992). Professors' communication styles: How they influence male and female seminar participation. *Teaching and Teacher Education, 8*(4), 405–418.

Hyman, R. (1987). Discussion strategies and tactics. In W. Wilen (Ed.), *Questions, questioning techniques, and effective teaching* (pp. 138–139). Washington, DC: National Educational Association.

Hymes, D. (1972). Models of the interaction of language and social life. In J. Gumperz & D. Hymes (Eds.), *Directions in sociolinguistics: The ethnography of communication* (pp. 419–429). New York: Holt, Rinehart & Winston.

Infante, D. A. (1995). Teaching students to understand and control verbal aggression. *Communication Education, 44,* 51–63.

Jaasma, M. A., & Koper, R. J. (1999). The relationship of student–faculty out-of-class communication to instructor immediacy and trust and to student motivation. *Communication Education, 48*(1), 41–47.

Jamieson, D. W., & Thomas, K. (1974). Power and conflict in the student–teacher relationship. *The Journal of Applied Behavioral Science, 10,* 321–336.

Jaques, D. (1992). *Learning in groups* (2nd ed.). Houston, TX: Gulf Publishing.

Javidi, M., Downs, V., & Nussbaum, J. (1988). A comparative analysis of dramatic style behaviors at higher and secondary educational levels. *Communication Education, 37,* 278–288.

Javidi, M., & Long, L. (1989). Teachers' use of humor, self-disclosure, and narrative activity as a function of experience. *Communication Research Reports, 1,* 47–52.

Johannesen, R. L. (1990). *Ethics in human communication.* Prospect Heights, IL: Waveland Press.

Johnson, D., & Johnson, E. (1991). *Joining together: Group theory and group skills* (4th ed.). Englewood Cliffs, NJ: Prentice Hall.

Johnson, D. W., & Johnson, R. (1985). Classroom conflict: Controversy versus debate in learning groups. *American Educational Research Journal, 22,* 237–256.

Johnson, R., & Johnson, D. (1985, July/August). Student–student interaction: Ignored but powerful. *Journal of Teacher Education, 36,* 22–26.

Jones, M. (1989). Gender issues in teacher education. *Journal of Teacher Education, 40,* 33–44.

Jordan, F. F., McGreal, E. A., & Wheeless, V. E. (1990). Student perceptions of teacher sex-role orientation and use of power strategies and teacher sex as determinants of student attitudes toward learning. *Communication Quarterly, 38,* 43–53.

Joss, M. W. (1999). *Looking good in presentations* (3rd ed.). Scottsdale, AZ: Coriolis.

Joyce, B., & Weil, M. (1986). *Models of teaching* (3rd ed.). Englewood Cliffs, NJ: Prentice Hall.

Karabenick, S., & Sharma, R. (1994). Perceived teacher support of student questioning in the college classroom: Its relation to student characteristics and role in classroom questioning process. *Journal of Educational Psychology, 86,* 90–103.

Karp, D. A., & Yoels, E. W. C. (1976) The college classroom: Some observations on the meanings of student participation. *Sociology and Social Research, 60,* 421–439.

Kearney, P., & Plax, T. G. (1987). Situational and individual determinants of teacher's reported use of behavior alteration techniques. *Human Communication Research, 14,* 145–166.

Kearney, P., Plax, T. G., & Burroughs, N. F. (1991). An attributional analysis of college students' resistance decisions. *Communication Education, 40,* 325–342.

Kearney, P., Plax, T. G., Richmond, V. P., & McCroskey, J. C. (1984). Power in the classroom III: Teacher communication techniques and messages. *Communication Education, 34,* 19–28.

Kearney, P., Plax, T., Richmond, V., & McCroskey, J. (1985). Power in the classroom IV: Teacher communication techniques as alternatives to discipline. In R. Bostrom (Ed.), *Communication yearbook, 8.* Beverly Hills, CA: Sage.

Kearney, P., Plax, T., Smith, V., & Sorensen, G. (1988). Effects of teacher immediacy and strategy type on college student resistance. *Communication Education, 37,* 54–67.

Keefe, J. (1982). Assessing student learning styles: An overview. In J. Keefe (Ed.), *Student learning styles and brain behavior.* Reston, VA: National Association of Secondary Principals.

Kelley, D. H., & Gorham, J. (1988). Effects of immediacy on recall of information. *Communication Education, 17,* 198–207.

Kelley, H. (1950). The warm–cold variable in first impressions of persons. *Journal of Personality, 18,* 433.

Kendon, A. (1967). Some functions of gaze-direction in social interaction. *Acat Psychologica, 26,* 22–63.

Kendrick, W. L. (1987). *Receiver clarifying in response to problems of understanding.* Unpublished doctoral dissertation, University of Washington, Seattle, WA.

Kendrick, W. L., & Darling, A. L. (1990). Problems of understanding in classrooms: Students' use of clarifying tactics. *Communication Education, 39,* 15–39.

Kepler, P., Royse, B., & Kepler, J. (1996). *Windows to the world.* Glenview, IL: Good Year Books.

Kinch, J. (1963). A formalized theory in self-concept. *American Journal of Sociology, 68,* 481–486

Kindaichi, H. (1975). *Hihonjin no gengohyogen.* Tokyo, Japan: Kodansha.

King, E. W. (1994). *Educating young children in a diverse society.* Boston: Allyn & Bacon.

Kirkwood, W. (2000). Stories that bring peace to the mind: Communication and the education

of feeling. *Southern Communication Journal, 66*(1), 16–26.

Klein, S. (1971). Student influence on teacher behavior. *American Educational Research Journal, 8,* 403–421.

Kleinfeld, J. (1994). Learning styles and culture. In W. J. Lonner & R. S. Malpass (Eds.), *Psychology and culture* (pp. 151–156). Boston: Allyn & Bacon.

Klopf, D. W. (1984). Cross-cultural apprehension research. A summary of Pacific basin studies. In J. A. Daly & J. C. McCroskey (Eds.), *Avoiding communication: Shyness, reticence and communication apprehension* (pp. 157–169). Beverly Hills, CA: Sage.

Klopf, D. W. (1991). Japanese communication practices: Recent comparative research. *Communication Quarterly, 39,* 130–143.

Knapp, M., & Hall, J. (1996). *Nonverbal communication in human interaction* (4th ed.). New York: Holt, Rinehart & Winston.

Knapp, M., & Vangelisti, A. (1996). *Interpersonal communication and human relationships* (3rd ed.). Boston: Allyn & Bacon.

Koblinsky, S. G., & Sugawara, A. I. (1984). Nonsexist curricula, sex of teacher, and children's sex role learning. *Sex Roles, 10,* 357–367.

Koester, J., & Lusting, M. (1991). Communicating curricula in the multicultural university. *Communication Education, 40,* 250–254.

Koff, E., Rierdan, J., & Stubbs, M. (1990). Gender, body image, and self-concept in early adolescence. *Journal of Early Adolescence, 10,* 37–55.

Kolbe, R., & LaVoie, J. C. (1981). Sex-role stereotyping in preschool children's picture books. *Social Psychology Quarterly, 44,* 369–374.

Koneya, M. (1976). Location and interaction in row and column seating arrangements. *Environment and Behavior, 8,* 265–282.

Kounin, J. S. (1970). *Discipline and group management in classrooms.* New York: Holt, Rinehart & Winston.

KPBS (Producer). (1994). *Frontline: School Colors.* San Diego: KPBS.

Kramarae, C., Schulz, M., & O'Barr, W. (Eds.). (1984). *Language and power.* Beverly Hills, CA: Sage.

Kramer, M., & Berman, J. (2001). Making sense of a university's culture: An examination of undergraduate students' stories. *Southern Communication Journal, 66*(4), 297–311.

Krasnow, J. H. (1992). *The social competency program of the reach out to schools project: Project report no. 3.* Wellesley College, MA: Stone Center for Development Services.

Kreidler, W. J. (1984, January). How well do you resolve…conflict? *Instructor, 93,* 30–34.

Krupnick, C. G. (1985, May). Women and men in the classroom: Inequality and its remedies. *On Teaching and Learning: The Journal of the Harvard-Danforth Center for Teaching and Learning, 18*–25.

Kunda, Z., & Sherman-Williams, B. (1993). Stereotypes and the construal of the individuating information. *Personality and Social Psychology Bulletin, 19,* 12–17.

Kurfill, J. (1988). Critical thinking: Theory, research, practice and possibilities. *ASHE-ERIC Higher Education Report, 2.*

Kurtz, E., & Ketcham, K. (1992). *The spirituality of imperfection: Storytelling and the journey to wholeness.* New York: Bantam.

Langer, E. (1989). *Mindfulness.* Reading, MA: Addison-Wesley.

Lapakko, D. (1997). Three cheers for language: A closer examination of a widely cited study of nonverbal communication. *Communication Education, 46,* 63–67.

Lawrenz, F. P., & Welch, W. W. (1983). Student perceptions of science classes taught by males and females. *Journal of Research in Science Teaching, 20,* 655–662.

Leach, M. (1990). Toward writing feminist scholarship into history education. *Educational Theory, 40,* 453–461.

Leatherman, C. (1994, June 15). The minefield of diversity. *The Chronicle of Higher Education,* A15.

Lee, C., & Galati, F. (1977). *Oral interpretation* (5th ed.). Boston: Houghton Mifflin.

Lee, C. R., Levine, T. R., & Cambra, R. (1997). Resisting compliance in the multicultural classroom. *Communication Education, 46,* 29–43.

Lehr, J., & Harris, H. (1988). *At-risk, low-achieving students in the classroom.* Washington, DC: National Education Association.

Lerner, R., Delaney, M., Hess, L., Javonovic, L. J., & VonEye, A. (1990). Early adolescent physical attractiveness and academic competence. *Journal of Early Adolescence, 10,* 4–20.

Lerner, R., Lerner, J., Hess, L., Schwab, J., Javonovic, J., Talwan, R., & Kucher, J. (1991).

Physical attractiveness and psychosocial functioning among early adolescents. *Journal of Early Adolescence, 11,* 300–320.

Lieberman, D. (1994). Ethnocognitivism, problem solving and hemisphericity. In L. Samovar & R. Porter (Eds.), *Intercultural communication: A reader* (7th ed., pp. 178–193). Belmont, CA: Wadsworth.

Lim, B. (1996). Student's expectations of professors. *The Teaching Professor, 10*(4), 3–4.

Littell, J., & Littell, J. (1972). *The language of man* (Vol. 1). Evanston, IL: McDougal Littell.

Littlejohn, S. W. (1989). *Theories of human communication* (3rd ed.). Belmont, CA: Wadsworth.

Lu, S. (1997). Culture and compliance gaining in the classroom: A preliminary investigation of Chinese college teachers' use of behavior alteration techniques. *Communication Education, 46,* 9–28.

Lutzker, M. (1995). *Multiculturalism in the college curriculum: A handbook of strategies and resources for faculty.* Westport, CT: Greenwood.

Macke, A. S., & Richardson, L. W. (1980). *Sex-typed teaching styles of university professors and student reactions.* Columbus: Ohio State University Research Foundation.

Malandro, L. A., & Barker, L. (1983). *Nonverbal communication.* Reading, MA: Addison.

Marshall, H., & Weinstein, R. (1984). Classroom factors affecting students' self evaluations: An interactional model. *Review of Educational Research, 54,* 301–325.

Martin, M., Behnke, R., & King, P. (1992). The communication of public speaking anxiety: Perceptions of Asian and American speakers. *Communication Quarterly, 3,* 279–288.

Martin-White, C., & Staton-Spicer, A. (1987). Instructional communication in the elementary gifted classroom. *Communication Education, 36,* 259–271.

Marzanno, R., Brant, R., Hughes, C., Jones, B., Presseisen, S., Rankin, S., & Shuor, C. (1988). *Dimensions of thinking: A framework for curriculum and instruction.* Alexandria, VA: Association for Supervision and Curriculum Development.

Maslow, A. H. (1954). *Motivation and personality.* New York: Harper and Row.

Maslow, A. H., & Mintz, N. L. (1956). Effects of esthetic surroundings: Initial effects of three esthetic conditions upon perceiving "energy" and "well-being" in faces. *Journal of Psychology, 41,* 254–257.

Mayer, R. (1968). *Developing an attitude toward learning.* Palo Alto, CA: Fearon.

McCaleb, J. L. (Ed.). (1987). *How do teachers communicate? A review and critique of assessment practices.* Teacher Education Monograph No. 7. Washington, DC: ERIC Clearinghouse on Teacher Education.

McCroskey, J. C., Andersen, J., Richmond, V., & Wheeless, L. (1981, April). Communication apprehension of elementary and secondary students and teachers. *Communication Education, 30,* 122–132.

McCroskey, J. C., & Dunham, R. E. (1974). Ethos: A confounding element in communication research. *Speech Monographs, 33,* 456–463.

McCroskey, J. C., Fayer, J., Richmond, V., Sulliven, A., & Barraclough, R. (1996). A multi-cultural examination of the relationship between nonverbal immediacy and affective learning. *Communication Quarterly, 44,* 297–307.

McCroskey, J. C., Holdridge, W., & Toomb, J. K. (1974). An instrument for measuring source credibility of basic speech communication instructors. *Speech Teacher, 23,* 30.

McCroskey, J. C., & McCroskey, L. L. (1986). The affinity-seeking of classroom teachers. *Communication Research Reports, 3,* 158–167.

McCroskey, J. C., & McVetta, R. W. (1978, March). Classroom seating arrangements: Instructional communication theory versus student preferences. *Communication Education, 27,* 101–102.

McCroskey, J. C., & Richmond, V. P. (1983). Power in the classroom I: Teacher and student perceptions. *Communication Education, 32,* 176–184.

McCroskey, J. C., & Richmond, V. P. (1990). Willingness to communicate: Differing cultural perspectives. *Southern Communication Journal, 56,* 72–77.

McCroskey, J. C., & Richmond, V. P. (1991). *Quiet children and the classroom teacher.* Urbana, IL: ERIC Clearinghouse on Reading and Communication Skills.

McCroskey, J. C., Richmond, V. P., Plax, T. G., & Kearney, P. (1985). Power in the classroom V: Behavior alteration techniques, communication training, and learning. *Communication Education, 34,* 214–226.

McCroskey, J. C., Richmond, V. P., Sulliven, A., Fayer, J., & Barraclough, R. (1995). A cross-cultural and multi-behavioral analysis of the relationship between nonverbal immediacy and teacher evaluation. *Communication Education, 44,* 281–306.

McCroskey, J. C., & Wheeless, L. R. (1976). *Introduction to human communication.* Boston: Allyn & Bacon.

McGuire, J. (1988). Sounds and sensibilities: Storytelling as an educational process. *Children's Literature Association Quarterly, 13,* 11–15.

McKeachie, W. (1986). *Teaching tips: A guidebook for the beginning teacher* (8th ed.). Lexington, MA: D. C. Heath.

McLaughlin, M., Erickson, K., & Ellison, M. (1980, January). A scale for the measurement of teachers' affective communication. *Communication Education, 29,* 21–32.

Medley, D., & Mitsel, H. (1963). Measuring classroom behavior by systematic observation. In N. W. Gage (Ed.), *Handbook of research on teaching* (p. 253). Chicago: Rand McNally.

Mehan, H. (1979). *The competent student. Sociolinguistic working paper number 61.* Austin, TX: Southwest Educational Development Lab. (ERIC Document Reproduction Service No. ED 250 934)

Merton, R., Reader, G., & Kendall, P. (1957). *The student physician.* Cambridge, MA: Harvard University Press.

Meyers, S. (1995). Student perceptions of teacher affinity-seeking and classroom climate. *Communication Research Reports, 12,* 192–199.

Midgley, C., Feldlaufer, H., & Eccles, J. (1989). Change in teacher efficacy and student self- and task-related beliefs in mathematics during the transition to junior high school. *Journal of Educational Psychology, 81,* 247–258.

Miskel, C., McDonald, D., & Bloom, S. (1983). Structural and expectancy linkages within schools and organizational effectiveness. *Educational Administration Quarterly, 19*(1), 49–82.

Mliner, J. (1977). *Sex stereotypes in mathematics and science textbooks for elementary and junior high schools: Report of sex bias in the public schools.* New York: National Organization for Women.

Montagu, M. F. A. (1971). *Teaching: The human significance of the skin.* New York: Columbia Press.

Morreale, S., & Andersen, K. (1999). Intense discussion at summer conference yields draft of NCA credo for communication ethics. *Spectra.* National Communication Association.

Morreale, S., & Jones, A. (Eds.). (1997). *Racial and ethnic diversity in the twenty-first century: A communication perspective.* Annandale, VA: National Communication Association.

Morris, T. L., Gorham, J., Cohen, S. H., & Huffman, D. (1996). Fashion in the classroom: Effects of attire on student perceptions of instructors in college classes. *Communication Education, 45,* 135–148.

Murray, H. G., (1985). Classroom teaching behaviors related to college teaching effectiveness. In J. G. Donals, & A. M. Sullivan (Eds.), *Using research to improve teaching* (pp. 21–34). San Francisco: Jossey-Bass.

Nadler, L., & Nadler, M. (1990). Perceptions of sex differences in classroom communication. *Women's Studies in Communication, 13,* 46–65,

Nakane, C. (1970). *Japanese society.* London: Werdenfeld & Nicholson.

Neer, M. (1987). The development of an instrument to measure classroom apprehension. *Communication Education, 36,* 154–166.

Neer, M. (1990). Reducing situational anxiety and avoidance behavior associated with classroom apprehension. *Southern Communication Journal, 56,* 49–61.

Neer, M. (1992). Reducing situational anxiety and avoidance behavior associated with classroom apprehension. *Southern Communication Journal, 57,* 49–62.

Neer, M., & Kircher, W. F. (1989). Apprehensives' perception of classroom factors influencing their participation. *Communication Research Reports, 6,* 70–77.

Nell, V. (1988). *Lost in a book: The psychology of reading for pleasure.* New Haven, CT: Yale University Press.

Neuliep, J. (1991). An examination of the content of high school teachers' humor in the classroom and the development of an inductively derived taxonomy of classroom humor. *Communication Education, 40,* 341–355.

Neuliep, J. (1995). A comparison of teacher immediacy in African-American and Euro-American college classrooms. *Communication Education, 44,* 267–277.

Neuliep, J., & McCroskey, J. (1998). *Ethnocentrism trait measurement: Intercultural communication research instruments.* International and Intercultural Communication Conference, School of Communication, University of Miami.

Nicklin, J. L. (1991). Teacher-education programs face pressure to provide multicultural training. *The Chronicle of Higher Education,* A16.

Nilsen, A. P. (1987). Three decades of sexism in school science materials. *School Library Journal, 33,* 117–122.

Nishida, H. (1985). Japanese intercultural communication competence and cross cultural adjustment. *International Journal of Intercultural Relations, 9,* 247–269.

Norton, R. W. (1977). Teacher effectiveness as a function of communicator style. In B. D. Ruben (Ed.), *Communication Yearbook 1* (pp. 525–555). New Brunswick, NJ: Transaction.

Norton, R. W. (1978). Foundation of a communicator style construct. *Human Communication Research 4,* 99.

Norton, R. W. (1983). *Communicator style: Theory, applications, and measures.* Beverly Hills, CA: Sage.

Nussbaum, J., & Scott, M. (1979). The relationship among communicator style, perceived self-disclosure, and classroom learning. In D. Nimmo (Ed.), *Communication Yearbook 3* (pp. 561–584). New Brunswick, NJ: Transaction.

Nussbaum, J., & Scott, M. (1980). Student learning as relational outcome of teacher–student interaction. In D. Nimmo (Ed.), *Communication Yearbook 4* (pp. 533–552). New Brunswick, NJ: Transaction.

Nyquist, J., & Wulff, D. (1990). Selected active learning strategies. In J. Daly, G. Friedrich, & A. Vangelisti (Eds.), *Teaching communication: Theory, research, and methods* (pp. 337–362). Hillsdale, NJ: Erlbaum.

Ogden, C. K., & Richards, I. A. (1927). *The meaning of meaning.* New York: Harcourt.

Olaniran, B. A., & Roach, K. D. (1994). Communication apprehension in Nigerian culture. *Communication Quarterly, 42,* 379–389.

Olaniran, B., & Stewart, R. (1996). Instructional practices and classroom community apprehension: A cultural explanation. *Communication Reports, 9,* 193–203.

O'Mara, J., Allen, J., Long, K., & Judd, B. (1996). Communication apprehension, nonverbal immediacy, and negative expectations for learning. *Communication Research Reports, 13,* 109–128.

Orem, R. A. (1991). Preparing adult educators for cultural change. *Adult Learning, 9,* 8–10.

Orenstein, P. (1994). *School girls.* New York: Doubleday.

Page, R. (1992). Feelings of physical unattractiveness and hopelessness among high school students. *The High School Journal, 75,* 150–156.

Pahnos, M. L., & Butt, K. L. (1992). Ethnocentrism—A universal pride in one's ethnic background: Its impact on teaching and learning. *Education, 112,* 113, 118–120.

Palmer, P. (1998). *The courage to teach: Exploring the inner landscape of a teacher's life.* San Francisco: Jossey-Bass.

Parsons, C. (1997, January 28). Uniform success in schools. *Chicago Tribune, Metro Chicago,* 1–5.

Patterson, M. (1999). Storytelling: The art form of painting pictures with your tongue. Available at http://www.hollowtop.com/storytelling.html

Paul, R. W. (1986). *Program for the fourth international conference on critical thinking and educational reform.* Rohnert Park, CA: Sonoma State University Center for Critical Thinking and Moral Critique.

Pearson, J. C., & West, R. (1991). An initial investigation of the effects of gender on student questions in the classroom: Developing a descriptive base. *Communication Education, 41,* 167–180.

Pemberton, G. (1988). *On teaching the minority student: Problems and strategies.* Brunswick, ME: Bowdoin College.

Peterson, K. (1994, September 7). Teens' tales from the classroom. *USA Today,* 1D–2D.

Peterson, S., & Lach, M. (1990). Gender stereotypes in children's books: Their prevalence and influence on cognitive and affective development. *Gender and Education, 2,* 185–197.

Plax, T. G., Kearney, P., McCroskey, J. C., & Richmond, V. P. (1986). Power in the classroom VI: Verbal control strategies, nonverbal immediacy and affective learning. *Communication Education, 35,* 43–55.

Postman, N., & Weingartner, G. (1969). *Teaching as a subversive activity.* New York: Dell.

Potter, W., & Emanuel, R. (1990). Student's preferences for communication styles and their relationship to achievement. *Communication Education, 39,* 234–249.

Powell, B. (1990). *Conflict resolution, communication, and problem solving.* Part IV of the Biloxi, Mississippi family English literacy curriculum. Biloxi, MS: Mississippi Board of Education.

Powell, J. (1990). *Why am I afraid to tell you who I am?* Allen, TX: Thomas More.

Prather, H. (1970). *Notes to myself.* New York: Bantam Books.

Proctor, R., Douglas, A., Garera-Izquierdo, T., & Wartman, S. (1994). Approach, avoidance, and apprehension: Talking with high California students about getting help. *Communication Education, 43,* 312–321.

Purcell, P., & Stewart, L. (1990). Dick and Jane in 1989. *Sex Roles, 22,* 177–185.

Qin, Z., Johnson, D., & Johnson, R. (1995). Cooperative versus competitive efforts and problem solving. *Review of Educational Research, 65,* 129–143.

Redfield, D., & Rousseau, A. (1981). A meta-analysis of experimental research on teacher questioning behavior. *Review of Educational Research, 51,* 237–246.

Reed, J. H., & Hallock, D. E. (1996, January). Encouraging ethical behavior in class. *The Teaching Professor, 10*(1), 1.

Remen, R. N. (1996). *Kitchen table wisdom: Stories that heal.* New York: Putnam.

Resnick, L., & Klopfer, L. (1988). Toward the thinking curriculum: Current cognitive research. Annandale, VA: Association for Supervision and Curriculum Development.

Richman, J., & Bowman, G. (1997). School failure: An eco–interactional–developmental perspective. In M. Fraser (Ed.), *Risk and resiliency in childhood: An ecological perspective* (pp. 95–116). Washington, DC: National Association of Social Workers.

Richman, J., Rosenfeld, L., & Bowen, G. (1998). Social support for adolescents at risk of school failure. *Social Work, 43,* 309–323.

Richmond, V. P. (1990). Communication in the classroom: Power and motivation. *Communication Education, 39,* 181–195.

Richmond, V. P., & Andriate, G. S. (1984, April). *Communication apprehension: Cross-cultural per-*

spectives. Paper presented at the annual meeting of the Eastern Communication Association, Philadelphia, PA.

Richmond, V. P., & Gorham, J. (1988). Language patterns and gender role orientation among students in grades 3–12. *Communication Education, 37*, 142–149.

Richmond, V. P., Gorham, J. S., & McCroskey, J. C. (1986). The relationship between selected immediacy behaviors and cognitive learning. In M. L. McLaughlin (Ed.), *Communication Yearbook 10*. Beverly Hills, CA: Sage.

Richmond, V. P., & McCroskey, J. C. (1984). Power in the classroom II: Power and learning. *Communication Education, 33*, 125–136.

Richmond, V. P., & McCroskey, J. C. (1995). *Communication apprehension, avoidance, and effectiveness*. Scottsdale, AZ: Gorsuch Scarisbrick.

Richmond, V. P., McCroskey, J. C., Kearney, P., & Plax, T. (1987). Power in the classroom VII: Linking behavior alteration techniques to cognitive learning. *Communication Education, 36*, 1–12.

Richmond, V. P., McCroskey, J. C., & Payne, S. (1987). *Nonverbal behavior in interpersonal relations*. Englewood Cliffs, NJ: Prentice Hall.

Richmond, V. P., & Roach, K. D. (1992). Power in the classroom: Seminal studies. In V. P. Richmond & J. C. McCroskey (Eds.), *Power in the classroom: Communication, control, and concern* (pp. 47–65). Hillsdale, NJ: Erlbaum.

Rierdan, J., Koff, E., & Stubbs, M. (1988). Gender, depression and body image in early adolescence. *Journal of Early Adolescence, 8*, 109–117.

Rierdan, J., Koff, E., & Stubbs, M. (1989). A longitudinal analysis of body image as a predictor of the onset and persistence of adolescent girls' depression. *Journal of Early Adolescence, 9*, 454–466.

Roach, K. D. (1991). Graduate teaching assistants' use of behavior alteration techniques in the university classroom. *Communication Quarterly, 39*, 178–188.

Roe, B., Ross, E., & Bums, P. (1984). *Student teaching and field experiences handbook*. Columbus, OH: Merrill.

Rogers, C. (1962, Fall). The interpersonal relationship: The core of guidance. *Harvard Education Review, 32*, 46.

Rogers, E., & Steinfatt, T. (1999). *Intercultural communication*. Project Heights, IL: Waveland Press.

Rogge, E. (1959). Evaluating the ethics of a speaker in a democracy. *Quarterly Journal of Speech, 45*, 419–425.

Rose, J., & Medway, F. (1981). Measurement of teachers' belief in their control over student outcomes. *Journal of Educational Research, 74*, 185–190.

Rosenfeld, L. (1973). *Human interaction in the small group setting*. Columbus, OH: Merrill.

Rosenfeld, L. (1983). Communication climate and coping mechanisms in the college classroom. *Communication Education, 32*, 170–176.

Rosenfeld, L., Grant, C., & McCroskey, J. (1995). Communication apprehension and self-perceived communication competence of academically gifted students. *Communication Education, 44*, 79–86.

Rosenfeld, L. B., & Jarrard, M. W. (1985). The effects of perceived sexism in female and male college professors on students' descriptions of classroom climate. *Communication Education, 34*, 205–213.

Rosenfeld, L., & Richman, J. (1999). Supportive communication and school outcomes, Part II: Academically "at-risk" low income high school students. *Communication Education, 48*, 294–307.

Rosenfeld, L., Richman, J., & Bowen, G. (1998). Supportive communication and school outcomes for academically "at-risk" and other low income middle school students. *Communication Education, 47*, 311–325.

Rosenthal, R., & Jacobson, L. (1968). *Pygmalion in the classroom*. New York: Holt, Rinehart & Winston.

Roth, M. (1987). Teaching modern art history from a feminist perspective: Challenging conventions, my own and others. *Women's Studies Quarterly, 15*, 21–24.

Rothman, H., & Cosden, M. (1995). The relationship between self-perception of a learning disability and achievement, self-concept, and social support. *Learning Disability Quarterly, 18*(3), 203–213.

Rothwell, J. D. (1995). In mixed company: Small group communication (2nd ed.). Fort Worth, TX: Harcourt.

Rowe, M. (1986, January–February). Wait time: Slowing down may be a way of speeding up! *Journal of Teacher Education, 36,* 43–48.

Rowe, M. (1987). Using wait time to stimulate inquiry. In W. Wilen (Ed.), *Questions, questioning techniques, and effective teaching* (pp. 95–106). Washington, DC: NEA.

Rubin, D. (1998). Help! My professor (or doctor or boss) doesn't talk English! In J. Martin, T. Nakayama, & L. Flores (Eds.), *Readings in cultural contexts* (149–160). Mountain View, CA: Mayfield.

Rubin, R. B., & Feezel, J. D. (1986). Elements of teacher communication competence. *Communication Education, 35,* 254–268.

Russ, T., Simonds, C., & Hunt, S. (2002). Coming out in the classroom…An occupational hazard? The influence of sexual orientation on teacher credibility and perceived student learning. *Communication Education, 51*(3), (in press).

Sadker, D. (2000). Gender equity: Still knocking at the classroom door. *Equity and Excellence, 33,* 80–83.

Sadker, M., & Sadker, D. (1981). The development and field trial of a nonsexist teacher education curriculum. *The High School Journal, 64,* 331–336.

Sadker, M., & Sadker, D. (1994). *Failing at fairness: How our schools cheat girls.* New York: Simon & Schuster.

Sammons, M. C. (1995, May). Students assess computer-aided classroom presentation. *T.H.E., Technological Horizons in Education, 22,* 74–92.

Samovar, L., & Porter, R. (1995). *Communication between cultures.* Belmont, CA: Wadsworth.

Samovar, L., & Porter, R. (2000). *Intercultural communication: A reader* (9th ed.). Belmont, CA: Wadsworth.

Samovar, L. A., & Porter, R. E. (2001). *Communication between cultures* (4th ed.). Belmont, CA: Wadsworth.

Sanders, J. A., & Wiseman, R. L. (1990). The effects of verbal and nonverbal immediacy on perceived cognitive, affective, and behavioral learning in the multicultural classroom. *Communication Education, 39,* 341–353.

Sandler, B. (1991). Women faculty at work in the classroom, or Why it still hurts to be a woman in labor. *Communication Education, 40,* 6–15.

Sandler, B., & Hall, R. (1986). *The campus climate revisited: Chilly for women faculty, administrators,* and graduate students. Washington, DC: Project on the Status and Education of Women, Association of American Colleges.

Schlesinger, A. M. (1992). *The disuniting of America: Reflections on a multicultural society.* New York: W. W. Norton.

Schlossen, L., & Algozzine, B. (1980, Spring). Sex, behavior, and teacher expectancies. *Journal of Experimental Education, 48,* 78–92.

Schmier, L. (1995). *Random thoughts: The humanity of teaching.* Madison, WI: Magna.

Schneider, M. J., & Jordan, W. (1981). Perception of the communicative performance of Americans and Chinese in intercultural contact: A literature review. *Intercultural Relations, 5,* 175–191.

Schumaker, D. (1986, April). What are thinking skills? In R. D. Feldman, *Instructor,* 37.

Sedlacek, W., Helm, E., & Prieto, D. (1997). The relationship between attitudes toward diversity and overall satisfaction of university students by race. (ERIC Document Reproduction Service, No. ED 411 752)

Semmel, M. I. (1978, March–April). Systematic observation. *Journal of Teacher Education, 29,* 27.

Shade, B., & New, C. (1993). Cultural influences on learning: Teaching implications. In J. Banks & C. Banks (Eds.). *Multicultural education: Issues and perspectives* (2nd ed., pp. 315–327). Boston: Allyn & Bacon.

Sharon, S., & Sharon, Y. (1965). *Small group teaching.* Englewood Cliffs, NJ: Educational Technologies Publications.

Shulman, L. (1987). The wisdom of the practitioner. In D. Berliner & B. Rosenshine (Eds.), *Talk to teachers* (p. 382). New York: Random House.

Sills, C. (1988). Interactive learning in the composition classroom. In J. Golub (Ed.), *Focus on collaborative learning* (p. 21). Urbana, IL: National Council of Teachers of English.

Simonds, C. J. (1995). *Have I made myself clear: The effects of teacher clarity on challenge behavior in the college classroom.* Unpublished doctoral dissertation. University of Oklahoma, Norman, Oklahoma.

Simonds, C. J. (1997a). Classroom understanding: Expanding the notion of teacher clarity. *Communication Research Reports, 14*(3), 279–290.

Simonds, C. J. (1997b). Challenge behavior in the college classroom. *Communication Research Reports, 14*(4), 481–492.

Simonds, C., & Cooper, P. (2001). Communication and gender in the classroom. In D. Borisoff and L. Arliss (Eds.), *Women and Men Communicating* (2nd ed., pp. 232–253). Fort Worth, TX: Harcourt.

Sinatra, R. (1986). *Visual literacy connections to thinking, reading and writing.* Springfield, IL: Charles C. Thomas.

Slavin, R. (1986). *Using student team learning.* Baltimore, MD: Johns Hopkins University Press.

Slavin, R., & Madden, W. (1989, February). What works for students at risk: A research synthesis. *Educational Leadership, 47,* 3–9.

Smagorinsky, P., & Fly, P. (1993). The social environment of the classroom: A Vygotskian perspective on small group process. *Communication Education, 42,* 159–171.

Sommer, R. (1969). *Personal space: The behavioral basis of design.* Englewood Cliffs, NJ: Prentice Hall.

Sommer, R., & Olsen, H. (1980). The soft classroom. *Environment and Behavior, 12,* 3–16.

Sommers, C. H. (2000). *The war against boys.* New York: Simon & Schuster.

Sorensen, G. (1989a). The relationship among teachers' self-disclosive statements, students' perceptions, and affective learning. *Communication Education, 38,* 259–276.

Sorensen, G. (1989b). Teaching teachers from East to West: A look at common myths. *Communication Education, 38,* 331–332.

Sorensen, G., Plax, T. G., & Kearney, P. (1989). The strategy selection–construction controversy: A coding scheme for analyzing teacher compliance-gaining message constructions. *Communication Education, 38,* 102–118.

Spender, D. (1989). *Invisible women: The schooling scandal.* London: Women's Press.

Sprague, J. (1992). Expanding the research agenda for instructional communication: Raising some unasked questions. *Communication Education, 41,* 1–25.

Staton, A. (1990). *Communication and student socialization.* Norwood, NJ: Ablex.

Staton, A., & Darling, A. (1986). Communication in the socialization of preservice teachers. *Communication Education, 35,* 215–230.

Staton, A., & Hunt, S. (1992). Teacher socialization: Review and conceptualization. *Communication Education, 41,* 110–137.

Stefani, L. (1997). The influence of culture on classroom communication. In L. Samovar & R. Porter (Eds.), *Intercultural communication: A reader* (8th edition, pp. 349–364). Belmont, CA: Wadsworth.

Steil, L. (1980). *Your personal listening profile.* Minneapolis, MN: Sperry Corporation.

Steinbeck, J. (1962). *Travels with Charley: In search of America.* New York: Viking.

Stepp, P. (2001). Sexual harassment in communication extra-curricular activities: Intercollegiate debate and individual events. *Communication Education, 50,* 34–51.

Sternglass, M. (1997, March). *Effects of race, class, and gender on writing: Report from a longitudinal study.* Paper presented at the meeting of the Conference on College Composition and Communication, Phoenix, AZ.

Stewart, J. (1999, April 7). Go figure: A closer look at equal pay. *Chicago Tribune,* sec. 8, 1.

Stewart, L., Cooper, P., & Stewart, A. (2003). *Communication and Gender.* Boston: Allyn & Bacon.

Stewart, J., & Thomas, M. (1990). Dialogue listening: Sculpting mutual meanings. In J. Stewart (Ed.), *Bridges not walls* (pp. 192–210). New York: McGraw-Hill.

Stone, P. (1996). Ghettoized and marginalized: The coverage of racial and ethnic groups in introductory sociology texts. *Teaching Sociology, 24,* 356–363.

Stuart, W., & Rosenfeld, L. (1994). Student perceptions of teacher humor and classroom climate. *Communication Research Reports, 11,* 87–97.

Sumner, W. (1906/1940). *Folkways.* Boston: Ginn.

Suzuki, T. (1973). *Kotoba to bunka (Language and culture).* Tokyo: Iwanami Shoten.

Swinton, M., & Bassett, R. (1981, April). Teachers' perceptions of competencies needed for effective speech communication and drama instruction. *Communication Education, 30,* 140–151.

Tetenbaum, T. J., & Pearson, J. (1989). The voices in children's literature: The impact of gender on the moral decisions of storybook characters. *Sex Roles, 20,* 381–395.

Teven, J., & Comadena, M. (1996). The effects of office aesthetic quality on students' perceptions of teacher credibility and communicator style. *Communication Research Reports, 13,* 101–108.

Teven, J., & McCroskey, J. (1996). The relationship of perceived teacher caring with student learning and teacher evaluation. *Communication Education, 46,* 1–9.

Thomas, C. E. (1994). *An analysis of teacher socio-communicative style as a predictor of classroom communication behaviors, student liking, motivation and learning.* Unpublished doctoral dissertation, West Virginia University, Morgantown, WV.

Thomas, C. E., Richmond, V. P., & McCroskey, J. C. (1994). The association between immediacy and socio-communicative style. *Communication Research RepoZrts, 11,* 107–114.

Thompson, J. J. (1973). *Beyond words: Nonverbal communication.* New York: Citation Press.

Thweatt, K., & McCroskey, J. (1996). Teacher non-immediacy and misbehavior: Unintentional negative communication. *Communication Research Reports, 13,* 198–204.

Thweatt, K. S., & McCroskey, J. C. (1998). The impact of teacher immediacy and misbehavior on teacher credibility. *Communication Education, 47*(4), 351–356.

Tiberius, R. G. (1990). *Small group teaching: A trouble-shooting guide.* Toronto: Ontario Institute for Studies in Education Press.

Tinto, V. (1993). *Building learning communities for new college students: A summary of research findings of the collaborative learning project.* University Park, PA: National Center on Post Secondary Teaching, Learning, & Assessment.

Todd-Mancillas, W. (1982). Classroom environment and nonverbal behavior. In L. Barker (Ed.), *Communication in the classroom* (pp. 77–97). Englewood Cliffs, NJ: Prentice Hall.

Totusek, T. (1978, November). *The relationship between classroom seating preference and student personality characteristics.* Paper presented at the meeting of the Speech Communication Association Convention, Minneapolis, MN.

Totusek, P., & Staton-Spicer, A. Q. (1982). Classroom speaking preference as a function of student personality. *Journal of Experimental Education, 50,* 159–163.

Tran, M. T., Young, R. K., & DiLella, J. D. (1994). Multicultural education courses and the student teacher: Eliminating stereotypical attitudes in our ethnically diverse classroom. *Journal of Teacher Education, 45,* 183–189.

Twain, M. (1923). *The adventures of Huckleberry Finn.* New York: Harper & Row.

U.S. Department of Education, National Center for Education Statistics (2000). *Educational Equity of Girls and Women* NCES 2000-030, by Y. Bae, S. Choy, C. Geddes, J. Sable, & T. Snyder. Washington, DC: U.S. Government Printing Office.

Van Note Chism, N., Cano, J., & Pruitt, A. (1989). Teaching in a diverse environment: Knowledge and skills needed by TAs. In J. Nyquist, R. Abbott, & D. Wulff (Eds.), *Teaching assistant training in the 1990s, new directions for teaching and learning, no. 39* (pp. 23–35). San Francisco: Jossey-Bass.

Vaughan–Roberson, C., Tompkins, G., Hitchcock, M., & Oldham, M. (1989). Sexism in basal readers: An analysis of male main characters. *Journal of Research in Childhood Education, 4*(1), 62–68.

Vernay, M. (1990). *Curriculum and instruction to reduce racial conflict.* New York: ERIC Clearinghouse on Urban Education, Document ED0-UD-89-7.

Vonnegut, K. (1992). Listening for women's voices: Revisioning courses in American public address. *Communication Education, 41,* 26–39.

Waldeck, J. H., Kearney, P., & Plax, T. G. (2001). Teacher e-mail message strategies and students' willingness to communicate online. *Journal of Applied Communication Research, 29*(1), 54–70.

Walker, E. J., & McKeachie, W. J. (1967). *Some thoughts about teaching the beginning course in psychology.* Belmont, CA: Brooks/Cole.

Wallach, J., & Metcalf, G. (1995). *Working with Americans: A practical guide for Asians on how to succeed with US managers.* New York: McGraw-Hill.

Walsh, P. (1986). *Tales out of school.* New York: Viking.

Waltman, M. (1995). An assessment of the discriminant validity of the checklist of behavior alteration techniques: A test of the item desirability bias in prospective and experienced teachers' likelihood-of-use ratings. *Journal of Applied Communication Research, 23,* 201–211.

Watson, A., & Monroe, E. (1990). Academic achievement: A study of relationships of IQ, communication apprehension, and teacher perception. *Communication Reports, 3,* 28–36.

Watson, K. W., Monroe, E. E., & Atterstrom, A. (1989). Comparison of communication apprehension across cultures: American and Swedish children. *Communication Quarterly, 37*, 67–76,

Weaver, J., & Kintley, M. (1995). Listening styles and empathy. *The Southern Communication Journal, 60*, 131–140.

Weaver, R. L., II. (1974). The use of exercises and games. *Speech Teacher, 23*, 302–311.

Webb, L. (1986). Eliminating sexist language in the classroom. *Women's Studies in Communication, 9*, 21–29.

Weiller, K., & Higgs, C. (1989). Female learned helplessness in sport: An analysis of children's literature. *Journal of Physical Education, Recreation and Dance, 60*(6), 65–67.

Weiner, H. (1986). Collaborative learning in the classroom: A guide to evaluation. *College English, 48*, 55–61.

Weitzman, L. J., Eifler, D., Hokada, E., & Ross, C. (1972). Sex role socialization in picture books for preschool children. *American Journal of Sociology, 77*, 1125–1150.

Weitzman, L. J., & Rizzo, D. (1975). Sex bias in textbooks. *Today's Education, 64*(1), 49–52.

Welch, L. (1991). College students need nurturing too. *The Teaching Professor, 5*, 7.

Wenburg, J., & Wilmot, W. (1973). *The personal communication process*. New York: John Wiley.

West, R. (1994). Teacher–student communication: A descriptive typology of students' interpersonal experiences with teachers. *Communication Research Reports, 7*, 109–118.

West, R., & Pearson, J. C. (1994). Antecedent and consequent conditions of student questioning: An analysis of classroom discourse across the university. *Communication Education, 43*, 299–311.

Wheeless, L. R. (1974). The relationship of attitude and credibility to comprehension and selective exposure. *Western Speech Communication, 38*, 88–97.

Wheeless, L. R. (1975). The relationship of four elements to immediate recall and student–instructor interaction. *Western Speech Communication, 39*, 131–140.

Wheeless, V. E., & Potorti, P. (1987). *Student assessment of teacher masculinity and femininity: A test of the sex role congruency hypothesis on student learning*. Paper presented at the Tenth Annual Communication, Language and Gender Conference, Milwaukee, WI.

Whitworth, R. (1988). Collaborative learning and other disasters. In J. Golub (Ed.), *Focus on collaborative learning* (p. 13). Urbana, IL: National Council of Teachers of English.

Whitworth, R., & Cochran, C. (1996). Evaluation of integrated versus unitary treatments for reducing public speaking anxiety. *Communication Education, 45*, 306–314.

Wilen, W. (1987). Effective questions and questioning: A classroom application. In W. Wilen (Ed.), *Questions, questioning techniques, and effective teaching*. Washington, DC: National Education Association.

Wilen, W., & Clegg, A. (1986). Effective questions and questioning: A research review. *Theory and Research in Social Education, 21*, 153–161.

Williams, V. G., & Winkworth, J. M. (1974, July). The faculty looks at student behavior. *Journal of College Student Personnel, 15*(4), 305–310.

Wilmot, W. W. (1976). *The influence of personal conflict styles of teachers on student attitudes toward conflict*. Paper presented at the annual meeting of the International Communication Association, Portland, OR.

Wolvin, A., & Coakley, C. (1991). A survey of the status of listening training in some fortune 500 corporations. *Communication Education, 40*, 152–164.

Wood, B. (1977). *Communication competencies: Grade 7–12*. Urbana, IL: ERIC/SCA.

Wood, D., & Wood, H. (1987). Questioning and student initiative. In J. Dillon (Ed.), *Questioning and discussion: A multidisciplinary study*. Norwood, NJ: Ablex.

Wood, J. (1989). *Feminist pedagogy in interpersonal communication courses*. Paper presented at the Speech Communication Association, San Francisco, CA.

Wood, J. (1997). *Gendered Lives*. (2nd ed.). Belmont, CA: Wadsworth.

Wood, J. (2001). *Gendered lives: Communication, gender, and culture* (4th ed.). Belmont, CA: Wadsworth.

Wood, J. T., & Lenze, L. F. (1991). Gender and the development of self: Inclusive pedagogy in interpersonal communication. *Women's Studies in Communication, 14*(1), 1–23.

Woolfolk, A. E., & Brooks, D. M. (1983). Nonverbal communication in teaching. In E. Gordon (Ed.), *Review or research in education*. Washington, DC: American Educational Research Association.

Wycoff, V. L. (1973). The effects of stimulus variation on learning from lecture. *Journal of Experimental Education, 41,* 85–90.

Young, R. L. (1993). Cross-cultural experiential
learning for teacher trainees. *Teacher Education
Quarterly, 20*(3), 67–76.

Zeichner, K. M. (1980). Myths and realities: Field-
based experience in pre-service teacher education. *Journal of Teacher Education, 31,* 45–55.

Zorn, T. E. (1993). Motivation to communicate: A
critical review with suggested alternatives.
Communication Yearbook, 16, 515–549.

INDEX

Credits

Amdion, Edmund and Hunter, Elizabeth. Excerpts from *Improving Teaching: The Analysis of Class-room Verbal Interaction*, copyright © 1966 by Holt, Rinehart and Winston and renewed 1992 by Edmund Amidon. Reprinted by permission of the publisher.

Backland, Phil and Black, Don. "Teacher Communication Rating Scale." Reprinted by permission of the authors, Central Washington University, Ellensburg, WA.

Brophy, Jere E. and Good, Thomas L. Excerpt from *Teacher–Student Relationships: Causes and Consequences*, copyright © 1974 by Holt, Rinehart and Winston. Reprinted by permission of the publisher.

Cooper, Laura E. Beth. "I Was Sure to Follow" Reprinted by permission of author.

Cooper, Laura E. Beth. "Pam" Reprinted by permission of author.

Cooper, Laura E. Beth. "The Spaces in Between" Reprinted by permission of the author.

Cornett, Claudia E. From *What You Should Know about Teaching and Learning Styles*. Fastback 191. Bloomington, IN: Phi Delta Kappa Educational Foundation, 1983. Used by permission.

Cullum, Albert. "Do You Love Your Teacher, Children" from *Blackboard, Blackboard on the Wall Who Is the Fairest of Them All?* Reprinted courtesy of Harlin Quist Books. Copyright © by Harlin Quist. All rights reserved.

Cullum, Albert. "It's June, and It's Over" from *The Geranium on the Window Sill Just Died But Teacher You Went Right On*. Reprinted courtesy of Harlin Quist Books. Copyright © by Harlin Quist. All rights reserved.

Cullum, Albert. "It's September Again" from *The Geranium on the Window Sill Just Died But Teacher You Went Right On*. Reprinted courtesy of Harlin Quist Books. Copyright © by Harlin Quist. All rights reserved.

Cullum, Albert. "On the Mornings You Tell Us about the Night Before" from *The Geranium on the Window Sill Just Died But Teacher You Went Right On*. Reprinted courtesy of Harlin Quist Books. Copyright © by Harlin Quist. All rights reserved.

Cullum, Albert. "The Robins Sang and Sang and Sang" from *The Geranium on the Window Sill Just Died But Teacher You Went Right On*. Reprinted courtesy of Harlin Quist Books. Copyright © by Harlin Quist. All rights reserved.

Cullum, Albert. "Teacher, Give me Back My 'I'" from *The Geranium on the Window Sill Just Died But Teacher You Went Right On*. Reprinted courtesy of Harlin Quist Books. Copyright © by Harlin Quist. All rights reserved.

Eliot, T. S. "The Love Song of Alfred J. Prufrock" from *Collected Poems 1909–1962*. Copyright © 1963 by Harcourt Brace & Company. Copyright © 1964, 1963 by T. S. Eliot. Reprinted by permission of the publisher.

Fisch, Linc. From "Using Responsive Questions to Facilitate Discussions" in *The Teaching Professor* (November 1992), Magna Publications. Used by permission.

Flanders, Ned. From *Analyzing Teaching Behavior*, 1970, Addison-Wesley Publishing Company, Inc., pp. 98–106. Copyright © 1970 by Ned Flanders. Reprinted by permission of the author.

Frost, Gerhard. "Deliver Us!" reprinted from *Bless My Growing*, copyright © 1974 Augsburg Publishing House. Used by permission of Augsburg Fortress.

Frost, Gerhard. "Let It Live" reprinted from *Bless My Growing*, copyright © 1974 Augsburg Publishing House. Used by permission of Augsburg Fortress.

Frost, Gerhard. "There Will Be Some Silence in Any Class" reprinted from *Bless My Growing*, copyright © 1974 Augsburg Publishing House. Used by permission of Augsburg Fortress.

Frost, Gerhard. "To Learn Is to Live" reprinted from *Bless My Growing*, copyright © 1974 Augsburg Publishing House. Used by permission of Augsburg Fortress.

Fulghum, Robert L. "Storytellers Creed" from *All I Really Need to Know I Learned in Kindergarten.* Copyright © 1986, 1988 by Robert L. Fulghum. Reprinted by permission of Villard Books, a division of Random House, Inc.

Gerritz, Kalle. "Dear Ms. McCrea, About That Conference Next Week" in *Learning* (February 1983), p. 46. Reprinted by permission of the author.

Good, Thomas L. and Brophy, Jere E. From *Looking in Classrooms,* 5th ed. Copyright © 1991 by HarperCollins Publishers, Inc. Reprinted by permission of Addison-Wesley Educational Publishers Inc.

Grant, B. M. and Hennings, D. G. From *The Teacher Moves: An Analysis of Non-Verbal Activity,* (New York: Teachers College Press, © 1971 by Teachers College, Columbia University. All rights reserved.), pp. 126–133. Reprinted by permission of the publisher.

Hart, Rod P. From "Communication Barriers to Effective Lecturing" in *Lecturing as Communication: Problems and Potentialities* (1973), pp. 10–14. Copyright © 1973, Purdue Research Foundation, West Lafayette, IN 47907. Used by permission.

Lim, Billy B. L. From "Students' Expectations of Professors" in *The Teaching Professor* (April 1996), Magna Publications. Reprinted by permission.

Littell, J. and Littell, J. "What Did You Not Say?" in *The Language of Man 1* (1972), p. 19. Copyright © 1972 by McDougal Littell, Inc. Used by permission.

Murray, Harry G. From "Teacher Behaviors Inventory" in *The Teaching Professor* (October 1988), Magna Publications. Reprinted by permission.

Prather, Hugh. From *Notes to Myself.* Copyright © 1970 by Real People Press. Used by permission of Bantam Books, a division of Bantam Doubleday Dell Publishing Group, Inc.

Stewart, L., Cooper, P., Stewart, A., and Friedley, S. From *Communication and Gender,* "Strategies for Change," pp. 166–170, Scottsdale, AZ: Gorsuch Scarisbrick. Copyright © 1996 by Allyn and Bacon. Reprinted by permission.

Weimar, Maryellen. From "A Hearing Aid: Improving Classroom Listening Skills" in *The Teaching Professor* (January 1993), Magna Publications. Used by permission.

Welch, Leona Nicolas. From "College Students Need Nurturing Too" in *The Teaching Professor* (December 1991), Magna Publication. Used by permission.